Arts-Based Research, Resilience and Well-being Across the Lifespan

Loraine McKay • Georgina Barton
Susanne Garvis • Viviana Sappa
Editors

Arts-Based Research, Resilience and Well-being Across the Lifespan

palgrave
macmillan

Editors
Loraine McKay
Education and Professional Studies
Griffith University
Brisbane, QLD, Australia

Georgina Barton
School of Education
University of Southern Queensland
Springfield, Brisbane, QLD, Australia

Susanne Garvis
University of Gothenburg
Göteborg, Sweden

Viviana Sappa
Swiss Federal Institute for Vocational
Education and Training
Lugano, Switzerland

ISBN 978-3-030-26052-1   ISBN 978-3-030-26053-8   (eBook)
https://doi.org/10.1007/978-3-030-26053-8

© The Editor(s) (if applicable) and The Author(s), under exclusive licence to Springer Nature Switzerland AG 2020
This work is subject to copyright. All rights are solely and exclusively licensed by the Publisher, whether the whole or part of the material is concerned, specifically the rights of translation, reprinting, reuse of illustrations, recitation, broadcasting, reproduction on microfilms or in any other physical way, and transmission or information storage and retrieval, electronic adaptation, computer software, or by similar or dissimilar methodology now known or hereafter developed.
The use of general descriptive names, registered names, trademarks, service marks, etc. in this publication does not imply, even in the absence of a specific statement, that such names are exempt from the relevant protective laws and regulations and therefore free for general use.
The publisher, the authors and the editors are safe to assume that the advice and information in this book are believed to be true and accurate at the date of publication. Neither the publisher nor the authors or the editors give a warranty, express or implied, with respect to the material contained herein or for any errors or omissions that may have been made. The publisher remains neutral with regard to jurisdictional claims in published maps and institutional affiliations.

This Palgrave Macmillan imprint is published by the registered company Springer Nature Switzerland AG.
The registered company address is: Gewerbestrasse 11, 6330 Cham, Switzerland

I would like to dedicate this book to:
My late father, Alistair Fyfe who I lost during the period of preparing this book. He was a great ambassador and role model for resilience, overcoming many challenges and living his life to the full along with the limitations later imposed by Kennedy's disease.
My mother, Christine Fyfe, my husband Scott McKay and my children Kate and Andrew who keep me accountable for my own self-care and well-being in a crazy, busy world.
My growing tribe of grandchildren who fill me with pure joy and remind me to take time to notice the beauty and wonder of the world.
I am lucky to be surrounded by a loving family who support my resilience and well-being from across the lifespan.
Loraine McKay

Acknowledgements

We would like to acknowledge the support from Griffith Institute of Educational Research and Swiss Federal Institute for Vocational Education and Training SFIVET for their financial contribution towards the preparation of this manuscript.

Loraine McKay
Georgina Barton
Susanne Garvis
Viviana Sappa

Contents

1 Introduction: Defining and Theorising Key Concepts of Resilience and Well-Being and Arts-Based Research   1
Georgina Barton, Loraine McKay, Susanne Garvis, and Viviana Sappa

2 Early Childhood Education, Arts-Based Research and Resilience   13
Susanne Garvis

3 How Arts-Based Methods Are Used to Support the Resilience and Well-Being of Young People: A Review of the Literature   29
Abbey MacDonald, Margaret Baguley, Georgina Barton, and Martin Kerby

4 Building Resilience Through Listening to Children and Young People About Their Health Preferences Using Arts-Based Methods   47
Jane Coad

Contents

5 Promoting Resilience in Youth Through Participation in an Arts-Based Mindfulness Group Program 63
Diana Coholic

6 Engendering Hope Using Photography in Arts-Based Research with Children and Youth 81
Sophie Yohani

7 Using Arts-Based Reflection to Explore the Resilience and Well-Being of Mature-Age Women in the Initial Year of Preservice Teacher Education 105
Loraine McKay and Kathy Gibbs

8 Joint Painting for Understanding the Development of Emotional Regulation and Adjustment Between Mother and Son in Expressive Arts Therapy 127
Rainbow Ho and Wong Chun Chiu

9 Empowering In-Service Teachers: A Resilience-Building Intervention Based on the Forum Theatre Technique 147
Viviana Sappa and Antje Barabasch

10 Overcoming a Lived Experience of Personal Impasse by Creating a Theatrical Drama: An Example of Promoting Resilience in Adult Education 169
Deli Salini and Marc Durand

11 Clowning Training to Improve Working Conditions and Increase the Well-Being of Employees 191
Reinhard Tschiesner and Alessandra Farneti

12 The Reflexive Practitioner; Using Arts-Based Methods and Research for Professional Development 209
Cecilie Meltzer

13	University Teachers' Professional Identity Work and Emotions in the Context of an Arts-Based Identity Coaching Program *Katja Vähäsantanen, Päivi Kristiina Hökkä, and Susanna Paloniemi*	233
14	"Colouring Outside the Lines": Employment and Resilience for Art-Makers with Disabilities *Tanya Riches, Vivienne Riches, and Bruce O'Brien*	257
15	Beating Stress, the Swedish Way: Time for a 'Fika' *Liisa Uusimäki*	279
16	Using Clay in Spiritually Ecological-Existential Art Therapy: To "See", to "Listen" and to "Understand" by Hands *Jaroslava Šicková-Fabrici*	301
17	Picturing Childhood Connections: How Arts-Based Reflection and Representation Strengthen Preservice Early Childhood Teachers' Understandings About Well-Being, Belonging, and Place *Alison L. Black*	317
18	Arts-Based Research Across the Lifespan and Its Contribution to Resilience and Well-Being *Loraine McKay, Georgina Barton, Viviana Sappa, and Susanne Garvis*	339
Index		347

Notes on Contributors

Margaret Baguley is a Professor in arts education at the University of Southern Queensland. Her contribution to quality learning, teaching and research has been recognised through a series of awards including a national citation for her outstanding contribution to student learning. Professor Baguley is also a practising artist who has received a number of significant awards throughout her career including the Australia Council's New Media Residency to Banff, Canada. Her work is part of an international touring exhibition funded by the Australia Council for the Arts and is currently being shown as part of the *Ten Days on the Island* statewide arts festival in Tasmania. Professor Baguley is currently the President of Art Education Australia (AEA), the peak body for visual art education in Australia. She has published extensively and recently co-edited *The Palgrave Handbook of Artistic and Cultural Responses to War* since 1914 (Kerby, Baguley & McDonald, 2019).

Antje Barabasch is a Professor and graduated in 2006 with a PhD in Educational Policy Studies and Social Foundations at Georgia State University in Atlanta. Over the following years, she worked as visiting professor and senior researcher at Universities in Germany, the United States and Canada before taking on a post as senior expert at CEDEFOP, an agency of the European Commission in 2011. Since 2015 she works at SFIVET as head of one of the three research areas. Her research is concerned with creativity development and creative approaches to VET education, learning cultures in enterprises, migration, policy transfer, digitalisation as well as resilience

Georgina Barton is a Professor and Associate Head of School—Research in the School of Education at the University of Southern Queensland in Australia where she is discipline lead for literacies and pedagogy. She has taught in a number of schools and has experience as an Acting Principal and working as a volunteer in South India teaching English. In the higher education context, Georgina has taught English and literacy, and arts education. She researches in the areas of the arts and literacy with diverse communities and has attracted over $1 million in research funding as both a project leader and member of teams. With over 100 publications, Georgina has utilised a range of methodologies in her research including arts-based research methods. She is a co-editor of the *Palgrave Handbook of Global Arts Education* with Associate Professor Margaret Baguley.

Alison L. Black is a Senior Lecturer in the School of Education at the University of the Sunshine Coast in Queensland, Australia. She is a scholar with a strong sense of professionalism and a commitment to innovative practice, collegial relationships, and knowledge construction. Her teaching, research and service seeks to foster knowledge and connectedness through the building of reflective and creative lives and through understanding the conditions that enhance meaning-making, well-being, and community. I bring creativity, strategy, enthusiasm, energy and professional expertise to this work.

Jane Coad is a Professor and has a strong background in both art and nursing, specifically cancer and complex care and undertakes a number of arts-based participatory qualitative methods, surveys and complex evaluation projects, her research portfolio being circa £7 million since 2010 as Professor in Children and Family Nursing. User Involvement across health and social care is central to Jane's portfolio. She also has a strong background in education, undertaking lecturing and Program Director posts. In terms of professional recognition, she was awarded a Royal College of Nursing Fellowship in 2013 for lifetime research and leads on a number of local, national and international groups holding substantive posts.

Diana Coholic obtained her PhD. at the University of New South Wales in Sydney, Australia, and her MSW degree at the University of Toronto. Diana is a practising clinical social worker with 20+ years of experience, and she has been a board member of the local chapter of the Ontario Association of Social Workers since 2005. At Laurentian University, she is a core member of the research group ECHO—Evaluating Children's Health Outcomes. Diana's research has focused on investigating the effectiveness of arts-based mindfulness group work for the improvement of resilience and self-concept, particularly in marginalised children and youth. In September 2016, she began a new three-year project (funded by the SSHRC) with youth aged 11–17 years old who are experiencing challenges with schooling. Information can be found on her research website: www.dianacoholic.com. Diana is also the Academic Director for the Northern Ontario Region of the YouthREX project.

Marc Durand is Honorary Professor at the University of Geneva. He is an expert of adult professional training and lifelong education. He got a PhD at the Universities of Paris and Montpellier (France) in the domains of psychology and education. He is Honoris Causa Doctor of the University of Louvain La Neuve (Belgium). He studies human activity in everyday situations and in specific practices such as working, artistic creation, high-performance sport, leisure, and education. He is simultaneously engaged in a technological research program aimed at designing educative situations promoting individual and collective human well-being, health, safety, efficacy and development.

Alessandra Farneti is full Professor of Developmental Psychology at the Free University of Bolzano/Bozen (Italy). Her research is currently focused mainly on two topics: three-generational relationships and the effects of the art of clowning on training processes. She previously worked at Bologna University, where she organised Master courses (*Clowning for people*) for those who use clowning in different settings (at school, in hospitals, in rest homes, etc.), to encourage self-irony and to improve self-image and well-being. Recently she organised training courses for hospital staff with the help of professional clowns.

Susanne Garvis is a professor at Gothenburg University, Gothenburg, Sweden and Guest Professor Stockholm University, Sweden. She researches in the field of early childhood education with a particular focus on quality, learning and family involvement. She has been involved in national and international research projects, provided consultancy to government agencies and NGOs and developed expert reports for various agencies around the delivery of early childhood education.

Kathy Gibbs has enjoyed an extensive teaching career in P-12 schools as a Head of Department, Counsellor, Deputy Principal and Acting Principal and over the past five years at the tertiary level within Education faculties at Queensland University of Technology and the Australian Catholic University. Since July 2016, she has been employed within the School of Education and Professional Studies, Griffith University as a contracted Level B and C academic and sessional lecturer in undergraduate and postgraduate studies, teaching a diversity of courses across three campuses. In conjunction with her teaching responsibilities, she has been involved in developing new courses within the Master of Special Needs and Intervention Education and the Masters of Secondary Teaching. Priority areas of teaching and convening include Primary and Secondary Education, Professional Experience and Initial Teacher Education, Inclusive Education and Psychology. Her publications centre on the schooling experience of adolescent boys with Attention Deficit Hyperactivity Disorder (ADHD).

Rainbow Ho PhD, REAT, BC-DMT, AThR, RSMT, CGP, CMA, is the Director of the Centre on Behavioural Health, Professor of the Department of Social Work and Social Administration, and the Director of the Master programs in Expressive Arts Therapy and Behavioural Health in the University of Hong Kong. She has been working as a researcher, therapist, educator and artist for many years. She has published extensively in refereed journals, scholarly books and encyclopedia, and has been the principal investigator of many research projects related to creative and expressive arts therapy, psychophysiology, mind-body medicine, and spirituality for healthy and clinical populations.

Päivi Kristiina Hökkä (PhD) is a researcher in education and adult education at the Department of Education, University of Jyväskylä, Finland. Her current research interests concern professional agency and identity, workplace learning, teacher education and leadership in education. Her recent research and publications focus on investigating promotion of professional agency, leadership in education, and emotions in adult learning.

Martin Kerby is a Senior Lecturer in Education at the University of Southern Queensland. His research focuses on historical and educational areas. His interest is in understanding the effect of educational and sociopolitical changes on people and institutions. He has an extensive publication history with his most recent publication being *The Palgrave Handbook of Artistic and Cultural Responses to War* since 1914 (Kerby, Baguley & McDonald, 2019). Dr. Kerby has received numerous awards and grants including a 2017 Queensland Government Anzac Centenary Spirit of Service grant, which encompassed a regional music tour and accompanying children's picture book with a culminating performance at the State Library of Queensland. In July 2018 Dr. Kerby was awarded a 12 month QANZAC100 Fellowship at the State Library of Queensland for his project *A War Imagined: Queenslanders and the Great War*.

Abbey MacDonald is a Senior Lecturer in Arts Education at the University of Tasmania, where she specialises in visual art curriculum, pedagogy and practice. Dr. MacDonald is a qualitative researcher with an interest in the applications of storying and Arts-based methodologies to support participant, researcher and teacher engagement in and with relational art inquiry. Her research contexts include professional learning collaboration, teacher embodiment and enactment of curriculum, interdisciplinarity and exploration of the intersections and spaces between practice, pedagogy and methodology. Her classroom teaching experience includes secondary visual arts, media arts and English, as well as residential education leadership. Dr. MacDonald is a curator and visual artist, working in oils and cross-media. She is Vice President of Art Education Australia (AEA), and Councillor of the Tasmanian Art Teachers Association (TATA).

Loraine McKay is a Senior Lecturer in the School of Education and Professional Studies at Griffith University, Australia. She was a teacher for over 20 years before completing her PhD in preservice teacher beliefs, transitions to teaching and inclusive education. She currently teaches in the Bachelor of Education first-year program and is the First Year Coordinator in that program. Her teaching and service roles align with her research interests, which include identity development of preservice teachers as they transition in, through and out of their teacher education program and into teaching. Her work involves capacity building to promote resilience, agency and efficacy within preservice and beginning teachers' professional identity. She is interested in exploring the role of arts in reflective practice within teacher education.

Cecilie Meltzer is an Associate Professor in Arts-based Learning at Oslo and Akershus University College. She has a Master of Arts from the National Academy of Arts, a Master in Special Needs Education from Oslo University and is a certified Psychotherapist in Arts therapy at the European Association for Psychotherapy. Her broad educational and vocational background developed her interest in the interface between these practice fields. At the Department of Vocational Teacher Education she often uses arts-based methodology when teaching subject-specific themes at the course Creative Communication and in other studies. This practice has confirmed the value of a teaching approach that includes the arts in professional educational courses. She found that this form of learning can enhance the learning process, release latent resources and opportunities, and help clarify what restricts and hinders development and change.

Bruce O'Brien is interested in promoting self-advocacy. He has presented at the Inclusive Research Network Conferences in Australia and New Zealand. He has held a number of administrative positions and currently is employed as a clerical assistant at Centre for Disability Studies, affiliated with the University of Sydney, Australia. Bruce's role includes interviewing for the inclusive research presentations, data entry and analysing the data.

Susanna Paloniemi (PhD) is a senior lecturer in education and adult education at the Department of Education, University of Jyväskylä, Finland. Her research has focused on professional identity and agency, lifelong work-related learning and creativity in healthcare, education and knowledge-intensive domains. Her most recent publications focus on the promotion of professional identity and agency, and leadership practices enabling learning and creativity at work. She is currently focusing on investigating the role of emotions in professional learning with a focus of integrating various methods in researching the field.

Tanya Riches is a Training, Development and Research Officer at the Centre for Disability Studies, an affiliate of The University of Sydney. Her research is located at the intersection of anthropology and human development, with a focus upon lived experience. She is interested in what makes life meaningful for people, including people with disabilities. Her PhD investigated intersections between the Dreaming and Christianity and how spirituality directs emergent development in Aboriginal and Torres Strait Islander-led organisations within Australia's urban cities.

Vivienne Riches is a Clinical Professor of Psychology at the Centre for Disability Studies, Northern Medical School, University of Sydney. She has undertaken significant research and development work for and with people with disability in areas including vocational training and employment, transition from school to post-school, classification and assessment of support needs, community living, social and interpersonal skills, well-being, mental and emotional health, behaviour of concern and forensic issues, and Active Support. She was recently awarded a position as Fellow of the Australasian Society for Intellectual Disability (ASID), and has been inducted into the *Disability Employment Australia Hall of Fame* 2013 in recognition of an outstanding contribution to Disability Employment.

Deli Salini is Senior Researcher, Lecturer and Advisor at the Swiss Federal Institute for Vocational Education and Training (SFIVET). She got a PhD at the Geneva University, Faculty of Psychology and Educational Sciences. Her domains of activity are the teacher training, adult education and advising. Her theoretical framework articulates the Peirce's semiotic and the enactive approach. Her studies focus on anticipatory dynamics; the valorisation of informal learning and the imaginative activity, related to lifelong learning.

Viviana Sappa is senior researcher and teacher educator at Swiss Federal Institute for Vocational Education and Training (SFIVET) in Lugano, Switzerland. She got her PhD in Social and Developmental Psychology at the University of Turin, Italy. She has substantial experience in research in education, VET and teacher education. She is expert in teachers' resilience, identity development and transitions in the life span. She has conducted a large study on teachers' resilience in VET and she is currently investigating the impact of theatre-based intervention to support teachers' resilience. She published various papers in scientific journals in the education and developmental psychology field.

Jaroslava Šicková-Fabrici is a professor at Comenius University Bratislava, Slovakia. She combines her expertise and qualifications in psychology, Fine Art and special education in her work as an art therapist. She is the President of Slovak Association of Art Therapists and has authored several books and articles in this area She exhibits her sculptures in Slovakia, Czech republic, Hungary, Germany, Austria, Bulgaria, Romania, Italy, Spain, USA, Japan, S. Korea, Australia and New Zealand. Jaroslava has participated in numerous international sculpture and art therapy symposiums.

Reinhard Tschiesner is an Associate Professor of Developmental and Educational Psychology at the Free University of Bozen/Bolzano (Italy). His research is currently focused on Burnout in Educational Settings, Early Childhood Development and Learning, Crisis and Diseases in Self-Harm Behaviour and Clowning in professional training. He previously worked at University of Teacher Education Styria in Graz (Austria) with nursery-school-teachers and primary-school-teachers as well as students in education and training, where he focused on interpersonal relationships in educational settings and their impact on well-being and personality development.

Liisa Uusimäki (PhD) is a Senior Lecturer with extensive teaching and research experience from the higher education sector from Sweden and Australia. Her work at Gothenburg University, Sweden between 2013 and 2015 involved acting as Chair (seconder) & Executive for Work, Health and Safety (HAMO, AMO—SACO, SULF) at the Department of Education and Special Education. Her teaching and research involves educational and pedagogical leadership, internationalisation, mentoring and teacher education.

Katja Vähäsantanen (PhD) works as a university researcher in education and adult education at the Department of Education, University of Jyväskylä, Finland. She has conducted her current research in different professional domains, including education, healthcare and information technology. Her recent research interests and publications focus on professional agency, identity and emotions, and training and leadership practices promoting professional learning at individual and collective levels. Her recent publications include articles in *Teaching and Teacher Education, Studies in Continuing Education, Professional Development in Education*, and *Educational Research Review*.

Wong Chun Chiu AThR, MExAT, RNP, is a registered arts therapist and holds a Master degree in Expressive arts therapy from The University of Hong Kong. He is a psychiatric nurse and has been working with people with severe mental illness in the psychiatric hospital for more than 20 years. Mr. Wong is currently working in the Castle Peak Hospital in Hong Kong.

Sophie Yohani is a psychologist and associate professor of counselling psychology in the Department of Educational Psychology. Her interests lie in multicultural counselling, community-based participatory research, and refugee/migrant mental health. Her research examines the mental health and psychosocial adaptation of refugees and migrants, based on pre- and post-migration experiences, and practice/policy implications in education, healthcare, and community settings. Dr. Yohani currently serves as co-director of the Faculty of Education's Division of Clinical Services, a training clinic for graduate students in the Counselling, School and Child Clinical Psychology programs at the University of Alberta. She is originally from Tanzania, and serves as an adjunct visiting professor in the Clinical Psychology Program, Department of Psychiatry and Mental Health at Muhimbili University of Health and Allied Sciences (MUHAS) in Tanzania.

Abbreviations

ABS	Australian Bureau of Statistics
ACER	Australian Council for Educational Research
ACL	Adjective Check List Self-Assessment Questionnaire
AD	Attachment Disorder
ADHD	Attention Deficit Hyperactivity Disorder
AEA	Art Education Australia
AIHW	Australian Institute of Health and Welfare
ASD	Autism Spectrum Disorder
ASEBA	Achenbach System of Empirically Based Assessment
ASID	Australasian Society for Intellectual Disability
BC-DMT	Board Certified Level of Dance/Movement Therapy Practice
CAMM	Child and Adolescent Mindfulness Measure
CEDEFOP	European Centre for the Development of Vocational Training
CIHR	Canadian Institute of Health Research
CRPD	Convention on the Rights of Persons with Disability
DECS	Department of Education, Culture, and Sport
DRS	Dynamic Re-enactment Sessions
EAT-MCR	Expressive Arts Therapy for Mother-Child Relationship
ECE	Early Childhood Education
ECHO	Evaluating Children's Health Outcomes
EQ-I	Emotional Quotient Inventory
HAP	Holistic Arts-Based Program
IVE	Institute of Vocational Education

JPP	Joint Painting Procedure
KT	Knowledge Translation
MBCT	Mindfulness-Based Cognitive Therapy
MBIs	Mindfulness-Based Interventions
MBSR	Mindfulness-Based Stress Reduction
MUHAS	Muhimbili University of Health and Allied Sciences
NDIS	National Disability Insurance Scheme
NIDA	National Institute of Dramatic Arts
OHS	Occupational, Health and Safety
PFA	Psychological First Aid
SBE	Small Business Enterprise
SD	Stage Director
SEEA	Spiritually Ecological-Existential Art
SES	Social Economic Status
SFIVET	Swiss Federal Institute for Vocational Education and Training
SSCV	SSCV Scale: For the Assessment of Susceptibility to Shame and Guilt
TATA	Tasmanian Art Teachers Association
TATE	Teaching and Teacher Education
TDR	*The Drama Review*
TLE	Theatre of Lived Experience
UNCRPD	United Nations' Convention on the Rights of Persons with Disability
VET	Vocational Education and Training
WHO	World Health Organization

List of Figures

Fig. 6.1	Hope story painted on a quilt	82
Fig. 6.2	Collage depicting images of hope	91
Fig. 6.3	Image of books as sources of hope	93
Fig. 7.1	Ellie's mask	114
Fig. 7.2	Kelly's mask looking in	117
Fig. 7.3	Donna's mask	119
Fig. 7.4	Nancy's mask	120
Fig. 8.1	The flow of the architecture of a session. (Adapted from Knill et al., 2005; Levine, 2014)	134
Fig. 8.2	Sketch of the *Peaceful World* game. The four Chinese words together mean world peace	136
Fig. 8.3	The "Peaceful World" game with the presence of dinosaurs-aerial view	138
Fig. 8.4	The "Peaceful World" game with the presence of dinosaurs-mid-shot	138
Fig. 8.5	These image illustrate the communication pattern between Jimmy and his mother	141
Fig. 12.1	'Predatory animals' competing for space	222
Fig. 12.2	A vibrant, coloured drawing expressing energy and zest	222
Fig. 12.3	'Hoofed animals', taking turns to draw on the paper	223
Fig. 12.4	A harmonious drawing filled with circles	224
Fig. 12.5	A group already 'on the move', ready to go	226

Fig. 12.6	A group with plenty of creativity but ambivalent to collaboration	226
Fig. 13.1	Examples of professional bodies	239
Fig. 14.1	Lisa Lanzi in *Fefu and her Friends*. (Photograph by Michael Errey, 2018)	267
Fig. 14.2	*Franciscan Beauty*. (Photograph by Keith Chidzey, 2017)	269
Fig. 14.3	Amy Winters. (Photography by Kym Thompson, 2017)	270
Fig. 15.1	The Nordic Model, Dølvik (2013)	282
Fig. 17.1	Rena: Fond memories	319
Fig. 17.2	Rena and her mother	319
Fig. 17.3	Rena's Nan and father	319
Fig. 17.4	Rena: Connecting with clay	320
Fig. 17.5	Rena's handmade bowls	320
Fig. 17.6	Rena's finished art making	320
Fig. 17.7	Amber: Finding my way back	323
Fig. 17.8	Cherished connections	326
Fig. 17.9	Grounded in the earth	328
Fig. 17.10	The Big Fig Tree	330
Fig. 17.11	Remembering and reconnecting	334
Fig. 18.1	Using collage for self care and reflection	342
Fig. 18.2	Thinking outside the box	346

List of Tables

Table 9.1	Questionnaire sample	157
Table 9.2	Interview sample	157
Table 9.3	Key concepts related to feelings	159
Table 10.1	Matrix with six components for the semiological analysis of actors' experience	175
Table 10.2	Excerpt from the protocol to analyse the data of participant J.	177
Table 10.3	Framework for the succession of TLE activities	178
Table 15.1	Swedish universal rights and benefits	284
Table 15.2	Causes of stress and symptoms	293

1

Introduction: Defining and Theorising Key Concepts of Resilience and Well-Being and Arts-Based Research

Georgina Barton, Loraine McKay, Susanne Garvis, and Viviana Sappa

---

G. Barton (✉)
School of Education, University of Southern Queensland, Springfield, Brisbane, QLD, Australia
e-mail: georgina.barton@usq.edu.au

L. McKay
Education and Professional Studies, Griffith University, Brisbane, QLD, Australia
e-mail: loraine.mckay@griffith.edu.au

S. Garvis
University of Gothenburg, Göteborg, Sweden
e-mail: susanne.garvis@gu.se

V. Sappa
Swiss Federal Institute for Vocational Education and Training, Lugano, Switzerland
e-mail: viviana.sappa@iuffp.swiss

Introduction

Arts-based research, resilience and well-being across the lifespan shares robust research that utilises arts-based research methods in diverse contexts and from across the globe. The main objective of research included in this volume is to investigate how arts-based research methods can influence participants' resilience and well-being at various stages of life and in various context. The book brings together a diverse range of contributors who work in the field.

We live in a time where change is the only constant. Increasing day-to-day pressures stem from a variety of sources such as, but not limited to work-life balance, social media influences, civil unrest, isolation, economic instability and new technologies. Understanding how both resilience and well-being can be supported is important in a world that is rarely stress-free. Recognising the effective personal tools of individuals and groups as well as how these skills are harnessed and utilised is important to counter the current marketisation of quick-fix solutions for the challenges that are faced.

A search of the literature makes it clear that resilience and well-being have been increasing areas of research in the last 20 years, conducted on various populations across the lifespan, including people from all walks of life and in multiple contexts (see, e.g., systematic literature reviews by Aburn, Gott, & Hoare, 2016 [defining resilience]; Chmitorz et al., 2018 [resilience intervention studies]; Dray et al., 2017 [child and adolescent resilience-focused interventions]; King, Renó, & Novo, 2014 [dimensions and measures of well-being]; Robertson, Cooper, Sarkar, & Curran, 2015 [resilience training in the workplace]). The topic is represented across multiple domains such as psychology, occupational therapy, sociology, adolescent and early childhood studies and education. The numerous lenses used to research resilience and well-being may contribute to the lack of clarity that exists around the definition of terms.

Resilience

Resilience is a slippery term. According to Aburn et al. (2016), no universal definition of resilience exists within the research literature. There are, however, common elements that have been identified that encapsulate a trait-oriented perspective with a process-oriented view. A trait-oriented view considers that individuals have a set of personal characteristics that determine their ability to cope with or adjust to adversity, although, Kalisch et al. (2017) suggest the empirical evidence to support this view is weak. More recently, resilience has been considered from a process-oriented approach that considers physical and emotional health can be sustained during or returned following adversity or hardship (Chmitorz et al., 2018). From this perspective, resilience is not a fixed entity but rather a dynamic process, and therefore, something that can be taught or developed (Masten, 2001). In their review of literature within education Mansfield, Beltman, Broadley, and Weatherby-Fell (2016) determined that resilience could be determined as a personal resource, a strategy, a contextual resource or an outcome. As a personal resource, resilience is a set of characteristics that acts as a buffer or protective coating during adversity. These qualities can be developed over time during context-personal interactions which suggests a certain amount of hardship needs to be experienced as part of the learning process in which strategies are also developed (Masten, 2001). Masten (2011) also suggests that it is through a complex set of interactions of factors: biological, personal, temporal and environmental, that resilience emerges.

For the purpose of this book resilience is defined as "the state in which an individual realises his or her own abilities, can cope with normal stresses of life, can work productively, and is able to make a contribution to his or her own community" (World Health Organization, 2014, p. 1). Resilience is related to the ideal of well-being as it refers to how people adapt to and adopt the ability to cope with challenges and new circumstances. When people are resilient, they are able to face others with confidence and positivity. Furthermore, they have the skills needed in different contexts and throughout one's life to maintain the positive approach to life that supports their well-being.

Well-Being

Well-being and resilience are closely linked, and like resilience, well-being is a multidimensional concept. According to Dodge, Daly, Huyton, and Sanders (2012), well-being occurs when individuals have "the psychological, social and physical resources they need to meet a particular psychological, social and/or physical challenge" (p. 230). The broader socioecological perspective of well-being is considered more holistically than previous measures that were limited to "objective measures of economic conditions, housing, education, and welfare" (King et al., 2014, p. 682). A socioecological perspective includes the quality of the social and material attributes of a person's life, such as employment, housing, health care, and education, as well as satisfaction, connectedness and autonomy associated with life circumstances (King et al., 2014). Well-being can be seen as an outcome of resilience (Mansfield et al., 2016) or as a precursor to developing resilience when personal resources including motivation, efficacy, optimism, high expectations and courage are activated to manage or move on from adversity (Dodge et al., 2012).

Arts-Based Research

One important area of development has been the *arts in health movement* with a focus on resilience and well-being. The *arts in health* field can be defined as compromising all activities that aim to use arts-based approaches to improve individual and community health, health promotion, healthcare or seek to enhance the healthcare environment through visual art and performances (Macnaughton, White, & Stacy, 2005). As such, arts are viewed as good for the health of society and viewed as essential for physical, social and mental well-being (Macnaughton et al., 2005). From such movements has come a focus on the importance of arts-based research for resilience and well-being across community health, medical perspectives and physical environment creations. Arts-based research can thus be described as:

> A research method in which the arts play a primary role in any or all of the steps of the research method. Art forms such as poetry, music, visual art, drama and dance are essential to the research process itself and central in formulating the research question, generating data, analysing data and presenting the research results. (Austin & Forinash, 2005, pp. 460–461)

The arts have an important role to play in providing different understandings and ways of supporting positive health development. Eisner (2008) argues that since not all knowledge is reducible to language, exploration of visual and sensory understanding provide opportunities for non-linguistic dimensions in research, which may allow us to represent different levels of experience, creating greater awareness and support for well-being and resilience.

The use of arts-based research also creates possibilities to engage in research with children. Broadly speaking, arts-based research help children communicate with others (Brooks, 2009), allowing problems from traditional research methods such as interviews to be overcome. Wright (2007, p. 24) notes:

> Language as a communicational medium is inadequate for the expression of everything that we think, feel or sense. Hence drawing, graphic-narrative play and other forms of artistic expression offer important and distinct forms of meaning-making through figurative communication, which is intricate, multifaceted, symbolic and metaphoric.

For example, asking children to create portraits allows children to also be more aware of their own emotions (Muri, 2007) as well as being able to condense their experiences and identity into a visual metaphor (Bagnoli, 2009). The different forms of representation provide alternate ways of expressing understanding and experience. In this sense, arts-based research is more inclusive of providing different opportunities for representation. It is for this reason arts-based research was considered for this book.

Examples of Arts-Based Methods for Resilience and Well-Being Across the Lifespan

The arts, and more specifically, arts-based research, provides opportunities for creative experiences and learning to occur in different ways. Craft, Cremin, Burnard, and Chappell (2007) propose five fundamental conditions of creative learning as described by the Qualification and Curriculum

Authority in England. These include providing opportunities to ask questions, to make connections, imagining possibilities, exploring options and reflecting critically. All that can be provided by the arts and more specifically arts-based research.

In this book we draw from Akkerman and Bakker (2011) and understand learning to include new knowledge and skills, transference of these skills into meaningful opportunities in our own lives, transformation of our belief system because of these meaningful opportunities and institutional development. We have deliberately adopted a broad definition of learning that can incorporate developing new knowledge and skills; adopting changes to belief systems; developing self regulatory behaviours, including emotional regulation; applying creativity across various stages of the lifespan and in multiple contexts. We propose that all learning requires reflection, which can take many forms and can be enriched through arts-based practices.

For some time, scholars have utilised the arts to support people's resilience and well-being. There is strong evidence to suggest that the arts allow the opportunity to express oneself through multiple means, enabling transformative practice and reflection. Leitch's (2006) work showed that when participants created images related to 'self' "new meanings, previously unaware, unvoiced, unexpressed, half-understood came to be significant and capable of being incorporated into the participants' social and/or emotional understanding of themselves, to the point that new actions or directions could be taken in their lives" (p. 566). Such work is critical when dealing with factors related to resilience and wellbeing as it enables participants to tap into areas of thought that may not always be conscious or present. In McNiff's (2008) study arts-based and creative approaches to reflection resulted in more "meaningful insights [that] often come by surprise, unexpectedly and even against the will of the creator" (p. 40). Such experience is important for transformed practice and different ways of knowing or being (Liamputtong & Rumbold, 2008).

Arts-based methods can assist researchers and their participants in having different perspectives about the subject of inquiry (Ewing & Hughes, 2008). Ewing and Hughes (2008) highlight how such approaches can promote more empathy and empathic understanding, thereby providing access to components of resilience and well-being. Many studies have used arts-based methods as a foundation of transformative practice and these have been across a range of disciplines including education, health, and professional contexts.

Clift's (2012) work, for example, notes that the arts can be utilised as a creative and public health resource. He recognised that "the field of arts and health is complex and multifaceted and there are challenges in moving beyond *practice-based* research, towards building a progressive body of knowledge that can provide a basis for future *evidence-based* practice in health care and public health" (p. 120). In this sense, it is important for arts-based researchers in the area of health to develop robust evidence when presenting research.

Similarly, Pearson and Wilson (2008) showed how arts-based methods can enhance well-being and resilience, resulting in long term changes. The authors use the notion of inner-life skills to explore emotions in the hope of improving therapeutic outcomes. They argue that creativity is "an in-built drive and a major goal within the psyche" (Pearson & Wilson, 2008, p. 3) therefore it makes sense to use arts-based approaches to support people's development of resilience and well-being.

Participating in arts-based practices can also improve resilience and well-being in various communities. Bungay and Vella-Burrows' (2013) work, for example, presented a comprehensive review of the literature exploring the effects of young people's (aged 11–18) participation in creative activities. Their review of the literature revealed that while there is evidence that creative activities are beneficial for students it is important that studies provide robust proof through rigorous and useful methods.

In this book we theorise how arts-based research methods can positively contribute to resilience and well-being. As such, the book will discuss ways in which researchers and educators can consider and implement such strategies. A range of arts-based practices being used to support the resilience and well-being of individuals and groups across the lifespan are presented. Drawing on a range of arts-based methodologies, each chapter examines these spaces at various junctures across the lifespan. The intention is to provide a holistic understanding of the research field that covers a range of arts-based methodologies at various junctures of life.

The book contains a total of eighteen chapters. The chapters are organised into a chronological sequence across the lifespan. Chapter 2 explores early childhood education, arts-based research and resilience. In this chapter, Garvis has a particular focus on how arts-based research can be chosen as an important tool to support refugee children and their families in early childhood settings. The focus in adolescence as a developmental phase is presented in Chap. 3 by MacDonald, Baguley, Barton and Kerby. The authors draw on their experiences as academics and arts educators who have worked with adolescent students, teachers and pre-service teachers to explore well-being and resilience. In particular, enablers to support young people's well-being are identified. The fourth chapter by Coad (Chap. 4), focuses on how arts-based methods can be used to build resilience with children aged 9–18 years. Real life case studies are presented that shows the importance of supporting young people's resilience in hospitals and transitions across health services. Coholic presents how to promote resilience with young through mindfulness group programs in Chap. 5. The program builds a variety of resiliencies including self-awareness, emotion regulation and self-esteem, allowing the importance of arts-based methods and processes when working with youth to be visible. Chapter 6 (Yohani) focuses on photography in arts-based research with children and youth with a particular focus on children in post-conflict countries living in Canada and Tanzania. The approach shows the importance of arts-based research for the development of child-centred approaches that allow active meaning-making.

The next section of the book moves into adulthood. In Chap. 7, McKay and Gibbs explore resilience and well-being of mature aged pre-service teachers who have returned to study following motherhood. A specific focus is made on arts-based reflection and its contribution to learning, transformation and growth related to resilience and well-being. Chapter 8 describes how Expressive Arts Therapy can be used to help a child with Autism Spectrum Disorder to express emotions and develop a better relationship with his mother. Ho and Wong show how joint painting approaches enable bi-directional communication between the mother and son. Chapter 9 provides insights into a resilience-building intervention based on the forum theatre technique. Sappa and Barabsch show how the technique can be used to empower in-service teachers. Salini and

Durand in Chap. 10 write how theatrical drama can be used to overcome the lived experience of personal impasse by promoting resilience in adult education. The experience allowed participants to gain value as an event triggering resilience and dynamic vitality. Still within adulthood, Chap. 11 focuses on improving the working conditions and increasing the well-being of employees through the use of clowning training. Tschiesner and Farneti show how the training allows individuals to rediscover themselves and grow resilience. Chapter 12 moves towards teachers and the reflexive practitioners, where Meltzer examines how arts-based approaches can be used to stimulate professional growth in teachers and learners. The approach provides deep learning and stimulates communication, exploration and creativity. Chapter 13 continues with the theme of teachers with a focus on the identity of university teachers' professional identity. Vähäsantanen, Hökkä and Paloniemi investigate professional identity work and emotions in the context of arts-based coaching programs. They uncover how professional identity work is an emotional endeavour that encompasses both pleasant and unpleasant emotions in the shaping of professional identity.

Riches, Riches and O'Brien in Chap. 14 share findings from a qualitative study that explored how the arts can build resilience amongst unemployed and underemployed Australians with disabilities. In the chapter, artistic endeavours are seen as acts of self-definition that play an important role in society's meaning-making. Chapter 15 shares experiences from the Swedish context with Uusimäki sharing specific cultural strategies prompted by arts-based reflection by reflecting on experiences as a university academic. She suggests a number of specific strategies to support workplace well-being. In Chap. 16, Šicková-Fabrici describes how clay can be used in spiritually ecological-existential art therapy with a specific focus on three-dimensional art expression. The use of clay and moulding as a means to stimulate senses and emotions is examined. Black in Chap. 17 demonstrates how arts-based reflection and representation strengthen preservice early childhood teachers' understandings about well-being, belonging and place. This understanding leads to better ways to support children's relationships and well-being through nature-rich environments and connections, bringing the life trajectory focus back around again from adult to child. In the final chapter (Chap. 18 by the editors) reflections are given on the overall themes across the book around resiliency and well-being. A particular focus is also made on the importance of arts-based research methods to support resiliency.

As you engage with the life trajectory across the book, we hope you also start to reflect on how arts-based methods could be useful to supporting resilience and well-being in your own life and the lives of those around you. We hope that for readers, the book opens up new possibilities for implementing arts-based methods in different educational settings and workplaces to begin a holistic focus on supporting resiliency and well-being for all.

References

Aburn, G., Gott, M., & Hoare, K. (2016). What is resilience? An integrative review of the empirical literature. *Journal of Advanced Nursing, 72*(5), 980–1000.

Akkerman, S. F., & Bakker, A. (2011). Boundary crossing and boundary objects. *Review of Educational Research, 81*(2), 132–169.

Austin, D., & Forinash, M. (2005). Arts-based inquiry. In B. Wheeler (Ed.), *Music therapy research* (2nd ed., pp. 458–471). Gilsum, NH: Barcelona.

Bagnoli, A. (2009). Beyond the standard interview: The use of graphic elicitation and arts-based methods. *Qualitative Research, 9*(5), 547–570.

Brooks, M. (2009). Drawing to learn. In M. Narey (Ed.), *Making meaning: Constructing multimodal perspectives of language, literacy, and learning through arts-based early childhood education* (Vol. 2, pp. 9–30). New York, NY: Springer.

Bungay, H., & Vella-Burrows, T. (2013). The effects of participating in creative activities on the health and well-being of children and young people: A rapid review of the literature. *Perspectives in Public Health, 133*(1), 44–52.

Chmitorz, A., Kunzler, A., Helmreich, I., Tüscher, O., Kalisch, R., Kubiak, T., … & Lieb, K. (2018). Intervention studies to foster resilience—A systematic review and proposal for a resilience framework in future intervention studies. *Clinical Psychology Review, 59*, 78–100.

Clift, S. (2012). Creative arts as a public health resource: Moving from practice-based research to evidence-based practice. *Perspectives in Public Health, 132*(3), 120–127.

Craft, A., Cremin, T., Burnard, P., & Chappell, K. (2007). Teacher stance in creative learning: A study of progression. *Thinking Skills and Creativity, 2*(2), 136–147.

Dodge, R., Daly, A. P., Huyton, J., & Sanders, L. D. (2012). The challenge of defining wellbeing. *International Journal of Wellbeing, 2*(3), 222–235.

Dray, J., Bowman, J., Campbell, E., Freund, M., Wolfenden, L., Hodder, R. K., … & Small, T. (2017). Systematic review of universal resilience-focused interventions targeting child and adolescent mental health in the school setting. *Journal of the American Academy of Child & Adolescent Psychiatry, 56*(10), 813–824.

Eisner, E. (2008). Arts and knowledge. In J. G. Knowles & A. L. Cole (Eds.), *Handbook of the arts in qualitative research: Perspectives, methodologies, examples and issues* (pp. 3–12). London, UK: Sage.

Ewing, R., & Hughes, J. (2008). Arts-informed inquiry in teacher education: Contesting the myths. *European Educational Research Journal, 7*(4), 512–522.

Kalisch, R., Baker, D. G., Basten, U., Boks, M. P., Bonanno, G. A., Brummelman, E., … & Geuze, E. (2017). The resilience framework as a strategy to combat stress-related disorders. *Nature Human Behaviour, 1*(11), 784.

King, M. F., Renó, V. F., & Novo, E. M. (2014). The concept, dimensions and methods of assessment of human well-being within a socioecological context: A literature review. *Social Indicators Research, 116*(3), 681–698.

Leitch, R. (2006). Limitations of language: Developing arts-based creative narrative in stories of teachers' identities. *Teachers and Teaching: Theory and Practice, 12*(5), 549–569.

Liamputtong, P., & Rumbold, J. (2008). *Knowing differently: Arts-based and collaborative research methods*. New York, NY: Nova Publishers.

Macnaughton, J., White, M., & Stacy, R. (2005). Researching the benefits of arts in health. *Health Education, 105*(5), 332–339.

Mansfield, C. F., Beltman, S., Broadley, T., & Weatherby-Fell, N. (2016). Building resilience in teacher education: An evidenced informed framework. *Teaching and Teacher Education, 54*, 77–87.

Masten, A. S. (2001). Ordinary magic: Resilience processes in development. *American Psychologist, 56*(3), 227.

Masten, A. S. (2011). Resilience in children threatened by extreme adversity: Frameworks for research, practice, and translational synergy. *Development and Psychopathology, 23*(2), 493–506.

McNiff, S. (2008). Art-based research. Handbook of the arts in qualitative research. In J. G. Knowles & A. L. Cole (Eds.), *Handbook of the arts in qualitative research: Perspectives, methodologies, examples, and issues* (pp. 29–40). Thousand Oaks, CA: Sage.

Muri, S. A. (2007). Beyond the face: Art therapy and self-portraiture. *The Arts in Psychotherapy, 34*, 331–339.

Pearson, M., & Wilson, H. (2008). Using expressive counselling tools to enhance emotional literacy, emotional wellbeing and resilience: Improving therapeutic outcomes with expressive therapies. *Counselling, Psychotherapy and Health, 4*(1), 1–19.

Robertson, I. T., Cooper, C. L., Sarkar, M., & Curran, T. (2015). Resilience training in the workplace from 2003 to 2014: A systematic review. *Journal of Occupational and Organizational Psychology, 88*(3), 533–562.

World Health Organization. (2014). *Mental health: A state of well-being*. Retrieved from: http://www.who.int/features/factfiles/mental_health/en/

Wright, S. (2007). Graphic-narrative play: Young children's authoring through drawing and telling. *International Journal of Education and the Arts, 8*(8), 1–27.

2

Early Childhood Education, Arts-Based Research and Resilience

Susanne Garvis

Introduction

Resilience is a complex construct with numerous definitions in the literature. For the purpose of the chapter, I will adopt the idea of resilience as described by DiClemente, Santelli, and Crosby (2009) as the ability to rebound from adverse life events by positively adapting to them. This means that when working with young children and early childhood settings, it relates to how children (and also their families) can work with difficult situations to make the most of their lives. The components of resilience can be broken into intrinsic as well as extrinsic factors. Intrinsic factors are those that are within the individual (or self) and include a sense of belonging, self-efficacy and self-esteem. Extrinsic factors are those that relate to outside influences such as secure attachments and relationships, access to wider support beyond the family and positive experiences at school and in the community.

S. Garvis (✉)
University of Gothenburg, Göteborg, Sweden
e-mail: susanne.garvis@gu.se

© The Author(s) 2020
L. McKay et al. (eds.), *Arts-Based Research, Resilience and Well-being Across the Lifespan*,
https://doi.org/10.1007/978-3-030-26053-8_2

Early childhood education is an important time for the building of resilience in a person's life. Children who are able to experience positive intrinsic and extrinsic factors can develop suitable skills to support resilience through to adulthood. It is important to note, however, that thinking about the development of resilience also extends to the child's family. The family plays an important role in fostering the child's sense of self and belonging. Thus, it is important that families are also supported and have positive experiences with early childhood settings and the community.

One way to support resilience in early childhood is through arts-based methods that can also act as a form of pedagogies. The arts can play an important role in supporting the development of self and lead to positive encounters with education settings and the community, allowing children and their families to also learn about themselves and others. Limited studies, however, have specifically looked at links between early childhood education, arts methods and resilience. While there is a strong field of research emerging around young people, arts experiences and mental health (see the systematic review by Zarobe & Bungay, 2017), similar studies have not yet been conducted in early childhood education.

This chapter has a specific focus on how arts-based methods can be used to work with refugee children and their families in early childhood settings to develop inclusive spaces and create senses of belonging for children and their families. The next section focuses on the importance of recognising refugee children and their families in early childhood settings, before exploring specific arts-based methods of narrative research. The chapter concludes with points for consideration when thinking about resilience in early childhood education and the importance of arts-methods to be used as pedagogies.

Working with Refugee Children and Their Families in Early Childhood Settings to Support Inclusive Spaces

School is an integral part of the lives of refugees, many of which come as young families with children to their host country. Without attending to the diverse lives of refugees and the complex history of forced migration and displacement, it is challenging to work with refugees in respectful, meaningful and engaging ways in schools that focus on inclusion. In these moments, encounters in school even hold the potential to become *miseducative* (Dewey, 1938). Young children and their families must make sense of unfamiliar school settings and educational narratives, narratives and experiences that hold the potential to bump up with their previous experiences and expectations. Without attention to those who are arriving, it is difficult to know how their familial and schooling narratives are being shaped as they arrive.

For some refugee families, preschool is the first contact with the new dominant culture (Adair & Tobin, 2008; Grieshaber & Miller, 2010) that provides opportunities for families with broader discourses of their new society (Vandenbroeck, Roets, & Snoeck, 2009). However, the nuances of early childhood education may not be easily understood by refugee families and could result in tension if left unattended. Few studies have investigated the transition experiences of refugee children and families into early childhood settings (De Gioia, 2015; Grieshaber & Miller, 2010). Poor transition experiences have been identified as a potential contributor to increased stress and longer-term health and well-being consequences for refugee children and their families (Sims & Hutchins, 2001). Given the increasing numbers of refugee children and families, it is important that the narrative of the transition process becomes the focus of inquiry. Refugee children and families require access to inclusive spaces in preschools to allow a sense of belonging, to shape meaningful stories in and of schooling and education, and to impact the long term inclusion of refugees into new places, new homes.

Research with refugee children and families is often shaped by a top-down approach, administered through statistical analysis of geographic movement and demographic characteristics. Within Sweden, it usually encompasses a psychological discourse. Such an approach, however, lacks the perspectives of refugee children and their families (Wigg, 2008). More qualitative, empirical studies in other disciplines as an important complement to existing psychological research on refugee children and their family is needed (Wigg, 2008). An inclusive approach allows the perspectives of refugee children and their families to be known, respecting the participants' experiences as sources of knowledge. Adair and

Tobin (2008) discuss the importance of listening to refugee parents and opening dialogues about their goals for their children. In one small Australian study, for example, Whitmarsh (2011) found that asylum-seeking mothers suggested non-tokenistic displays of cultural inclusivity were important to ongoing feelings of being welcomed. In interviews with mothers, De Gioia (2015) also found that creating spaces that allowed conversations between refugee mothers and educators was important for the family to build social capital.

The relationships and initial trust between child, family and preschool are important for all. This can be extremely complex for some families and their children if they have had traumatic experiences from war and being a refugee. Angel, Hjern, and Hernandez (2004) suggest that preschool is one of the most important initiatives for the development and learning needs of newly arrived children. The preschool provides newly arrived children a structure in everyday life where both children and parents can access the support they need. It also provides an opportunity for parents to meet other adults—an important resource for families who left their old network behind and have not yet had time to establish new networks. Start days, contact days, parent-teacher meetings, relationships with staff and other activities is a natural opportunity for parents to get to know other adults within the preschool and society (Lunneblad, 2006). The introduction into preschool can have a decisive impact on children's later school success and the full integration of family longitudinally within Swedish society. ECE is the best economical investment in preventing risk of social exclusion, marginalisation and alienation (Doyle, Harmon, Heckman, & Tremblay, 2009; Heckman, 2006). Preschool staff, therefore, have an important function for the families' long-term integration within Sweden.

The importance of parental interaction is reinforced both in national and international research (Bunar, 2010; Suárez-Orozco, Pimentel, & Martin, 2009). In today's preschool, parents are expected to play an active role (Bouakaz, 2007; Dalli, 2002; Tallberg Broman, 2009). Daily meetings between parents and teachers at preschool are situations where different conceptions of what it means to be a parent are made visible and how these beliefs carry meanings around class, gender, ethnicity and normality (Crozier, 2001; Tallberg Broman, 2009). The importance of cooperation and dialogue with parents is also something important for children and families who carry with them the memories of war and persecution. Research done in clinical psychology around refugee children's health highlights the role of preschool can play in offering children a stable living environment. Studies show how the preschool can serve as a support where the children can have a structure in their daily lives and access to stable adults if their parents feel stressed/overwhelmed (Angel et al., 2004).

Educational research on new arrivals, and children often focuses on multilingual development and mother tongue importance. The situation for many newly arrived children is that they should learn a new culture while also learning a new language (Cummins, 2001; Hyltenstam & Tuomela, 2004; Sims & Hutchins, 2001). For example, in Sweden, research has shown that the Swedish language is described as a key to getting ahead in Swedish society. In preschool, teachers take the role as the bearer of Swedish culture and language. A linguistic regime is implemented based on language.

Australian research has highlighted the importance of the relationship between teacher and refugee family (De Gioia, 2015; Sims & Hutchins, 2001). Refugee mothers have described the importance of feeling welcomed into preschools as well as having signs displayed in their own language as important to a sense of belonging in the preschool. In Sweden, Lunneblad (2017) has also identified fostering strategies aimed to teach parents to adjust to routines and norms in Swedish preschools used by teachers. This includes flexible routines during the children's breakfast to accommodate children who arrive at different times. He argues that the approach provides a sense of ontological security for parents who are in an unfamiliar situation who may not understand routines within the preschool. Lunneblad (2017) found, however, that while teachers expressed values related to ideas about how to act as parents in a Swedish preschool, actual references to multicultural policy was absent in the teachers' narratives.

In Finland, Lappalainen (2003) argues that international and multicultural weeks have become a popular pedagogic tool in multicultural preschools. Yet, Lappalainen's ethnographic study in a Finnish preschool reveals that differences rather than similarities between cultures were discussed during the multicultural week in the investigated preschool. Despite Finland's largest minority group being Swedish-speaking Finns, Lappalainen states that only cultures and countries outside the Nordic countries were mentioned during these discussions. There is a pressing need for alternative narratives to emerge within education.

Preschools can create places of belonging, identity making and agency (Hilppö, Lipponen, Kumpulainen, & Rainio, 2016) for refugee children and their families by creating inclusive spaces. Inclusive spaces are spaces where dignity and safety are norms, diversity is recognised and accepted, and everyone feels encouraged, supported, and included. They are spaces where a balance of power shifts is realised/emerges. Inclusive spaces provide opportunities for identity building based on relationships, respects and responsibility. The space also allows authentic interaction and learning to occur between different parties. The design of such spaces aligns with the European Commission's (2015) "new policies for fairness in education from an early age" goal.

Arts-Based Research

One way to explore the experiences of refugee children and their families is with arts-based research. Arts-based research provides new ways to understand children's lives and perspectives, as well as those of families and early childhood teachers. There is agreement in the research field that the use of artistic methods within qualitative research provides opportunities to uncover phenomenon not accessible through other means (Bagnoli, 2009; Garvis, 2017; Ledger & Edwards, 2011; Shannon-Baker, 2015). Arts-based research is described as:

> a research method in which the arts play a primary role in any or all of the steps of the research method. Art forms such as poetry, music, visual art, drama and dance are essential to the research process itself and central in formulating the research question, generating data, analysing data and presenting the research results. (Austin & Forinash, 2005, pp. 460–461)

Arts-based methods can take on many different forms, however literature available on different methods within the field of early childhood

2 Early Childhood Education, Arts-Based Research and Resilience

education is scarce, given the originality of the qualitative approach. Some approaches have included photographs (Driessnack & Furukawa, 2012), videography (Kozinets & Belk, 2006), drawings (Fleer, 1997; Papandreou & Terzi, 2011; Robbins, 2009; Wright, 2007), photostory (Wang & Burris, 1997), and digital photographs (Clark, 2010; Cook & Hess, 2007; Einarsdottir, 2014).

Another popular approach has been the use of narratives (Garvis, 2015). This approach respects the individual and allows participants to take a strong sense of agency over their experiences. The approach is and located within an interpretivist paradigm (Garvis, 2015). A narrative approach highlights gaps between policy and practice as it highlights how narratives of experience relate to each other (Garvis, 2010, 2015). Narratives of experiences are always shifting, "each with a unique spiralling pattern, necessarily involving many plotlines, which, in turn, bring multiple meanings" (Craig, 2007, p. 4). In a narrative approach, individuals' narratives of experience relate to each other (Garvis, 2010). Their narratives of experience are always shifting, "each with a unique spiralling pattern, necessarily involving many plotlines, which, in turn, bring multiple meanings to bear on teachers' knowledge as shaped in their reforming school contexts" (Craig, 2007, p. 4). Through this approach, "a constellation of factors ... including the moralities and mores of teachers" (Schwab, 1970, pp. 8–10), is brought to the surface for discussion and analysis. Through this approach, key ideas become known for discussion and analysis (Garvis, 2010).

The narrative approach is highly important when working with refugee children and their families. To study forced population shifts of children and their families through narratives of experience (Connelly & Clandinin, 1990), many types of understanding are needed. According to Clandinin et al. (2006), "we need to understand ...embodied, narrative, moral, emotional, and relational knowledge as it is expressed in [context]" (p. 172). Also, in order to make sense of refugees as culturally situated and shaped human beings who have been geographically displaced, we must pay attention to culture, which is "the sum of the stories we tell ourselves about who we are and want to be, individually and collectively" (Maxwell, 2001, p. 1). Cultural stories, Maxwell claims, are the "staging ground" (p. 1) for identity narratives or stories to live by (Connelly & Clandinin, 1999), the narrative inquiry term. These stories to live by, in Stone's (1988) words, "give messages and instructions; ... offer blueprints and ideals; [and]... issue warnings and prohibitions" (p. 5). Clandinin and Connelly (2000) explain that "narrative is the closest we can come to experience... [The] guiding principle... is to focus on experience and to follow where it leads" (p. 188). The overarching *priority* of narrative inquiry, then, is "to compose research texts that [animate] the lives of participants" (Clandinin & Murphy, 2009, p. 600), who, in this proposed study, are refugee children, their families and their teachers. Furthermore, the lives of refugees are embedded in social circumstances that are "puzzling, intractable, [and] no longer amenable to existing theoretical frameworks and social discourse" (Connelly, Phillion, & He, 2003, p. 366). In such situations, the need for flexible inquiry—inquiry that holds everything open to scrutiny—is even more important (Dewey, 1938). Narrative methods, therefore, provide the possibility for children and their families to participate in well-being and resilience research. Young children are able to express themselves about their own life and well-being (Estola, Farquhar, & Puroila, 2018).

Children's perspectives about their own well-being and resilience are rarely explored (McAuley & Rose, 2010). Only a handful of studies have attempted to gain insights into the experiences of refugee children and their families through the use of narratives. The first was a study of refugee children's sandplay narratives in immigration detention in Canada (Kronick, Rousseau, & Cleveland, 2018). The sandplay method was chosen as it allowed young children to express themselves in a nonverbal and imaginative way. Kronick et al. (2018, p. 425) also argue that:

> previous research has suggested that parents of varying cultural backgrounds may be more comfortable with an arts-based interview method rather than direct discussion with pre-adolescent children... Arts or creative expression based modalities are developmentally well-suited for children who share their inner worlds through play. Children's play may serve as a metaphor for past experience and therefore, has the possibility of generating knowledge of their lived realities.

Sandplay is considered an arts and narrative based method—within a broader approach of narrative-based research. Sandplay has been used in previous studies to work with immigrant and refugee children to allow the representation of difficult experiences (such as tsunamis) (Lacroix et al., 2007). The experience with sandplay provides opportunities for children to permit the transformation of traumatic events into children's inner worlds and lived experience, also providing a therapeutic potential for children (Lacroix et al., 2007).

In the study of refugee children in Canada (Kronick et al., 2018), three broad themes emerged; (1) confinement and surveillance; (2) loss of protection; and (3) human violence. The experiences shared by the children also reinforced the absence of stories of normality, with the children focusing on a simple, stress experience. The authors conclude that sandplay provides an opportunity for an ethical and culturally safe research method to create qualitative data (alongside children) because it is developmentally appropriate and permits indirect (nonverbal) and direct (verbal) expression. The approach also provided opportunities for "reconstruction and transformation of traumatic narratives in a way which extinguishes distressing affect" (Kronick et al., 2018, p. 435). The children involved were able to work through difficult experiences by retelling stories in ways which allowed them to regain a sense of control of their experiences. The approach became an empowering experience for children to understand and make meaning out of their experiences.

The importance of listening to refugee children's stories of their adaption experiences and the narratives of their families into American early childhood classrooms has also been reported by Prior and Niesz (2013). Engaging in narrative inquiry, the stories of young children's adaption, cultural dissonance and belonging were explored within early childhood contexts. The researchers collected drawings that were created by the children, as well as oral and written stories. Stories from the children's families were also collected to allow a multiperspective narrative of the child's experience. The findings from the study showed a change in orientation by the children to school over time. Initially, the children were sad but through schooling, were able to bridge divides in their experience. The children were able to find connection between home and school and build friendships in the classroom (Prior & Niesz, 2013). The children were able to share strategies of how they were able to find belonging, especially after cultural dissonance. Some of the children focused their stories on finding commonalities with peers to provide connections in the short and long-term. The children also discussed the importance of educators for supporting their inclusion and how they felt valued. As such, Prior and Niesz (2013, p. 14) describe the importance of multimodal (oral, written and arts-based) stories from children and their families as a research method that allows a "richer and more multifaceted understanding of 'storied' experiences". The method also appeared to aid the children's adaption to the early childhood setting. The researchers conclude that (Prior & Niesz, 2013, p. 15):

> As a greater number of children and families are finding refuge in new communities across the globe, it is essential for educators to understand how refugees of all ages are making meaning of their experiences and provide them with opportunities to tell their stories. These can teach us how to support children's and families' adaptation into a new community, how to foster smooth transitions, and how to adapt our classrooms to provide students with the best educational experiences possible.

Narrative research as an arts-based method, therefore, has enormous power to bring change to educational settings for children, families and educators. The approach provides opportunities to explore the experiences of refugee children and their families to provide educators with a better understanding of how they can understand the child and family and provide the necessary support to build resilience.

Key Points for Consideration About Early Childhood, Arts-Based Research and Resilience

This chapter provided a brief overview of the literature around early childhood education, arts-based research and resilience. A specific focus was made on working with refugee children and their families. Across the literature, it becomes evident that narrative research methods provide important opportunities for new understanding of everyday experience around resilience. While there is limited research in the field, key messages can be made about the importance of engaging with arts-based research (such as narratives) to support the development of resilience within early childhood education. The key messages are:

1. Arts-based research is an important tool for allowing new ways of understanding resilience in early childhood education. Different perspectives can be shown from the child and the family that, to date, have rarely been explored in the research literature. The different perspectives differ from the everyday perceptions of resilience that have largely come from an adult or medical perspective.
2. Narrative methods (as arts-based research) are an important tool for working with refugee children and their families in early childhood education settings. The approach allows the lived experience to become known to educators and policy-makers, providing important insights into resilience at points in time. The approach works directly with the reality of the child and the family, allowing their voices to be heard. The approach is respectful of the research participant and provides space for them to share their lived experience in their own time. Thus, the approach can be used to assist supporting and developing resilience with children and their families.
3. Narrative methods (as arts-based research) provide opportunities for educators to also develop skills and knowledge around how to support the development of resilience when working with refugee children and their families. The examples of multimodal and sandplay were given. By listening to the narratives, educators also begin to reflect on their pedagogical practices and ways of working with refugee children and their families. It is hoped that through self-reflection, change can be enacted that provides supportive approaches for resilience. By allowing the perspective of the child and the family to emerge, new understandings about how educators and key stakeholders can support refugee families become known. The approach provides care and consideration and allows a "bottom-up" approach to research, building from the lived experiences of young children and their families around resilience
4. Resilience is an emerging research field within early childhood education. To date, there is limited research in the literature that has explored resilience within the field of education. The perspective has largely

been based on medical or health perspectives. It is important that the perspective of resilience and early childhood education continues to develop and includes the viewpoints of children and families.

The preschool is an important context for consideration in building resilience when working with refugee children and their families. The preschool is often the first point of connection with society and the role of the educators extends to also supporting and community inclusion of the family. It is important for educators to understand their role in supporting young children and their families in developing resilience.

As the importance of arts-based research begins to grow, it is hoped more researchers implement suitable techniques that bring more discussion about the child's perspective about their own well-being and resilience. The discussion allows respect for the child and family and brings together supportive methods to hopefully enact change. In particular, it is hoped that key stakeholders and policy-makers are able to reflect on the important messages from refugee children about their own resilience.

References

Adair, J., & Tobin, J. (2008). Listening to the voices of immigrant parents. In C. Genisha & A. Lin Goodwin (Eds.), *Diversities in early childhood education. Rethinking and doing* (pp. 137–150). New York, NY: Routledge.

Angel, B., Hjern, A., & Hernandez, J. (2004). *Att möta flyktingar* [To meet refugees]. Lund, Sweden: Studentlitteratur.

Austin, D., & Forinash, M. (2005). Arts-based inquiry. In B. Wheeler (Ed.), *Music therapy research* (2nd ed., pp. 458–471). Gilsum, NH: Barcelona Publishers.

Bagnoli, A. (2009). Beyond the standard interview: The use of graphic elicitation and arts-based methods. *Qualitative Research, 9*(5), 547–570.

Bouakaz, L. (2007). *Parental involvement in school: What hinders and what promotes parental involvement in an urban school* (Unpublished doctoral thesis). Malmö, Sweden: Malmö Lärarutbildningen.

Bunar, N. (2010). *Nyanlända och lärande* [New arrivals and learning]. Stockholm, Sweden: Vetenskapsrådet.

Clandinin, D. J., & Connelly, F. M. (2000). *Narrative inquiry: Experience and story in qualitative research*. San Francisco, CA: Jossey-Bass.

Clandinin, D. J., Huber, J., Huber, M., Murphy, S., Murray Orr, A., Pearce, M., & Steeves, P. (2006). *Composing diverse identities: Narrative inquiries into the interwoven lives of children and teachers*. New York, NY: Routledge.

Clandinin, D. J., & Murphy, M. S. (2009). Relational ontological commitments in narrative research. *Educational Researcher, 38*(8), 598–602.

Clark, A. (2010). Young children as protagonists and the role of participatory, visual methods in engaging multiple perspectives. *American Journal of Community Psychology, 46*(1–2), 115–123.

Connelly, F. M., & Clandinin, D. J. (1990). Stories of experience and narrative inquiry. *Educational Researcher, 19*(5), 2–14.

Connelly, F. M., & Clandinin, D. J. (1999). *Shaping a professional identity: Stories of educational practice* (p. 184). New York, NY: Teachers College Press.

Connelly, F. M., Phillion, J., & He, M. F. (2003). An exploration of narrative inquiry in multiculturalism in education: Reflecting on two decades of research in an inner-city Canadian community school. *Curriculum Inquiry, 33*(4), 363–384.

Cook, T., & Hess, E. (2007). What the camera sees and from whose perspective. Fun methodologies for engaging children in enlightening adults. *Childhood, 14*(1), 29–45.

Craig, C. (2007). Story constellations: A narrative approach to situating teachers' knowledge of school reform in context. *Teaching and Teacher Education, 23*(2), 173–188.

Crozier, G. (2001). Excluded parents: The deracialisation of parental involvement. *Race Ethnicity and Education, 4*(4), 329–341.

Cummins, J. (2001). *Negotiating identities: Education for empowerment in a diverse society*. Los Angeles, CA: California Association for Bilingual Education.

Dalli, C. (2002). From home to childcare: Challenges for mothers, teachers and children. In H. Fabian & A. W. Dunlop (Eds.), *Transitions in the early years. Debating continuity and progression for young children in early education* (pp. 38–51). New York, NY: Routledge.

De Gioia, K. E. (2015). Immigrant and refugee mothers' experiences of the transition into child care: A case study. *European Early Childhood Education Research Journal, 23*(5), 662–672.

Dewey, J. (1938). *Experience and education*. New York, NY: Collier Books.

DiClemente, R., Santelli, J., & Crosby, R. (2009). *Adolescent health: Understanding and preventing risk behaviours*. Hoboken, NJ: Jossey-Bass.

Doyle, O., Harmon, C. P., Heckman, J. J., & Tremblay, R. E. (2009). Investing in early human development: Timing and economic efficiency. *Economics & Human Biology, 7*(1), 1–6.

Driessnack, M., & Furukawa, R. (2012). Arts-based data collection techniques used in child research. *Journal for Specialists in Pediatric Nursing, 17*(1), 3–9.

Einarsdottir, J. (2014). Children's perspectives on the role of preschool teachers. *European Early Childhood Education Research Journal, 22*(5), 679–697.

Estola, E., Farquhar, S., & Puroila, A. M. (2018). Well-being narratives and young children. *Educational Philosophy and Theory, 46*(8), 929–941. https://doi.org/10.1080/00131857.2013.785922

European Commission. (2015). *Education and training*. Retrieved February 12, from http://ec.europa.eu/education/policy/school/early-childhood_en.htm

Fleer, M. (1997). A cross-cultural study of rural Australian aboriginal children's understandings of night and day. *Research in Science Education, 27*(1), 101–116.

Garvis, S. (2010). *An investigation of beginning teacher self-efficacy for the arts in the middle years of schooling (years 4–9)* (Unpublished doctoral thesis). Brisbane, Australia: School of Music, University of Queensland.

Garvis, S. (2015). *Narrative constellations*. Rotterdam, The Netherlands: Sense Publishers.

Garvis, S. (2017). Arts-based research with young children across health and education. In G. Barton & M. Baguley (Eds.), *Palgrave handbook of global arts education* (pp. 461–473). London, UK: Palgrave.

Grieshaber, S., & Miller, M. (2010). Migrant and refugee children, their families and early childhood education. In O. Saracho & B. Spodek (Eds.), *Contemporary perspectives on language and cultural diversity in early childhood education* (pp. 167–190). Charlotte, NC: Information Age Publishing.

Heckman, J. J. (2006). Skill formation and the economics of investing in disadvantaged children. *Science, 312*(5782), 1900–1902.

Hilppö, J., Lipponen, L., Kumpulainen, K., & Rainio, A. (2016). Children's sense of agency in preschool: A sociocultural investigation. *International Journal of Early Years Education, 24*(2), 157–171.

Hyltenstam, K., & Tuomela, V. (2004). *Svenska som andraspråk: i forskning, undervisning och samhälle* [Swedish as a second language: In research, teaching and society]. Lund, Sweden: Studentlitteratur.

Kozinets, R. B., & Belk, R. W. (2006). Videography. In V. Jupp (Ed.), *Sage dictionary of social research methods*. Retrieved from http://srmo.Sagepub.com/view/the-sage-dictionary-of-social-research-methods/n221

Kronick, R., Rousseau, C., & Cleveland, J. (2018). Refugee children's sandplay narratives in immigrant detention in Canada. *European Child and Adolescent Psychiatry, 27*, 423–437.

Lacroix, L., Rousseau, C., Gauthier, M. F., Singh, A., Giguère, N., & Lemzoudi, Y. (2007). Immigrant and refugee preschoolers' sandplay representations of the tsunami. *The Arts in Psychotherapy, 34*(2), 99–113.

Lappalainen, S. (2003). Celebrating internationality: Constructions of nationality at preschool. In D. Beach, T. Gordon, & E. Lahlema (Eds.), *Democratic education: Ethnographic challenges* (pp. 80–91). London, UK: The Tufnell Press.

Ledger, A., & Edwards, J. (2011). Arts-based research practices in music therapy research: Existing and potential developments. *The Arts in Psychotherapy, 38*(5), 312–317.

Lunneblad, J. (2006). *Förskolan och mångfalden: En etnografisk studie på en förskola i ett multietniskt område*. Göteborg, Sweden: Acta Universitatis Gothoburgensis.

Lunneblad, J. (2017). Integration of refugee children and their families in the Swedish preschool: Strategies, objectives and standards. *European Early Childhood Education Research Journal, 25*(3), 359–369.

Maxwell, R. (Ed.). (2001). *Culture works: The political economy of culture*. Minneapolis, MN: University of Minnesota Press.

McAuley, C., & Rose, W. (2010). Child well-being: Current issues and future directions. In C. McAuley & W. Rose (Eds.), *Child well-being. Understanding children's lives* (pp. 207–240). London, UK: Jessica Kingsley.

Papandreou, M., & Terzi, M. (2011). Exploring children's ideas about natural phenomena in kindergarten classes: Designing and evaluating "eliciting activities". *Review of Science, Mathematics and ICT Education, 5*(2), 27–47.

Prior, M. A., & Niesz, T. (2013). Refugee children's adaptation to American early childhood classrooms: A narrative inquiry. *The Qualitative Report, 18*(39), 1–17.

Robbins, J. (2009). Analyzing young children's thinking about natural phenomena: A sociocultural/cultural historical perspective. *Review of Science, Mathematics and ICT Education, 3*(1), 75–97.

Schwab, J. (1970). *The practical: A language for curriculum*. Washington, DC: National Education Association.

Shannon-Baker, P. (2015). "But I wanted to appear happy": How using arts-informed and mixed methods approaches complicate qualitatively driven research on culture shock. *International Journal of Qualitative Methods, 14*(2), 34–52.

Sims, M., & Hutchins, T. (2001). Transition to child care for children from culturally and linguistically diverse backgrounds. *Australasian Journal of Early Childhood, 26*(3), 7–11.

Stone, E. (1988). *Black sheep and kissing cousins: How our family stories shape us.* New York, NY: Penguin Books.

Suárez-Orozco, C., Pimentel, A., & Martin, M. (2009). The significance of relationships: Academic engagement and achievement among newcomer immigrant youth. *Teachers College Record, 111*(3), 712–749.

Tallberg Broman, I. (2009). "No Parent Left Behind": Föräldradeltagande för inkludering och Effektivitet. *Educare, 2–3,* 221–240.

Vandenbroeck, M., Roets, G., & Snoeck, A. (2009). Immigrant mothers crossing borders: Nomadic identities and multiple belongings in early childhood education. *European Early Childhood Education Research Journal, 17*(2), 203–216.

Wang, C., & Burris, M. A. (1997). Photovoice: Concept, methodology and the use for participatory needs assessment. *Health Education and Behavior, 24*(3), 369–387.

Whitmarsh, J. (2011). Othered voices. Asylum-seeking mothers and early years education. *European Early Childhood Education Research Journal, 19*(4), 535–551.

Wigg, U. (2008). *Bryta upp och börja om.: Berättelser om flyktingskap, skolgång och identitet* [Break up and start over. Stories about refugees, schooling and identity] (Doctoral dissertation). Linköpings Universitet, Sweden.

Wright, S. (2007). Graphic-narrative play: Young children's authoring through drawing and telling. *International Journal of Education and the Arts, 8*(8), 1–27.

Zarobe, L., & Bungay, H. (2017). The role of arts activities in developing resilience and mental wellbeing in children and young people a rapid review of the literature. *Perspectives in Public Health, 137*(6), 337–348.

3

How Arts-Based Methods Are Used to Support the Resilience and Well-Being of Young People: A Review of the Literature

Abbey MacDonald, Margaret Baguley, Georgina Barton, and Martin Kerby

Introduction

Young people are navigating challenges today that were not necessarily present in earlier generations (Chaplin & John, 2007; Schmitz & Tyler, 2016). These challenges are so foreign to older generations that they are often at a loss in knowing how to support young people in successfully negotiating

---

A. MacDonald (✉)
University of Tasmania, Hobart, TAS, Australia
e-mail: Abbey.MacDonald@utas.edu.au

M. Baguley • G. Barton • M. Kerby
School of Education, University of Southern Queensland,
Springfield, Brisbane, QLD, Australia
e-mail: margaret.baguley@usq.edu.au; georgina.barton@usq.edu.au;
martin.kerby@usq.edu.au

© The Author(s) 2020
L. McKay et al. (eds.), *Arts-Based Research, Resilience and Well-being Across the Lifespan*,
https://doi.org/10.1007/978-3-030-26053-8_3

the challenges that shape or threaten their resilience and well-being. As a result of technological advancements, transmobility of people within and across geographic borders, and social and cultural environments continue to become more and more complex (Bertaux & Thompson, 2017; Karvonen, Rimpelä, & Rimpelä, 1999), young people find themselves navigating increasingly complex issues related to families, communities, political agendas and governments. Such concerns compound for young people, especially those from non-dominant populations, due to limited access to resources and appropriate support. Chaplin and John (2007) and Schmitz and Tyler (2016), for example, note that many marginalised youth are expected to carry out significant domestic roles, such as looking after younger siblings, budgeting home affairs and/or caring for elderly members of the family. This is further problematised by the fact that, one in six young people in Australia (aged 15–24) are reportedly living in poverty and at risk of becoming, or are already homeless (Homelessness Australia, 2016).

It is of particular relevance to this chapter and review of the literature, presented herein, to ascertain the factors and circumstances that characterise what it means to be a young person growing up, particularly in Australia, and assemble a sense of how resilience and well-being collectively unfold within this experience. If an understanding of the effectiveness of existing strategies enacted to support young peoples' development and capacity to maintain resilience and well-being can be ascertained, we are ultimately better positioned to offer the best support for young people. An analysis of recent literature facilitates an examination of the experience of adolescents in contemporary Australia, if not globally, and how the arts can be used to cultivate resilience. In achieving this, the chapter is able to identify the most appropriate resources to support adolescents as they face increasingly complex and diverse challenges.

Process Taken to Map the Literature Related to Young Peoples' Resilience, Well-Being and the Arts

This chapter opens its discussion with an exploration of the substructural literature that offers conceptualisations and applied definitions of resilience and well-being of young people in education contexts. The mapping undertaken for this project was conducted systematically (Pickering & Byrne, 2014). In employing mapping as method, the authors adopt a process that aligns powerfully with the socioecological lens brought to examine the interrelationship between resilience and well-being, where such "mapping of pertinent literature embraces a process of networked, relational and transversal thinking" (Coleman & Collins, 2006, p. 232). In providing a means through which to articulate fresh interconnections and possibilities within existing terrain, the method of mapping synergises with the role of arts-based methods in resisting the tracing of something that came before. This mapping method employed within our systematic review of literature makes way for possible other terrain to emerge through "setting out the co-ordination points for worlds in progress, for subjectivities to come" (O'Sullivan, 2006, p. 35). In perceiving the systematic review of literature as inherent to arts-based methods and in relation to a socioecological perspective, our connections and potentialities converge within the object of the map, "where the object itself is movement" (Deleuze & Guattari, 1987, p. 61).

The goal of the mapping was to explore research literature that has sought to ascertain how arts-based methods have been used to support the development of resilience and well-being in adolescents (Clarke, 2018). The mapping exercise collated the bibliographic details of each resource, a brief overview, the type of resource (i.e., journal article, book, blog, written document or university guide), what information or recommendations were being offered as most useful in relation to young people, resilience and well-being, and any issues or barriers. Our review of literature did not outset parameters upon search dates as it sought to include and ascertain an evolution of how arts-based methods have and are being employed in cultivating resilience and well-being for adolescents. This is consistent with the mapping method employed as it enabled the gathering of literature to remain open for new potentialities to emerge from existing terrain. The initial abstract pitched for this chapter as part of the proposal process provided an impetus statement, from which four prevailing search terms were identified by the team; these being *resilience, well-being, arts-based* and *adolescents*. The initial gathering of literature unfolded from these four key search terms, from which particular attention was paid to the key and/or prevalent terms noted in individual items. This iterative process informed the collation and mapping of literature, feeding into and from the search and subsequent mapping, from which 55 items (see reference list) were meaningfully engaged with as part of the process and ensuing product of this book chapter. Notes regarding specific resources' abstract and pertinent keywords aligning with the keywords that emerged for this chapter were collated and referred back to by the authors as the chapter evolved. The key search terms distilled from the above iterative process were used in a variety of search browsers and databases including Google Scholar, Informit, ProQuest and JSTOR. These prevalent search terms evolved to include (but were not limited to):

- Adolescents and adolescence
- Arts-based interventions
- Resilience
- School/community
- Well-being
- Young people

Following the initial mapping exercise, the authors then engaged with the collective literature, and met at various stages throughout the drafting process to discuss emerging themes, and settle upon the overarching thematic *throughlines* or threads (Bland, 1992) that would be used to frame the ensuing post-review discussion. Upon determining the overarching points for discussion, the authors also collectively distilled a set of recommendations and directions that might further enhance practice to support the cultivation of resilience and well-being in adolescents in educational contexts.

Defining Resilience and Well-Being for Diverse Disciplinary Contexts

In conceptualising this chapter, the authors ascertained individual understandings; how we have collectively encountered in our respective education contexts the challenges impacting on young people's capacity to cultivate resilience and well-being. In intersecting our individual perceptions and perspectives, we were able to settle upon a definition of resilience that acknowledged and embraced the diversity of our discipline contexts, which spanned the arts (predominantly music; and media and visual art), English and history.

Having insight into the historical evolution of resilience allowed us to determine how young people, and those who support them in education contexts, have engaged with one another to enable or inhibit resilience and well-being. The term resilience originates from the Latin word *resilire*, meaning to rebound, bounce back or referring to one's ability to cope and prevail despite adversity (Heise, 2014). In the field of social work, which operates in close or entwined proximity to education in terms of aspiration and challenges, Greene (2007) describes resilience as the development of clusters of self-protective behaviours and strengths. The broader field of study straddling education and social work pertaining to resilience emerges from the field of prevention, or preventative measures, which within the context of youth development programs became prominent in extrapolating the prevention of drug and alcohol abuse (Aisenberg & Mennen, 2000; Rhodes & Schechter, 2014).

As noted in Chap. 1 of this volume, resilience and well-being are interrelated. To investigate these interrelationships, a socioecological perspective of well-being is the framework around which this chapter is conceptualised. The points at which various factors converge or resist in the interrelationship between resilience and well-being allow us to see the interplay of factors through a socioecological lens. In order for this interplay to be articulated, distinctions, synergies and nuances between definitions of resilience and well-being as captured within a socioecological perspective help us to ascertain interrelatedness. For this chapter, Panter-Brick and Leckman's (2013) definition of resilience as inextricably linked to well-being is embraced within "a process of harnessing biological, psychosocial, structural, and cultural resources to sustain wellbeing" (2013, p. 333). The interconnectedness of resilience and well-being is reiterated within a socioecological perspective, where students can be assisted to become aware of entwined factors, such as social relationships, family, peers, their schooling and the environment that exists between themselves, others and more broadly within society (Chen, Lau, Tapanya, & Cameron, 2012). King, Renó, and Novo's (2014) view of well-being further encompasses the socioecological perspective by including employment opportunities, health care and education, however they highlight the impact of these on young people in marginalised communities. Bourdieu's (1986) concept of cultural capital explains how important it is that students have access to creative pursuits in order to enhance meaning in their lives and subsequently well-being (DiMaggio & Mukhtar, 2004). Approaches to improving cultural capital have the potential to draw on the cultural and social strengths of youth rather than from a deficit perspective (Barton, 2019).

It is interesting to note however, that there is a prevalence of deficit language in prevention research, which tends to emphasise the problems of youth, using negative labels such as delinquent, deviant, or dysfunctional (Aisenberg & Mennen, 2000; Krovetz, 2007). Deficit storylines have the capacity to be reimagined as generative spaces for possibility and consequently resilience can thrive (MacDonald, Hunter, Ewing, & Polley, 2018). Careful reflection and caution however should be exercised when seeking to address concerns surrounding the cultivation of resilience and well-being, as language can be powerfully enacted to reiterate disempowerment or aspirations to mobilise change.

Exposure and Affect

Awareness of the scope and prevalence of adolescents being exposed to, or affected by, traumatic experiences is important for any professional person working with young people to understand. Adolescents can be particularly vulnerable. It has been suggested, that approximately 90% of people will be exposed to at least one traumatic event at some point in their life (Breslau, 2002). This experience may lead people to develop post-traumatic stress related issues (Cavanaugh, 2016; Hyman, Zelikoff, & Clarke, 1988). Despite the prevalence of traumatic experiences and the impact upon a diverse demographic of children (Yatham, Sivathasan, Yoon, da Silva, & Ravindran, 2018), most individuals survive and many thrive (Ibeagha, Balogun, & Adejuwon, 2004).

In relation to potential outcomes that can eventuate from adolescents' exposure to traumatic events, it is pertinent to consider some of the broader risks and adversities regarded as typical within adolescence. According to Rosenman and Rodgers (2004), "childhood adversity is an important moderator of the effects of trauma" (p. 695). The same researchers' longitudinal community study of psychological health in the Canberra region of Australia revealed that 59.5% of the sample group (7485 randomly selected subjects in 20–24, 40–44 and 60–64 year age bands) had experienced some form of childhood adversity, with domestic conflict, parental psychopathology and/or substance use (Rosenman & Rodgers, 2004) identified as typical common adversities. While there is growing recognition that some people exposed to adversities will not experience disruptions in life (Everly, Smith, & Lating, 2009; Westphal & Bonanno, 2007), there still remains the question why some people cope but others crumble in similar circumstances (Heise, 2014). Within the spaces where resilience is either forged or impeded, engagement with and in the arts emerges as a means for assisting young people to cultivate a healthy sense of well-being, and build capacity to successfully navigate adversity.

Arts encounters or intervention mechanisms that embrace creative sensibilities and encourage us to examine propensities that may be judged unsociable, disruptive or unruly, can position us to understand relationships between exposure and affect. Through these engagements in or encounters with the arts, young people can be emboldened to come to terms with inhibitors as well as embracing the enablers of resilience (Coholic, 2011). In these ways, the arts can contribute constructively to the health of society and are integral to positive physical, social and mental well-being (Macnaughton, White, & Stacy, 2005).

Our ability to elicit meaning of affect (Biesta, 2010; Massumi, 2002) through the arts in relation to what might be traditionally viewed as resilient or thriving, or conversely declining, within education contexts, can position us to reimagine, and where necessary interrupt, a contemporary politics of aspiration (MacDonald et al., 2018). Where arts-based methods or interventions are embraced in our examination of exposure and affect of circumstances that impact upon resilience and well-being, we can create spaces and provide the means for young people to express themselves metaphorically or symbolically without requiring explicit reliving or retelling of adverse challenges. Further to this, we can listen and affirm, but not try to solve their problems, and focus on the individual's strengths and assets and use these as a source of communication and emancipation (Heise, 2014).

Arts-Based Methods to Cultivate Resilience and Well-Being in Young People

A number of studies have explored various ways in which the arts can be employed to improve the experience of young people, and in particular those from marginalised communities (Kay & Arnold, 2014; Krovetz, 2007; Yatham et al., 2018). Whether through direct experiences of working with arts practice or exploring arts-based methods for meaning-making and communication, these studies have shown both significant and diverse impacts on young people's capacity to develop and maintain resilience and a sense of personal health and well-being (Coholic, 2011; Diamond & Lee, 2011). Underpinning the research that advocates for arts engagement as capacity building and a means for bolstering young people's resilience and well-being are investigations that have demonstrated how arts multimodality and ways of knowing support the engagement necessary to cultivate positive mindsets, confidence and competence in young people (Barton, 2019). Communication through different modes is important as sometimes those who are suffering need *more than words* to express their emotions (Livermore, 1998). Further, if working with young people from culturally and linguistically diverse backgrounds, and potentially with English as a Second Language, it is important that opportunities are provided where language is not the dominant mode of communication (Lynch, 2007). The arts and other ways of knowing and being can assist people in feeling safe and supported (Payne, 1993).

Irwin (2006) argues that working with and in arts-based activities can be enormously engaging and satisfying for young people and it is this capacity to "stimulate a desire to create, express hidden wishes, and relieve tension" (p. 305) that makes arts-based methods and interventions attractive and inclusive for young people from diverse backgrounds. Further to the arts capacity to embrace, include and receive people, James (1989) describes the enjoyment it can create that keeps young people emotionally receptive and open to positive messages about self and other.

The importance of positive messaging that can be promoted, celebrated and accessed through arts-based experiences align powerfully with mindfulness programs and interventions in schools which have been shown to be an effective way for children and adolescents to reframe stress, modulate their response to stress, and improve their focus (Napoli, Krech, & Holley, 2005). Coholic (2011) describes how mindfulness-based practices "have the potential to help young people in need learn to focus on their feelings and thoughts without judging these experiences thereby promoting the development of self-awareness" (p. 314). Regular practice of these mindfulness interventions, either within or parallel to engagement in and with the arts may further augment capacity to hold attention and regulate emotions (Diamond & Lee, 2011; Klatt, Harpster, Browne, White, & Case-Smith, 2013), which positively correlates with young people's demonstration of inhibitory control (Oberle, Schonert-Reichl, Lawlor, & Thomson, 2011). When arts-based methods are entwined purposefully with mindfulness initiatives in schools, young people are provided with a means of and for multi-modal exploration to cultivate self-awareness and aspects of resilience, including "improved coping and social skills, problem solving skills, and feelings of self-esteem" (Coholic, 2011, p. 315).

Aspiration

The role of aspiration in relation to young people's resilience and well-being emerges as an area of key interest, and potentially under-examined in regard to how their aspirations, education priorities and agendas, educators, community and citizenship do not always align. When individual aspirations are not acknowledged, or identified as misaligning with the collective, young people's sense of self-worth and resilience has the potential to become destabilised. Hunter and MacDonald's (2017) exploration of *dark play*, and attention given to an alternative politics of aspiration posits the questions "what social inquiry has been undertaken to map young people's aspirations, in young people's terms?" (p. 10). The notion of dark play is the naming up of a space which questions the conceptualisation of a particular type of aspiration, purpose and meaning of education, which risks overlooking opportunities for transformation and achievement through alternative means (Hunter & MacDonald, 2017). Rankin (2018) describes the importance of paying attention to the power of culture, and the need to remain open to and vigilant about everyone's right to thrive. This is imperative to ensuring all sections of society are heard, visible, included and not contained by deficit discourses that might seek to demonise or render stories invisible and citizenry vulnerable.

It is interesting to note that these exercises of investigation, or attentive enquiry mostly occur beyond the formal environments of school, in the extra-curricular domain. An example of this can be seen in Tasmania, where the arts-community organisation *Kick Start Arts*' multiyear *The Happiness Project* was designed to support positive mental health and digital literacy by involving the Tasmanian community (all ages) in creating and producing short broadcast-quality films about their everyday lives. Such a project is anchored in a purposeful process of artistic collaboration where teachers role-model the "kinds of positive education pedagogies and outcomes for which many schools strive—creative, critical, collaborative, communicative, and very 21st century" (Hunter & MacDonald, 2017, p. 14). When teaching and learning is driven by a heightened ethics of care for context that priorities access, accomplishment and care above regimes of testing and ranking, the aspirations of young people can be made visible and tangible through "hidden" and extra-curricular contexts and real world applications and accomplishment. These are the kinds of projects that can richly bolster resilience and well-being, where aspiration of the individual is empowered through arts-centric methods that "enable participants to make as many marks for and with others, as for themselves" (Hunter & MacDonald, 2017, p. 17).

Arts-Based Approaches to Improving Resilience and Well-Being for Young People: Thematic Throughlines

The preceding discussion provides an overview of reading that emerged as pertinent (reflecting a spread of seminal to more recent emerging literature) to young people's capacity to cultivate resilience and well-being in and through arts-based methods and practices. Ongoing searches occurred until the mapped themes reached saturation, that is, that the same themes kept reoccurring. The next section of this review explores the key themes in relation to young people's participation in the arts and how they can support development of resilience and well-being, as settled upon by the authorship team.

How the Arts Can Empower People

It is clear from our study of the literature that the arts can be transformative (Ewing, 2011). When young people are uncertain of how to improve their lives, the arts can assist them to flourish in, through and from examples of adversity they may find themselves navigating. Indeed, Kay (2000) highlights how the arts can be used to regenerate communities. He notes that the arts assist communities in recognising their own identities, culture and support people to work together. The arts are appropriate in wider community development programs (Kay, 2000) and are versatile enough to be used across discipline areas, contexts and cultures. Nissley (2010) reports on how the arts were utilised for learning at work in the area of business such as in relation to strategic transformation. Strategic transformation is, according to Nissley (2010), "when the business integrates the arts in areas such as vision and values, creativity and innovation, branding and marketing" (p. 12) but also in supporting work colleagues to express themselves, affording access to "deep interior lives" (p. 13).

Thompson, Molina, Viswanath, Warnecke, and Prelip (2016) argue that the arts can reduce health disparities as they empower individual and communities to "become major players in solving their own health problems" (p. 1424). They highlight how empowerment is a community process and has potential to equalise power distribution. This is particularly relevant to young people living in less than optimal conditions. From our review of the literature, it is apparent that it takes more than one person for empowerment to occur. The arts are collaborative and build teamwork practices and therefore enable transformative practice in young people's lives.

The Arts as a Different Way of Knowing and Communicating

The fact that the arts are multimodal allows for young people, regardless of background and academic outcomes, to express meaning in a range of contexts. Much research notes the importance of the arts in marginalised communities as they provide opportunities and access to having a voice and as stated above feel empowered. Muraco, for example, states that:

> Arts organizations can teach… a variety of skills and processes that are not emphasised in the normal curriculum… These skills are… intuitive and qualitative skills. The arts can teach communication and presentation; team building and problem solving; or product and systems innovation. Arts based training can be designed to teach… the allowance for failure and risk-taking. (Muraco as cited in Nissley, 2010, p. 9)

Even though Muraco was referring to corporate contexts, it is important to note that the arts were used in these situations due to their capacity to express meaning through multiple means. Further, Barton (2019) reveals that the arts have been identified as improving literacy learning and communication skills in general due to the increase in the ways in which young people communicate with each other, across cultural and social borders. The arts directly improve students' confidence and self-esteem (Bungay & Vella-Burrows, 2013), compassion and empathy (Barton, Baguley, Kerby, & MacDonald, 2019), and resilience and well-being (Perso, Nutton, Fraser, Silburn, & Tait, 2011).

The Arts Are Important in Marginalised Communities

The power of the arts in transforming communities that face more hardship than others is clearly apparent in the literature. Many arts-based projects in these communities have resulted in improved outcomes for young participants across a range of areas. Ngo, Lewis, and Maloney Leaf's (2017) work, for example, showed how the arts fostered sociopolitical and critical thinking for youth in marginalised areas. They were able to analyse texts and agendas in their community with the view of exploring their own differences, and how they belong amongst their community members. Similarly, Nunn (2018) showed that arts-based practices supported resettled young people into regional cities in Australian and the United Kingdom. She observes that marginalised communities often have poor access to arts activities despite the evidence that the arts are beneficial in such populations. The benefits described in this study included:

- Gaining creative skills
- Building personal capacities, including confidence, leadership skills, teamwork
- Having fun and
- Sharing ideas and experiences with each other and with audiences

The program involved in this study explored social justice issues and engaged young people in order "to generate and communicate innovative, affective and embodied knowledge and understandings" (p. 6).

Future Imaginings and Directions

It is clear that the arts and/or arts-based approaches to working with young people, particularly in marginalised communities, make a difference to their resilience and well-being. Through a range of participatory strategies the arts provide young people with a powerful voice and a means by which can express who they are. This in turn improves their capacity to be resilient and improves well-being. What is also clear is that it takes a community to support young people. In addition, these communities must be built on strengths-based rather than deficit perspectives on young people as the issues they face are largely out of their control. Critical and community reflection is needed when addressing the concerns of young people. As such, the use of language needs to be considered as it can powerfully influence the ways in which young people feel empowered or alternatively disempowered and can either mobilise or inhibit change.

References

Aisenberg, E., & Mennen, F. (2000). Children exposed to community violence: Issues for assessment and treatment. *Child and Adolescent Social Work Journal, 17*, 341–360.

Barton, G. M. (2019). *Developing the arts and literacy in schools*. London: Routledge.

Barton, G. M., Baguley, M., Kerby, M., & MacDonald, A. (2019). Exploring how quality children's literature can enhance compassion and empathy in the classroom context. In G. M. Barton & S. Garvis (Eds.), *Compassion and empathy in educational contexts*. London: Palgrave Macmillan.

Bertaux, D., & Thompson, P. (2017). *Pathways to social class: A qualitative approach to social mobility*. Abingdon, UK: Routledge.

Biesta, G. J. (2010). Why 'what works' still won't work: From evidence-based education to value-based education. *Studies in Philosophy and Education, 29*(5), 491–503.

Bland, C. J. (1992). Characteristics of a productive research environment: Literature review. *Academic Medicine: Journal of the Association of American Medical Colleges, 67*(6), 385–397.

Bourdieu, P. (1986). The forms of capital. In J. Richardson (Ed.), *Handbook of theory and research for the sociology of education* (pp. 241–258). New York: Greenwood.

Breslau, N. (2002). Epidemiologic studies of trauma, post-traumatic stress disorder, and other psychiatric disorders. *Canadian Journal of Psychiatry, 47*(10), 923–929.

Bungay, H., & Vella-Burrows, T. (2013). The effects of participating in creative activities on the health and well-being of children and young people: A rapid review of the literature. *Perspectives in Public Health, 133*(1), 44–52.

Cavanaugh, B. (2016). Trauma-informed classrooms and schools. *Beyond Behavior, 25*(2), 41–46.

Chaplin, L. N., & John, D. R. (2007). Growing up in a material world: Age differences in materialism in children and adolescents. *Journal of Consumer Research, 34*(4), 480–493.

Chen, J., Lau, C., Tapanya, S., & Cameron, C. A. (2012). Identities as protective processes: Socio-ecological perspectives on youth resilience. *Journal of Youth Studies, 15*(6), 761–779.

Clarke, T. (2018). Do arts subjects matter for secondary school students' wellbeing? *Thinking Skills and Creativity, 29*, 97–114.

Coholic, D. A. (2011). Exploring the feasibility and benefits of arts-based mindfulness-based practices with young people in need: Aiming to improve aspects of self-awareness and resilience. *Child & Youth Care Forum, 40*(4), 303–317.

Coleman, S., & Collins, P. (2006). *Locating the field: Space, place and context in anthropology* (ASA series). Oxford, UK: Berg Publishers.

Deleuze, G., & Guattari, F. (1987). *Dialogues*. London: Athlone Press.

Diamond, A., & Lee, K. (2011). Interventions shown to aid executive function development in 4 to 12 year olds. *Science, 333*, 959–964.

DiMaggio, P., & Mukhtar, T. (2004). Arts participation as cultural capital in the United States, 1982–2002: Signs of decline? *Poetics, 32*(2), 169–194.

Everly, J. G., Smith, K. J., & Lating, J. M. (2009). A rationale for cognitively-based resilience and psychological first aid (PFA) training: A structural modeling analysis. *International Journal of Emergency Mental Health, 11*(4), 249–262.

Ewing, R. (2011). *The arts and Australian education: Realising potential*. Melbourne, VIC: ACER.

Greene, R. R. (2007). *Social work practice: A risk and resilience perspective*. Monterey, CA: Brooks/Cole.

Heise, D. (2014). Steeling and resilience in art education. *Art Education, 67*(3), 26–30.

Homelessness Australia. (2016). *Homelessness and young people*. Australia: Homelessness Australia. Retrieved from https://www.homelessnessaustralia.org.au/sites/homelessnessaus/files/2017-07/Young%20People.pdf

Hunter, M. A., & MacDonald, A. (2017). Dark play: On an alternative politics of aspiration. In P. O. Connor & C. Gómez (Eds.), *Playing with possibilities* (pp. 16–33). Newcastle-upon-Tyne, UK: Cambridge Scholars Publishing.

Hyman, I. A., Zelikoff, W., & Clarke, J. (1988). Psychological and physical abuse in the schools: A paradigm for understanding post-traumatic stress disorder in children and youth. *Journal of Traumatic Stress, 1*(2), 243–267.

Ibeagha, P. N., Balogun, S. K., & Adejuwon, G. A. (2004). Resiliency of inner-city Yoruba University undergraduates in South Western Nigeria. *Studies of Tribes and Tribals, 2*(2), 125–129.

Irwin, E. C. (2006). Peter: A study of cumulative trauma from 'robot' to 'regular guy'. In L. Carey (Ed.), *Expressive and creative arts methods for trauma survivors* (pp. 93–113). London, UK: Jessica Kingsley Publishers.

James, B. (1989). *Treating traumatized children: New insights and creative interventions*. New York, NY: The Free Press.

Karvonen, S., Rimpelä, A. H., & Rimpelä, M. K. (1999). Social mobility and health related behaviours in young people. *Journal of Epidemiology & Community Health, 53*(4), 211–217.

Kay, A. (2000). Art and community development: The role the arts have in regenerating communities. *Community Development Journal, 35*(4), 414–424.

Kay, L., & Arnold, A. (2014). Order from chaos: An arts-based approach to counteract trauma and violence. *Art Education, 67*(3), 31–36.

King, M. F., Renó, V. F., & Novo, E. M. (2014). The concept, dimensions and methods of assessment of human well-being within a socioecological context: A literature review. *Social Indicators Research, 116*(3), 681–698.

Klatt, M., Harpster, K., Browne, E., White, S., & Case-Smith, J. (2013). Feasibility and preliminary outcomes for move-into-learning: An arts-based mindfulness classroom intervention. *The Journal of Positive Psychology, 8*(3), 233–241.

Krovetz, M. L. (2007). *Fostering resilience: Expecting all students to use their minds and hearts well.* Thousand Oaks, CA: Corwin.

Livermore, J. (Ed.). (1998). *More than words can say: A view of literacy through the arts.* Canberra, ACT: Australian Centre for Arts Education, Faculty of Education, University of Canberra.

Lynch, P. (2007). Making meaning many ways: An exploratory look at integrating the arts with classroom curriculum. *Art Education, 60*(4), 33–38.

MacDonald, A., Hunter, M. A., Ewing, R., & Polley, J. (2018). Dancing around drawn edges: Reimagining deficit storylines as sites for relational arts teacher professional learning collaboration. *Australian Art Education, 39*(3), 455.

Macnaughton, J., White, M., & Stacy, R. (2005). Researching the benefits of arts in health. *Health Education, 105*(5), 332–339.

Massumi, B. (2002). Introduction. In B. Massumi (Ed.), *A shock to thought: Expression after Deleuze and Guattari* (pp. xiii–xxxix). London, UK: Routledge.

Napoli, M., Krech, P. R., & Holley, L. C. (2005). Mindfulness training for elementary school students: The attention academy. *Journal of Applied School Psychology, 21*, 99–125.

Ngo, B., Lewis, C., & Maloney Leaf, B. (2017). Fostering sociopolitical consciousness with minoritized youth: Insights from community-based arts programs. *Review of Research in Education, 41*(1), 358–380.

Nissley, N. (2010). Arts-based learning at work: Economic downturns, innovation upturns, and the eminent practicality of arts in business. *Journal of Business Strategy, 31*(4), 8–20.

Nunn, C. (2018). *Dispersed belongings: A participatory arts-based study of experiences of resettled refugee young people in regional cities in Australia and the United Kingdom. A report for project partners*. Manchester, UK: Manchester Centre for Youth Studies.

O'Sullivan, S. (2006). *Art encounters Deleuze and Guattari: Thought beyond representation*. London, UK: Palgrave Macmillan.

Oberle, E., Schonert-Reichl, K. A., Lawlor, M. S., & Thomson, K. C. (2011). Mindfulness and inhibitory control in early adolescence. *The Journal of Early Adolescence, 20*, 1–24.

Panter-Brick, C., & Leckman, J. F. (2013). Editorial commentary: Resilience in child development—Interconnected pathways to wellbeing. *Journal of Child Psychology and Psychiatry, 54*(4), 333–336.

Payne, H. (1993). *Handbook of inquiry in the arts therapies: One river, many currents*. London: Jessica Kingsley Publishers.

Perso, T., Nutton, G., Fraser, J., Silburn, S. R., & Tait, A. (2011). *'The Arts' in education: A review of arts in schools and arts-based teaching models that improve school engagement, academic, social and cultural learning*. Darwin, NT: Menzies School of Health Research.

Pickering, C., & Byrne, J. (2014). The benefits of publishing systematic quantitative literature reviews for PhD candidates and other early-career researchers. *Higher Education Research & Development, 33*(3), 534–548.

Rankin, S. (2018). *Cultural justice and the right to thrive* (Platform papers, no. 57) (pp. 8–9). Sydney, NSW: Currency House.

Rhodes, A. M., & Schechter, R. (2014). Fostering resilience among youth in inner city community arts centers: The case of the artists collective. *Education and Urban Society, 46*(7), 826–848.

Rosenman, S., & Rodgers, B. (2004). Childhood adversity in an Australian population. *Social Psychiatry and Psychiatric Epidemiology, 39*(9), 695–702.

Schmitz, R., & Tyler, K. (2016). Growing up before their time: The early adultification experiences of homeless young people. *Children and Youth Services Review, 64*, 15–22.

Thompson, B., Molina, Y., Viswanath, K., Warnecke, R., & Prelip, M. L. (2016). Strategies to empower communities to reduce health disparities. *Health Affairs, 35*(8), 1424–1428.

Westphal, M., & Bonanno, G. A. (2007). Post-traumatic growth and resilience to trauma: Different sides of the same coin or different coins? *Applied Psychology, 56*(3), 417–427.

Yatham, S., Sivathasan, S., Yoon, R., da Silva, T. L., & Ravindran, A. V. (2018). Depression, anxiety, and post-traumatic stress disorder among youth in low and middle income countries: A review of prevalence and treatment interventions. *Asian Journal of Psychiatry, 38*, 78–91.

4

Building Resilience Through Listening to Children and Young People About Their Health Preferences Using Arts-Based Methods

Jane Coad

Introduction

This chapter describes how arts-based approaches can be used in effectively eliciting the views children and young people about their health preferences in a range of settings in order to develop resilience and well-being (Hart, Aumann, & Heaver, 2010). Arts-based approaches are not new but work to develop resilience in terms of in-depth human understanding. This is important if we are to understand the world through children and young people's eyes but also contribute to their overall well-being.

Many writers over the last two decades have reported that in order to listen to children and young people effectively one way to do this is use age and development appropriate arts-based approaches (Christensen & James, 2008; Clark & Moss, 2011; Coad & Hambly, 2011; Garbarino

---

J. Coad (✉)
School of Health Sciences; Faculty of Medicine and Health Sciences, The University of Nottingham, Nottingham, UK
e-mail: Jane.Coad@nottingham.ac.uk

& Stott, 1989; Gibson, Aldiss, Horstman, Kumpunen, & Richardson, 2010; McCleod, 2011). Whilst authors offer guidance about the use of different approaches and techniques there is less critical evidence surrounding using choice of arts-based activities in terms of specific groups of children and young people. This is important in order that their engagement is meaningfully captured and characteristics of resilience such as confidence and a feeling of positive well-being are fostered.

Background

The first thing to think about in using any visual arts-based approach is that using such methods can evoke interesting responses. This is because we all have visual images around us every minute of every day and in turn they permeate our work, lives, conversation and dreams (Pink, 2001). Arts-based approaches therefore will unleash a response. It is true to say that the facilitator may want that, but even experienced facilitators can be surprised, even astounded, at the results. Young children can find it difficult to convey feelings verbally so arts-based activities can provide an opportunity to express fears and feelings through such approaches. Other writers have reported that the all children and young people, whatever their age and/or stage of development, really enjoy and gain much benefit from such activities (Christensen & James, 2008; Lewis, Kellett, & Robinson, 2003). That said, it is interesting that arts-based techniques and activities remain under-used and even under-valued in eliciting children and young people's views. We are arguing in this chapter that children and young people, including those who have diverse literacies or have speech and language needs, can use visual arts-based techniques and activities to communicate effectively as they can provide child-centred structures to enable them to describe their environments such as health care settings (Dose, 2006; McLeod, 2011; Roulstone & McLeod, 2011).

In terms of variety of approaches the list seems endless but arts-based approaches that have been used with children and young people in health-related work, with variable success, include examples such as paintings and drawings, photographs, graffiti walls, collages, mapping, textiles, clay, storytelling, woodwork and scrapbooks to name but a few (Coad, Plumridge, & Metcalfe, 2009).

Other disciplines such as early years educators, psychologists, arts therapists, play workers and arts therapists have also repeatedly noted that the use of arts-based approaches may act as symbolic languages in their own right and are thus central to the process of early development and learning (Angell, Alexander, & Hunt, 2015; Blaisdell, Arnott, Wall, & Robinson, 2018; Punch, 2002). Another point that the author of this chapter has observed is that in order to use arts-based approaches with children and young people, the facilitator does not necessarily have to have well developed personal artist skills or qualifications. Clearly, arts-based training or working with an experienced arts-based facilitator will be invaluable but these are suggestions as of more relevance is that the facilitator has a real understanding of the diverse development of children and young people and a genuine desire to hear their voices. Children and young people will see that genuine interest [or not] very quickly and usually respond accordingly (Einarsdóttir, 2007). However, there is one final point here which is whilst arts-based approaches are an interactive process in order to really enhance resilience and well-being the power relationship between adult facilitator and child/young person participant, must be underpinned by a belief that they are competent and capable research participants and in some cases, co-producers and/or co-researchers (Lundy, McEvoy, & Byrne, 2011).

Having presented an overview, a range of focused arts-based approaches will now be described with their application to listening to children and young people. They are discussed in terms of three broad and yet flexible groups as using them very much depends on the child's development. They include Pre-School (Below age 5 years) School-age (Age 6–12 years) and Teenagers/Young People (Age 13–18 years). Literature and work undertaken by the author is drawn upon.

Which Approach Shall I Use?

The first considerations in using arts-based approaches with children and young people is that the facilitator must be clear about what method they wish to use and if that method will work to achieve the objectives set out. In all of this author's arts-based work (Coad), a practice run through is undertaken with aim of helping team members to prepare. At the same time, the team are then hopefully more familiar and confident that the prepared arts-based approaches are fit for purpose, are fun and appear to be spontaneous to the children and young people. This is important to ensure that the children and young people feel relaxed and safe in talking through the feelings. It is envisaged that this helps the facilitators collate authentic information required but more so in turn it facilitates resilience and well-being of the children and young people.

The choice of which method to use is often the most challenging aspect of conducting research with children so a range of different arts-based approaches are set out in Box 4.1 which will be further explored in the groups within the chapter. However, it is worth noting that facilitators may also need to consider if the approach is a supplement or be the main approach to other techniques such as interviews. Each group will be discussed in relation to three broad groups of Pre-School (Below age 5 years) School-age (Age 6–12 years) and Teenagers/Young People (Age 13–18 years).

Box 4.1 Suggestion for Arts-Based Approaches Used with Children and Young People

Visual Arts-based

Drawing and sketching
Colouring and painting
Craft techniques such as clay, making masks, pottery, woodwork
Craft materials such as pipe cleaners, feathers, glue, glitter, stickers, textiles
Modelling and mapping
Puppets and storytelling
Collages and scrapbooking
Using shapes such as clouds, speech bubbles

Writing-based

Diaries and journals
Scrapbooking and memos (also visual as above)
Creative writing such as letters and poetry
Graffiti walls /Mapping to write ideas
Flipchart and pens/post its
Using posters to prompt response

Film or Digital-based
Photographs (taking them or viewing them)
Video
Use of Information Technology
Social media
Mobile Applications

Visual Arts-Based Approaches

Drawing, sketching, colouring and painting have been used the most frequently with children and young people across a spectrum of settings with variable success (Coad et al., 2009). What is most important is that participation in a group visual arts activity can stimulate a sense of belonging (Skudrzyk et al. 2009), develop new social experiences and interactions (Askins & Pain, 2011) and improves inclusivity such as for those with non-verbal or learning needs (MacPherson, Hart, & Heaver, 2012).

One example includes Gibson et al. (2010) used age-appropriate, arts-based techniques over 6 months with a range of children and young people with cancer aged 4–19 years. Arts-based approaches included draw and write, play and puppets, supplementary interviews and an 'activities day'. This was important to ask children and young people about their cancer in this way as little is known about whether cancer services actually meet their needs, that is from their perspectives, as the majority of previous research had sought the views of parents/legal guardians as proxies. Using participatory arts-based approaches enabled the team to build resilience including rapport, confidence and a sense of well-being with the children and young people. Their accounts were subsequently instrumental in voicing their preferences such as the importance of having familiar environments in order to ensure they gradually become a central part of the communication process and thus in time shift to being in the foreground of any communication exchange.

This team and others have thus concluded that these are valuable techniques in that they encourage children and young people to participate in the project in a way that was meaningful but also enabled the adult researcher to have insight into the child's mind in a way that they may not have had through other methods. Arguably at the core of this meaningful relationship is building resilience and trust.

However, one challenge in using such visual arts-based approaches is that the actual creation of a drawing or an art piece might be threatening to them. As a technique it may not be enhancing resilience and well-being at all in this scenario. Indeed, many adults will also proclaim '*I cannot draw*'. Further, for some pre-school children or those with physical needs creating a visual piece of art may be challenging in that it they simply do not have the have the ability. With young people they can become so over stylized the aim of the activity does not remain focused. To overcome such challenges, supplementary techniques can be used to help develop resilience and well-being. One suggestion is that, once the drawing or picture is complete the facilitator should spend time with the children or young people to enable them to talk through the drawing and can be invited to (or the adult facilitator can) add labels or cards to capture meanings (Angell et al., 2015).

Writing-Based Approaches

Writing-based approaches can be used as a single data collection tool but in terms of arts-based approaches are often used alongside visual methods. The group includes diaries, journals, letters, poetry, Graffiti walls and/or mapping activities. Facilitators will use flipchart and pens/post its to write down ideas and beliefs. Using arts-based methods with writing or using writing in arts-based way can be useful to extract data but more importantly this will reaffirm voices and build confidence, all fundamental for developing resilience and a sense of positive well-being.

Diaries or journals are commonly used with children and young people to record their views and have been found to reduce some of the difficulties of trying to reconstruct events from memory within the interview format. By asking children or young people to create a written (or notes based) diary they are able to give their views freely and creatively. But using diaries with children and young people have been critiqued as being limited if reliant on writing text only or when parents/adults are overzealous to help. To overcome this, a more recent development is the use of videos to allow the child or young person to have that autonomy and thus build their confidence and resilience.

Arguably, a useful alternative arts-based approach supplemented with written-based words or sentences might be scrapbooking. Scrapbooking is a hugely popular method for preserving personal and family history in the form of photographs, printed media, and memorabilia contained in decorated albums, or scrapbooks (Bragg & Buckingham, 2008). Whilst that actual design is based on the *Rule of Odds* which visually means that our eyes are drawn to those items arranged in odd numbers to be more natural and pleasing, arguably it is the notion of keeping printed materials of personal interest that helped it gain such popularity. A central feature in all scrapbooks is the use of *memorabilia* which refers to items that help recreate the memories but needs careful handling with children and young people. Examples might include programs, ticket stubs, postcards, invitations, awards and pamphlets. A further feature is that of *Journaling which refers to the accompanying* text that describes, explains, or accents the photographs on a scrapbook page. *Contemporary journaling* can thus take many forms such as reflective stories; personal notes or lists of words; song lyrics; quotes and poems. Consequently, a rich visual based narrative can be collated for health research which clearly is useful in capturing and understanding the views and perspectives of children and young people.

Film or Digital-Based

The final approach to be considered this chapter is film or digitally based methods. This can include photographs whether taking them or viewing them, use of video, use of Information Technology, social media and Mobile Applications *or Apps*. Overall, this group allows participants to make or comment on visual records and some of this group such as still photographs have been long established as a data collection tool in many disciplines including anthropologists, psychologists and educationalists (Winston, Cronin and Becker from Prosser, 1998). In particular, there is a dearth of work in the mid-1970s undertaken by Sontag (1977). Becker (1978) and Wagner (1979) (cited in Prosser, 1998). Therefore, these are not new. However, there has been a move especially with the massive global increase of the use of social media and Information technology sources enabling download of film-based records to be easily taken and more accessible worldwide. Many participatory facilitators have used such techniques with children and young people as many of their worlds are embedded with social media. Arguably, facilitators need to feel as confident as the children and young people in using these as arts-based approaches but can be a useful platform for building resilience and trust.

Critical Discussion of Arts-Based Techniques Across the Life Span in Building Resilience and Well-being

This chapter has to date introduced a number of practical arts-based approaches in the broadest sense. This chapter will now discuss how the author used arts-based approaches across the life course in a variety of settings to elicit information about health (Under-fives; School-age and Teenagers/Young People) to facilitate children and young people to have their say in a way that made sense to them.

Under-Fives

Recent work undertaken in a large national UK study known as *Child Talk*, which was led by Professor Susan Roulstone from The University of West of England, Bristol and the author of this chapter was part of the team (See Roulstone et al., 2015). One part of the large study was to seek the views of pre-school children, age two to five years with speech and language needs, and what activities could potentially work (or not) in supporting their needs. Twenty-four children with a variety of needs from diverse backgrounds from two UK children's centres and one nursery class. The children agreed and families consented for them to take part in a range of activities using an observational approach to capture their responses and experiences. Activities were varied by using picture resources or real-world objects, familiar or unfamiliar items. The resources and activities selected were tailored to reflect each particular group members' developmental stage and abilities by speech and language therapists on the research team.

To evidence the process, children were also filmed during a series of arts-based sessions, with innovative head mounted cameras worn by the children and supported by researcher field notes. Framework analysis (Smith & Firth, 2011) was then used to analyse the data based on the body movement, vocalisation and visual attention of the children during these sessions. The findings highlighted that children expressed enjoyment and engagement in a range of speech and language therapy activities through combinations of body language, vocalisation, and visual attention.

The team believed by developing unique and novel methods, we would gain the trust of the pre-school children and they would feel safe in expressing their experiences of the therapy situation. Being facilitated to express their feelings about their experiences may in turn enable an early sense of resilience and well-being (Flewitt, 2005).

School-Age Children

Work by the author of this chapter (See Coad, 2007) included 35 school age children age 9 and 10 years in two schools in the UK who were invited to highlight aspects that were *'good'* about their local community in terms of improving their health and aspects that they would like to see improved in services.

Arts-based methods included photographs, collage/poster making and mapping exercises. They were partnered into twos based on their regular teacher's advice and quickly settled into the activity. The children were asked throughout the activities to write responses as important key words or notes on post-cards based on the task following which they were invited to post their cards into a large prepared visual wallet. They were also told that they could choose to post the cards forwards the group if they were happy for everyone to see them or turn them over if they only wanted the adult facilitator to read them.

Thematic analysis was used to analyse the data. Children had good knowledge of health, what made then healthy and it was evident that the groups cared very much about the absence of and accessibility to healthy-based facilities and professionals. Findings included that they liked the locality but felt public places like parks were *scary* and *dirty* which impacted on their health. Many of them reported wanting more safe places for children to play. Many reported that they felt 'ignored' by professionals when they were sick and that much communication exchange took place between their parents/carers not them. This case study approach highlighted that the children liked the interactive approach and it was effective in obtaining their views in this age group. Overall, this enabled the adults to explore what the children perceived about their local communities but also what health services they would ideally like.

Another case study drawn from a team the author was part of was in Dublin, Ireland (See Lambert, Coad, Hicks, & Glacken, 2014a, 2014b). The project aim was to ascertain children and young people's views across a broad range of ages (up to 18 years) and abilities about a purpose-built Children's Unit in a new hospital build (Dublin, Ireland). The novelty of the approach was that it was driven by the opinions of children and young people through the use of child-friendly multi-methods, based on a combination of interviews; drawing; artwork and questionnaires in order to explore preferences about décor, colour and environmental textures. Twelve older children and young people (aged 10–18 years) volunteered to act as an 'advisory expert group' to the project. The group were given supportive ongoing training, and with carefully planned adult support, developed all data collection tools and validated data analysis. The aim of the group was to contribute to the project collaboratively in order to gain insight into other children's perspectives but also it was hoped that this would have additional impact on the planning and design of the Children's Unit.

Teenagers and Young People

In 2013, this author was Chief Investigator (CI) of a large team across the UK which sought to explore the experiences of young liver transplant recipients transitioning to adult services and determine what they require in order to achieve a successful move. The research also explored the possibility of using a mobile phone application (app) as a tool to support transition. (Toft et al., 2018). The team used novel arts-based focus groups and one-to-one interviews. Twenty-one young people aged 16–25 years, 16 health-care professionals involved in their care, and seven young people as follow-up took part using arts-based methods alongside an interview format. Methods included collages/images, post-its and the use of interactive discussion activities such as using Target Boards (designed by Coad and Toft resembling an archery board) upon which participants could place post it notes to show which aspects were more important than others. The overall goal of these arts-based approaches was to allow all participants to engage in a safe environment in order that resilience and confidence was facilitated so the team could collect detailed and in-depth data about their experiences of transition.

Data highlighted the variability of transition pathways in England for young people moving from child to adult health services. The results showed that teenagers and young people wanted clearer information regarding transition processes including specific medical information and that there was a shortfall in such information. They also wanted health-care transitions to be more individualized and based upon transition readiness rather than age, although the research showed that age cut-offs were still used. This was an important study in hearing this under-represented group.

Critical Reflections

There is a body of evidence which demonstrates the pragmatic value of well-designed arts-based approaches in building resilience from planning to exiting the field or event. Macpherson, Hart, and Heaver (2012) list out a number in their robust work in this area, adapted below in following list:

1. Using visual arts to help communicate pro-health, pro-resilience messages;
2. Using visual arts to help children and young people cope with difficult feelings which may be difficult/impossible to articulate;

3. Using skills-based visual arts workshops to help children and young people develop a range of core components of resilience;
4. Using arts activities to help foster social empowerment and communicate the lived experience of participants to wider communities;
5. Using visual arts methods to help children and young people talk about their own resilience individually or in a group;
6. Choosing a component of arts practice (such as mindfulness of feelings) which is known to be resilience-promoting and focusing on this activity.

However, there is also a wider arts-based evidence which highlights that any co-production or participation is likely to enhance overall wellbeing (Clift et al., 2009). One might ask what are the challenges and limitations then?

One limitation is that with children and young people a one size fits all approach is not helpful. The facilitators in their planning need to consider a range of arts-based approaches and be prepared for all eventualities. These approaches take careful planning, time and creativity to enact. In short, they must be taken as seriously as developing more traditional approaches like a questionnaire.

A further consideration in the planning phase of arts-based approaches are the resources that are available in the project. In the experience of this author children and young people appear to enjoy the spontaneity of using arts-based methods but the materials must be appear well considered and need to be to hand (purchased and prepared) in good time. You do not need to buy the most expensive materials, but you do need to be considerate to aspects such as new crayons, clean paper/card and fresh imagery to encourage children and young people's participation.

Children or young people's consent (or assent) should be ascertained on an ongoing basis in all research. In terms of arts-based approaches children and young people before you start any activity you need to re-clarify the purpose and talk the group/child/young person through what will happen. Coad and Hambly (2011) suggest ways to support children and young people having a say and even controlling the end.

Being involved in an arts-based activity with a child or young person can be an effective way of establishing a rapport in a relatively short time and thus build resilience. However, the author of this chapter has found challenging it the balancing of power with the flexibility of undertaking an arts-based approach. In many environments where the arts-based approaches are used you will find they are directed, managed or influenced by adults including health environments. Preparation of those adults before the event is thus vital. During the event, you might also think about how to either include the adults to develop their confidence or have another area nearby for the adults to talk together. Both have worked for the author of this chapter.

Finally, exiting is always a challenging task as many time children and young people are so engrossed and engaged that they do not want you to leave. Some will also work at different rates to others depending on need. Often proud of their artwork produced and many are used to writing their name on such pieces. This author always tells them at the start how long it will take and pre-warns them at a time point before the end. In order to build resilience and a sense of well-being, feedback and reward are fundamental to valuing the activity and the child or young person. However, any reward needs to be appropriate to the age/cognitive development and needs. At the end of the arts-based activities children and young people and the adults should also be given feedback about what will happen to the work and how it will be used.

Conclusion

Building resilience through listening to children and young people about their health preferences using arts-based methods can be hugely rewarding and is important if they are to have a real voice in shaping their worlds. This chapter has set out how a number of arts-based approaches can be used to elicit the views children and young people in a range of settings. Literature and field work undertaken by the author has been drawn upon from health settings to inform critical discussion of not only using arts-based approaches with children and young people in *real world* settings but how they can be used to positively impact on children's resilience and well-being. This chapter throughout has highlighted that using such approaches needs a flexible approach and open mind in order to encourage the active participation of children and young people in order to understand their preferences, desires and views. This is important if we are to build resilience and enhance well-being.

References

Angell, C., Alexander, J., & Hunt, J. A. (2015). 'Draw, write and tell': A literature review and methodological development on the 'draw and write' research method. *Journal of Early Childhood Research, 13*, 17–28.

Askins, K., & Pain, R. (2011). Contact zones: Participation, materiality, and the messiness of interaction. *Environment and Planning D: Society and Space, 29*(5), 803–821. https://doi.org/10.1068/d11109

Blaisdell, C., Arnott, L., Wall, K., & Robinson, C. (2018). Look who's talking: Using creative, playful arts-based methods in research with young children. *Journal of Early Childhood Research.* ISSN 1476-718X, https://doi.org/10.1177/1476718X18808816

Bragg, S., & Buckingham, D. (2008). 'Scrapbooks' as a resource in media research with young people. In P. Thomson (Ed.), *Doing visual research with children and young people* (pp. 114–131). London, UK: Routledge. https://www.researchgate.net/publication/42797438_%27Scrapbooks%27_as_a_resource_in_media_research_with_young_people. Accessed 22 May 2019.

Christensen, P., & James, A. (2008). *Research with children: Perspectives and practices* (2nd ed.). London, UK: Falmer Press. ISBN-10: 0415416841/ISBN-13: 978-0415416849.

Clark, A., & Moss, P. (2011). *Listening to young children: The mosaic approach* (2nd ed.). London, UK: National Children's Bureau.

Clift, S., Camic, P. M., Chapman, B., Clayton, G., Daykin, N., Eades, G., & White, M. (2009). The state of arts and health in England. *Arts & Health: An International Journal for Research, Policy and Practice, 1*(1), 6–35.

Coad, J. (2007). Using art-based techniques in engaging children and young people in health care consultations and/or research. *Journal of Nursing, 12*(5), 487–497.

Coad, J., & Hambly, H. (2011). Listening to children and young people with speech, language and communication needs through arts-based methods. In S. Roulstone & S. McLeod (Eds.), *Listening to children and young people with speech, language and communication needs* (p. 132). Surrey, UK: J&R Press.

Coad, J., Plumridge, G., & Metcalfe, A. (2009). Involving children and young people in the development of art-based research tools. *Nurse Researcher, 16*, 4.

Dose, L. (2006). *National network for the arts in health: Lessons learned from six years of work*. First Published May 1. Royal Society for Public Health. Accessed at https://doi.org/10.1177/1466424006064299

Einarsdóttir, J. (2007). Research with children: Methodological and ethical challenges. *European Early Childhood Education Research Journal, 15*(2). https://doi.org/10.1080/13502930701321477

Flewitt, R. (2005). Is every child's voice heard? Researching the different ways 3-year-old children communicate and make meaning at home and in a preschool playgroup. *Early Years: An International Journal of Research and Development, 25*(3), 207–222.

Garbarino, J., & Stott, F. M. (1989). *What children can tell us: Eliciting, interpreting and evaluating information from children*. San Francisco, CA: Jossey-Bass.

Gibson, F., Aldiss, S., Horstman, M., Kumpunen, S., & Richardson, A. (2010). Children and young people's experiences of cancer care: A qualitative research study using participatory methods. *International Journal of Nursing Studies, 47*(11), 1397–1407. https://doi.org/10.1016/j.ijnurstu.2010.03.019

Hart, A., Aumann, K., & Heaver, B. (2010). *Boingboing resilience research and practice*. Accessed from www.boingboing.org.uk

Lambert, V., Coad, J., Hicks, P., & Glacken, M. (2014a). Young Children's perspectives of ideal physical design features for hospital-built environments. *Journal of Child Health Care, 18*(1), 57–71.

Lambert, V., Coad, J., Hicks, P., & Glacken, M. (2014b). Social spaces for young children in hospital. *Child: Care, Health and Development, 40*(2), 195–204.

Lewis, V., Kellett, M., Robinson, C., et al. (2003). *The reality of research with children and young people*. London, UK: Sage Publications.

Lundy, L., McEvoy, L., & Byrne, B. (2011). Working with young children as co-researchers: An approach informed by the United Nations convention on the rights of the child. *Early Education and Development, 22*, 714–736.

MacPherson, H., Hart, A., & Heaver, B (2012). *Connected communities: Building resilience through collaborative community arts practice*. Accessed at: https://www.boingboing.org.uk/wp-content/uploads/2017/02/cc-report-for-web.pdf

McLeod, S. (2011). Listening to children and young people with speech, language and communication needs. Who, why and how? In S. Roulstone & S. McLeod (Eds.), *Listening to children and young people with speech, language and communication needs*. Guildford, UK: J&R Press.

Pink, S. (2001). *Doing visual ethnography*. London, UK: Sage.

Prosser, J. (1998). *Image-based research: A sourcebook for qualitative researchers psychology press*. ISBN: 075070649X, 9780750706490.

Punch, S. (2002). Interviewing strategies with young people: The 'secret box', stimulus material and task-based activities. *Children and Society, 16*(1), 45–56.

Roulstone, S., & McLeod, S. (Eds.). (2011). *Listening to children and young people with speech, language and communication needs*. Surrey, UK: J&R Press.

Roulstone, S. E., Marshall, J. E., Powell, G. G., Goldbart, J., Wren, Y., Coad, J., … Coad, R. A. (2015). Evidence- based intervention for preschool children with primary speech and language impairments: Child talk – An exploratory mixed-methods study. In *Programme Grants for applied research, no. 3.5*. Southampton, UK: NIHR Journals Library.

Skudrzyk, B., Zera, D. A., McMahon, G., Schmidt, R., Boyne, J., & Spannaus, R. (2009). Learning to relate: Interweaving creative approaches in group counselling with adolescents. *Journal of Creativity in Mental Health, 4*(3), 249–261.

Smith, J., & Firth, J. (2011). Qualitative data analysis: Application of the framework approach. *Nurse Researcher, 18*(2), 52–62.

Toft, A., Taylor, R., Claridge, L., Clowes, C., Ferguson, J., Hind, J., … Coad, J. (2018). The experiences of young liver patients transferring from Children's to adult services and their support needs for a successful transition. *Progress in Transplantation*, 244–249. https://doi.org/10.1177/1526924818781567

5

Promoting Resilience in Youth Through Participation in an Arts-Based Mindfulness Group Program

Diana Coholic

Introduction

In collaboration with colleagues, I have been testing the benefits and effectiveness of an arts-based mindfulness group program for over 10 years. Our 12-week group program is called Holistic Arts-Based Program or HAP and it was recently published in its entirety in *Facilitating Mindfulness: A Guide for Human Service Professionals* (Coholic, 2019). HAP is a strengths-based program to develop mindfulness skills and resilience. The goals of HAP include learning mindfulness, improving self-awareness, developing self-compassion and empathy, and shoring up strengths. Arts-based activities are used to assist participants to develop mindfulness-based skills such as paying attention to one's thoughts/feelings and decreasing negative self-judgment. For one example, we sometimes encourage group participants to sculpt out of clay or draw a picture of what they are imagining as they listen to a short guided imagery

D. Coholic (✉)
Laurentian University, Sudbury, ON, Canada
e-mail: dcoholic@laurentian.ca

reading or meditation. Creating something while they are practising listening and paying attention helps them achieve success with the meditation.

Through our current research project, we hope to assist marginalised youth who are experiencing challenges with schooling to learn skills and develop strengths that will assist them to engage with learning. For instance, some students need to learn how to focus and sustain attention over time before they can fully engage in learning, and mindfulness-based interventions (MBIs) are proving effective in developing these skills (Broderick, 2013). Relevant to our work, the link between childhood maltreatment and poor educational outcomes may be caused in part by a disruption in developmental processes such as emotion regulation and sense of agency (Romano, Babchishin, Marquis, & Frechette, 2014). Participating in HAP can improve the youths' mindfulness and resilience, which includes self-awareness, emotion regulation, feelings of confidence, self-esteem, and improved mood and coping skills, and thus, their engagement with schooling. In HAP, we understand resilience as a conceptual umbrella for characteristics and abilities that are found to modify the impact of adversities including a sense of mastery, a sense of relatedness, and an ability to regulate emotions (Prince-Embury & Courville, 2008). In general, preventative interventions such as HAP that promote increased self-regulation may assist youth towards a more positive developmental trajectory (Feagans Gould, Dariotis, Mendelson, & Greenberg, 2012).

Mindfulness-Based Interventions with Marginalised Youth

The goals of MBIs usually include becoming fully aware of one's moment-to-moment stream of consciousness and to be accepting of these experiences. There is emphasis on improving concentration and attention, building emotion regulation, gaining self-knowledge, and improving empathy and compassion (Greenberg & Harris, 2012). Mindfulness training in the conscious control of attentional resources benefits learning (Huppert & Johnson, 2010) and with increased understanding of one's feelings and thoughts, a youth can make better choices regarding their emotional expression, which can lead to improved functioning at school, home, and with peers (Coholic, 2011). Mindfulness can help a youth to view negative thoughts as passing events rather than valid reflections of reality (just because someone believes a thought does not mean the thought is correct or true), and can promote flexible responses as opposed to ruminating (Ciarrochi, Kashdan, Leeson, Heaven, & Jordan, 2011).

We begin to teach the concept and practice of mindfulness in HAP using an activity called *Thoughts Jar*. Using a jar half filled with water, we drop in beads representing the feelings and thoughts we have experienced that day. As the beads are dropped into the water, the participants can share what feeling or thought is represented. After a lid is screwed on, the beads are swirled around in the jar, which represents a mind that is distracted, anxious and so on. It is difficult to identify what is in the jar when this is happening. But when the beads are left to settle to the bottom of the jar, we can identify what it is we have been thinking and feeling. Discussion can be focused on the power mindfulness provides us to identify our feelings and thoughts in order to make effective choices rather than acting out or drifting mindlessly through our day.

Many MBIs for youth have been adapted from programs originally developed for adults by shortening breathing meditations and adding experiential activities. The two most widely studied MBIs have been Mindfulness-Based Stress Reduction (MBSR) (Kabat-Zinn, 1990) and Mindfulness-Based Cognitive Therapy (MBCT) (Segal, Williams, & Teasdale, 2002). Researchers have reviewed the evidence for MBCT for improving self-regulation in youth and found promising results in that youth were able to improve self-regulation and coping skills (Perry-Parrish, Copeland-Linder, Webb, Shields, & Sibinga, 2016). Also, researchers conducting a systematic review and meta-analysis of MBIs for youth with anxiety reported that MBIs are effective for the treatment of anxiety in youth (Borquist-Conlon, Maynard, Esposito Brendel, & Farina, 2017).

This being said, research investigating the effectiveness of MBIs with children and youth is a developing field. A plethora of MBIs have been developed and studied with some being developed for use in schools

(Black & Fernando, 2014; Ricarte, Latorre, & Beltran, 2015; Vickery & Dorjee, 2016) while others have been developed for specific youth populations and challenges such as incarcerated youth (Le & Proulx, 2015), youth suffering headaches (Hesse, Holmes, Kennedy-Overfelt, Kerr, & Giles, 2015) and eating disorders (Atkinson & Wade, 2015), youth with substance use disorders (Himelstein, 2011), and many more. A variety of benefits have also been reported often depending on the focus and aims of the MBI. Common outcomes include improved emotion regulation and mood, decreases in stress and depressive/anxiety symptoms, and improved well-being (Coholic, Dano, Sindori, & Eys, 2019).

In our current research program, we are testing the benefits of HAP for a diverse population of marginalised youth aged 11–17 years old who are experiencing challenges with schooling. These challenges are diverse and could include academic, mental health, and social challenges including anxiety, poor peer relationships and emotion regulation, social exclusion, and inabilities to focus and pay attention. For example, while Sarah performs well academically and has not suffered any childhood traumas, she experiences anxiety and worries throughout her day about her abilities, popularity, family members, and so on. The constant worry affects her self-esteem, confidence, and ability to sleep; she seldom participates in school because she is worried about being negatively judged. She is dependent on her parents for constant reassurance, seldom takes risks to experience new things, and believes there is something wrong with her. On the other hand, some of the youth in our program have suffered childhood traumas such as witnessing violence, being subjected to abuse, and other traumas and losses that would necessitate becoming involved with the child welfare system. These youth can suffer from a host of challenges including poor emotion regulation, persistent feelings of anxiety, sadness and/or anger, poor boundaries in relationships, and so on. Much has been written about the deleterious effects of abuse, loss, trauma, and family dysfunction on children's physical, cognitive, emotional, social, and behavioural development (Flisher et al., 1997; Pagani, Japel, Vaillancourt, Cote, & Tremblay, 2008) including that these youth have a greater likelihood of poor long-term functional outcomes (Racusin, Maerlender, Sengupta, Isquith, & Straus, 2005).

Our current research question asks: Is an arts-based mindfulness group program beneficial and/or effective for youth experiencing challenges with schooling, and if so, what are these benefits and how do these benefits assist youth to cope and learn? Perceived benefits will be evidenced (or not) by way of qualitatively analysing individual pre- and post-group interviews with the youth; youth are interviewed following their participation in HAP and then again 12 weeks later. Effectiveness will be assessed by quantitatively analysing pre- and post-group scores on self-report inventories measuring mindfulness (Greco, Baer, & Smith, 2011) and resilience (Prince-Embury & Courville, 2008), and scores from caregiver assessments of behaviour and coping (Achenbach & Rescorla, 2001).

While we are just beginning to analyse the data we have collected over the past three years, in previous studies we found that HAP helped children/youth to develop self-awareness and improved mood, coping and social skills, confidence and self-esteem, empathy, and an ability to pay attention and focus, which helped some of the children/youth to better engage with learning and develop positive peer and familial relationships (Coholic & Eys, 2016; Coholic, Eys, & Lougheed, 2012). Anecdotally, we are seeing positive benefits from the youth we are currently working with. In fact, one of our challenges is trying to accommodate all of the youth who desire to participate in HAP a second time. The youth tell us that they can be authentic in the program and greatly appreciate making connections with peers. Of particular relevance to this chapter is the fact that the youth participants all discuss how they enjoy the arts-based approach and experience it as non-threatening, inclusive, and *fun*.

An Arts-Based Approach

Not all youth, especially youth who are marginalised due to challenging life circumstances such as abuse, bullying, social exclusion, poverty, family dysfunction and so forth, have the interests or capacities for engaging in traditional mindfulness education and training; hence the importance of using arts-based methods. When we began our research program exploring how learning mindfulness-based practices and concepts could help children develop resilience, based on our previous practice experiences and knowledge about trauma and loss, we knew that we had to facilitate mindfulness in a manner that was going to engage the children and foster success; at the time, we were working with children in the care of the local child welfare agency. Traditional MBIs such as MBSR are often adapted for use with children/youth but we believed that shortening a breathing meditation, for one example, was not going to be engaging and effective enough for these children who can have chaotic lives internally and externally. Indeed, many of the children who came to HAP in the early development of the program had trouble remaining physically still and listening to the facilitators and each other. Also, many of the children/youth we have worked with tell us that they are not interested in talking about their problems or going to "counseling." We wanted to develop activities and processes that the children would find relevant and meaningful, and that would keep them coming back for more.

Using creative methods with youth has long been accepted within helping professions as it is understood that youth communicate many of their thoughts/feelings nonverbally through creative activity (Goodman, 2005). Certainly, creative methods have strong potential to engage marginalised youth (Leckey, 2011; Olson-McBride & Page, 2012) especially in group work (Coholic, Dano, et al., 2019). Moreover, the most important element of a program might be that it involves activities youth enjoy so that they will devote effort and time to engaging with the activities (Flook et al., 2010). One of the most important things that I have learned over the years of doing this work is that the experience of fun is vital for children/youth, and they can learn important skills and concepts through these enjoyable experiences, that is, change and growth does not have to be a difficult or pain-filled process. For example, sometimes we have had youth in our groups who are reluctant or unable to engage with the group and the activities. They might sit with the group but with their arms crossed or they might refuse to share their creations with the group. Recently, we had a youth in our group that engaged in the drawing activities but ripped up her creations when she was done before anyone else could see what she had created. However, these youth keep coming back week after week and usually over time, we can help them participate more actively. We understand these behaviours as related in part to poor attachments formed by these youth earlier in their lives. Understandably, trusting peers and facilitators takes time for youth who are afraid of being vulnerable and anticipate others hurting or letting them down. An arts-based approach focused on strengths can accommodate diversity in capacities and can create a safe context wherein youth who feel vulnerable can be helped over time to take risks to share some aspects of their lives, thoughts, and feelings.

Since the 1970s, art therapists have argued for connections between using art and improving aspects of resilience (Malchiodi, 2007). Others have explained how arts-based counseling can foster improved well-being and resilience (Pearson & Wilson, 2008), and how arts-based activities can improve self-esteem and resilience in adolescents and young adults (Jang & Choi, 2012; Roghanchi, Mohamad, Mey, Momeni, & Golmohamadian, 2013). Some have argued that visual arts practices can improve resilience, and that even short-term interventions can impact on a youth's resilience (Macpherson, Hart, & Heaver, 2015). In HAP we use an activity called *Warm Fuzzies* to help youth participants understand and accept positive qualities about themselves. In this activity, every group member decorates an envelope with their name on it. These are hung on a string in the group room for the duration of the program symbolising our connection and belonging to the group. In every session the youth write down things they like about the other members, depositing these in the envelopes. In the process of doing so, they learn about both self-compassion and empathy.

Sinding, Warren, and Paton (2014) reported that social workers use arts-based methods to help people express themselves, and to help us make sense of someone else's experiences. Based on their developmental stages, this is especially the case when working with children and youth who may need to learn to identify their feelings first before they can effectively express them. In HAP, we use many activities aimed at helping youth identify and express feelings, for instance, encouraging them to paint what short clips of different types of music make them feel. Arts-based creations can also be a profound way to learn about someone's experiences. For example, one of the first activities we facilitate in HAP is called *Me as a Tree* in which everyone draws themselves as a tree. This is usually an enjoyable and creative way to get to know each other and it can also build self-awareness. However, on one occasion in a group with teenage girls, Cathy (all names in this chapter are pseudonyms) drew a tree that looked dead: it was drawn in pencil and the tree had no leaves, and was located behind a barbed-wire fence. In discussion about her tree drawing, Cathy admitted that she thought of dying and had suicidal thoughts. Drawing the tree enabled Cathy to let us know how she felt when she might not have been able to do so directly in conversation. Thus, there are rationales for facilitating mindfulness using arts-based methods that are based both on the effectiveness of these methods (creating art can be an enjoyable, empowering, and enlightening experience), and on the characteristics of the youth one is working with (children and youth may lack language and understanding to express their thoughts and feelings).

Recently, we reported on a study where we tested HAP with youth admitted to a short-term inpatient mental health program situated within our local hospital. We reported the results by writing a vignette/story using the youths' own words organised according to the main themes of the thematic analysis (Coholic, Schinke, et al., 2019). Composite vignettes are short storied narratives that feature the depth of each theme utilising language and description accessible to the participants. In this study, regarding the arts-based approach, the youth explained that engaging with the arts-based activities connected them with other youth and helped them express themselves, for instance,

> [B]efore coming to the group, I didn't know how to formulate my words and thoughts but with art, you have all the colors in the world to share your thoughts more and to express yourself. I am starting to observe that I really enjoy being able to express myself in a way I never thought I could. (p. 11)

They also reported that the arts-based activities helped them cope, for example,

> You don't realize it but when you're doing art it's actually a way of coping… I learned that art can keep you grounded and feeling peaceful. In the group, there were lots of fun activities and it helped me find myself and find peace within myself. (p. 11)

In general, I think we need to do better within the helping professions listening to children and youth about what they need and want. We have learned from the hundreds of youth we have worked with in HAP that most are in need of spaces where they can join with peers and build positive relationships, and they need to be engaged in activities that are strengths-based, engaging, and that foster success. I am continually surprised at how many of the youth we work with lack adults in their lives who really listen to them and places where they can be authentic. Indeed, a report produced by UNICEF Canada examining youths' opinions about mental health found that relationships and a sense of belonging were identified as vitally important for children and youth; friendship, belonging, and caring relationships were dominant themes identified with youth well-being (UNICEF Canada, 2017).

Writing the vignette mentioned above was a way for us to present findings in a much more accessible and interesting way emphasising the youths' voices. In the future, we would like to involve youth in co-constructing vignettes so as to involve them in a more meaningful way in the research process. Reflecting a strengths-based and social constructionist approach, and aiming to work with youth participants in meaningful and equalitarian ways, we have involved youth in several arts-based processes aimed at disseminating our research.

Dissemination of Research Findings Using Arts-Based Methods

Sharing the results of research in a variety of ways for various stakeholders is vital to disseminating knowledge in ways that will influence practice and policy development. Also, involving research participants in these processes is another way of building resilience in children and youth involved in research projects. For instance, we have involved HAP youth participants in the making of short films that have aimed to present their experiences in our program. These processes provided the participants with additional skill-building as they learned about cinematography and film editing, and the films constitute creative knowledge transfer from the perspectives of the youths themselves providing youth, their caregivers, teachers, and other knowledge users with examples of effective pathways to learning in accessible and engaging language and art. This process can help to empower the youth through the research process, in turn contributing to the authenticity and usefulness of the results (Blodgett et al., 2011).

For example, one film is called *Self-Growth and Group Work: A Lesson from Nature* (Cheu & Coholic, 2015). This is a short Claymation film available on YouTube. In this one-day process, we began by showing the youth participants some preliminary themes with examples from the analysis of their post-HAP interviews. We asked them to choose the themes that resonated the most for them and then using these themes we helped them create a storyboard for the film (they led the process and it is their story that is depicted in the film). The youth decided to begin with drawing themselves as trees, which is one of the arts-based activities we use early in the HAP program mentioned earlier in this chapter. The tree drawing that begins the film shows a tree that has been cut down but has a small growth on the stump. The boy who drew this tree stated that he felt like he had been cut down but now feels hopeful that he can grow and heal. The youth developed a story in which forest animals nurture the tree that has been cut down. The story ends with statements that they thought encapsulated some of the lessons they learned in HAP such as *self-expression helps you grow, creativity helps you develop your mind, body, spirit, take time to appreciate life's moments,* and *love yourself first.*

More recently, for our University's Research Week SciArt show (a show that encourages researchers and students to present their research using art), we asked three different HAP groups to create something that depicted the science and art of learning mindfulness. The creations show the youths' understandings of mindfulness and how learning mindfulness-based practices and concepts has helped them. These creations took place as the HAP groups were ending, which explains the group participants' understandings about the benefits of practising mindfulness. For example, in an older girls' group, Beth who is 16 years old, explained that:

"Mindfulness is like a balloon. It's about being able to let thoughts come and choose to hold on to them or let them go. Mindfulness gives me the ability to accept and make choices for myself."

Sue, who is 17 years old, described her drawing:

This is half a heart. Half of mindfulness is what you see on the outside but the other half happens in the inside of ourselves, and not everyone gets to see that. Being mindful is like riding waves; you learn to see a choice, then respond, then let it be without resistance.

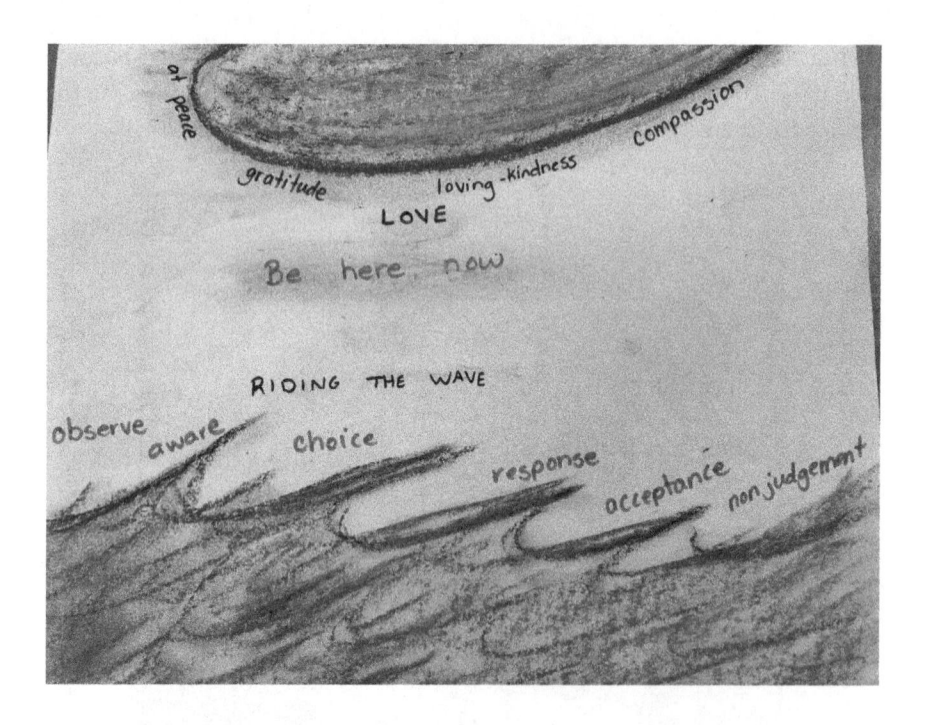

A HAP group of girls aged 11–12 decided to create a drawing together. The girls drew their brains before and after learning mindfulness. With mindfulness, they feel like they can control the important parts of their lives. They feel in control when they make choices that are good for themselves and others. When they make effective choices, they feel like smart, calm, and understanding people. The power of mindfulness is this ability to make choices about one's feelings, thoughts, and behaviours rather than acting out. Presenting youths' experiences and learning by way of their own arts-based creations brings research processes and findings to life in an interesting, engaging, and accessible manner.

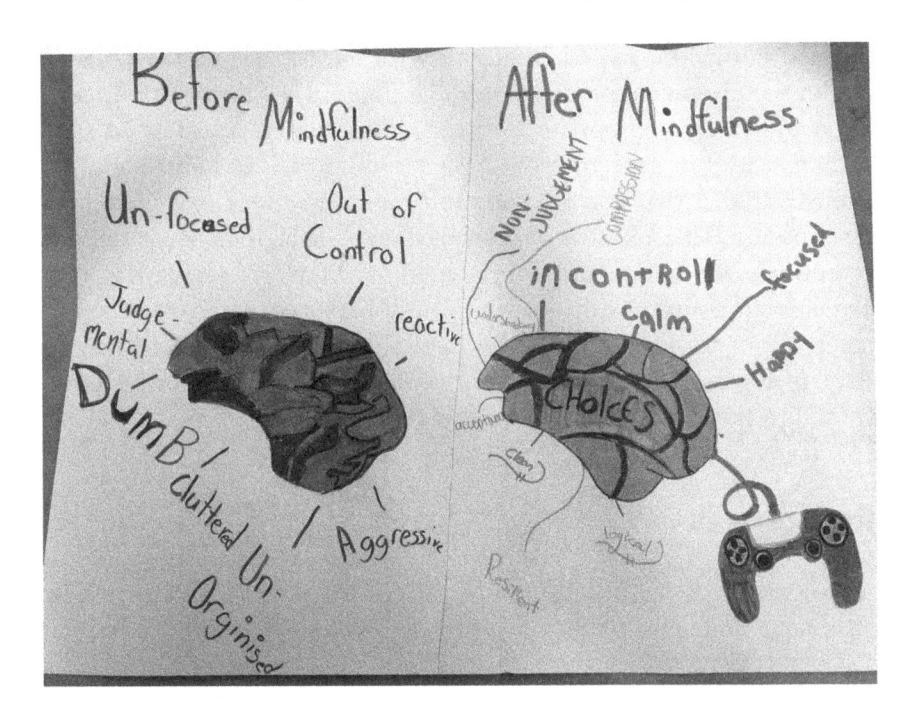

Conclusion

In our current milieu, many youth are struggling with anxiety, social exclusion, family dysfunction, the pressures of schooling, and despair about their futures. In our experiences, youth desire places where they can find support and positive relationships. Our HAP program meets some youths' needs by offering a mechanism by which they can improve their resilience through learning and practising mindfulness, forming positive relationships with others, and being creative. For some youth, HAP meets their needs and they leave feeling better about themselves with increased confidence in their abilities to cope with daily living. For other youth who might require a more intensive helping intervention such as one-to-one counselling, HAP serves as bridge and warms them up to the helping process, assisting them to be more successful in individual treatment as they have some basic skills and competencies they can draw on.

Importantly, the arts-based approach in the delivery of the program and in the dissemination of the research findings is enjoyable, engaging, developmentally appropriate, and can accommodate a variety of skills and capacities or lack thereof. HAP builds capacities and focuses on strengths rather than focusing on problems and what is going wrong or not working. The youth we have worked with are incredibly creative and accepting of diversities, and these strengths are nurtured as we work in an equalitarian manner with the youth, in a context where creativity and compassion are emphasised. The arts-based approach also helps us develop as practitioners as we are encouraged to draw on our own creativity and to experience fun with the group participants.

References

Achenbach, T., & Rescorla, L. (2001). *Manual for ASEBA school-age forms & profiles*. Burlington, VT: University of Vermont, Research Center for Children, Youth, & Families.

Atkinson, M. J., & Wade, T. D. (2015). Mindfulness-based prevention for eating disorders: A school-based cluster randomized controlled study. *International Journal of Eating Disorders, 48*(7), 1024–1037. https://doi.org/10.1002/eat.22416

Black, D. S., & Fernando, R. (2014). Mindfulness training and classroom behavior among lower-income and ethnic minority elementary school children. *Journal of Child and Family Studies, 23*, 1242–1246. https://doi.org/10.1007/s10826-013-9784-4

Blodgett, A. T., Schinke, R. J., Peltier, D., Fisher, L. A., Watson, J., & Wabano, M. J. (2011). May the circle be unbroken: The research recommendations of Aboriginal community members engaged in participatory action research with university academics. *Journal of Sport and Social Issues, 35*(3), 264–283.

Borquist-Conlon, D., Maynard, B., Esposito Brendel, K., & Farina, A. (2017). Mindfulness-based interventions for youth with anxiety: A systematic review and meta-analysis. *Research on Social Work Practice*, 1–11. https://doi.org/10.1177/1049731516684961

Broderick, P. (2013). *Learning to breathe: A mindfulness curriculum for adolescents to cultivate emotion regulation, attention, and performance*. Oakland, CA: New Harbinger Publications.

Cheu, H., & Coholic, D. (2015). *Self-growth and group work: A lesson from nature*. https://www.youtube.com/watch?v=jd0fLNzDQ3Q

Ciarrochi, J., Kashdan, T., Leeson, P., Heaven, P., & Jordan, C. (2011). On being aware and accepting: A one-year longitudinal study into adolescent well-being. *Journal of Adolescence, 34*, 695–703. https://doi.org/10.1016/j.adolescence.2010.09.003

Coholic, D. (2011). Exploring the feasibility and benefits of arts-based mindfulness-based practices with young people in need: Aiming to improve aspects of self-awareness and resilience. *Child and Youth Care Forum, 40*(4), 303–317. https://doi.org/10.1007/s10566-010-9139-x

Coholic, D. (2019). *Facilitating mindfulness: A guide for human service professionals*. Whitby, ON: Northrose Educational Resources.

Coholic, D., Dano, K., Sindori, S., & Eys, M. (2019). Group work in mindfulness-based interventions with youth: A scoping review. *Social Work with Groups*. https://doi.org/10.1080/01609513.2019.1571764

Coholic, D., & Eys, M. (2016). Benefits of an arts-based mindfulness group intervention for vulnerable children. *Child & Adolescent Social Work Journal, 33*(3), 1–13. https://doi.org/10.1007/s10560-015-0431-3

Coholic, D., Eys, M., & Lougheed, S. (2012). Investigating the effectiveness of an arts-based and mindfulness-based group program for the improvement of resilience in children in need. *Journal of Child and Family Studies, 21*, 833–844. https://doi.org/10.1007/s10826-011-9544-2

Coholic, D., Schinke, R., Oghene, O., Dano, K., Jago, M., McAlister, H., & Grynspan, P. (2019). Arts-based interventions for youth with mental health challenges. *Journal of Social Work*. https://doi.org/10.1177/1468017319828864

Feagans Gould, L., Dariotis, J., Mendelson, T., & Greenberg, M. T. (2012). A school-based mindfulness intervention for urban youth: Exploring moderators of intervention effects. *Journal of Community Psychology, 40*(8), 968–982. https://doi.org/10.1002/jcop.21505

Flisher, A. J., Kramenr, R. A., Hoven, C. W., Greenwald, S., Bird, H. R., Canino, G., ... Moore, R. E. (1997). Psychosocial characteristics of physically abused children and adolescents. *Journal of American Academy of Child and Adolescent Psychiatry, 36*, 123–131. https://doi.org/10.1097/00004583-199701000-00026

Flook, L., Smalley, S., Kitil, M. J., Galla, B., Kaiser-Greenland, S., Locke, J., ... Kasari, C. (2010). Effects of mindful awareness practices on executive functions in elementary school children. *Journal of Applied School Psychology, 26*, 70–95. https://doi.org/10.1080/15377900903379125

Goodman, T. (2005). Working with children: Beginner's mind. In C. Germer, R. Siegel, & P. Fulton (Eds.), *Mindfulness and psychotherapy* (pp. 197–219). New York, NY: Guilford Press.

Greco, L., Baer, R., & Smith, G. T. (2011). Assessing mindfulness in children and adolescents: Development and validation of the child and adolescent mindfulness measure (CAMM). *Psychological Assessment, 23*(3), 606–614. https://doi.org/10.1037/a0022819

Greenberg, M. T., & Harris, A. R. (2012). Nurturing mindfulness in children and youth: Current state of research. *Child Development Perspectives, 6*(2), 161–166. https://doi.org/10.1111/j.1750-8606.2011.00215.x

Hesse, T., Holmes, L. G., Kennedy-Overfelt, V., Kerr, L. M., & Giles, L. L. (2015). Mindfulness-based intervention for adolescents with recurrent headaches: A pilot feasibility study. *Evidence-Based Complementary and Alternative Medicine, 2015*, 1–9. https://doi.org/10.1155/2015/508958

Himelstein, S. (2011). Mindfulness-based substances abuse treatment for incarcerated youth: A mixed method pilot study. *International Journal of Transpersonal Studies, 30*(1–2), 1–10. https://doi.org/10.24972/ijts.2011.30.1-2.1

Huppert, F., & Johnson, D. (2010). A controlled trial of mindfulness training in schools: The importance of practice for an impact on well-being. *The Journal of Positive Psychology, 5*, 264–274. https://doi.org/10.1080/17439761003794148

Jang, H., & Choi, S. (2012). Increasing ego-resilience using clay with low SES (social economic status) adolescents in group art therapy. *The Arts in Psychotherapy, 39*, 245–250. https://doi.org/10.1016/j.aip.2012.04.001

Kabat-Zinn, J. (1990). *Full catastrophe living: Using the wisdom of your body and mind to face stress, pain and illness.* New York, NY: Delta.

Le, T. N., & Proulx, J. (2015). Feasibility of mindfulness-based intervention for incarcerated mixed-ethnic Native Hawaiian/Pacific Islander youth. *Asian American Journal of Psychology, 6*(2), 181–189. https://doi.org/10.1037/apa0000019

Leckey, J. (2011). The therapeutic effectiveness of creative activities on mental well-being: A systematic review of the literature. *Journal of Psychiatric and Mental Health Nursing, 18*, 501–509. https://doi.org/10.1111/j.1365-2850.2011.01693.x

Macpherson, H., Hart, A., & Heaver, B. (2015). Building resilience through group visual arts activities: Findings from a scoping study with young people who experience mental health complexities and/or learning difficulties. *Journal of Social Work*, 1–20. https://doi.org/10.1177/1468017315581772

Malchiodi, C. (2007). *The art therapy sourcebook* (2nd ed.). New York, NY: McGraw-Hill.

Olson-McBride, L., & Page, T. (2012). Song to self: Promoting a therapeutic dialogue with high-risk youths through poetry and popular music. *Social Work with Groups, 35*, 124–137. https://doi.org/10.1080/01609513.2011.603117

Pagani, L., Japel, C., Vaillancourt, T., Cote, S., & Tremblay, R. (2008). Links between life course trajectories of family dysfunction and anxiety during middle childhood. *Journal of Abnormal Child Psychology, 36*, 41–53. https://doi.org/10.1007/s10802-007-9158-8

Pearson, M., & Wilson, H. (2008). Using expressive counselling tools to enhance emotional literacy, emotional wellbeing and resilience: Improving therapeutic outcomes with expressive therapies. *Counselling, Psychotherapy, and Health, 4*(1), 1–19.

Perry-Parrish, C., Copeland-Linder, N., Webb, L., Shields, A. H., & Sibinga, E. (2016). Improving self-regulation in adolescents: Current evidence for the role of mindfulness-based cognitive therapy. *Adolescent Health, Medicine and Therapeutics, 7*, 101–108. https://doi.org/10.2147/AHMT.S65820

Prince-Embury, S., & Courville, T. (2008). Comparison of one-, two-, and three-factor models of personal resiliency using the resiliency scales for children and adolescents. *Canadian Journal of School Psychology, 23*(1), 11–25. https://doi.org/10.1177/0829573508316589

Racusin, R., Maerlender, A., Sengupta, A., Isquith, P., & Straus, M. (2005). Psychosocial treatment of children in foster care: A review. *Community Mental Health Journal, 41*(2), 199–221. https://doi.org/10.1007/s10597-005-2656-7

Ricarte, J., Latorre, J., & Beltran, M. (2015). Mindfulness-based intervention in a rural primary school: Effects on attention, concentration, and mood. *International Journal of Cognitive Therapy, 8*(3), 258–270. https://doi.org/10.1521/ijct_2015_8_03

Roghanchi, M., Mohamad, A. R., Mey, S. C., Momeni, K. M., & Golmohamadian, M. (2013). The effect of integrating rational emotive behavior therapy and art therapy on self-esteem and resilience. *The Arts in Psychotherapy, 40*, 179–184. https://doi.org/10.1016/j.aip.2012.12.006

Romano, E., Babchishin, L., Marquis, R., & Frechette, S. (2014). Childhood maltreatment and educational outcomes. *Trauma, Violence & Abuse*, 1–20. https://doi.org/10.1177/1524838014537908

Segal, Z., Williams, J., & Teasdale, J. (2002). *Mindfulness-based cognitive therapy for depression: A new approach to preventing relapse.* New York, NY: Guilford Press.

Sinding, C., Warren, R., & Paton, C. (2014). Social work and the arts: Images at the intersection. *Qualitative Social Work, 13*(2), 187–202. https://doi.org/10.1177/1473325012464384

UNICEF Canada. (2017). *My cat makes me happy: What children and youth say about measuring their well-being.* Toronto, ON: UNICEF Canada. Retrieved from http://www.unicef.ca/sites/default/files/2017-08/UNICEF_One%20Youth%20Report.pdf

Vickery, C., & Dorjee, D. (2016). Mindfulness training in primary schools decreases negative affect and increases meta-cognition in children. *Frontiers in Psychology, 6*(2025), 1–13. https://doi.org/10.3389/fpsyg.2015.02025

6

Engendering Hope Using Photography in Arts-Based Research with Children and Youth

Sophie Yohani

First I was in Africa and we had a war. They were killing people. Some people were carrying things on their heads like food and clothes. We traveled to XXX. From XXX we flew to Canada. When we arrived, we stayed in a hotel until we could find an apartment. After that, about a month, we went to school. When I finish university, I would like to become a doctor. (Akinyi, 14-year-old refugee girl). (Yohani & Larsen, 2009, p. 253)

I met Akinyi, an energetic and friendly Canadian youth of African origin, when she was 14 and living with her mother and siblings in a midwestern city in Canada. Akinyi had been displaced from her West African country as a result of conflict spanning the late 1990s into early 2000s. On first looking at Akinyi's quilt drawing (Fig. 6.1), one is drawn to the images associated with trauma, loss, and displacement—stories that are all too familiar in the popular media. Yet this same picture takes on a new meaning when you learn that Akinyi drew this picture to illustrate a story

---

S. Yohani (✉)
University of Alberta, Edmonton, AB, Canada
e-mail: sophie.yohani@ualberta.ca

Fig. 6.1 Hope story painted on a quilt

of hope. Through the lens of hope, Akinyi's story maintains its horror, but other aspects of her experience emerge—including survival, opportunities, and a future. Her story illustrates the importance of viewing refugee children's stories holistically, paying attention to both the positive and negative aspects of the whole. In her own words, Akinyi illustrates that successful outcomes under conditions of adversity often encompasses relationships between risks, resources and contexts (McCubbin & McCubbin, 2013; McCubbin, Thompson, & Thompson, 1995; Rutter, 1987).

Research on children who have experienced armed conflict or political oppression often focuses on identifying psychopathology, with psychological trauma being the main focus of research (Yohani, 2015). Furthermore, research on children with adverse life experiences often relies on the perspectives of adults, providing few opportunities for children to represent their own experiences using developmentally-appropriate methods (Yohani & Larsen, 2009). To date, there is little research about how refugee and other children who have experienced adversity "maintain a hopeful outlook on life, while negotiating and interpreting their experiences during their early years of adjustment"

(Yohani & Larsen, 2009, p. 247), following conflict or resettlement in new countries. Yet, increasingly, there is a growing number of researchers whose work illuminates how children navigate, and even overcome, adverse experiences towards increased well-being and resilience (see Denov & Akesson, 2016).

An important aspect of resilience-based research is the consideration given for research methods that are appropriate for the contextual and developmental needs of children. This chapter will reflect on the use of arts-based research with children and youth who have experienced adversity, and how art offers a safe, relational, and respectful approach to explore experiences while engendering hope. The chapter will specifically draw on my experience of using photography in arts-based research to explore hope with children and youth. I will demonstrate for readers: (a) How theory is used to guide photography in research with children, (b) Practical information and considerations for data collection methods, (c) Approaches to data analysis, and (d) Knowledge translation activities in child-centred research.

Context: Researching Hope with Refugee Children

The curiosity to better understand what influences children, and youth like Akinyi, to maintain a sense of well-being was explored through the lens of hope. Guiding this inquiry were the questions:

- What are the hope-engendering and hindering experiences of school-age children who are recent immigrants and refugees from war-torn countries?
- What do these children and important people in their lives perceive to be helpful in aiding their psychosocial adjustment in resettlement countries?

The project used hope and human ecology theories and a qualitative case study design and took place in an early intervention program for refugee and immigrant children in a western Canadian city, with 17 children between ages 8 and 18 years, 12 program staff, and 7 parents (see Yohani, 2008). Sources of information included interviews, observations, and artefacts, all using arts-based activities (drawing, storytelling, collages, quilt making, and photography). The majority of program participants were recent newcomers (less than five years) from war-affected countries. The use of a hope perspective was employed to bring to light positive as well as negative experiences associated with adjustment. In studying hope, researchers discuss hope as involving a creative process (Jevne, 1993; Salander, Bergknut, & Henriksson, 2014). As such, stories and other creative methods (e.g., photographs and drawings) deemed helpful in describing personal experience associated with hope (Desmond, Kindsvatter, Stahl, & Smith, 2015; Jevne, Nekolaichuk, & Boman, 1999) were used in this research with children.

A human ecological framework (i.e., Bronfenbrenner, 1986) was used as a broader lens to understand children's experiences. This involved broadening the focus on children's perspectives to include views of hope in children from individuals in the children's life contexts (including program staff, cultural brokers, and parents). This contextualised perspective was also used to guide data collection activities that allowed children to reflect on experiences beyond the research setting. For practical purposes, a thematic analysis method (Colaizzi, 1978) was used as a general guideline to analyse both the children and adults' data. The use of a holistic and hope-focused approach required a shift from a focus on psychosocial adjustment through the detection and outlining of trauma symptoms in participants, to a stance that tried to understand children's perspectives regarding their current experiences. Through this process, I embraced a child-centred stance that allowed children to share as much as they wanted in ways that were most comfortable to them (see Barker & Smith, 2012). I was not positioned as the expert searching for evidence, but rather the learner being taught by and learning with the children. As noted previously, a significant aspect of this approach was the use of creative methods to engage children, and I specifically returned to a photography method I had used successfully to explore hope with youth in

Tanzania, East Africa (Parkins, 1997). The use of photographs allowed me to engage with the children in their current life contexts as captured well in the words of Judy Weiser:

> I would offer the suggestion that rather than being able to walk in their (children and youth) shoes for a day in order to really experience the world as they do, let us instead ask to step behind their cameras in order to see what (and how) they see; to pose for them under their direction of how we should be (or pose) for the camera; to reflect with them upon the meanings, feelings, memories, and thoughts stimulated by a photo-catalyst. (Weiser, 1988a, p. 372)

The outcome was a focus on process, on discovery, and what was personally important to participants rather than the search for evidence of preconceived notions of participants' experiences. This approach and emerging results eventually led me to review and re-appreciate the work of Judith Herman. In *Trauma and Recovery* (2015), Herman maintains that adjustment or recovery from trauma and loss requires the reconstruction of meaning, the rebuilding of hope, and the sense of empowerment needed to regain control of one's being and life. For Herman, strengths-based psychological processes such as hope are worthy of focus in recovery given the many negative psychological processes associated with challenging life events.

The rest of this chapter discusses the uses and usefulness of photography and photo-assisted interviews when conducting resilience-based research (in this case hope) with children and adolescents. First, I situate the use of photography within a historical and theoretical context, as a basis for guiding research with children. Next, I reflect on practical considerations for data collection methods, including incorporating collage making and story-telling *with* photography, I then discuss approaches to data analysis, ethical considerations, and knowledge translation activities that maintain the integrity of child-centred research. While I refer mostly to the hope project with refugee children in Canada, I also draw examples from my work with youth in Tanzania.

Photography in Qualitative Research

The camera as a research tool is well documented in disciplines such as anthropology and sociology (Collier & Collier, 1986; Hogan & Pink, 2010; Schwartz, 1989). Collier and Collier's book *Visual Anthropology: Photography as a Research Method* is one of the pioneering works addressing research procedures, observations and interpretations of visual data in anthropology. These researchers view photography as a bridge for communication and introduce the idea of interviewing participants using photographs. Through their experience, Collier and Collier noted that photographs enhance interviews by interpreting experiences, inviting open expression, while maintaining concrete and explicit reference points (i.e., the photograph). They reported that participants are more relaxed and tell their stories more spontaneously when the focus is not on them but on the photographs at issue.

The photo-interviews that Collier and Collier (1986) described used photographs taken by researchers, and this approach of researcher-photographer (as opposed to participant-photographer), was the most common approach earlier in qualitative research (Collier & Collier, 1986; English, 1988; Schwartz, 1989). Ziller (1990) later introduced another approach to photo-interviews by providing participants with cameras and instructing them to record their own images associated with various feelings:

> Through the insider's (participant) view via photography, the researcher becomes a part of the phenomenon, and a personal knowledge is achieved. The researcher begins to "see as they see" and "feel as they feel." The purpose of observation is not in simple description and analysis but understanding. (Ziller, 1990, p. 21)

Ziller traced this approach back to Worth and Adair who in 1966 asked Indigenous Navajo people in the United States to take motion pictures of their own lives. However, it has only been in the last decade, that arts-based research has become mainstream, and photography-based methods such as PhotoVoice (Plunkett, Leipert, & Ray, 2013; Wang, Yuan, & Feng, 1996), are now well documented research methods and tools for facilitating research and social change with children (Johnson, 2011) and youth (Delgado, 2015).

Photography in Qualitative Research with Children

Photography began to show up in research with children in the mid- to late 1970s, involving intervention studies with children struggling with emotional difficulties (Ammerman & Fryrear, 1975; Gallagher, 1983; Nelson-Gee, 1975), children with hearing impairments (Bodner, 1975; Weiser, 1988b), children with language development problems, and children form whom English is a second language (Nath, 1979), youth with behavioural challenges (Fryrear, Nuell, & White, 1977), and institutionalised (Milford, Fryrear, & Swank, 1983) and hospitalised adolescents (Savedra & Highley, 1988). These researchers used photography to facilitate verbal expression (Bodner, 1975; Nath, 1979; Weiser, 1988b), to enhance self-esteem (Ammerman & Fryrear, 1975; Fryrear et al., 1977; Milford et al., 1983) to enhance social skills (Gallagher, 1983; Nelson-Gee, 1975; Weiser, 1988a), to learn how adolescents view an experience (Savedra & Highley, 1988), and to assist in understanding children (Aitken & Wingate, 1993).

The overall message in these studies is that the use of photography in research works well, enriches studies, and is a rewarding experience for both the researcher and participants. In the words of one researcher:

> The student's enthusiasm was obvious to all who observed any of the photographic activities… The photography social skills unit was judged highly successful and will be implemented again. The theme, 'Photography—A Joyful Experience', permeated the entire series of lessons. (Gallagher, 1983, p. 45)

These early child researchers found photography to be particularly useful for work with nonverbally expressive groups such as children with language difficulties (Bodner, 1975; Nath, 1979; Weiser, 1988b). Further, experimental studies reported improved social skills and higher self-esteem scores in children with emotional and behavioural problems after completing photograph-based projects (Ammerman & Fryrear, 1975; Fryrear et al., 1977; Gallagher, 1983). Photography has had a resurgence in research in the past two decades (Barker & Smith, 2012), and this is also reflected in research with children (Eskelinen, 2012; Proveda, Matsumoto, Morgade, & Alonso, 2018; Whiting, 2015).

Although Hagedorn (1994) referred to photographs as a medium to capture visual data of experience just as audiotaping records verbal descriptions of experience, there are potential limitations in using photographs as the only data source. Photographs, like any form of art, can be interpreted in many ways. Highley and Ferentz (1989) maintained that the process of incorporating photography in research conversations often leads to uncovering misconceptions (held by the researcher) and arriving at more reality-based understandings of phenomena. Likewise, English (1988) noted that the use of written data with photography ensures congruence in determining the significance of the images to the context from which they were generated. Thus a combination of photographs and accompanying narratives adds richness to data in a study. This approach of using photographs and accompanying narratives was also supported by Schwartz (1989, p. 120) who stated that "in order to benefit social research, the use of photographic methods must be grounded in the interactive context in which photographs acquire meaning". Photo-elicited or photo-assisted interviews have since been used in research with children (Cappello, 2005; Epstein, Stevens, McKeever, & Baruchel, 2006; Whiting, 2015). A number of theoretical frameworks can be used as a basis for using photo-assisted interviews in research, specifically with children and adolescents.

Phenomenology and Hermeneutic as Theoretical Frameworks: From the Eye of a Child

Ziller and Smith (1977) first elaborated a phenomenological basis for the use of photography as a research tool whereby photographs are images of the photographer's information processing and part of the photographer's interaction with the physical and social environment. Phenomenological inquiry attempts to gain entry into the conceptual world of individuals in order to understand the meanings they construct around daily events in their lives (Bogdan & Biklen, 1992; Plunkett et al., 2013). The use of images taken by a camera appears to be one significant tool for gaining such understanding. According to Ziller and Smith, extending the phenomenological approach to the medium of photography has two main advantages: (a) the camera documents a person's perceptual orientation with minimal training and without the disadvantages of verbal report techniques, (b) and instead of the researcher selecting material, the participant is able to do so. Although photographs and verbal reports have their disadvantages, the use of photo-assisted interviews compliments the limitations of the two mediums.

Hagedorn (1994) on the other hand, introduced hermeneutic photography, an aesthetic technique grounded in hermeneutic and aesthetic philosophy, as a research method that provides insight into knowledge about the human experience by seeing and interpreting. In hermeneutics, artistic expressions, ideas, sculpture, and photographic interpretations are regarded as text (Van Manen, 1994). Thus hermeneutic photography highlights the importance of seeing and interpreting as a means of understanding experiences by grasping symbols that reflect experience. Hagedorn (1994) stated that "the images captured with photography invite human beings to speak about these experiences with a reflective depth. Photographs not only gather interpretations of images of experience, but also enrich and extend the communication of the experiences" (p. 46).

Van Manen (1984) recommended using creative ways for obtaining personal experience descriptions from children who may not be verbally expressive or reflective in traditional interviews and often cannot sit for long periods of time without tiring, by suggesting researchers gain access to the experience of young children "play with them, puppeteer, paint, draw, follow them into their play spaces and into the things they do while remaining aware of the way it is for children" (p. 18). In other words, Van Manen emphasised the importance of understanding developmental differences in children and adults in determining the methods of collecting data in research.

Considerations for Children's Cognitive Development: "Photographing" Our Thoughts

Piaget's theory of cognitive development may be used to argue for the usefulness of photo-assisted or elicited interviews with children and adolescents. According to Piaget, development of cognition is acquired through sequences starting with the sensorimotor stage of coordinating sensory perceptions and simple motor behaviours, and ending with the formal operational stage where the ability to think abstractly and systematically is acquired (Piaget, 1964). In middle childhood (ages 6–12 years), children are *concrete thinkers*, which means operational thinking allows them to mentally combine order in the presence of objects and events being thought about. This has enormous implications when conducting research on abstract and elusive concepts such as experiences of hope. Creative approaches must then be taken to make full use of children's participation (e.g., see Cook & Hess, 2007). In such cases, photo-assisted interviews is one reasonable method for exploring abstract concepts with children since the images are concrete reference points for the children to express thoughts and feelings (Cappello, 2005; Cook & Hess, 2007). Since adolescents have recently emerged from the world of concrete thinking, the use of photographs as a basis for verbal interviews is familiar and perhaps more valuable for adolescents who are late developers.

Practical Considerations for Arts-Based Data Collection and Analysis Methods

Preparing Children for the Photo-Assignment

Before giving child participants cameras with instructions for a project, time must be spent preparing them to take pictures related to the research question. Preparation is necessary since it helps participants with the technical aspects of taking pictures and also places the photo assignment in the context of something larger (i.e., the concept or issue being researched). In my studies, the concept being explored was hope as experienced and represented in the lives of children and adolescents. With this in mind, participants were prepared to answer my research question through a series of workshops to introduce them to the notion of presenting an idea or experience through visual images. I have done this by inviting a guest photographer to speak to the participants about some technical and artistic aspects of photography. This workshop approach also allowed me to introduce the idea of representing hope through images and talking about our creations by constructing collages (see Fig. 6.2). These pre-photo activity workshops were particularly useful for my work with children and adolescents who were still learning English and new to Canada. It eased any anxiety about taking photos, and introduced an element of playfulness and relaxation with images and storytelling. A word about cameras. Early photo researchers used polaroid cameras. Since then we have seen the evolution from regular cameras and film, to disposable cameras, and now digital cameras in a variety of forms ranging from phones to iPads. The choice of type of camera is up to the researcher and study goals. Regardless of the type of camera used, this should be incorporated into the training workshop(s).

Fig. 6.2 Collage depicting images of hope

The Photo-Assignment: What and How to Ask Questions?

Instructions for taking photographs may vary depending on the research question. Participants can be given a set of instructions adapted from those previously used by Ziller and Smith (1977).[1] Versions of the same instructions have been used in other studies (Aitken & Wingate, 1993; Ziller & Lewis, 1981). For the hope project, I gave disposable cameras with 27 pictures to participants with the following set of instructions (adapted from Ziller & Smith, 1977):

> Ask yourself the question "what is hope for me?" To do this we would like you to take **24 photographs** that capture or represent hope to you. The photographs can be of anything just as long as they tell something about your hope. Don't worry about your skills as a photographer. Keep in mind that the photographs should represent **your own** experience of hope. When you have taken each photograph, you will be asked to tell the story of 12 of your pictures, that is why you chose each one as a representation of hope to you. The stories could either be written or recorded onto a tape recorder so that someone else will write them for you. When you finish this project, you will have a book/portfolio about your own hope that is made up of 24 photographs. Remember, these photographs are simply to tell something about **your** hope.

Using Ziller and Smith's instructions as a framework is particularly useful since it outlines the instructions in a relatively simple and straightforward manner. These instructions also highlight the phenomenological aspect in that participants are taking photographs of their own experience. A sheet of paper with written instructions can be used for planning the pictures by having participants sketch their images in drawn boxes. Although I gave my participants the option of writing down their reflections, most students chose to participate in the photo-assisted interviews. Figure 6.3 shows an image of a bookshelf taken by a 12-year-old participant who reflected on her the process of learning to read in English

---

[1] Ziller and Smith (1977) used these instructions in studies using photography to understand orientations (personal frames of reference) associated with self-concept.

Fig. 6.3 Image of books as sources of hope

as hope enhancing. A separate activity had the participants create *photo books* where they selected and glued photos into a book along with reflections to go with their images. An assistant supported the participants who needed assistance with writing.

How Are Photo-Assisted Interviews Conducted?

Photo-assisted interviews can take on the nature of regular qualitative interviews ranging from structured to unstructured interviewing. In the hope project, I used photographs as the basis of the interviews by employing a semi-structured approach. I began the interviews by asking the participant to tell me why she or he had chosen the photograph as a representation of hope. For example, in Fig. 6.2, the young participant stated, "This is about books…it makes me to learn. If I can learn something and my teacher helps me to read or sometimes she helps me to pronounce lots of things that I did not know, then I have hope." From there I typically ask questions for clarification and elaboration. Regardless of the approach taken, the participant must be comfortable and preferably in their own environment to reduce anxiety relating to the interview process. In my view, photo-assisted interviews are actually more relaxing and easy to conduct than regular interviews, both for the interviewer and child participant. One reason may be the focus was on the photographs and not the participant. The externalised images probably put the participants at ease as they were not the *object* under study. Another reason may be that in many cases the photographs seem to quickly evoke emotions and stories, thus facilitating the interview process. All participants appeared to enjoy talking about their pictures.

The following is an excerpt from photo-assisted interview with a 14-year-old female participant in my Tanzanian study.

Sophie: Tell me about your second picture Mary,[2] why does it represent hope to you?

Mary: This is my family. In my family we were seven. My brother died, so we are now four children, my father and my mother. [spends some time point out each sibling in photograph and telling me their names and school grades they are in]

Sophie: In what way does your family represent hope to you, Mary?

Mary: Why my family is my hope is because they are around me every time. Even if I am in a bad condition they are around me. Once when I was a little kid, I got an accident when I was playing Rede, do you know Rede?

Sophie: Yes, babua kati? [another Swahili name for a type of ball game]

Mary: Yes (laughing) back then I was trying my best to make the ball not to hit me and then I fell down and I hurt my teeth.

---

[2] This is a pseudonym to maintain the participant's anonymity. Likewise, I have not included material that is identifying in this excerpt.

	One tooth fell down and the other was like coming out but it was still in there. And then I had to get braces. And then I was not able to eat food like rice, only soft food like biscuits, uji [porridge]. And then I was like not able to go out and play, so if I needed something my brother or my sister would get it for me. And they were always all around me, telling me sorry and things like that.
Sophie:	So they were there for you?
Mary:	Yeah. Even now they are there for me. They are hope for me. It is important to me that I have them to turn to.

How Are Photo-Assisted Interviews Analysed?

Like traditional verbal interviews, analysis of photo-assisted interviews can be conducted in a variety of ways depending on the theoretical framework that the researcher is using, the research objective, questions, or general intervention goals. From a qualitative perspective, an inductive analytical approach allows patterns to emerge from the photographs and narratives as opposed to a deductive approach where a specific research hypothesis guides what is searched for (Patton, 2002). As such, researchers can draw from a number of analytical approaches including *thematic analysis*, narrative analysis, interpretive phenomenological analysis or content analysis. In both of my hope projects, I chose to conduct a thematic analysis of the interviews using Colaizzi's (1978) method as a general guideline as it provides a clear and logical approach to analysis. A thematic analysis of the narratives refers to the "recovering of a theme or themes that are embodied and dramatized in the evolving meanings and imagery of the work" (Van Manen, 1994, p. 78). I began by reading each transcribed interview, then extracting significant sentences or phrases. Instead of formulating meanings from the significant phrases, I paraphrased the significant statements then clustered the paraphrases into the categories. Finally, I pulled together related categories into larger themes. Colaizzi ends the analysis by defining the essential structure of the concept under study. Another approach can combine thematic analysis of interviews and a separate content analysis of photographs. *Content analysis* of photographs is used mostly in studies that use photographs alone (for a discussion on content analysis of photographs see Highley & Ferentz, 1989).

Ethical Considerations: Do They Differ When Using Photographs?

In what way do ethical considerations differ when using photography in research? In studies that utilise photographic material, ethical issues can become important for a variety of reasons. For instance, concerns may arise regarding consent to take photographs, ownership of photographic images, and even cultural differences in meanings attached to photography. Ethical issues may also arise regarding maintaining anonymity of participants or people in photographs. Usual ethics in research requires that anonymity of participants be assured and no names be connected to results unless a participant wishes to have their name retained. This is a tricky issue in photography since some images may include identifying objects. These issues must be considered beforehand and discussed in detail with participants.

Hannes and Parylo (2014) suggest that the most critical factor in gaining access and consent is a reasonable approach that is sensitive to the individual being photographed. In studies where participants take photographs, clear instructions to obtain the permission of people (e.g., family members) with clear explanations if the photographs will be used in research must be given. I found the participants in the hope study to be very creative with this matter. For example, a number of participants whose family member was unavailable, chose to take a picture of something that represented that member (e.g., a Mother's Day card to represent their mother). Savedra and Highley (1988) relate initial concern regarding consent issues and possible irresponsibility on the part of adolescents using cameras in their study. They go on to report that in actuality gaining consent was not a problem and adolescents used the cameras in a responsible manner. More recently, Whiting (2015) echoes this sentiment when noting that even young children seem to understand consent with regard to visual images and are able to use cameras appropriately.

Using photo-assisted interviews involves gaining consent from participants to access both narratives and photographs. Signed permission from participants to use photographs must be obtained as soon as the pictures are developed. Like any study, participants who are minors must gain permission by parents or guardians to participate in a study. In cross-cultural studies, local ethical procedures must be followed and honoured. For example, in the Tanzanian study, the school principal was in charge of granting permission for students to take part in the study on behalf of parents. In addition to obtaining permission from the principal, students were instructed to report their participation to their parents and guardians. Participants should also be given the freedom to withdraw from the study, withdraw their photographs from the study, or obtain copies of their photographs at any time and without repercussion. For publication purposes, check with journals about their policies on publishing photographs which may include additional signed consent from photographer and use of black and white pictures only. Like all research procedures, respecting the decisions of the participants is of utmost importance in studies using photography.

Knowledge Translation Activities in Child-Centred Research

The primary goal of knowledge translation (KT) is to ensure that key messages are delivered in an audience-specific manner such that they align with the needs of integrated knowledge users (Canadian Institute of Health Research [CIHR], 2014). Since resilience-based research with children and youth is centred on honouring and including child and youth participants in the research journey, including them in knowledge translation activities is important. For the hope project, participants chose to showcase their photographs (and other pieces of work that was part of the project including collages and a quilt) in a variety of community settings.

These included having an exhibition at the host immigrant-serving agency, and at a local hospital, university and a number of local schools. Youth were present at the opening of these exhibitions and were able to interact directly and share their experiences of resettling in Canada with stakeholders such as settlement service providers, education, and healthcare professionals. The use of art mediums allowed them to communicate their experiences in a manner that was not threatening and reduced language barriers.

Reflections on Researching Hope with Refugee Children Using Arts-Based Research: Reconstructing Stories After Loss and Trauma

In many ways, this hope project was about finding another side to refugee and immigrant stories. In my attempt to better understand what was missing in mental health literature, I began to understand the bigger story of these children's lives—stories that involve challenges as well as successes. The idea of story has particular relevance to this population of children. If our lives are a constant process of recreating story (Freedman & Combs, 1996), then disconnecting experiences such as migration require the reconstruction of life stories to incorporate new experiences. Traumatic experiences associated with war, loss, and adjustment also bring with them the need to reconstruct life stories.

In his book, *The Politics of Storytelling*, Jackson (2002) argues that reconstituting events in a story shifts the storyteller from a passive subject in disempowering circumstances to actively reworking events, which enhances a sense of agency. However, because of the perpetuation of silencing children through disempowering experiences (i.e., challenges that hinder hope), many refugee children feel disconnected and don't have a structure to tell the story of their lives. They have lost their homes due to war, have had to endure the harsh life of refugee camps and in resettlement countries, they continue to struggle with language, culture, and financial barriers. One approach to helping children reconstruct personal narratives is by providing them with an arts-based structure to do this. In trauma literature, telling of the "trauma story" means that the stressful event must be reconstructed and processed within a structure where the traumatised person feels like a competent human being rather than a victim.

The hope-focused approach described in this study provides one structure whereby children can begin to connect to what is important and in doing so begin to weave their personal narratives, using art (photography in this particular example). As Jackson (2002) pointed out, reconstituting events through the lens of hope can help shift children from passive subjects in disempowering circumstances to active agents in their own lives. Therefore, rather than bringing forward the part that is disempowered by focusing on traumatic experiences, asking the children to explore hope using photographs gave voice to the aspect that is empowered in the children. That is, a part of the children that has somehow come through despite the many challenges they have had and continue to experience. Asking about hope taps into how a person remains connected to life, how they find meaning, and in this structure, life stories are continually constructed.

References

Aitken, S. C., & Wingate, J. (1993). A preliminary study of the self-directed photography of middle-class, homeless, and mobility-impaired children. *The Professional Geographer, 45*(19), 65–67.

Ammerman, M. S., & Fryrear, J. L. (1975). Photographic self-enhancement of children's self-esteem. *Psychology in the Schools, 12*, 317–325.

Barker, J., & Smith, F. (2012). What's in focus? A critical discussion of photography, children and young people. *International Journal of Social Research Methodology, 15*(2), 91–103.

Bodner, B. A. (1975). The eye of the beholder: Photography for deaf preschoolers. *Teaching Exceptional Children, Fall*, 18–22. https://doi.org/10.1177/004005997500800106

Bogdan, R. C., & Biklen, S. K. (1992). *Qualitative research for education: An introduction to theory and methods*. Boston, MA: Allyn and Bacon.

Bronfenbrenner, U. (1986). Ecology of the family as a context for human development: Research perspectives. *Developmental Psychology, 22*, 723–742.

Canadian Institute of Health Research (CIHR). (2014). *More about knowledge translation at CIHR.* Ottawa, ON: Author. Retrieved from www.cihr-irsc.gc.ca/e/39033.html

Cappello, M. (2005). Photo interviews eliciting data through conversations with children. *Field Methods, 17*(2), 170–182.

Colaizzi, P. F. (1978). Psychological research as a phenomenologist views it. In R. S. Valle & M. King (Eds.), *Existential-phenomenological alternatives for psychology* (pp. 48–71). New York, NY: Oxford University Press.

Collier, J., & Collier, M. (1986). *Visual anthropology: Photography as a research method.* Albuquerque, NM: University of New Mexico Press.

Cook, T., & Hess, E. (2007). What the camera sees and from whose perspective. Fun methodologies for engaging children in enlightening adults. *Childhood, 14*(1), 29–45.

Delgado, M. (2015). *Urban youth and photovoice: Visual ethnography in action.* New York, NY: Oxford University Press.

Denov, M., & Akesson, B. (Eds.). (2016). *Children affected by armed conflict: Theory, method, practice.* New York, NY: Columbia University Press.

Desmond, K. J., Kindsvatter, A., Stahl, S., & Smith, H. (2015). Using creative techniques with children who have experienced trauma. *Journal of Creativity in Mental Health, 10*(4), 439–455.

English, F. W. (1988). The utility of the camera in qualitative inquiry. *Educational Researcher, 17*(4), 8–15.

Epstein, I., Stevens, B., McKeever, P., & Baruchel, S. (2006). Photo elicitation interview (PEI): Using photos to elicit children's perspectives. *International Journal of Qualitative Methods, 5*(3), 1–11.

Eskelinen, K. (2012). Children's visual art and creating through photographs. *Procedia—Social and Behavioral Sciences, 45,* 168–177. https://doi.org/10.1177/160940690600500301

Freedman, J., & Combs, G. (1996). *Narrative therapy. The social construction of preferred realities.* New York, NY: W. W. Norton & Company.

Fryrear, J. L., Nuell, L. R., & White, P. (1977). Enhancement of male juvenile delinquents' self-concepts through photographed social interactions. *Journal of Clinical Psychology, 33*(3), 833–838.

Gallagher, P. (1983). Social skills and photography. *The Pointer, 27*(37), 42–45.

Hagedorn, M. (1994). Hermeneutic photography: An innovative esthetic technique for generating data in nursing research. *Advances in Nursing Science, 17*(1), 44–50.

Hannes, K., & Parylo, O. (2014). Let's play it safe: Ethical considerations from participants in a photovoice research project. *International Journal of Qualitative Methods, 13*(1), 255–274.

Herman, J. (2015). *Trauma and recovery. The aftermath of violence—From domestic abuse to political terror*. New York, NY: Basic Books.

Highley, B. L., & Ferentz, T. C. (1989). The camera in nursing research and practice. In C. L. Gillis, B. L. Highly, B. M. Roberts, & I. M. Martinson (Eds.), *Toward a science of family nursing*. Menlo Park, CA: Addison-Wesley.

Hogan, S., & Pink, S. (2010). Routes to interiorities: Art therapy and knowing in anthropology. *Visual Anthropology, 23*(2), 158–174.

Jackson, M. (2002). *The politics of storytelling. Violence, transgression and intersubjectivity*. Copenhagen, Denmark: Museum Tusculanum Press.

Jevne, R. (1993). Enhancing hope in the chronically ill. *Humane Medicine, 9*(2), 121–130.

Jevne, R., Nekolaichuk, C., & Boman, J. (1999). *Experiments in hope. Blending art & science with service*. Edmonton, AB: The Hope Foundation.

Johnson, G. (2011). A child's rights to participation: Photovoice as methodology for documenting experiences of children living in Kenyan orphanages. *Visual Anthropology Review, 27*(2), 141–161.

McCubbin, H. I., Thompson, E. A., & Thompson, A. I. (1995). *Resiliency in ethnic minority families: Native and immigrant American families* (Vol. 1). Madison, WI: University of Wisconsin System.

McCubbin, L. D., & McCubbin, H. I. (2013). Resilience in ethnic family systems: A relational theory for research and practice. In D. S. Becvar (Ed.), *Handbook of family resilience* (pp. 175–195). New York, NY: Springer.

Milford, S. A., Fryrear, J. L., & Swank, P. (1983). Phototherapy with disadvantaged boys. *The Arts in Psychotherapy, 10*, 221–228.

Nath, J. (1979). Ronnie and the magic of photography. *The B.C. Teacher, 1*, 112–113.

Nelson-Gee, E. (1975). Learning to be: A look into the use of therapy with polaroid photography as a means of recreating the development of perception and the ego. *Art Psychotherapy, 2*, 159–164.

Parkins, S. Y. (1997). *Exploring hope: A journey with Tanzanian adolescents in a school setting* (Unpublished thesis). University of Alberta, Edmonton, Canada.

Patton, M. Q. (2002). *Qualitative evaluation and research methods* (3rd ed.). Newbury Park, CA: Sage.

Piaget, J. (1964). Part I: Cognitive development in children: Piaget development and learning. *Journal of Research in Science Teaching, 2*(3), 176–186.

Plunkett, R., Leipert, B. D., & Ray, S. L. (2013). Unspoken phenomena: Using the photovoice method to enrich phenomenological inquiry. *Nursing Inquiry, 20*(2), 156–164.

Proveda, D., Matsumoto, M., Morgade, M., & Alonso, E. (2018). Photographs as research tool in child studies: Some analytical metaphors and choices. *Qualitative Research in Education, 7*(2), 170–196.

Rutter, M. (1987). Psychosocial resilience and protective mechanisms. *American Journal of Orthopsychiatry, 57*(3), 316–331.

Salander, P., Bergknut, M., & Henriksson, R. (2014). The creation of hope in patients with lung cancer. *Acta Oncologica, 53*(9), 1205–1211.

Savedra, M. C., & Highley, B. L. (1988). Photography: Is it useful in learning how adolescents view hospitalization? *Journal of Adolescent Health Care, 9*(3), 219–224.

Schwartz, D. (1989). Visual ethnography: Using photography in qualitative research. *Qualitative Sociology, 12*(2), 119–153.

Van Manen, M. (1984). *Doing phenomenological research and writing: An introduction* (Monograph no. 7). Department of Secondary Education, University of Alberta, Edmonton, Canada.

Van Manen, M. (1994). *Researching lived experience.* London, ON: Althouse Press.

Wang, C., Yuan, Y. L., & Feng, M. L. (1996). Photovoice as a tool for participatory evaluation: The community's view of process and impact. *Journal of Contemporary Health, 4*, 47–49.

Weiser, J. (1988a). Phototherapy: Using snapshots and photo-interaction in therapy with youth. In C. Schaefer (Ed.), *Innovative interventions in child and adolescent therapy.* New York, NY: Wiley.

Weiser, J. (1988b). "See what I mean?": Phototherapy as nonverbal communication in cross cultural psychology. In F. Poyatos (Ed.), *Cross-cultural perspectives in nonverbal communication.* Lewiston, NY: Hogrefe.

Whiting, L. S. (2015). Reflecting on the use of photo elicitation with children. *Nurse Researcher, 22*(3), 13–17.

Yohani, S. C. (2008). Creating an ecology of hope: Arts-based interventions with refugee children. *Child & Adolescent Social Work Journal, 25*(4), 309–323.

Yohani, S. C. (2015). Applying the ADAPT psychosocial model to war affected children and adolescents. *SAGE Open July–September*, 1–18. https://doi.org/10.1177/2158244015604189

Yohani, S. C., & Larsen, D. J. (2009). Hope lives in the heart: Refugee and immigrant children's perceptions of hope engendering sources during early years of resettlement. *Canadian Journal of Counselling, 43*(4), 246–264.

Ziller, R. C. (1990). *Photographing the self: Methods for observing personal orientation*. New York, NY: Sage.

Ziller, R. C., & Lewis, D. (1981). Orientation: Self, social, and environmental precepts through auto-photography. *Personality and Social Psychology Bulletin, 7*(2), 338–343.

Ziller, R. C., & Smith, D. E. (1977). A phenomenological utilization of photographs. *Journal of Phenomenological Psychology, 7*(2), 172–185.

7

Using Arts-Based Reflection to Explore the Resilience and Well-Being of Mature-Age Women in the Initial Year of Preservice Teacher Education

Loraine McKay and Kathy Gibbs

Introduction

As academics, we are interested in using various arts-based tools to support the process of reflection within teacher education. Because transition into university can be a challenging time for all new students (Briggs, Clark, & Hall, 2012; Busher, James, & Piela, 2016) we were particularly interested in how arts-based reflection might support students during this period. In this chapter, we report on the experiences and reflections of four mature-age preservice teachers collected during their first year at university and the distinct set of challenges they encountered. We also examine the personal and contextual resources and strategies that they

---

L. McKay (✉)
Education and Professional Studies, Griffith University,
Brisbane, QLD, Australia
e-mail: loraine.mckay@griffith.edu.au

K. Gibbs
Griffith University, Brisbane, QLD, Australia
e-mail: k.gibbs@griffith.edu.au

© The Author(s) 2020
L. McKay et al. (eds.), *Arts-Based Research, Resilience and Well-being Across the Lifespan*,
https://doi.org/10.1007/978-3-030-26053-8_7

implemented to navigate those challenges. Finally, we consider how arts-based reflection contributed towards the women's resilience and well-being during their transition into university.

Literature Review

The transition into university is a challenging process for many students, especially those students from non-traditional backgrounds (Basit, 2012; Busher et al., 2016), including mature-age women (O'Shea, 2014). Failing to develop a sense of belonging (Cramp, 2011; Pokorny, Holley, & Kane, 2017), time management, self-discipline, managing paid employment, navigating institutional systems and accessing academic support (Blair, 2017), financial issues, and balancing family and personal commitments (O'Shea & Stone, 2011) are a few examples of the challenges that students face. Deciding to complete a university degree with the goal of embarking on a new career can also evoke a range of mixed feelings.

The implications of returning to study in higher education for mature-age women include changes in their relationships and their personal identity. O'Shea and Stone (2011) reported on the changing dynamics and roles within the households of women returning to university, including active resistance from partners that, in some cases, contributed to relationship breakdowns. Moreover, as women became more confident in their knowledge and opinions, their perceptions of themselves changed. They developed clearer definition of themselves and their future goals, along with an increasing sense of worth. Identifying and exploring these new insights is important as it can lead to competencies and skills to help cope with new demands in the future (Keller-Schneider, 2014) especially in relation to their future role as teacher. Therefore, rather than characterising challenges encountered during transition as barriers, they can be utilised and reconsidered as opportunities to activate personal and contextual resources and practical strategies to support resilience and well-being.

In teacher education, engaging personal and contextual resources to support resilience and well-being is essential to balance the demands on a preservice teacher's personal life and their developing professional identity

(Mantas & Di Rezze, 2011). Teaching can be a highly stressful job that requires a teacher to deal simultaneously with a range of personalities, roles, responsibilities, social, and political factors within and across varying contexts. In addition, the personal expectations to which preservice teachers hold themselves accountable, resulting from individual beliefs, values and attitudes developed through past experiences, can support or stifle transformation and growth and add to the challenges beginning teachers experience early in their careers (McKay, 2013). Therefore, it is useful for mature aged women to recognise, harness and support their own resilience and well-being during initial teacher education.

Resilience and Well-Being

According to Beltman, Mansfield, and Harris (2016) resilience is a contextually embedded construct that can be developed over time. Resilience theory (Fregeau & Leire, 2016) suggests resilience develops when adverse situations are resolved by utilising personal resources, contextual factors or strategies. Some of these resources could include core qualities such as courage and flexibility (Korthagen, 2017). Resilient teachers develop and employ a range of strategies such as humour and building networks of support. Family support, relationships and a strong sense of self, may act as protective factors. Resilient traits such as social competence, problem solving skills and autonomy are then able to flourish (Gonzales, 2003). As a consequence, job satisfaction and well-being are supported as a result of professional growth, commitment, and job performance (Wright & Cropanzano, 2000).

Together, these features of resilience are reflected in Mansfield, Beltman, Price, and McConney's (2012) multidimensional view of a resilient teacher. Within the social dimension, resilient teachers are found to develop networks and a sense of belonging. They seek help and advice as they build reciprocal relationships. Teachers who demonstrate qualities within the motivational dimension are persistent and assume an improvement focus while displaying confidence in themselves and others. Importantly, resilient teachers know how to manage their emotions and through a sense of optimism and self-care, employ ways to manage stress.

Resilient teacher qualities identified within the professional dimension include being a problem solver, organised, flexible and reflective. These dimensions are linked with well-being.

Dodge, Daly, Huyton, and Sanders (2012, p. 230) refer to well-being as having "the psychological, social and/or physical resources [required] to meet a particular psychological, social and/or physical challenge." When an individual has strategies such as goal setting, and communication skills to access and action the personal resources and contextual resources available, well-being is likely to be enhanced. Personal resources include motivation, efficacy, optimism, high expectations and courage. Contextual factors include trust, collaborative partnerships and networks, strong relationships in the workplace, recognition and autonomy. Clearly, there is a distinct overlap in the skills, strategies and traits identified in the resilience and well-being literature.

Reflection and Reflective Practice as a Protective Barrier in Teaching and Teacher Education

Regular reflective practice can contribute to a protective layer of resilience and has been identified as critical for self-care for those working in high stress jobs (Moffatt, Ryan, & Barton, 2016). Because regular reflection is identified as a tool to support self-care, it is an important process to develop during teacher education (Skovholt & Trotter-Mathison, 2011).

Reflection helps preservice teachers to understand the complexity of teaching (Unrath & Nordlund, 2009). Kenny, Finneran, and Mitchell (2015) note space needs to be created for reflection in teacher education to add value to the participatory activities that preservice teachers tend to privilege, such as practical courses and in-school experiences. Mantas and Di Rezze (2011) note the relational aspect of teaching, examined through reflection is often placed secondary to knowledge transmission and measureable outcomes as proof of learning within teacher education. Furthermore, evidence in the literature champions the notion that reflective processes can be enhanced via modes such as images, sound and/or gesture, claiming that reflection that relies on words alone can reduce people's expression of emotions (King et al., 2014; Lavina, Fleet, & Niland, 2017; Power & Bennett, 2015).

Method and Methodology

A phenomenological case study approach was used to explore the perspectives of four mature-aged female, preservice teachers who were enrolled in the first year of a Bachelor of Education undergraduate degree. A phenomenology approach was chosen as it "illuminates a phenomenon from the perspectives of those experiencing it" (Fregeau & Leire, 2016, p. 65). Furthermore, phenomenology takes a philosophical approach to research as a means to explore human experiences through the consciousness of the experiencer (Giorgi, 2009). These experiences are examined and understood through qualitative evidence, with the intent to give them meaning (Ayres & Guilfoyle, 2013). This project focused on the phenomenon of how four mature-aged preservice teachers, through their personal accounts, perceive their resilience and well-being in the first year of their study.

Three research questions guide this study. They are:

1. What challenges do mature-age women face in their first year at university?
2. What personal and contextual resources and strategies do they implement to navigate those challenges?
3. Does arts-based reflection support resilience and well-being during the transition into university?

The four female participants were in the same age demographic (28–38 years of age) and have family responsibilities, each with at least two children. Two participants were raising their children as single parents, often without extended family support, and two women had other carer roles for extended family members. Three women also worked outside the home in part-time paid employment. Individual descriptions are not included to protect the anonymity of the participants. Approval to conduct the study was granted by the university's Human Research Ethics Committee and to comply with ethical clearance, data were collected during workshop activities held at irregular intervals throughout the second half of the first year of study once the first author had completed teaching responsibilities with the participants.

Seven workshops were held in total over six months. Six of those workshops ranged from one to two hours while the seventh workshop was held over a full day. The activities were designed to: (1) develop participants' understanding of the term resilience and the vocabulary associated with it; (2) build trust in the group so open and honest reflection could occur; (3) investigate the challenges participants identified; and (4) understand the ways the participants were responding to them.

Author 1, was teaching in the first year program and had a service role as First Year Coordinator. Through weekly contact in these roles, during the first six months of the degree, Author 1 built a strong rapport with participants. Author 2 conducted interviews and focus groups after establishing rapport during the full day workshop. The case notes prepared using each participant's data were shared with that participant for verification that their perceptions had been captured correctly. Triangulation of data occurred through multiple data sets.

Data Collection Tools and Arts-Based Reflection

The data set for each participant included collage (My resilient self) and written deconstruction; photo elicitations (How I see myself as a teacher); timelining, an emotion continua with written reflections (What challenges and enablers have you encountered in the first year? How did you respond?); construction of a collaged mask (Inner side: Represent the teacher you want to be; Outside: represent the enablers and blockers to being that person); and two semi-structured group interviews. An individual interview was also conducted with each participant to explore the written reflection that accompanied the mask activity and then a final focus group interview was conducted. The individual interview promoted a breadth of views on how the design of the mask related to the challenges and enablers in the first year of university and further opportunity to access information that might not be yielded during the written reflection. The group interview enabled all participants to share their ideas about their first year at university and allowed the interviewer to make a comparison of the data collection from the group and one-to-one interviews.

The data collection tools are explained in the following section.

Rip and paste collage involved the selection of materials, including magazine images and art supplies, to represent an event or phenomena. Participants then responded to a series of questions based on the work of Simmons and Daley (2013) to examine the process, and open-ended questions to explore the representations. The first collage activity was completed on paper with the size determined by the participant. The second collage activity involved the creation of a mask.

Timelining is a process of guided reflection where participants recall six emotions they have experienced in relation to their first two trimesters in their first year of their university degree. Next they describe or draw an event related to the identified emotion and then organise the events on a continua depending on the level of control they perceived they had over the event. Participants then considered possible future responses.

Photo elicitation involved choosing an image from a random selection of commercially produced photos. Examples included a range of images of natural and built environments, families, celebrations and household items. Participants were asked to select an image that resonated with them in relation to their studies in Trimester 2. Brief notes were created during individual reflection, and then as a group they shared their thoughts and emotions extending their jotted notes in depth and detail.

Data Analysis

Initially a formal profile for each participant was created starting with demographic information. Next, the data set completed by each participant (collage and mask, photo elicitation, and timelining) including relevant sections of the transcripts of the focus group interview and the individual interviews were analysed by each of the authors. Each data set was read in its entirety first with margin annotations and highlighting in order to identify key words, phrases, and excerpts and possible relationships between each. Both researchers shared and compared their early analysis of each case.

Data were analysed using a constant comparison method as outlined by Thomas (2011). This method of analysis is a flexible method for analysing qualitative data and can be used to identify emerging themes within the data. The emerging themes are organised into major themes based on the questions asked to the interviewees. The coding process occurs several times (a distillation process), comparing each of the emerging themes. The distillation process identified the group's experiences of the challenges and enablers encountered in the first year of university, rather than the experience of one person. Overriding the constant comparison method of data analysis was the materialisation of sub-themes that helped to better capture the context of the data and formed a draft of the analysis. Furthermore, through colour coding, physically manipulating chunks of transcribed data and preparing visual organisers of the analysis (Bazeley, 2013), broad themes such as high risk, new and changing relationships, prioritising time, changing views of myself, self care, and new confidences emerged. These themes were then organised into a framework for reporting.

Findings and Discussion

In the following section the authors report on the distilled essence of the four participants: Kelly, Donna, Nancy and Ellie (pseudonyms). The report is structured using aspects of the resilient teacher model proposed by Mansfield et al. (2012) with dimensions of social well-being identified by Dodge et al. (2012).

Social Dimension

All participants noted the importance of meeting new like-minded people that extended to the formation of friendships during the transition into university. A recurring element in the collage activities was a link to new friends. Similar to the findings of Ayres and Guilfoyle's (2013) and Hamilton and O'Dwyer (2018), these four women noted their peers as an important source of support and friendship. They recognised four roles the friendships filled besides academic support. First, they were all mothers who could empathise with the challenges they faced juggling family responsibilities. Second, the friendships helped to reaffirm that they belonged at university and to overcome the fear that they would be seen as a "social pariah, sitting at the front [alone]" (Ellie). Third, their group served as a sounding board where they could vent in a safe environment without feeling judged. Finally, they recognised these new friends would form part of their professional network once they graduated. This final point is particularly notable because the positive impact of developing strong support networks during their teacher preparation will also act as a protective contextual factor that will be required to maintain or buoy their resilience and well-being in the early stages of their career (Väisänen, Pietarinen, Pyhältö, Toom, & Soini, 2017).

Relationships with staff, family and partners changed or were solidified during the first year. Participants saw their age, life experience, and commitment to their studies helped them to develop strong relationships with staff because as enthusiastic students they attended and actively engaged in lectures and tutorials. They recognised that these relationships were their entry points into the profession.

Relationships with spousal partners reportedly changed during the first year. Unlike the study of O'Shea and Stone (2011), Kelly noted her relationship with her partner was strengthened as she transitioned to university and together they made decisions to make her study less stressful. Downsizing their home allowed her to reduce the hours of work in paid employment allowing study to be prioritised. The two other women who had partners also noticed a shift in the parenting and domestic responsibilities (O'Shea, 2014). Self-confessed as "house-proud", Nancy noticed a change in her priorities as she "let things go" around the house. She also noted a shift in domestic roles and recognised the extra help offered by her husband, which allowed her to focus on her studies and her own self-care. These incidents were turning points in the value these participants placed on their needs in comparison to others. Learning to attend to self-care and well-being can be taught during teacher education and will be significant in their future roles as teachers.

Echoing the findings of Väisänen et al. (2017) in their study of 40 preservice teachers in Finland, asking for help was something that the preservice teachers in the current study described did not come to them naturally. Donna and Ellie acknowledged they found it "easier to power through" (Donna) rather than to delegate or find help. Ellie explained the use of excessive sticky tape on her mask (Fig. 7.1) represented times when "things kind of fall apart" and being able to "put it back together as best as you can, and just keep going". Originally Nancy expressed a similar concern but came to realise it was in her

Fig. 7.1 Ellie's mask

and her family's best interest for her to seek help when it was required. She also noted that her experiences as a parent had prepared her to find ways to have her voice heard which she drew on during a difficult situation at a professional experience when she felt her personal beliefs were being compromised. Resilient people know where and when to access help, and therefore it is in the best interests of all participants' long-term well-being to nurture help seeking practices (Väisänen et al., 2017).

Participants noted that simply being part of the research project and the reflection processes helped to strengthen their well-being because of the caring vibe among the group. For example, the workshop tasks, such as collage making, provided opportunities for informal sharing of experiences and contributed to the establishment of a safe and caring research environment (McKay & Sappa, 2019). Participating in the workshops provided an additional avenue of emotional support and also scaffolded the reflection process. Kelly explained the process of collaging and,

> creating the visual representation was fun but it also prompted some much needed conversation … We are certainly working towards a collective of supportive colleagues which adds to my resilience. (Kelly)

She also explained that she was "overwhelmed by the support of the [other] women" which was important to her as the project was "the only thing [she] was currently doing just for [herself]." These findings resonate with Le Cornu's (2009) study of preservice teachers where peer support, especially partnerships that offered reciprocity, were found to foster resilience.

Motivational Dimension

Akin to the findings of Ayres and Guilfoyle (2013) the participants were all highly self-motivated. Being a role model for their children, personal fulfilment and the high stakes (temporary financial burden, risk in being unsuccessful, future employment opportunities, loss of family time, strain on relationships) they associated with their decision to come to university were the common factors the women identified that kept them motivated.

The participants had a strong focus on learning, self-improvement and personal satisfaction. Donna's confidence increased as she "learnt to trust her abilities and be proud of everything [she had] achieved". In turn, long-term aspirations emerged, supported by her early success. She explained,

> I do actually see myself coming back to uni… I don't want to get stuck in a rut and I am always looking for ways to further my knowledge… Doing things I want to do will mean being successful and in turn add to my happiness.

During the workshops and interviews, Nancy consistently referred to the importance of fun in learning. As a parent, however, she reported seeing classrooms where the students "were starved for fun, creativity, [and] affection." Nancy identified that as a teacher, her "duty [was] to instil [students] with confidence" and recognised that she needed to have confidence in herself to achieve this. She explained that, "in the first year I got a strong sense of who I am and where I want to be. I know [coming to university] is the right journey [although] I don't have enough knowledge yet to consider myself a teacher."

While these comments indicate an internal change in how Nancy and the other women defined themselves, and are comparable to the findings of O'Shea (2014), it also indicated a growing confidence in the transformational possibilities that they may facilitate in the future. This desire to improve the lives of themselves and others was a motivating force and despite the various challenges each of the participants faced, they remained optimistic about their studies and their decision to undertake university studies.

Nancy recalled her feelings in relation to her first year and noted the growth in herself and her peers in the process.

> I felt brave the entire time… It was really hard at some points but I stuck to it. That was really gratifying … I gave up money. I've given up time with

my family. It's made my marriage harder. We (her peers) are a bit more assertive with our needs. (Nancy)

The lion's mane on Kelly's mask (Fig. 7.2) also represented bravery. She explained,

It took courage to come back to university at my age … and to make me a priority. I hadn't really been a priority in my life. I hadn't made myself a priority or my goals or my dreams a priority. I've just done what I had to do to keep money and keep rolling and keep the family running. So finally deciding what it is I want to do with my life and changing careers … to be a teacher. I want to do this for myself.

The current study extends the work of Stone and O'Shea (2013) by providing a forum for mature-age women to explore the gendered challenges

Fig. 7.2 Kelly's mask looking in

and other tensions they faced during the first year of university. By reflecting in a safe, supportive, non-judgemental environment using arts-based methods to support the process, a network for problem solving, sharing empathetic viewpoints and empowering autonomy evolved and contributed positively towards the development of personal and contextual resources that support resilience and well-being.

Emotional Dimension

As mothers, Nancy and Kelly commented they had not made themselves a priority in recent years. Nancy recognised that "taking care of yourself [was] not selfish" and a difference noted by all participants in their first year of university was the change in where they placed themselves in their order of priority. While time management and flexibility was a skill the participants indicated was part of their lives prior to commencing university, how they used their time was re-organised to create ways to manage university and family demands while also addressing their own well-being. These findings resonate with Stone and O'Shea (2013) who also found women tailored their study time around other responsibilities, however, in the current study, perhaps encouraged through guided reflection, the women went on to find ways to improve their self-care. They did this by speaking out about their own needs such as getting more help from a spouse to make time not only for study, but for some kind of activity to provide balance, such as doing craft, reading for enjoyment, taking time to exercise or meet with friends for coffee.

Some kind of highlighting around the eyes, or additional eyes glued onto the masks of most participants illustrated the strong feeling of being watched or judged by family, friends and teachers they knew or met during the first year (See Figs. 7.3 and 7.4). Nancy explained she started university feeling very overwhelmed with self-doubt and while feeling "watched and judged" she came to realise that "when [she] put too much pressure on [her]self to do well … [she was] creating less space for other things that might also make [her] happy." By the end of the first year she claimed she was "less burdened by [her] own standards" and decided to "choose to be calm", to back herself and her ability to be a good teacher

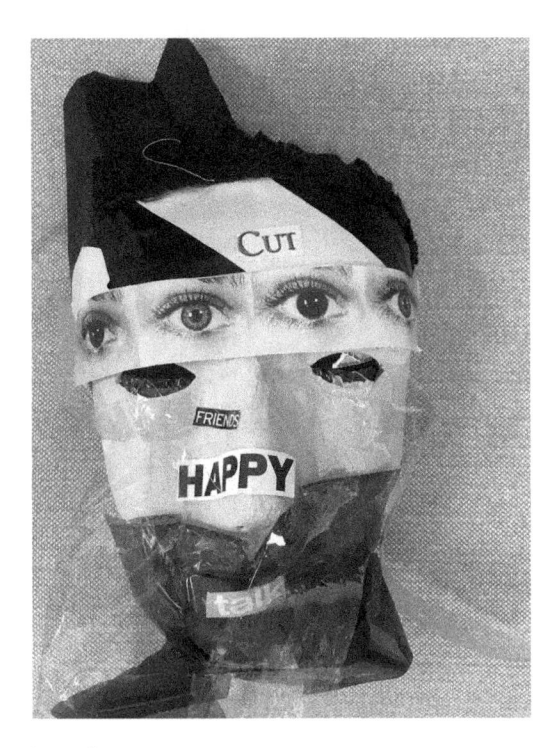

Fig. 7.3 Donna's mask

and noted "self-love and happiness go together." Choice, happiness and calm were words used more frequently by Nancy towards the latter part of data collection and reflected the positive actions she employed at the same time, such as accessing a tutor early in the trimester, increasing child care arrangements for her young children, and volunteering to mentor commencing students.

The participants generally tried to remain positive and optimistic, but at times they were dragged into a downward emotional spiral because of high workloads, frustrating interactions with other students and staff, and attempting to meet their inflated personal expectations. A variety of resources was used at these times. Music and humour were strategies participants identified that they used as coping mechanisms. In addition, social networks became increasingly important for academic and emotional support. Despite realising they functioned more efficiently as

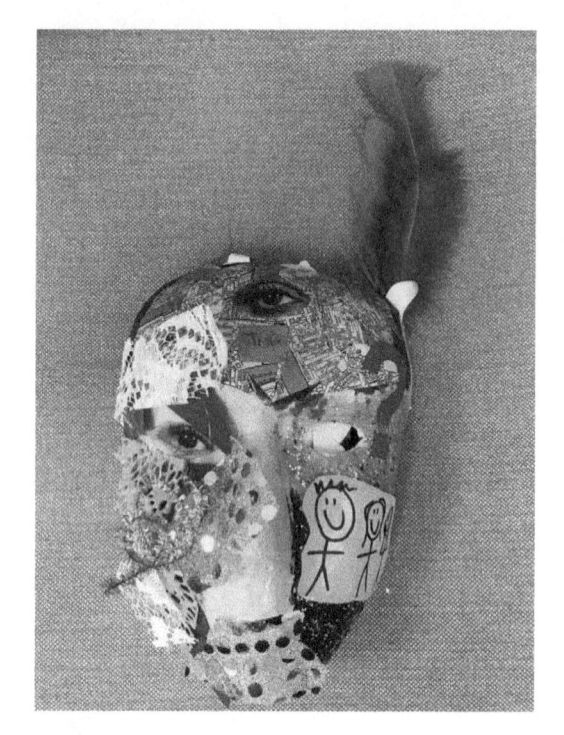

Fig. 7.4 Nancy's mask

parents and students when they took time out for themselves, some students found relinquishing control, adjusting self-expectations and putting themselves, first required intentional decision making.

Professional Dimension

The unexpectedly high level of academic success in their first trimester had a two-fold effect. While it raised their confidence and self-belief, it also led to personal pressure to maintain a particular standard. The greatest change noted in relation to learning, however, was the shift in the participants' focus from gaining high grades to developing new knowledge and skills, especially those they referred to as the soft skills of teaching. These skills referred to interpersonal and communication skills that they valued in the future teacher they strived to become. The shifting focus reaffirmed "it is okay not to know everything now" (Ellie) and it is "okay not to control everything" (Kelly). The change in thinking was closely linked with a readjustment in the expectations they held of themselves and others.

Participants were emotionally invested in becoming a teacher, and acknowledged the sacrifices they were making to get there. Kelly chose an image of a jetty leading out over the water to describe her feelings of being on the right path while also confirming she "had a long way to go until she gets on the boat" (becomes a teacher). Nancy saw herself as a ladybug on a leaf to illustrate her learning journey as ongoing and herself "as a small entity in a larger world". Even though at the end of her first year she did not consider she had "enough knowledge yet to consider [her]self a teacher," she did note "I am discovering I am both stronger and more vulnerable that I gave myself credit for" (Nancy). In line with Hamilton and O'Dwyer's (2018) study that compared the learning approaches of direct entry and mature age learners in undergraduate degrees, the process of learning was important in their end goal to become a teacher by each of the women in the current study.

Donna recognised teaching as "a really big responsibility" and noted she was "a bit scared of burning out." However, through ongoing reflection she noted "if you get too bogged down in all the negativity you'll become negative yourself … knowing when to step away, take a breath and refocus is a major part of developing my personal resilience."

Ellie's comments reflected the value of reflection participants associated with professional development. She noted that, "you can be blindsided by your own views" and went on to explain how the reflection activities undertaken freed up her thinking and willingness to share personal feelings and views. For Ellie, the arts-based supported reflection was helpful because "sometimes your thoughts can't be articulated, or you might be apprehensive about talking about them with other people so having another way to express yourself is helpful." For each of these women, reflection was important to their learning associated with self-care and well-being.

Conclusion and Limitations

There is no doubt the first year of university was a turbulent but transformative time for these four participants. The perceived high stakes decision to return to university magnified their initial fear of failure that was linked with letting down their family (Busher et al., 2016). While their confidence was enhanced through positive feedback and results, their need to sustain a high grade point average increased the expectations to which they held themselves accountable, often at the expense of their own well-being. Their perceptions of themselves changed with their increasing confidence and a greater sense of competence as they challenged the limitations of systemic processes and practices.

Identifying and managing the emotions they experienced was difficult. Feelings of guilt, incompetence, inadequacy and fear were experienced at various times throughout the year. Sensing they were shirking responsibilities, particularly related to their families, added stress on top of tight deadlines for assignments. The current study adds to the work of O'Shea and Stone (2011) illustrating that when the mature age women were supported through arts-based reflection to turn their attention to self-care, they prioritised their own needs and they found they were able to function far more efficiently and effectively as a mother, wife, student and friend. Shifting their focus to self-care and fun while re-assessing what it meant to be a good teacher allowed the participants to turn the first year at university from a time of survival into a time to thrive.

The emotional dimension appears to be the most at risk in these first year preservice teachers. As participants experienced success in many forms it reaffirmed their decision to return to university was a positive choice. Success and confidence bred success and confidence and increased their sense of well-being and love of learning. As future teachers, this outcome is likely to be of personal benefit to the participants as well as their family and the future generations of students they teach. Therefore, addressing the emotional dimension of preservice teacher resilience should be a primary concern of teacher education programs.

Furthermore, relationship building and interpersonal skills were highly important in helping the participants to navigate first year challenges. Strong social networks, built on mutual respect and trust helped to support a sense of belonging and enhanced positive emotional responses to university. Having a group of like-minded friends with whom they could share the challenges and humour helped to sustain their commitment to their studies despite the obstacles they faced.

Illustrated within the experiences of these four women is the potential offered by arts-based practices to support reflection that can help to sustain resilience and well-being. In the short term, what these women learnt about themselves supported their transition into teaching. However, given the demands on teachers and the challenges faced within the teaching profession, it is important to foreground resilience and well-being in teacher education as part of a long-term strategy to support professional identity. As these participants progress through their studies and move into a beginning teacher role it will be important that they continue to foster an ongoing commitment to their personal resilience and well-being.

While this chapter reports on only four participants and it may be seen as a limitation, it does provide an in-depth perspective of their first year experience. Given the increasing number of mature age students, particularly women, who are gaining access and returning to study in higher education, future research that includes a wider inquiry would be helpful for those charged with providing support for students' making the transition to university. Similarly, focusing on a male perspective would also add a gendered lens to future discussions.

As a final note, while this chapter illustrates the benefits of using arts-based practices to support reflection, it is noted a range of external, contextual factors and supports have also been present in the lives of these four women. Consequently, while not a sole influence, arts-based supported reflection has contributed to the learning, transformation and growth related to resilience and well-being that these women experienced. As Siegesmund and Cahnmann-Taylor (2008) contend,

> Arts-based educational research is particularly well-suited for understanding – and demystifying – the human relationships that enhance … the structures of deep learning. The outcome of such learning is personal agency: autonomous individuals who have the capacity to imaginatively shape their own lives by having the courage to write their own stories. (Siegesmund & Cahnmann-Taylor, 2008, p. 244)

Through higher education these women are re-writing their futures. Learning, in the form of arts-based reflection, has supported their journey.

References

Ayres, R., & Guilfoyle, A. (2013). Social support and sense of community for mature age women studying psychology. *The International Journal of Adult, Community and Professional Learning, 19*(4), 29–43.

Basit, T. N. (2012). 'I've never known someone like me go to university': Class, ethnicity and access to higher education. In T. N. Basit & S. Tomlinson (Eds.), *Social inclusion and higher education* (pp. 173–192). London, UK: Policy Press.

Bazeley, P. (2013). *Qualitative data analysis. Practical strategies.* London, UK: Sage.

Beltman, S., Mansfield, C. F., & Harris, A. (2016). Quietly sharing the load? The role of school psychologists in enabling teacher resilience. *School Psychology International, 37*(2), 172–188.

Blair, A. (2017). Understanding first-year students' transition to university: A pilot study with implications for student engagement, assessment, and feedback. *Politics, 37*(2), 215–228.

Briggs, A. R., Clark, J., & Hall, I. (2012). Building bridges: Understanding student transition to university. *Quality in Higher Education, 18*(1), 3–21.

Busher, H., James, N., & Piela, A. (2016). On reflection: Mature students' views of teaching and learning on access to higher education courses. *International Studies in Sociology of Education, 25*(4), 296–313.

Cramp, A. (2011). Developing first-year engagement with written feedback. *Active Learning in Higher Education, 12*(2), 113–124.

Dodge, R., Daly, A. P., Huyton, J., & Sanders, L. D. (2012). The challenge of defining wellbeing. *International Journal of Wellbeing, 2*(3), 222–235.

Fregeau, L., & Leire, R. (2016). Two Latina teachers: Culture, success, higher education. *Taboo: The Journal of Culture and Education, 15*(1), 61–78.

Giorgi, A. (2009). *The descriptive phenomenological method in psychology: A modified Husserlian approach.* Pittsburgh, PA: Duquesne University Press.

Gonzales, J. (2003). *Cesar Chavez: A case study of a resilient child's adaptation into adulthood* (ERIC document reproduction service no. ED47).

Hamilton, M., & O'Dwyer, A. (2018). Exploring student learning approaches on an initial teacher education programme: A comparison of mature learners and direct entry third-level students. *Teaching and Teacher Education, 71*, 251–261.

Keller-Schneider, M. (2014). Self-regulated learning in teacher education. The significance of individual resources and learning behaviour. *Australian Journal of Educational & Developmental Psychology, 14*, 144–158.

Kenny, A., Finneran, M., & Mitchell, E. (2015). Becoming an educator in and through the arts: Forming and informing emerging teachers' professional identity. *Teaching and Teacher Education, 49*, 159–167.

King, V., Garcia-Perez, A., Graham, R., Jones, C., Tickle, A., & Wilson, L. (2014). Collaborative reflections on using island maps to express new lecturer's academic identity. *Reflective Practices, 15*(2), 252–267.

Korthagen, F. (2017). Inconvenient truths about teacher learning: Towards professional development 3.0. *Teachers and Teaching, 23*(4), 387–405. https://doi.org/10.1080/13540602.2016.1211523

Lavina, L., Fleet, A., & Niland, A. (2017). The varied textures of an arts-informed methodology: Exploring teachers' identities through artful expressions. *Journal of Curriculum and Pedagogy, 14*(2), 143–163.

Le Cornu, R. (2009). Building resilience in pre-service teachers. *Teaching and Teacher Education, 25*(5), 717–723.

Mansfield, C. F., Beltman, S., Price, A., & McConney, A. (2012). Don't sweat the small stuff: Understanding teacher resilience at the chalkface. *Teaching and Teacher Education, 28*(3), 357–367.

Mantas, K., & Di Rezze, G. (2011). On becoming "wide-awake": Artful research and co-creative process as teacher development. *International Journal of Education & the Arts, 12* (S1.4). Retrieved from http://www.ijea.org/v12sil/

McKay, L., & Sappa, V. (2019). Harnessing creativity through arts-based research to support teachers' identity development. *Journal of Adult and Continuing Education.* https://doi.org/10.1177/1477971419841068

McKay, L. M. (2013). *Transforming perceptions and responses to student difference: The journey of seven beginning teachers* (Unpublished doctoral dissertation). Queensland University of Technology, Brisbane, Australia.

Moffatt, A., Ryan, M., & Barton, G. M. (2016). Reflexivity and self-care for creative facilitators: Stepping outside the circle. *Studies in Continuing Education, 38*(1), 1–18. https://doi.org/10.1080/0158037X.2015.1005067

O'Shea, S. (2014). Transitions and turning points: Exploring how first-in-family female students story their transition to university and student identity formation. *International Journal of Qualitative Studies in Education, 27*(2), 135–158. https://doi.org/10.1080/09518398.2013.771226

O'Shea, S., & Stone, C. (2011). Transformations and self-discovery: Mature-age women's reflections on returning to university study. *Studies in Continuing Education, 33*(3), 273–288.

Pokorny, H., Holley, D., & Kane, S. (2017). Commuting, transitions and belonging: The experiences of students living at home in their first year at university. *Higher Education, 74*(3), 543–558.

Power, A., & Bennett, D. (2015). Moments of becoming: Experiences of embodied connection to place in arts-based service learning in Australia. *Asia-Pacific Journal of Teacher Education, 43*(2), 156–168.

Siegesmund, R., & Cahnmann-Taylor, M. (2008). The tensions of arts-based research in education reconsidered: The promise for practice. In M. Cahnmann-Taylor & R. Siegesmund (Eds.), *Arts-based research in education: Foundations for practice*. New York, NY: Routledge.

Simmons, N., & Daley, S. (2013). The art of thinking: Using collage to stimulate scholarly work. *The Canadian Journal for the Scholarship of Teaching and Learning, 4*(1), 1–11. https://doi.org/10.5206/cjsotl-rcacea.2013.1.2

Skovholt, T. M., & Trotter-Mathison, M. (2011). *The resilient practitioner: Burnout prevention and self-care strategies for counselors, therapists, teachers, and health professionals* (2nd ed.). New York, NY: Taylor & Francis. https://doi.org/10.4324/9780203893326

Stone, C., & O'Shea, S. E. (2013). Time, money, leisure and guilt—The gendered challenges of higher education for mature-age students. *Australian Journal of Adult Learning, 53*(1), 95–116.

Thomas, G. (2011). *How to do your case study: A guide for students and researchers*. Los Angeles, CA: Sage.

Unrath, K. A., & Nordlund, C. Y. (2009). Postcard moments: Significant moments in teaching. *Visual Arts Research, 35*(1), 91–105.

Väisänen, S., Pietarinen, J., Pyhältö, K., Toom, A., & Soini, T. (2017). Social support as a contributor to student teachers' experienced well-being. *Research Papers in Education, 32*(1), 41–55.

Wright, T. A., & Cropanzano, R. (2000). Psychological well-being and job satisfaction as predictors of job performance. *Journal of Occupational Health Psychology, 5*(1), 84.

8

Joint Painting for Understanding the Development of Emotional Regulation and Adjustment Between Mother and Son in Expressive Arts Therapy

Rainbow Ho and Wong Chun Chiu

I don't know how to say it, I just feel the changes in me. After the artmaking sessions, I discover that I have funny and silly characteristics. My mum could be funny and silly too. (Jimmy)

I am mostly impressed that Jimmy could calm down his anger and apologize to me. He said, 'Mum, sorry for hurting you'. He has never done this before the intervention. (Jimmy's mother)

Introduction

Pertaining to the development of a child's ability in emotional regulation and resilience, the parent-child relationship is important (Fonagy, 2001). Working on the communication and interactions between par-

---

Rainbow Ho (✉)
University of Hong Kong, Pok Fu Lam, Hong Kong
e-mail: tinho@hku.hk

Wong Chun Chiu
Castle Peak Hospital, Tuen Mun, Hong Kong

ents and children thus become crucial in helping children develop appropriate strategies in emotional adjustment. However, usually it is not easy for children to express emotions through language and verbal communication. Due to the difficulty the children may encounter in social interaction, communication and emotional expression, for children with Autism Spectrum Disorder (ASD), this task becomes more complex. Special attention has thus to be placed not only on verbal communication but also on expressions through other appropriate means. Given the playfulness and nonverbal component during the process, an arts-based approach is one of the alternative solutions. This chapter starts with an overview of the challenges in working with parents and children, followed by an introduction of the Expressive Arts Therapy as an alternative therapeutic approach, and then the description of the joint painting procedure which serves as both the therapeutic and evaluation tool. A case study of applying joint painting game in the Expressive Arts Therapy with a boy with ASD and his mother is used to demonstrate the dynamic interactions and changes between the son and his mother.

Parent-Child Relationship

Throughout decades, researchers have been extensively investigating the importance of parent-child relationship in the psychosocial development of children. Erik Erikson's psychosocial theory of human development specifies that in the process of growing up, all individuals must experience eight developmental stages, during which one would need to resolve the corresponding psychosocial conflicts (Erikson, 1963, 1993). In particular, interactions between parents and children are essential in the first three stages: basic trust versus mistrust (infant–18 months), autonomy versus shame and doubt (18 months–3 years old), and initiative versus guilt (3 years old–5 years old) (Berger, 1988). As suggested by John Bowlby, positive interaction between caregivers and children in the first two years of life is conducive to the establishment of secure attachment (Bowlby, 1969). Such affectionate bonding is powerful in helping children develop independence and better coping strategies to deal with various forms of emotional distress and personality disturbance experienced in their later development (Bowlby, 1977). Recently, the parent-child relationship is also reported to be important in the development of abilities in emotional regulation and resilience among children (Fonagy, 2001). Studies have shown that in the process of emotional regulation, harsh parenting has both direct and indirect effects on child aggression (Chang, Schwartz, Dodge, & McBride-Chang, 2003). More specifically, maternal harsh parenting has a stronger effect on children's emotional regulation than paternal, whereas paternal harsh parenting affects more on sons than daughters (Chang et al., 2003).

Challenges Faced in the Field

While it is well understood that enhancing the communications and interactions between parents and children is important in helping children develop appropriate strategies in emotional adjustment, practitioners still face an obstacle that children are not easy to express emotions through language and verbal communications, not to mention those working with developmental disorders, that is, Autism Spectrum Disorders (ASD). Children with ASD are characterised with a deficit in social interactions, communications, and emotional expressions (Attwood, 2006). Brookman-Frazee and her colleagues indicated that as the task becomes more complicated, frustration and negative emotions may be experienced by therapists when serving children from such population (Brookman-Frazee, Drahota, Stadnick, & Palinkas, 2012). Specifically, emotional challenges can result from difficulties in serving children with ASD, related to slow progress, perceived ineffectiveness of psychotherapeutic strategies, and the constraint of the system in the special education and mental health services (Brookman-Frazee et al., 2012). Consequently, distinct attention has to be placed not only on verbal communications but also on expressions through other appropriate means.

Working with Children Using Expressive Arts Therapy

Expressive Arts Therapy refers to the therapeutic use of different art modalities, including visual arts, music, dance/movements, drama and poetry/writing with intermodal or multimodal approaches (Malchiodi, 2012). *Decentering* and *intermodal transfer* are the major concepts and principles in Intermodal Expressive Arts Therapy, a process in which one can step back from the literal reality and move into the alternative world of imagination. By so doing, it can help people develop and explore different perspectives and insights through the language of arts, play and imagination (Knill, Levine, & Levine, 2005; Levine, 2014). *Intermodal transfer* refers to moving from one art modality to another. And through the transfer, people may become more sensitive towards the possibilities of particular modalities or develop new perspectives or insights, thus intensifying and expanding their experiences. A deeper connection and expression of the feelings are consequently afforded (Knill, Barba, & Fuchs, 2004).

Thus, some professionals have chosen to use art expression as an alternative to communicate with children. Given that art expression is believed to be a natural language for most children and can enhance their communication and participation during the therapeutic process, Malchiodi introduced art expression as a helpful way to be adopted in therapy (Malchiodi, 2012). She further pointed out that art expression can lower the level of anxiety and help children feel more at ease, thereby increase their memory retrieval ability and better assist them to organise their own story. Waller demonstrated that in dealing with children's emotional, developmental and behavioural problems, art can act as a safe vessel through which children can communicate and express difficult emotions (Waller, 2006). Various studies also supported the advantages of using drawing to facilitate and enhance communications in children (Driessnack, 2005; Gross & Hayne, 1998; Rollins, 2005). In Wikström's study, hospitalised children used expressive arts to express and communicate difficult emotions such as fear, powerlessness and longing, with the therapist. For example, a child embroidered a boat without any oars to represent the feeling of out of control and powerlessness. Several weeks later, the child was able to create a tiny little oar representing her being able to manage the situation. Wikström suggested that expressive arts could be a powerful medium for children to symbolically express their feelings and ideas. By providing a safe and containing environment, children were able to gradually master and reduce their negative emotions, and eventually subdue the situation (Wikström, 2005).

Studies have also revealed that art is a helpful tool for therapists working with children diagnosed with ASD. Schweizer, Knorth and Spreen indicated that art therapy might enhance self-image, communication and learning skills among children in this population (Schweizer, Knorth, & Spreen, 2014). Besides, the use of art might contribute to their improvement in social communication problems, restrictive and repetitive behaviour patterns. For instance, some therapists use art to engage in relationships and develop face processing and recognition skills (Martin, 2008) as well as emotional recognition (Richard, More, & Joy, 2015). Improvisational music therapy was also found to have similar positive effects on communicative behaviour, language development, emotional responsiveness, attention span and behavioural control (Wigram & Gold, 2006). Scharoun and her colleagues reviewed different studies in dance/movement therapy which helped children with ASD in their social behaviours, emotional instabilities, and also other characteristics of ASD (Scharoun, Reinders, Bryden, & Fletcher, 2014). They concluded that dance/movement therapy can provide physical and psychological benefits for children with ASD and are successful in both individual and group settings. The pilot theatrical intervention conducted by Corbett and her colleagues further illustrated that theatre as a therapeutic approach to children with ASD was effective in improving facial recognition, skills in the theory of mind and social functioning (Corbett et al., 2011).

Case Study

Case Background

Jimmy (pseudonym) is an 11-year-old boy with Autism Spectrum Disorder (ASD). He studies in a conventional primary school in Hong Kong, but has poor academic performance. Jimmy has normal intellectual ability but his younger brother is suspected to be suffering from developmental delay. His parents were divorced when he was 8 and he did not have much contact with his father since. Jimmy's mother reported that Jimmy had many behavioral problems, including social difficulties and had temper tantrums easily when he was nearly 8. He was then assessed by a psychiatrist and diagnosed with ASD. Jimmy's mother said that she did not know how to teach him and deal with his behavioral and emotional problems. She disclosed that she was also having emotional problems herself and would use physical punishment when she could not tolerate his misbehaviors. Jimmy had experienced domestic violence and found to have some self-mutilation behaviors. Found by his school teacher with multiple bruise marks over his body, Jimmy was sent to a children's home and was separated from his mother under the order of the Family Court when he was 9. The family was labelled at risk and a social worker followed up the case. Jimmy was arranged to have regular interviews with a social worker and a clinical psychologist. Jimmy's mother was also required to receive counselling service in a Christian counselling center. Thereafter, she became calmer and was more willing to take up her parental role. At the age of 10, Jimmy was allowed to live with his mother again. He mentioned that his mother has changed and has become kinder towards him. His mother exerted no more violent behaviors on him, and he had not been found to have self-mutilation behaviors again.

Although Jimmy has returned home, his control of temper has still not improved. His mother described him being bad-tempered and threw a tantrum easily especially when his requests got rejected. During his temper outburst, he would shout aloud and break things at home. Sometimes, he would run away from home too. At school, he had assaulted his classmates when he felt disappointed. Sometimes, Jimmy would stay alone in the corner of his classroom and isolate himself for over an hour. His school teachers reported that they could not calm him down with verbal instructions alone. Once, they needed a team of six men to stop Jimmy while he was out of control. Afterwards, they brought him into a room to let him calm down. Besides having emotion dysregulation, he also had social and communication problems and did not have friends in school. He did not seem to understand what others think and could not identify with other people's emotions. These issues are raised as typical characteristics of ASD, in particular, the deficit of the ability to recognize and understand emotions. Moreover, his mother reported that he has hypersensitivity on tactile sensation. He would become agitated when people touched him even if it was just a friendly pat on the shoulder. His psychiatrist has prescribed tranquilizers for him to be used when necessary, but his mother rarely gave them to him. Furthermore, he was not able to engage with his school teacher or social worker. Jimmy has been referred to receive Expressive Arts Therapy for emotion regulation by the Christian counselling center.

Presenting problems

- Dysfunction in emotion regulation;
- Poor awareness of emotions;
- Maladaptive emotion regulation goals; and
- Limited emotion regulation strategies.

These problems are shown in his negative thoughts and inappropriate emotion expressions, such as seeing things in negative ways, or outburst of anger through breaking things or assaulting others.

Based on the background of this case, an Expressive Arts Therapy which comprised of 23 sessions was provided for Jimmy. As suggested by Gross and Jazaieri, emotion regulatory capacity is influenced by three essential factors, namely awareness of emotions, emotion regulation goals, and strategies in emotion regulation (Gross & Jazaieri, 2014). The intervention was designed to have three phases accordingly. In phase one (sessions 1–5), the objective was to enhance his awareness of emotions. In phase two (sessions 6–16), the objective was to help Jimmy set up his adaptive emotion regulation goals. In phase three (sessions 17–23), the objective was to enhance his strategies in emotion regulation. Eventually, the whole intervention lasted nine months.

Intermodal Expressive Arts Therapy

In each phase of the treatment, the architecture of the Intermodal Approach developed by Knill et al. (2005) was followed. Each session was divided into four parts: (1) filling-in; (2) decentering through play, art-making and imagination; (3) aesthetic analysis; and (4) harvesting (Knill et al., 2005; Levine, 2014) (see Fig. 8.1). Joint painting was mainly used in phase two to understand the interactions between Jimmy and his mother.

```
┌─────────────────────────────────────────────────────────┐
│                      Filling-in                         │
│      Focusing on the issues that needed to be worked on │
└─────────────────────────────────────────────────────────┘
                            ↓
┌─────────────────────────────────────────────────────────┐
│        Decentering through play, artmaking and imagination │
│           Entering into an alternative world of experience │
└─────────────────────────────────────────────────────────┘
                            ↓
┌─────────────────────────────────────────────────────────┐
│                    Aesthetic analysis                   │
│     Working on the imaginary reality and developing new │
│     perspectives from the artworks and the artistic process │
└─────────────────────────────────────────────────────────┘
                            ↓
┌─────────────────────────────────────────────────────────┐
│                       Harvesting                        │
│   Integrating the ideas and meaning from the decentering │
│            process in relation to the issues            │
└─────────────────────────────────────────────────────────┘
```

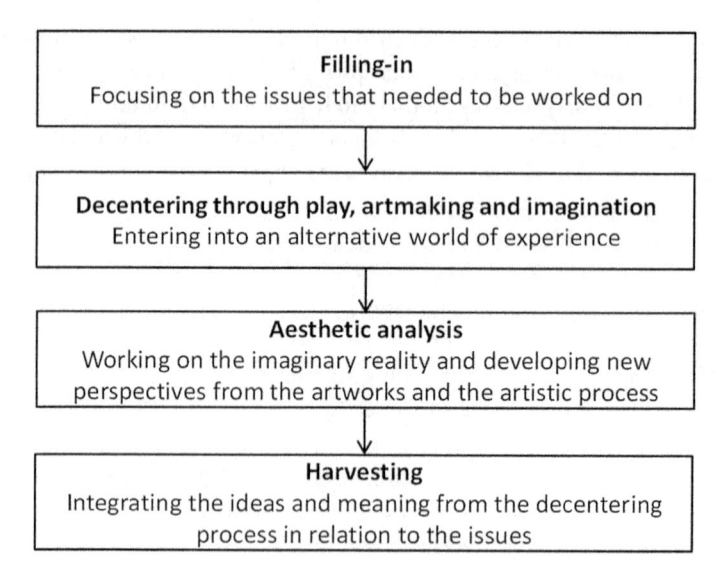

Fig. 8.1 The flow of the architecture of a session. (Adapted from Knill et al., 2005; Levine, 2014)

Joint Painting Procedure

Children with difficulties in emotional regulation and communication usually display problems in developing positive relationships with others, including with their parents. Given all the advantages in using the arts-based approach to work with the parent-child relationship, that is, more effective in expressing feelings in conscious and unconscious ways (Lai, 2011; Proulx, 2002), arts-based assessment tools which can help evaluate the process and progress of the parent-child relationship are nonetheless rarely available. Developed by Gavron (Gavron, 2012, 2013), the Joint Painting Procedure (JPP) has been used to evaluate the parent-child communication pattern in middle childhood (aged 6–12), and it has also been utilised in various clinical settings like parent-child art psychotherapy (Gavron, 2013; Gavron & Mayseless, 2015). The JPP consists of a child and his/her parent painting together on the same sheet of paper involving the following five steps (Gavron & Mayseless, 2015):

1. Pencilling a personal space on the paper;
2. Painting their own individual spaces;
3. Drawing a frame around one's own space to protect oneself;
4. Making a path from one's frame to the frame of the other; and
5. Drawing together in the shared area on the same paper.

Such procedures allow the expert/therapist to closely assess the process of change between the parent and the child. In general, the first three steps allow the expression of one's own internal world in the presence of the other. The fourth step provides the opportunity for them to express their motivation to be connected, and the last step demonstrates their ability to stay together in the relationship (Gavron & Mayseless, 2015).

The following is a case study using Expressive Arts Therapy on Jimmy (Wong, 2016), an 11-year-old boy with ASD who had dysfunction in emotional regulation and conflicts with his mother. A joint painting game named *Peaceful World* was used in this case.

Peaceful World is a traditional paper game which was very popular in the 80s and 90s in Southern China and Hong Kong (Fig. 8.2). It starts with two persons drawing at the two ends of the same paper. Each person has to draw a castle first, then the two persons will play the hand game, rock-paper-scissors. The one who wins can draw a flag (up to three flags) on his/her own castle, and then, add protective shields (up to five layers), drawing one item at a time. After building up all the shields, the one who wins the hand game can start to draw aircraft and cannons, and then start to attack the other person's castle and shields. An item damaged by another person can only be repaired when the person wins the rock-paper-scissors hand game. Finally, the person whose weapons, protective shields and castles are all damaged will lose the game. To a certain extent, this joint-painting game is similar to the JPP (Gavron, 2012, 2013).

Session 11 of Phase Two: Joint Painting for Understanding the Needs of the Client

In the past ten sessions, various games such as paper ball game, doodling, and tic-tac-toe, were used on Jimmy to help distract him from his negative emotions. At first, Jimmy only enjoyed the fun but resisted to men-

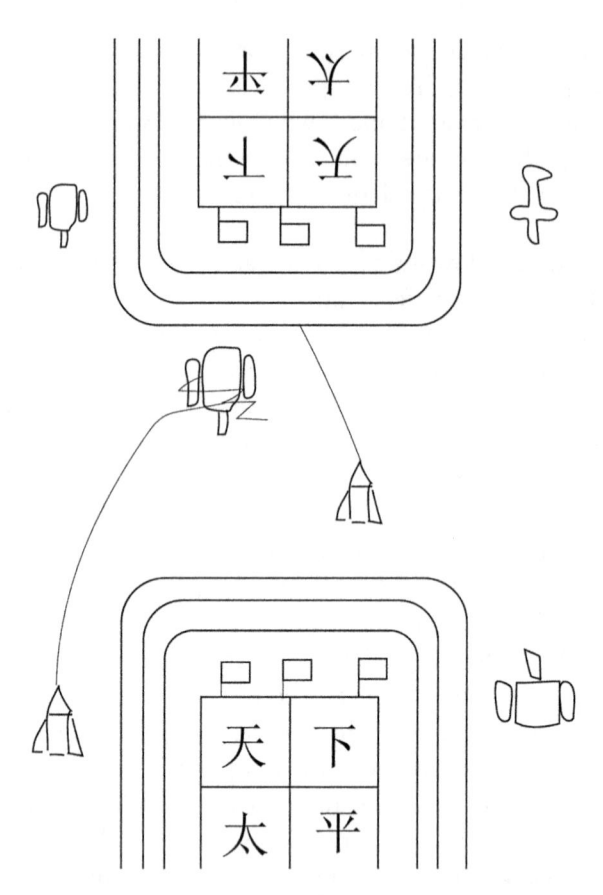

Fig. 8.2 Sketch of the *Peaceful World* game. The four Chinese words together mean world peace

tion the sources of his negative emotions. Thus, the treatment process appeared to be stuck at the very beginning of this phase leaving the therapeutic objective unreached. The situation, however, changed when a joint painting game called *Peaceful World* was introduced in session 11.

Filling-In

Meanwhile, Jimmy was more aware of his strengths and positive emotions. Nonetheless, he still did not know how to handle his negative emotions appropriately. While only paying attention to his short-term concerns, which were to avoid or ventilate his uneasy and uncomfortable feelings immediately, social relationships and the consequences of his temper outburst or other issues remained yet unresolved.

Reflection: After working with Jimmy for ten sessions to build up his strengths, we started to think about working with Jimmy on expressing or handling his negative emotions. We suspected that the imbalance between Jimmy's short-term (difficulty in expressing his negative emotions) and long-term concerns (established emotional regulation strategies) to be the major factor that he adopted maladaptive emotion regulation strategies. Thus this became the focus of this stage of treatment.

Decentering Through Play, Art-Making and Imagination

During the process of working on the *Peaceful World* game, Jimmy was encouraged to make sounds and move while creating his own army or destroying the opponents. Later, everyone in the room imitated the bombing sound together whenever the opponent was destroyed, and the victor cheered and sang loudly. When the sound component was included in the game, Jimmy's creativity was further stimulated. He suggested introducing his toy dinosaurs into the game. According to what he described, the white dinosaur was the good guy while the brown was the bad one. With his further elaboration, it became known that the white dinosaur represented him while the brown represented his mother. Thereafter, the *Peaceful World* game was played with the two dinosaurs putting inside the castles (see Fig. 8.3). Given that the victor could make a posture of victory among the dinosaurs (see Fig. 8.4), Jimmy finally ventilated his disappointment by making different postures in an interesting and humorous manner.

Reflection: During the process of the joint-painting game, shouting and singing loud helped Jimmy to become more relaxed. It also stimulated and activated his inner energy. His suggestion of introducing the two dinosaurs into the game represented his desire to interact with other people, and here, his mother, as he had expressed his longing to play with his mother. This should be the opportunity to explore this issue with him.

Fig. 8.3 The "Peaceful World" game with the presence of dinosaurs-aerial view

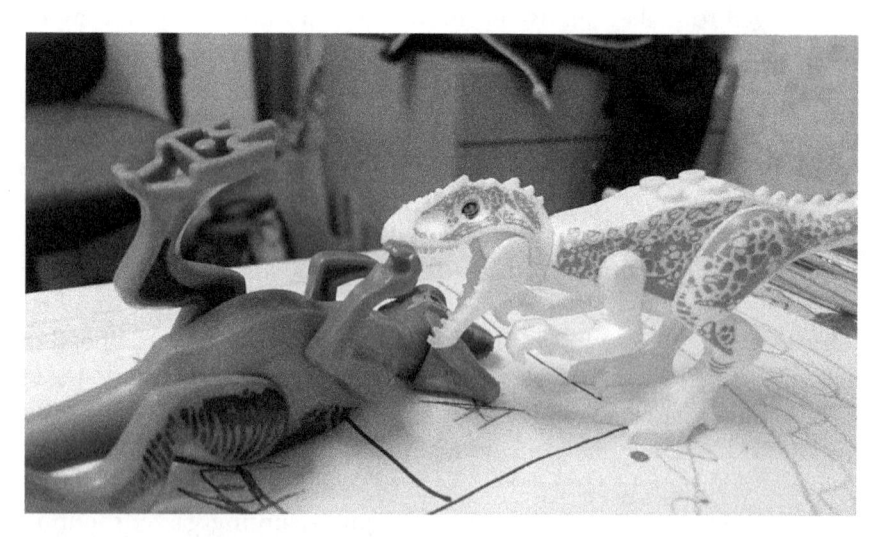

Fig. 8.4 The "Peaceful World" game with the presence of dinosaurs-mid-shot

Aesthetic Analysis

After the game, Jimmy mentioned that regardless of the result, he felt delighted and relaxed. All of a sudden, he disclosed that he wanted to have a father as one of the therapists. Concerning his desire to have a father in the game, the therapist invited Jimmy to share about the qualities he thought were essential to be a good father. He said that the qualities should include open-mindedness, acceptance and willingness to play with him. The therapist suggested that perhaps these qualities were also possibly found in his mother. Jimmy appeared to be in doubt and he mentioned that his mother had not played with him for a long time. Eventually, he expressed his desire to play with his mother together again. His real desire was explored through aesthetic analysis.

Reflection

The act of destructing the opponent helped Jimmy ventilate his negative emotions. This process was greatly enhanced by the addition of different arts modalities. Besides, he could use dinosaurs as symbolic representations of himself and his mother, and created his own way of expressing feelings towards his mother. We were delighted that Jimmy could finally ventilate his negative emotions. At this point, the relationship issue between Jimmy and his mother was brought to the surface, we could thus start to think about working on this.

Session 15 of Phase Two: Joint Painting for Revealing the Communication Pattern

Filling In

An incident happened a few days before this session. Jimmy strived for cycling with his mother but she finally turned down his request. Jimmy was unhappy about this and he reckoned his mother broke a promise.

The relationship between them became tensed and effective communication was almost impossible.

Reflection: Parent-child conflict always involves the fighting of authority, in particular when the child is on his way to establish autonomy. Nonetheless, crisis may bring about opportunities. Having been working on Jimmy's emotional expressions for a few sessions, this could be a good chance to explore how he could express and communicate emotions with his mother. The joint-painting game was used to explore their communication pattern as well as what emotion regulation strategies Jimmy might use on his mother.

Decentering Through Play, Art-Making and Imagination

In the beginning, at one end of the paper, Jimmy drew an army of soldiers while his mother drew a serene island with butterflies and flowers at the other end. Interesting patterns emerged when they crossed the joint area, which was the middle part of the paper. In response to Jimmy pressing his army forward, his mother frowned. Immediately, Jimmy drew more soldiers, tanks and battle aircraft. Then, his mum said, "they scare me," and she drew a barrier in the middle of the paper to block the path (Fig. 8.5a). Such process represented their communication pattern—Jimmy had his temper heightened when his mother chose to flee. They also recognised the similarities in their real-life situation.

Aesthetic Analysis

In the time to follow, Jimmy and his mother were asked to look at the drawing they created. While staying in the "imaginary reality", they were invited to think about in what way they wanted to change the drawing. At first, Jimmy thought that his mother drew two monsters to attack him, but when he looked at the drawing carefully, he found that they were just butterflies. The son then drew two angels and some diamonds on his side to show his benevolence towards his mother (Fig. 8.5b).

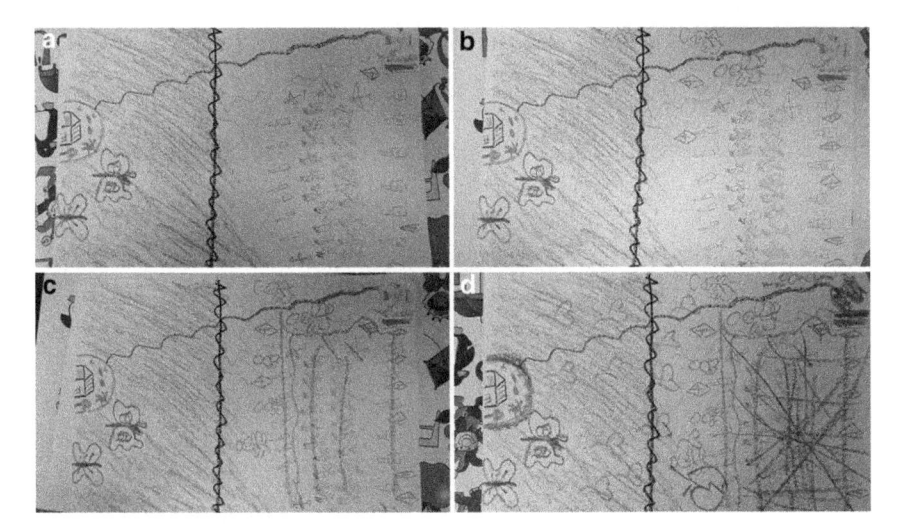

Fig. 8.5 These image illustrate the communication pattern between Jimmy and his mother

Finding that the mother still felt frightened, Jimmy then drew more angels and diamonds, and crossed out the soldiers to show his goodwill (Fig. 8.5c). In response, his mother drew some flying hearts crossing the midline of the paper, which finally motivated Jimmy to disarm to the full (Fig. 8.5d).

Harvesting

After the game, both Jimmy and his mother gained more insights into their communication patterns when encountering conflicts in real-life situations. Jimmy shared that he realised that his anger could scare people (i.e., in this case, his mother), like the soldiers and tanks in the game. Also, his mother understood that avoidance was her usual practice (like drawing a barrier in the game) when facing Jimmy's temper outbursts, leading to his greater frustration when he felt ignored.

Reflection: Through the experience, Jimmy and his mother could feel their love for each other, and also learn the importance of adaptive emotion regulation goals in maintaining a good relationship between them. This reminded them to reappraise the situation. Instead of following the tendency to fight or flight, they could decide which regulation strategies to be adopted in favour of the long-term concern in emotion regulation.

Discussion

Through working with the mother, the child will learn what works and what does not work. Therefore, the mother-child relationship is important for a child to develop efficient communication and emotional regulation strategies. The developed pattern will become a modal that the child will use in the future to deal with other people and the real world. For children with ASD, this developmental process becomes particularly difficult as their emotional recognition and expression are usually hindered. The arts-based therapeutic approach which allows nonverbal communication, and also playfulness, has special advantages in working with children who have ASD. Schweizer and co-workers made a similar recommendation after reviewing 18 relevant studies conducted between 1985 and 2012 (Schweizer et al., 2014). They concluded that art therapy is able to help children with ASD in two specific areas: social communicative problems and restricted and repetitive behaviour patterns.

In this chapter, the joint painting game was introduced in the case example during the decentering process. According to the Intermodal Expressive Arts Therapy framework, the joint painting game served as the therapeutic agent in creating the "alternative world of experience". The alternative space (the paper) and time (the game) allowed the boy and his mother to interact in a funny and playful way. As the boy always lost his control and temper whenever his mother wanted to interact with him, this was essential in resolving the conflicts between them. With this approach, the boy and the mother could exercise their strategies in communication, explore their communication in the imaginary reality (the painting game), and develop new ways of interactions in this special world. It also showed how the boy developed appropriate strategies to relate to and work with his mother, and how his mother also realised her interacting pattern and made changes. This joint painting approach enables bi-directional communication between the mother and the son, and appears to be both the therapeutic agent as well as the arts-based evaluation tool. Although this case was conducted three years ago, Gavron and Mayseless' newly published work reported similar findings with the JPP in 87 mother-son dyads (Gavron & Mayseless, 2018). The JPP may further help uncover the hidden processes between parents and children, thus be able to contribute to the transformation process.

As discussed by Gavron, the joint painting procedure has a number of advantages as an arts-based assessment: the possibility of examining the parent-child relations within a framework of time, space and procedures; allowing the identification of the dynamic relation between the parent and the child with a focus on the emotional needs of the child; and its suitability of applying to middle childhood. Additional benefit as demonstrated in this case is also its applicability to children with special needs, although the original JPP depends mainly on the use of visual art. In this case, we observed that when additional art forms (sounds, role play, and movements) were added into the process, the expression of emotions in the child became much intensified and reinforced. This result echoed well with the principle of Expressive Arts Therapy as described by Rogers: "by moving from art form to art form, we release layers of inhibitions that have covered our originality, discovering our uniqueness and special beauty" (Rogers, 1993, p. 43). Although in this case, the child has hindrance in expressing emotions, shouting with sound and moving with the dinosaurs during the joint painting games helped him to relax and thus deeper emotions can be released.

The benefit of using the joint painting game in expressive arts therapy also applied to the mother. Through playing together with the son, the mother could recognise her son's emotional expressions and made immediate adjustments to her own reaction, resulting in witnessing how her son also changed his attitude and emotions in response to her changes. The dynamic process allowed the mother to understand the adjustment process of his son's emotions and thoughts towards her and also the bi-directional interaction of emotional expressions and communication between themselves. This is important in the finding of a suitable interacting pattern to sustain a long-term relationship.

Implications and Conclusions

The mother-child relationship is crucial for the development of effective emotional regulation strategies as well as the social interactions of a child. For a child with ASD, due to its playfulness and allowing for nonverbal communication, the use of expressive arts therapy has special benefits. The art making process allows the child to enter into an alternative space and time not only to distract from the issues and reality, but also to explore creative solutions and ways out of the difficulties. The joint painting process provided a good platform in working with the mother and the child. Adding additional art forms, that is, voice and drama, into the painting process, further helped in expanding the range of play and imagination, and deepened the engagement of the participants as well as the process. To conclude, not only can the joint painting approach assess the parent-child relationship, the co-creation process of arts can also enable the dynamic and mutual transformation of parent-child in therapeutic works. Lastly, although the joint painting procedure has been mainly used for working with the mother-child relation, its co-creative process can potentially be applied to other works related to relational issues such as marital and intergeneration relations. Further application and research may help validate its suitability for application in other areas.

References

Attwood, T. (2006). *The complete guide to Asperger's syndrome.* London, UK: Jessica Kingsley Publishers.

Berger, K. S. (1988). *The developing person through the life span.* New York, NY: Worth Publishers.

Bowlby, J. (1969). *Vol 1. Attachment.* New York: Basic Books.

Bowlby, J. (1977). The making and breaking of affectional bonds: I. Aetiology and psychopathology in the light of attachment theory. *The British Journal of Psychiatry, 130*(3), 201–210.

Brookman-Frazee, L., Drahota, A., Stadnick, N., & Palinkas, L. A. (2012). Therapist perspectives on community mental health services for children with autism spectrum disorders. *Administration and Policy in Mental Health and Mental Health Services Research, 39*(5), 365–373.

Chang, L., Schwartz, D., Dodge, K. A., & McBride-Chang, C. (2003). Harsh parenting in relation to child emotion regulation and aggression. *Journal of Family Psychology, 17*(4), 598.

Corbett, B. A., Gunther, J. R., Comins, D., Price, J., Ryan, N., Simon, D., … Rios, T. (2011). Brief report: Theatre as therapy for children with autism spectrum disorder. *Journal of Autism and Developmental Disorders, 41*(4), 505–511.

Driessnack, M. (2005). Children's drawings as facilitators of communication: A meta-analysis. *Journal of Pediatric Nursing, 20*(6), 415–423.

Erikson, E. H. (1963). *Childhood and society*. New York, NY: Norton.

Erikson, E. H. (1993). *Childhood and society*. New York, NY: W. W. Norton & Company.

Fonagy, P. (2001). Changing ideas of change: The dual components of therapeutic action. In J. Edwards (Ed.), *Being alive: Building on the work of Anne Alvarez*. New York, NY: Brunner-Routledge.

Gavron, T. (2012). *Joint painting as an assessment of implicit mother-child relationships in middle childhood* (Unpublished master's thesis). Israel.

Gavron, T. (2013). Meeting on common ground: Assessing parent-child relationships through the joint painting procedure. *Art Therapy, 30*(1), 12–19.

Gavron, T., & Mayseless, O. (2015). The joint painting procedure to assess implicit aspects of the mother-child relationship in middle childhood. *Art Therapy, 32*(2), 83–88.

Gavron, T., & Mayseless, O. (2018). Creating art together as a transformative process in parent-child relations: The therapeutic aspects of the joint painting procedure. *Frontiers in Psychology, 9*, 2154. https://doi.org/10.3389/fpsyg.2018.02154

Gross, J., & Hayne, H. (1998). Drawing facilitates children's verbal reports of emotionally laden events. *Journal of Experimental Psychology: Applied, 4*(2), 163.

Gross, J., & Jazaieri, H. (2014). Emotion, emotion regulation, and psychopathology: An affective science perspective. *Clinical Psychological Science, 2*(4), 387–401. https://doi.org/10.1177/2167702614536164

Knill, P. J., Barba, H. N., & Fuchs, M. N. (2004). *Minstrels of soul: Intermodal expressive therapy* (2nd ed.). Toronto, ON: Palmerston Press.

Knill, P. J., Levine, E. G., & Levine, S. K. (2005). *Principles and practice of expressive arts therapy: Toward a therapeutic aesthetics*. London, UK: Jessica Kingsley Publishers.

Lai, N. H. (2011). Expressive Arts Therapy for Mother-Child Relationship (EAT-MCR): A novel model for domestic violence survivors in Chinese culture. *Arts in Psychotherapy, 38*(5), 305–311.

Levine, E. G. (2014). *Play and art in child psychotherapy: An expressive arts therapy approach*. London, UK: Jessica Kingsley Publishers.

Malchiodi, C. A. (2012). *Handbook of art therapy* (2nd ed.). New York, NY: The Guilford Press.

Martin, N. (2008). Assessing portrait drawings created by children and adolescents with autism spectrum disorder. *Art Therapy, 25*(1), 15–23.

Proulx, L. (2002). Strengthening ties, parent-child-dyad: Group art therapy with toddlers and their parents. *American Journal of Art Therapy, 40*(4), 238–258.

Richard, D. A., More, W., & Joy, S. P. (2015). Recognizing emotions: Testing an intervention for children with autism spectrum disorders. *Art Therapy, 32*(1), 13–19.

Rogers, N. (1993). *The creative connection: Expressive arts as healing*. Palo Alto, CA: Science & Behavior Books.

Rollins, J. A. (2005). Tell me about it: Drawing as a communication tool for children with cancer. *Journal of Pediatric Oncology Nursing, 22*(4), 203–221.

Scharoun, S. M., Reinders, N. J., Bryden, P. J., & Fletcher, P. C. (2014). Dance/movement therapy as an intervention for children with autism spectrum disorders. *American Journal of Dance Therapy, 36*(2), 209–228.

Schweizer, C., Knorth, E. J., & Spreen, M. (2014). Art therapy with children with autism spectrum disorders: A review of clinical case descriptions on 'what works'. *The Arts in Psychotherapy, 41*(5), 577–593.

Waller, D. (2006). Art therapy for children: How it leads to change. *Clinical Child Psychology and Psychiatry, 11*(2), 271–282.

Wigram, T., & Gold, C. (2006). Music therapy in the assessment and treatment of autistic spectrum disorder: Clinical application and research evidence. *Child: Care, Health and Development, 32*(5), 535–542.

Wikström, B. M. (2005). Communicating via expressive arts: The natural medium of self-expression for hospitalized children. *Pediatric Nursing, 31*(6), 480–485.

Wong, C. C. (2016). *A case study on the use of intermodal approach of expressive arts therapy on a child with Asperger's syndrome* (Unpublished master's thesis). The University of Hong Kong, Hong Kong.

9

Empowering In-Service Teachers: A Resilience-Building Intervention Based on the Forum Theatre Technique

Viviana Sappa and Antje Barabasch

Introduction

The increasing rate of burnout among teachers and the issue of teacher attrition have stimulated a growing scientific and political interest in understanding how to support schoolteachers to maintain their professional and personal well-being despite the challenges they are exposed to on a daily basis (Beltman, Mansfield, & Price, 2011; Day & Gu, 2014).

Around this problem, the literature on teachers' resilience has been growing, with the main intent to understand why some teachers are able to cope positively with their everyday stressful professional challenges, while

---

V. Sappa (✉)
Swiss Federal Institute for Vocational Education and Training, Lugano, Switzerland
e-mail: viviana.sappa@iuffp.swiss

A. Barabasch
Swiss Federal Institute for Vocational Education and Training, Zollikofen/Bern, Switzerland
e-mail: Antje.Barabasch@ehb.swiss

© The Author(s) 2020
L. McKay et al. (eds.), *Arts-Based Research, Resilience and Well-being Across the Lifespan*,
https://doi.org/10.1007/978-3-030-26053-8_9

others succumb to the stress, even to the point of burning out (Beltman et al., 2011; Day & Gu, 2014). The individual and contextual resources that contribute to improving the resilience of teachers are particularly informative in designing specific resilience-building interventions as well as in promoting the general conditions that favour teachers' well-being (Le Cornu, 2009; Mansfield, Beltman, Broadley, & Weatherby-Fell, 2016).

Within this framework, arts-based methods play an interesting role. The potential of the arts to empower people and communities, as well as to emotionally and cognitively support individuals in the face of adversities, has been widely demonstrated (McKay & Barton, 2018). In particular, artistic creativity (Gouthro, 2018) has the potential to stimulate individuals to generate new understandings and ways of dealing with problematic experiences. Moreover, it can support people in seeing problems and adversities from different perspectives (Metzl & Morrell, 2008) while allowing them to question their responses and move beyond the oppressive habits ensnaring them. This chapter illustrates a resilience-building intervention conducted with in-service vocational school teachers in Switzerland. The arts-based method adopted is the Forum theatre, a participatory drama technique based on August Boal's *Theatre of the Oppressed* (Boal, 1979).

In the following sections, we first illustrate the concept of teacher resilience adopted in the study. Next, we describe the Forum theatre technique and its potentialities for enhancing teachers' resilience. Then we provide a detailed description of the resilience-building intervention applied with vocational school teachers in Switzerland. The methods of data collection and analysis are also explained. The subsequent section of the paper includes a description of the main findings of the study. Finally, the conclusions are outlined, including the limitations of the study and the implications for research in the fields of resilience and arts-based methods.

Teacher Resilience: An Interactive and Context-Sensitive Definition

As widely reported in this book, resilience deals with an individual's ability to bounce back from adversity and thus be strengthened to face future adversity. The concept of resilience has been largely applied in the study of individuals faced with disruptive events, including children exposed to wars, abuse or traumatic experiences (Masten, Best, & Garmezy, 1990; Masten & Narayan, 2012). More recently, resilience has been investigated with respect to the everyday challenges in people's professional and personal lives. Professions in the social, education and health fields are considered particularly relevant in studying resilience as they are associated with a high risk of burnout.

Within this framework, a number of studies have been conducted on teacher resilience. Gu and Day (2013) have argued that what threatens the well-being of teachers is the ongoing exposure to daily difficulties. The multiple challenges related to teaching include the high emotional and relational labour implied in any educative profession (Le Cornu, 2009; Mansfield, Beltman, Price, & McConney, 2012). Such labour is particularly demanding for teachers in secondary schools, as the students are experiencing the delicate and complicated phase of adolescence. In this period, the relationships with students and students' parents become more complex and emotionally demanding for teachers. An excessive workload and the demands of school reforms are additional sources of job dissatisfaction and frustration (Boldrini, Sappa, & Aprea, 2019; Gu & Day, 2013). In addition, conflicting relationships with colleagues and school principals make everyday professional life more complicated for teachers, particularly when they feel trapped in an oppressor-oppressed dynamic.

Although a conceptualisation of resilience as an individual trait or ability is still part of the scientific debate on resilience, the majority of scholars approach teacher resilience from an interactive and context-sensitive perspective (Le Cornu, 2009; Mansfield et al., 2012). Adopting this perspective, we conceptualise resilience as a dynamic and functional outcome of the interplay between perceived adversity and resources (Sappa, Boldrini, & Barabasch, 2019). Resilient teachers are those who cope positively with professional adversities by activating appropriate resources that favour their personal and professional well-being.

The scientific literature on teacher resilience has pointed out the multiple dimensions of resilience and the multiple contextual and individual resources that contribute to supporting teachers to be resilient (Beltman et al., 2011; Mansfield et al., 2012; Sappa & Barabasch, 2019). Three types of resources are particularly relevant for this study: the ability to regulate one's emotions, the ability to reflect on one's experiences and behaviour, and a positive relational climate in schools.

Emotional regulation strategies include the ability to change the emotional impact of a stressor by interpreting the situation from a less threatening or more positive perspective (Troy & Mauss, 2011). The ability to regulate negative emotions in the face of stressors is also crucial in order to trigger active coping strategies around them, instead of accepting the stressors passively and waiting for an external solution. In addition, Tugade and Fredrickson (2007) emphasised the ability to maintain or increase positive emotional experiences as a key resource in promoting resilience. Resilient individuals are particularly able to capitalise on positive emotions when coping with negative emotional experiences. In this respect, a sense of humour and irony has been shown to contribute to the resilience process, as it allows individuals to see problems from an ironic perspective, thus lightening them, while at the same time enhancing their coping mechanisms and moderating the intensity of their emotional reactions (Earvolino-Ramirez, 2007). Mansfield et al. (2012) have also described a sense of humour as an important part of the resilience of teachers.

Second, *the ability of teachers to reflect on their practices and experiences* at school has been shown to empower them in the face of difficulties (Beltman et al., 2011; McKay & Sappa, 2019). The ability to reflect on their own practices facilitates teachers to understand the complexity of the professional situations they are involved in and enlarges the spectrum of possible actions in dealing with them (Leroux & Théorêt, 2014). Moreover, reflection promotes the processes of self-awareness and agency in individuals confronting difficulties by supporting them to identify personal, strategic and contextual resources that can help them to be more resilient (McKay & Barton, 2018).

Third, a *positive relational climate at school* is crucial to support teacher resilience. As reported in various studies (Day & Gu, 2014; Sappa et al., 2019; Steward, 2014) positive relationships with colleagues and school leaders are essential in supporting teachers to face adversities. Moreover, collegiality and a sense of belonging to the school community play an important role in preventing teachers from feeling alone in adverse situations. In this respect, teachers need to overcome the isolation that is typical of this profession in order to share and exchange problems, experiences and possible solutions. At the organisation level, this means creating a culture of sharing that relates not only to procedures and standards but also to feelings, problems and possible solutions. At the individual level, it implies the ability to seek help when needed as well as the capacity to cope positively with relational and communication problems.

In our study, the Forum theatre technique was selected as an appropriate arts-based method to support teacher resilience because of its potential to empower teachers and schools from an emotional, cognitive and social perspective, as detailed described in the next section.

The Forum Theatre as an Instrument to Promote Teacher Resilience

Forum theatre is a participatory drama technique based on Augusto Boal's *Theatre of the Oppressed* (Boal, 1979). In a Forum theatre workshop, participants are encouraged to confront real or realistic problems, mainly relational ones, within a theatre play involving an oppressed-oppressor dynamic. In this respect, the Forum theatre aims to overcome the distinction between actor and audience, with the main intent of transforming "people from spectators (objects) into actors (subjects) in their own lives and to make audiences aware of oppressed-oppressor relationships and how the consequences of such relationships can be avoided" (Hakkarainen & Vapalahti, 2011, p. 314).

Specifically, professional actors represent on the stage relational conflicts usually implying an oppressed-oppressor dynamic. The theatre script is typically designed around a real-life situation that hits close to home in the participants' everyday personal or professional lives. In our study, the script was based on teacher resilience and burnout research data, including a narrative inquiry conducted in the same region where the workshop took place (Boldrini et al., 2019).

The characters of the Forum theatre include the protagonist (the oppressed), the antagonist (the oppressor) and the tritagonist, that is, a neutral character who often attempts to mediate between the other two. The designed performance does not provide a "happy ending", in the sense that there are no fixed solutions or answers to the represented problems. Rather, the performance seeks to stimulate the audience to go on stage and propose strategies to solve the relational conflict. Particularly, participants are invited to replace an actor on the stage in order to propose their strategies. Additional actors who are present on the stage react spontaneously to the new proposed strategy. The original script progressively changes based on what is proposed by the "spect-actors" and the reaction of the other characters.

On the emotional side, the Forum theatre aims to provoke an empathetic feeling in the audience with respect to the protagonist being oppressed. This empathy is crucial in activating a feeling of *emotional dissonance* and *emotional disturbance* to motivate the participants to react to the oppressive dynamics (Boal, 1995). The emotional dissonance basically implies a negative feeling, that is, a sense of anger or frustration that stimulates a reaction to the oppressive situation. This feeling is fundamental in provoking the activation of the audience in order to empower the oppressed. This activation is the basis of the *catharsis process* described by Boal (1995). Specifically, as reported by Meisiek (2004), Boal claims that

> only the physical involvement of the audience during the play can lead to the kind of catharsis that serves to motivate action. The crucial purpose of his theatrical techniques is to overcome the divide between actors and audience in order to encourage social change. (p. 810)

The emotional dissonance aims at activating such a change, primarily on the aesthetic space of the stage. However, other emotions can be additionally activated. The Forum theatre design proposed in our study included sense of humour as a key means to engage the audience as well as to highlight critical issues in a theatrical performance, which typically would be avoided in other circumstances. Relational conflicts were presented in an ironic way, by emphasising the peculiarities of each character and the events in a humoristic sense. The aim was to make the audience laugh while reflecting on what happens in the school setting.

At the cognitive level, the Forum theatre technique has the potential to stimulate a dialogue between multiple perspectives, including those of the actors, spectators and spect-actors (i.e., participants who move from the audience to stage). Moreover, multiple perspectives are activated within the spect-actor him/herself, who shifts from the aesthetic space of the stage to real life. This activation of multiple perspectives is favoured by three specific attributes of the theatre: the plasticity, the dichotomy and the "tele-microscopy". By plasticity, Boal refers to the malleable nature of theatre: everything is possible on the stage, with the help of fantasy. Thus, the spectrum of possible actions can be enlarged in the aesthetic space of the theatrical performance. Second, the dichotomy of the stage refers to the division or doubling of self which occurs in the subject who comes on stage as a spectator and actor (i.e., spect-actor). This dichotomy leads to a process of self-observation. Finally, the tele-microscopic property magnifies everything and makes everything present, "allowing us to see things which, without it, in smaller or more distant form, would escape our gaze" (Boal, 1995, p. 28). Being embedded in a dialogue between multiple perspectives enhances reflection and self-reflection by stimulating a broader understanding of the represented situation.

Finally, the Forum theatre is a social event, as it involves an entire community or organisation. In our study, teachers and school leaders employed in the same school attended the theatre workshop. Thus, emotion and reflection are proposed in a collective environment that invites a sharing process. The collective setting allows the portrayal of real-life interpersonal confrontations. The realistic situations represented on the stage lead the participants to discuss common problems that are often omitted in the everyday discourses at school. Moreover, the dichotomy between function and reality offers the participants the opportunity to gradually move the discussion away from what happens in the aesthetic space of the stage to what happens in their everyday professional life.

The Forum theatre technique has been applied in various educational and professional contexts, particularly with adults. Multiple studies have demonstrated its potential in activating individual and collective reflection as well as in creating a positive attitude toward problem solving by focusing on individual agency and self-empowerment (McClimens & Scott, 2007; Souto-Manning, 2011).

The Workshop

This study is based on a resilience-building continuing training workshop proposed to in-service school teachers in Canton of Ticino, the Italian-speaking part of Switzerland. The workshop was designed and conducted in collaboration with teacher educators and actors in a cantonal project called L.i.n.e.a., which aimed to support teachers' well-being (see https://www4.ti.ch/decs/linea/chi-siamo/presentazione/). The project was financed by the local Ministry of Education (Department of Education, Culture, and Sport [DECS], Canton of Ticino). This study also was conducted at the mandate of the DECS ministry.

Consistent with the Forum theatre technique, the workshop involved a four-hour training session, including the following three phases:

- Phase I (traditional performance): Professional actors played a set of four scenes representing relational conflicts at school, mainly described in terms of an oppressed-oppressor dynamic.
- Phase II (interactive performance): The scenes were replicated, and the audience was invited to suggest and act out possible strategies to solve the conflicts by replacing the actors on the stage. A professional actor playing the role of the "joker" was in charge of persuading the spectators to participate. The participants were free to propose any strategies and to replace any actor on the stage to change the situation. However, the joker encouraged participants to propose strategies empowering the "oppressor" or tritagonist instead of focusing on the oppressed only. Additional actors involved in the scenes reacted to the proposed strategies, offering improvised feedback to the participant. The audience was then invited to share comments and ideas about the proposed strategies and to suggest possible alternatives.
- Phase III (final feedback): A final collective debriefing and discussion was conducted by the teacher educators in which the audience was invited to share their feelings and thoughts about what they had experienced.

The workshop was conducted in the school setting, and all of the teachers were invited to participate, including the principal.

The represented story took place at an imaginary high school in the Canton of Ticino where a school leader pressed teachers to improve a new L2 learning project. The main character was a female teacher who was very stressed out about this project due to a lack of support from the school and her colleagues. She felt oppressed in this situation, without perceiving any possible control over it. This scenario formed the framework of the entire performance, serving as the basis for the other scenes. The conflicting and oppressive relationship with the school principal was the focus of the first scene. The school principal was the oppressor, and a colleague took part in the interaction more passively as the witness. The second scene emphasised conflicting and unsupportive relationships among colleagues, with the same female teacher serving as the oppressed. Another colleague played the role of the oppressor, while two additional colleagues served as witnesses to the conflicting interaction between the oppressor and the oppressed. The third scene focused on a difficult relationship between the oppressed teacher and a student's mother whose behaviour was very aggressive. Other colleagues passively took part in the scene. The final scene took place in the oppressed teacher's home, where the stress she accumulated in the workplace turned into a source of family conflicts.

Aims of the Study

In a previous publication, we demonstrated how the Forum theatre method has favoured participants' proactive engagement in finding strategies to cope with relational problems represented on the stage (Sappa & Barabasch, 2019). In addition, critical awareness and reflectivity were activated during the workshop, and active coping strategies to face relational conflicts were also promoted. In this paper, we aim at exploring the emotional, cognitive and social impact of the theatre-based technique by investigating the participants' perceived impacts at the end of the workshop and one month after.

Method

Data were collected by means of a self-reported questionnaire and a semi-structured interview.

All participants were invited to complete a self-reported questionnaire, which included three open-ended questions, at the end of the workshop. The following main question is the object of this paper:

- How did you feel during the workshop?

The respondents were invited to answer by using two to five keywords.

The semi-structured interviews were conducted individually with a sub-sample of participants, including teachers and school leaders. The interview data were collected one month after the workshop. The interview guideline entailed questions about the perceived impacts of the theatre-based workshop on teachers and the school as a whole.

Sample

The questionnaire sample included the total number of participants in the theatre-based workshops. As reported in Table 9.1, four vocational schools and a total of 230 teachers were involved in the study. About 41% of them were female. Due to the large number of teachers employed at school one, we provided two workshop sessions, thus creating two groups from the teacher population.

The participants were all adults who had been working as teachers for at least one year. More precisely, 27.2% were in the early phase of their career (1–7 years of teaching in vocational schools), 26.3% were in the middle phase (8–15 years in vocational schools), 34.2% were in the middle-late phase (16–30 years in vocational schools) and 12.3% were in the late phase (over 30 years of teaching in vocational schools).

The interview sample (Table 9.2) consisted of 11 participants, including the school leaders and some teachers at each school. The sample is well balanced by gender. The interviewees agreed voluntarily to participate.

Table 9.1 Questionnaire sample

Gender	Vocational school 1		Vocational school 2	Vocational school 3	Vocational school 4	Total
	Session 1	Session 2				
Female	15	21	14	7	38	95
	27.30%	39.60%	35.90%	31.80%	62.30%	41.30%
Male	40	32	25	15	23	135
	72.70%	60.4%	64.10%	68.20%	37.70%	58.70%
Total	55	53	39	22	61	230
	100%	100%	100%	100%	100%	100%

Table 9.2 Interview sample

Gender	Vocational school 1	Vocational school 2	Vocational school 3	Vocational school 4	Total
Female	–	2	–	3	5
Male	3	1	2	–	6
Total	3	3	2	3	11

Data Analysis

Data gathered through the questionnaire consisted of a list of keywords related to the perceived emotions participants felt during the workshop. In this study, we referred to emotions in a general sense, including feelings, sentiments or sensations. Therefore, we accepted any answer related to any state of mind, including those more strictly related to primary or secondary emotion and those related to other cognitive and emotional processes. By using an inductive categorical analysis, keywords were clustered into key concepts, and the frequency of each key concept was calculated. In addition, cross-tabulation analyses were performed to investigate differences by gender and stage of career. The analyses were supported by T-Lab software.

The interview data were analysed by means of thematic analysis. As described by Braun and Clarke (2006), thematic analysis aims at identifying, analysing and reporting themes within data that are related to a specific research question or topic. Referring to our study, the focus of the thematic analysis was on the perceived impacts of the theatre-based workshop at the emotional, cognitive and social levels. As suggested by Braun and Clarke (2006), the following five steps were followed: (1) we familiarised ourselves with the data by re-reading and searching for meaning and patterns; (2) we generated initial codes; (3) we searched for themes by attributing different codes to potential themes; (4) we reviewed the themes by re-elaboration on the basis of coded data extracts, but also on the entire data set; and (5) we defined and named the themes.

Results

Feelings and Emotions During the Interactive Performance

As illustrated above, we asked participants to report their feelings during the performance using two to five keywords. We collected a total of 631 keywords reported by the 230 participants. As expected, both positive and negative feelings were reported, although positive feelings were strongly dominant. As shown in Table 9.3, by means of an inductive categorical analysis, we identified 18 key concepts: 12 referred to positive feelings (clustering 583 keywords, 92.3% of the total corpus), whereas six dealt with negative feelings (clustering 48 keywords, 7.7% of the total corpus).

Generally speaking, most of the participants reported *sentiment of amusement* (171 keywords), *personal engagement* (130 keywords), *interest* (104 keywords) and *sense of well-being* (52 keywords). Thus, the interactive performance promoted a general relaxing and convivial atmosphere during the workshop. In addition, 12 keywords dealt with more intense positive emotions, such as *enthusiasm* and *passion*. A further set of keywords represented the concepts of *empathy* (33 keywords) and *sharing* (27 keywords). Those feelings suggested the activation of personal and collective identification with the represented situations. The interactive performance was additionally perceived as something completely different from what they are used to doing in the school setting. Some participants denoted a *sense of astonishment* (17 keywords), including a sort of emotional and cognitive disorientation in the midst of the arts-based technique. Finally, cognitive states of minds were mentioned in terms of *reflection* (26 keywords) and *self-awareness* (3 keywords).

Table 9.3 Key concepts related to feelings

Key concepts	Single keywords (examples)	N	%
1. Positive feelings			
Amusement	Amused, amusement, smiling, laughing	171	27
Personal engagement	Engaged, stimulated, participation, activated	130	20.6
Interest	Motivated, interested	104	16.5
Well-being	Well-being, pleasure, happy, sense of safety	52	8.2
Empathetic feeling	Empathetic, identified with the situation, mirroring	33	5.2
Sense of sharing and collaboration	Sharing, collaboration, welcoming, embedded in a dialogue	27	4.3
Reflection and reflectivity	Reflective, reflecting, reflectivity, self-reflection, self-examining	26	4.2
Astonishment	Surprised, astonished, disoriented, being involved in an alternative experience	17	2.6
Enthusiasm	Enthusiastic, passionate, exited, touched	12	1.9
Learning	Learning, informative, transformed	8	1.4
Self-awareness	Self-aware	3	0.4
Sub-total		**583**	**92.3**
2. Negative feelings			
Sense of impotence	Worried, powerlessness	13	2.1
Bitterness	Irritated, annoyed, angry, frustrated	12	1.9
Detachment	Get bored, detached, passive	9	1.4
Embarrassment	Embarrassed, awkward	9	1.5
Stress	Stressed, tired, weary	5	0.8
Sub-total		**48**	**7.7**
Total		**631**	**100**

On the negative side, a *sense of impotence* (13 keywords) and *bitterness* (12 keywords) constituted the two most mentioned concepts. These two feelings can be considered as part of the emotional dissonance and disturbance that the Forum theatre aims to provoke in order to motivate the participants to act. On the contrary, the *sense of detachment* (9 keywords) has to be interpreted as a negative outcome. Although only a limited number of participants reported this feeling, it is clear that they referred to a lack of involvement, interest and satisfaction with the theatre-based experience. Finally, the responses of *embarrassment* (9 keywords) and *stress* (5 keywords) evoked the difficulties teachers experienced in participating in an active way. This is because, due to the interactive process, the

Forum theatre technique requires participants to expose themselves at a cognitive and emotional level. This kind of involvement is not easy, particularly in front of colleagues and the school leader.

Differences by gender and career phase were explored by a cross-tabulation procedure. The findings showed that females reported more frequently a feeling of amusement ($\chi2 = 24.18$, $p < 0.05$), while a sense of interest ($\chi2 = 10.75$, $p < 0.05$), engagement ($\chi2 = 10.74$, $p < 0.05$) and sharing were more likely to be indicated by males ($\chi2 = 3.95$, $p < 0.05$). In addition, the sense of impotence was prevalently indicated by teachers in the middle career phase (16–30 years of teaching experience in VET schools) ($\chi2 = 10.5$, $p < 0.05$). This latter finding is particularly interesting as the middle career phase was found to be particularly delicate. A survey conducted on the same population involved in this study showed that teachers who have 16–30 years of teaching experience are more exposed than other colleagues to a low sense of professional well-being in the face of adversities (Boldrini et al., 2019). It is reasonable to suppose that the performance re-activated the sense of impotence they feel—more than other colleagues do—during their everyday professional life.

Perceived Impacts of the Forum Theatre Workshop

The thematic analysis led us to identify seven themes related to the participants' perceived impacts at the emotional, cognitive and social levels.

Three themes refer to emotional factors. The first theme deals with *empathetic feelings*. The interviewees reported that they were profoundly touched by the represented scenes, as they were extremely realistic. They said that the theatre gave them the opportunity to "live" the oppressive relationship and to subsequently reflect upon that. The experience of being embodied in the oppressor-oppressed dynamic was perceived as very profound. In addition, the interviewees underlined that this opportunity was not only related to the act of going on the stage. Certainly, those who moved to the stage were much more actively involved in the identification process. However, feelings of empathy arose even while observing the actors and spect-actors performing on the stage.

The second theme deals with *sense of humour*. Specifically, the interviewees reported that the theatre experience gave them the opportunity to see everyday conflicts from a humorous perspective. In addition, the sense of humour performed on the stage was perceived as extremely contagious, and the audience was prompted to laugh about those conflicts that usually stressed them. As a consequence, it got easier and easier to discuss those conflicts in a constructive way, not only during the workshop but also afterwards in the school context. The sense of humour also helped the participating teachers overcome the "victim" mentality they often assume in relational difficulties.

The last emotional theme refers to *emotional dissonance*, as described by Boal (1995). Consistent with Boal's concept, the following teacher described how the conflicts represented in the theatre scenes caused a profound sense of irritation, anger and frustration among the audience. The conflicting dynamic was perceived as not acceptable. Such a feeling was so strong as to provoke the need to act, to intervene and to change the situation. This feeling led some participants to find the courage to go on the stage to propose their strategies to resolve the conflict. This is exactly the nature of the catharsis process described by Boal.

> I moved to the stage as what was represented was not acceptable. I was clear that the oppressed should react! Nobody [among the audience] raised their hand… but it was clear… and, at some point, I decided to intervene and explain my viewpoint. It was not easy to go on the stage… but I did it.

However, other teachers, although reporting a similar need to act, declared an inability to go on the stage. One of them, for example, declared that she did not want to go on the stage as she does not have a flair for drama performance. She feared that if she expressed her feelings, she would be asked to go to the stage. Therefore, she felt very frustrated and was not satisfied with the experience.

> I very much felt the need to stop the scene and say that something should be changed. However, I knew that I would be asked to go on the stage. I absolutely did not want to go on the stage. I do not have a flair for drama. I forced myself to not raise my hand… it was hard… I would have liked to give my opinion without going to the stage. It was very frustrating.

At the cognitive level, almost all the interviewees described the theatre experience as an opportunity to reflect on their relational conflicts at school. In this respect, the first theme deals with a *better understanding and higher awareness* of those conflicts. Specifically, the workshop promoted a higher awareness and a better understanding of the relational and communicative mechanism that cause conflicts at school. As illustrated in the following extract, the participants realised how relational conflicts often arise from biased interpretations or trivial misunderstandings of other colleagues' behaviours.

> Drama has the potential to activate a reflection. I was really engaged to think about relational conflicts. Sometimes they arise from some stupid misunderstanding. It is incredible... The performance was very good in describing that.

The performance allowed the participants to see the conflicts from multiple perspectives, including those of the oppressors, the oppressed and the other neutral individuals involved in the conflicting situations. Thus, a multiple perspective-taking process was activated, and a dialogue between the different perspectives was facilitated by offering a more comprehensive view of the situation.

A second cognitive theme concerns *self-reflection*. The interviewees declared to have recognised themselves in some of the represented characters. In this respect, they gained a better understanding of how their behaviours and relational approaches could be externally interpreted. Consequently, a significant process of self-awareness was activated. However, other interviewees argued that the potential impact of the theatre experience in terms of self-awareness is limited by the individuals' attitudes to self-questioning. Although the Forum theatre was recognised as very powerful in facilitating self-observation, some interviewees emphasised that those teachers who are more likely to be oppressive with respect to their colleagues are also less likely to be able and willing to question themselves. The risk in this is a limited impact of the theatre experience at the organisational level, as the most problematic teachers were excluded from the reflecting and transformative process. In fact, behaviour and relational transformation of those teachers who are particularly conflicting and oppressive would require them to get aware of their negative attitudes and to accept to question and change themselves. Despite the high potential of the Forum Theatre, a single session is not sufficient to activate a so complex process.

Finally, at the social level, two themes were outlined. The first theme refers to the opportunity to *laugh together about relational conflicts*. The following interviewee told us that, some weeks after the theatre-based training workshop, he and his colleagues still evoked the represented scenes and characters to joke about the relational conflicts that happen at school.

> Just yesterday, I joked with a colleague about a situation that happened at school. It was so similar to what was represented by the drama performance… it was so hilarious and we laughed about it.

In addition, the opportunity to recall a funny shared experience contributed to increasing the cohesion among colleagues.

The second social theme concerns the *increasing of reciprocal knowledge among colleagues*. Some interviewees declared that the interactive drama allowed them to better know their colleagues. In particular, the workshop offered them the opportunity to see their colleagues outside the formal professional relationship. In addition, they had the opportunity to understand how their colleagues interpreted and approached the represented conflicts.

Conclusion

As shown in this chapter, the Forum theatre technique can be considered a powerful arts-based method to support the emotional, cognitive and social resources necessary for building teachers' resilience. On the one hand, by representing relational problems in a humoristic mode, the theatre-based workshop led teachers to interpret their everyday conflicts from a less-threatening perspective. Although humour is not part of the traditional Forum theatre technique, we found that the opportunity for participants to laugh with other colleagues about the relational problems they experience was very much appreciated by the participants. In particular, humour made it possible to activate a dialogue around those problems that were perceived as too stressful to be shared. The opportunity to talk about a problem is the first step in searching for a constructive and collective solution. On the other hand, the oppressor-oppressed relationships represented on the stage caused a sense of anger, frustration and impotence among the participants. Most of the interviewees related those emotions to the catharsis process, as theorised by Boal. The represented scenes, although presented in a humorous way, led the participants to a profound emotional disturbance that stimulated them to act. The sense of impotence was thus transformed into an active involvement to solve the problem. This agentic positioning in the face of problems is a fundamental step toward a resilient approach to the problems.

Moreover, the theatre-based workshop promoted reflection and self-reflection processes. In this respect, two key outcomes of this experience included a better understanding of the problems threatening relationships and a higher awareness about the importance of facing these actively. The role of reflection and self-reflection in teacher resilience is widely demonstrated in the literature. The Forum theatre technique is a powerful method to empower such reflective processes. Furthermore, the shared experience favoured a collective humoristic dialogue about typical school conflicts. In addition, an increase in reciprocal knowledge was reported as an effect of the interactive drama performance.

However, some limitations of the theatre-based method were also revealed. Some participants reported a sense of frustration as they felt unable to participate in the interactive performance. They blocked themselves from participating on the stage as they did not want to stand out and did not feel they had a flair for drama performance. Therefore, while using arts-based methods, particularly drama methods, it is important to consider the individual attitudes to arts and creativity as well as the courage that is needed to expose oneself in front of colleagues. We can assume this exposure to be particularly threatening to teachers in the middle-phase career because of their particular identity defence mechanisms. Small groups could therefore encourage more active participation on the part of reluctant individuals. In addition, repeated Forum theatre sessions could help to better familiarise individuals with this practice. Repeated sessions could also facilitate a more diffused impact by including those teachers who are particularly conflict prone and oppressive.

In conclusion, we are aware of other limitations of the study as well. First, only self-reported data were adopted. Although the individuals' perceived perspectives are fundamental to investigating emotional and cognitive issues, observation data would have allowed us to reach a more comprehensive understanding of individuals' behaviours when faced with adversity. In addition, further investigation is needed in order to verify the long-term effects of the emotional, reflective and social processes activated through the interactive drama workshop. On the emotional side, our study demonstrated the potentialities of the Forum theatre method to activate emotional regulation processes. However, the actual lasting impact of such a potential on individual emotional regulation skills needs to be confirmed. Similarly, the reflective processes simulated through the theatre-based method need to be more deeply investigated in a long-term perspective in order to understand if they actually support teachers in facing stressful situations over time.

Despite these limitations, some implications for teacher resilience and arts-based research can be outlined. First, the Forum theatre technique has multiple potentialities to support the resilience of teachers and schools. This interactive, theatre-based method is thus worth considering for resilience-building interventions in educational settings. Second, the Forum theatre technique is additionally very informative about individual and collective ways to manage relational conflicts. The active involvement of teachers on the aesthetic space of the stage might offer an interesting observatory from which to capture people's coping strategies and approaches to adversity. Arts-based research could therefore take advantage of this technique for a variety of research purposes.

Finally, the Forum theatre technique is particularly interesting to apply with in-service teachers. Although application with preservice teachers is possible (Desai, 2017), in-service teachers are more likely to identify with the conflicting situations represented on the stage. In addition, the opportunity to share the experience with colleagues working in the same institution is likely to be much more effective in supporting resilience at the organisational level.

References

Beltman, S., Mansfield, C., & Price, A. (2011). Thriving not just surviving: A review of research on teacher resilience. *Educational Research Review, 6*, 185–207.

Boal, A. (1979). *Theater of the oppressed.* London, UK: Pluto Press.

Boal, A. (1995). *The rainbow of desire. The Boal method of theatre and therapy.* London, UK: Routledge.

Boldrini, E., Sappa, V., & Aprea, C. (2019). Which difficulties and resources do vocational teachers perceive? An exploratory study setting the stage for investigating teachers' resilience in Switzerland. *Teachers and Teaching, 25*(1), 125–141.

Braun, V., & Clarke, V. (2006). Using thematic analysis in psychology. *Qualitative Research in Psychology, 3*(2), 77–101.

Day, C., & Gu, Q. (2014). *Resilient teachers, resilient schools: Building and sustaining quality in testing times.* Oxford, UK: Routledge.

Desai, S. R. (2017). Utilizing theatre of the oppressed within teacher education to create emancipatory teachers. *Multicultural Perspectives, 19*(4), 229–233.

Earvolino-Ramirez, M. (2007). Resilience: A concept analysis. *Nursing Forum, 42*(2), 73–82.

Gouthro, P. (2018). Creativity, the arts, and transformative learning. In M. Milana, S. Webb, J. Holford, R. Waller, & P. Jarvis (Eds.), *The Palgrave international handbook on adult and lifelong education and learning.* London, UK: Palgrave Macmillan.

Gu, Q., & Day, C. (2013). Challenges to teacher resilience: Conditions count. *British Educational Research Journal, 39*(1), 22–44.

Hakkarainen, P., & Vapalahti, K. (2011). Meaningful learning through video-supported forum-theater. *International Journal of Teaching and Learning in Higher Education, 23*(3), 314–328.

Le Cornu, R. (2009). Building resilience in pre-service teachers. *Teaching and Teacher Education, 25*, 717–723.

Leroux, M., & Théorêt, M. (2014). Intriguing empirical relations between teachers' resilience and reflection on practice. *Reflective Practice, 15*(3), 289–303.

Mansfield, C. F., Beltman, S., Broadley, T., & Weatherby-Fell, N. (2016). Building resilience in teacher education: An evidenced informed framework. *Teaching and Teacher Education, 54*, 77–87.

Mansfield, C. F., Beltman, S., Price, A., & McConney, A. (2012). "Don't sweat the small stuff": Understanding teacher resilience at the chalkface. *Teaching and Teacher Education, 28*, 357–367.

Masten, A. S., Best, K. M., & Garmezy, N. (1990). Resilience and development: Contributions from the study of children who overcome adversity. *Development and Psychopathology, 2*(4), 425–444.

Masten, A. S., & Narayan, A. J. (2012). Child development in the context of disaster, war, and terrorism: Pathways of risk and resilience. *Annual Review of Psychology, 63*, 227–257.

McClimens, A., & Scott, R. (2007). Lights, camera, education! The potentials of forum theater in a learning disability nursing program. *Nurse Education Today, 27*(3), 203–209.

McKay, L., & Barton, G. (2018). Exploring how arts-based reflection can support teachers' resilience and well-being. *Teaching and Teacher Education, 75*, 356–365.

McKay, L., & Sappa, V. (2019). Harnessing creativity through arts-based research to support teachers' identity development. *Journal of Adult & Continuing Education*. Online first: https://doi.org/10.1177/1477971419841068

Meisiek, S. (2004). Which catharsis do they mean? Aristotle, Moreno, Boal and organization theatre. *Organization Studies, 25*(5), 797–816.

Metzl, E. S., & Morrell, M. A. (2008). The role of creativity in models of resilience: Theoretical exploration and practical applications. *Journal of Creativity in Mental Health, 3*(3), 303–318.

Sappa, V., & Barabasch, A. (2019). Forum-theatre technique to foster creative and active problem solving: A resilience-building intervention among in-service teachers. *Journal of Adult and Continuing Education*. On line first: https://doi.org/10.1177/1477971419842884

Sappa, V., Boldrini, E., & Barabasch, A. (2019). Teachers' resilience in vocational education and training (VET). In S. McGrath, M. Mulder, J. Papier, & R. Stuart (Eds.), *Handbook of vocational education and training*. Cham, Switzerland: Springer. (online first).

Souto-Manning, M. (2011). Playing with power and privilege: Theatre games in teacher education. *Teaching and Teacher Education, 27*(6), 997–1007.

Steward, J. (2014). Sustaining emotional resilience for school leadership. *School Leadership & Management, 34*(1), 52–68.

Troy, A. S., & Mauss, I. B. (2011). Resilience in the face of stress: Emotion regulation as a protective factor. *Resilience and Mental Health: Challenges Across the Lifespan, 1*(2), 30–44.

Tugade, M. M., & Fredrickson, B. L. (2007). Regulation of positive emotions: Emotion regulation strategies that promote resilience. *Journal of Happiness Studies, 8*(3), 311–333.

10

Overcoming a Lived Experience of Personal Impasse by Creating a Theatrical Drama: An Example of Promoting Resilience in Adult Education

Deli Salini and Marc Durand

Introduction

This chapter presents elements for interpreting the effects of theatrical practice to accompany adults with histories marked by serious pathology or traumatic episodes resulting in an impasse (Assal, Durand, & Horn, 2016). The Theater of Lived Experience (TLE) has proven effective, thus prompting an investigation to identify (a) the lived experience of TLE participants in order to (b) better understand its effects

D. Salini (✉)
Swiss Federal Institute for Vocational Education and Training (SFIVET), Lugano, Switzerland
e-mail: deli.salini@iuffp.swiss

M. Durand
University of Geneva, Geneva, Switzerland
e-mail: marc.durand@unige.ch

and determine which elements would provide a basis for designing training dispositive that, like TLE, articulate artistic aims, care and education.

Theatrical practices for therapeutic, educational and social promotion purposes date back to ancient times. The notion of catharsis has been variously interpreted (Darmon, 2011) and is at the heart of psychoanalytically inspired therapeutic theatrical practices (e.g., Moreno, 1959). Other theatrical proposals have educational aims in the schools (e.g., Mages, 2016) or the adult education field (Salgado, 2008). Theatrical proposals have also targeted inclusion or social promotion, having been inspired by the *Theater of the Oppressed* (Boal, 1985) and the critical pedagogy stream (Freire, 1970), with one example being the Playback Theater (e.g., Fox, 1986). The practices underline the power of theatre as a dialogical tool for exploring lived experience that participants return to and actors then re-enact. These practices are characterised by the search for pleasure, mutual understanding, and individual and collective achievement and provide a frame within which participants learn to express themselves better and regain self-confidence.

Within this diverse panorama of practices, the purpose of TLE is neither to efface a past painful episode nor to provide an outlet for suffering: it instead offers a way to elaborate step-by-step a lived experience and transform it theatrically, thereby giving it new meaning. TLE is part of the humanist tradition of education for personal development, providing support for individuals seeking to exceed personal limits and find meaning.

Created in the context of *therapeutic education* by Jean-Philippe Assal, professor of medicine and diabetologist, and Marcos Malavia, writer, director and performer (Assal, Malavia, & Roland, 2009), TLE offers help to the chronically ill and has involved hundreds of participants in Europe, Africa and Latin America (Assal et al., 2016). It is also used for educational purposes with a range of populations. TLE is now acknowledged as leading to positive transformations in (a) participants' daily behaviour, (b) their relations with their entourage or (c) their illness or traumatic life events, (d) the way they view their existence and, in some cases, (e) their physical and mental health status (Assal et al., 2016).

In a TLE workshop, five or six participants meet in a theatre for three days, along with facilitators whose principal occupations are in adult education, caregiving and theatre (directors, performers and sound and lighting technicians). The participants are asked to: (a) write a text about "an important episode in their lives," (b) stage it, and (c) direct the theatre professionals up to its performance before a limited audience. Round tables punctuate each phase of the workshop. The participants present the facts of their lived experience, comment on those of their peers, and engage in shared reflexivity to enrich the co-construction of the collective history of these three days. The workshop dynamics are characterised by facilitator prompts, support and other forms of aid, and by mutual support, mutual aid and solidarity among the participants.

To organise a space for artistic expression, TLE workshops follow the same pattern, and their dramatic and educational value resides in the collective activity (Salini, Durand, & Goudeaux, 2016). The professionals in education, healing and theatre are highly competent. They assure the participants of respect and no value judgments about their productions or lived experience. They are, moreover, a bit removed from their usual practices: they are doing their jobs without really doing them. They are the guarantors of a process of theatricalisation and accompany the participants in bringing their works to completion, although most of the time the latter are not familiar with theatrical codes. As they accompany the participants, they must respect their tastes, artistic choices and, most importantly, the expression of what lies deep within them. They do not focus on cures or healing or training but act according to a "negative capability" (Keats, 1899). And despite the uncertainty of the situation, they care for the participants, trusting in their potential for development and the impact of the artistic process. A balance is struck in these workshops between artistic, therapeutic and educational aims (Assal et al., 2016) that are in triadic relationship: each is in relation with the relationship between the other two (Durand, 2016).

The chapter focuses in particular on the experience of the participants. It has four sections: the theoretical and methodological framework, the context and a summary of the field study results, the elements that structure TLE and punctuate the course of the workshop, and a conclusion on the implications of this type of proposal in adult education.

Theoretical and Methodological Framework

Course of action theory—based on the enactive approach (Varela, Thompson, & Rosch, 1991)—is the frame of reference for our studies on human activity and its transformations in adult education (Durand, 2013; Durand & Poizat, 2015; Theureau, 2003, 2006, 2015). In this chapter, we present only the parts of this theoretical framework that concern the study of the TLE participants: the centrality of experience in human activity as pre-reflexive consciousness, its signifying dimension that makes it a semiosis and its contribution to processes of appropriation and individuation.

Activity-Experience

Experience is the "living out" of human activity, or pre-reflexive consciousness (Sartre, 1943/1983). This modality of consciousness consists of being present to oneself—consubstantially with activity—in such a way that individuals can be said to understand and know their activity (Theureau, 2003, 2006). Experience is an uninterrupted and constantly changing flow that Peirce (1994) hypothetically organised and modelled in three categories. Firstness concerns the Possible, referring to the propensities that may or may not be actualised in a situation; it characterises an actor's commitment to an open and undetermined but delimited situation. Secondness concerns the Actual, referring to perceptions and the meaningful and specific reactions of and in the real world; it is characterised by the event of updating some of the openings in the actor's engagement—that is, what the actor does in the here and now. Thirdness concerns the Virtual, referring to generalisations as mediations emerging from interactions between the other two categories; it is characterised by the possible extensions that actors confer on all or part of their activity in the present situation, which are likely to document future engagements.

The experience associated with the actor's commitment to an activity at a given moment can be conceptualised as the "surface effect" of this activity, in the sense that it is inherent and cannot be detached from it. It is also conceptualised as (a) the actor's path to his/her own activity: experience is the source of knowledge and consciousness of activity;

(b) an object that actors are likely to express; for example, by communicating the contents of experience to other actors under certain conditions (which are exploited and described in the "Methods" section below).

The actor's experience is further conceptualised as the condition for and product of a permanent dynamic of constituting meaning of and in activity. In other words, the experience that an actor elaborates of his/her activity *in situ* is a chain of local meanings that aggregate into more extensive meanings. This prompted Theureau (2006) to extend Peirce's (1994) *thought-sign* concept to the flow of human activity-experience. Experience is the way that actors signify—or give meaning to—what they do moment by moment in a concatenation and aggregation of units of meanings: semiosis.

Ordinary activity-experience can provoke aesthetic or artistic fulfilment, which is thus not reserved for extraordinary productions but instead belongs to and transcends the dimension of everyday human activity. An aesthetic experience is a relationship with the environment that is more vivid and amplified than what usually occurs in everyday situations. According to Dewey (1934), it is the experience of experience—that is, experience appreciated in itself. While preserving the generic features of ordinary experience, artistic practice amplifies and enhances it through creative imagination. As Dewey (1934) noted, artistic practice is accompanied by a fully absorbed *authentic experience* and aesthetic pleasure. In an aesthetic experience, the actors are both active and contemplative: they experience themselves with immediacy and artistic sensitivity. In the pleasure of experience as experience, artistic emotion emerges to exalt the ordinary experience. This experience of fullness can then be communicated and become the object of comment, reflection, analysis, and so on.

Human experiential dynamics are both a continuity and a succession of discontinuities, these last occurring in connection with changes in the environment that are also due to the dynamics of the activity itself. When discontinuities occur, they are sources of surprise or doubt, and an inquiry is engaged that may well transform meanings (Peirce, 2014). This movement is initiated by feelings of uncertainty and indeterminacy, followed by questions, recombination of old meanings, hypotheses, internal dialogues or collective discussions, assertions, and so on—up to the consolidation and extension of beliefs or old habits or the constitution of new meanings (Peirce, 1994, 2014). The iconic components of semiosis are essential elements of these dynamics, especially metaphors as hypotheses of interpretation (Fisette, 2009; Lakoff & Johnson, 1980; Peirce, 1994). Similarly, the dialogical dimension of thought is such that we are always either in relationship with others or involved in conversation between different states of mind or consciousness—as a dialogue between real or imagined individuals, between acts of thought and concrete acts, or between the doubts, hypotheses and beliefs punctuating an inquiry (Peirce, 1994, 2014).

Transformations in the activity-experience flow are generally labile (like transient adjustments to one-off changes), but some are permanent. They punctuate the dynamics of self-construction (or individuation) through a process of appropriation. This consists of the partial or total integration of concrete/technical or symbolic objects into the semiosis, which implies (a) assigning meaning to a previously irrelevant element in the environment that now stands out against an undifferentiated background and (b) inserting this element into the current or a future semiosis. Appropriation transforms and enriches current and future activity-experience and drives the dynamics of individuation, which is the permanent self-construction of living beings by a process of integration into successive and increasingly coherent and vast totalities. The trajectories of individuation gradually propagate but may also undergo abrupt and qualitative re-organisations. The successive states emerging from this process are the actualisations of possible contents from earlier pre-individuated phases. Individuals are thus conceived as phases in the individuation process, in the sense that they are not always already constituted and are always part of an ongoing trajectory (Poizat & Goudeaux, 2014; Simondon, 1992).

Methods

The components of lived experience are identified using a semiological framework for activity analysis, as well as (a) an ethnographic approach, (b) ethical and methodological positioning to ensure data reliability and a non-objectifying relationship with others, and (c) a method that facilitates access to actors' pre-reflexive awareness and the analysis of the experience categories (Theureau, 2006). Specifically, pre-reflexive consciousness is accessed by focusing on what in their activity actors consider meaningful and can demonstrate, recount, mime and comment on. The expression of these elements is facilitated in dynamic re-enactment sessions (DRS) with self-confrontation using traces (often video recordings) of their past activity. In these sessions (which are also recorded), the actors are encouraged to "relive" the recorded situations and describe and comment on the meaningful elements; the traces facilitate contextualised access to the lived activity (Gallese, 2005; Theureau, 2006) and the researcher reminds them to remain focused on the lived experience of the past activity.

The contents of the experience categories are first identified with protocols for mapping the transcripts of the activity (verbal and nonverbal behaviour) in the natural situation to the DRS contents. The data are then analysed using a matrix with six components (Table 10.1) that refer to Peirce's three experience categories:

Table 10.1 Matrix with six components for the semiological analysis of actors' experience

Actual	**[U] Unit of the course of experience**
	The actor's practical actions, communications to others or internal discourse, and lived emotions
	[R] Representamen
	What is meaningful for the actor at a given instant, taking into account the focus of attention. This component also includes "ruptures in anticipation" or those elements that contradict previous expectations
Possible	**[E] Engagement**
	Horizons of possible (intentional states, preoccupations, openings) arising from the actor's past actions, personal and professional history, and habits. It is also characterised by an affective state
	[A] Anticipation
	What an actor expects or plans to do in successive units of meaning
	[S] Situated knowledge
	Knowledge, rules for action, habits, past lived situations that are actualised and, more generally, all elements of the actor's own culture
Virtual	**[I] Interpretant**
	New assertions, rules for action and generalisations, as well as the manifestations of inquiry cycles: doubts, questions, and emerging hypotheses

This analytical or deconstructive approach is followed by a phase of generalisation or reconstruction: the typical dimensions of each actor's experience and then that of several actors are categorised thematically to identify the main elements in both the individual and collective dynamics of meaning.

Field Study and Results

The study lasted three years and included five TLE workshops. Participants had all experienced challenging biographical episodes: chronic illness, personal family or societal traumas, catastrophic events. They were aged 20–65, not having a particular theatrical culture. Data collection focused on the activity of all actors[1]: participants ($n = 18$) and facilitators ($n = 11$), through (a) ethnographic observations and audio/video recordings of three workshops, and (b) recordings of participants' and facilitators' verbalisations of their experience during the DRS. These data were supplemented by one to three post-TLE interviews with some of the participants ($n = 10$) in their homes, at intervals of three months to two years.

For the semiological analysis of the actors' experience, what each individual said was first organised into a structured chronicle of the activities specific to the TLE frame and then analysed by identifying the main components of the three experience categories (Table 10.2).

The next step in processing was identifying the components of the experience evaluated as typical at the individual and interindividual levels. The judgments of typicality were based on the frequency of occurrence in the sample and the judgments that emerged during the DRS.

The study alternated between phases of data collection, corpus processing, modelling, and intermediary interpretative hypothesising. It

---

[1] By actors, we refer to all those who participated in this research: the participants who benefited from the TLE, the facilitators who made it work, and the theater professionals who performed the mini-plays.

Table 10.2 Excerpt from the protocol to analyse the data of participant J.

Observed situation	DRS	Actual	Possible	Virtual
Start of the staging: J. is next to the stage director (SD) in front of the empty stage and facing the actors	So here, it's really vague... How can I present the experience I had? It's remained the most difficult moment in my existence, knowing what happened to her the day before I'm wondering how we are going to show this We need signposts to build the play. Start with something, a short concrete image to get it going so the play can unfold. I had a hard time seeing how to start	U. try to see how to represent his experience R. the memory of his wife the day before her death U. look for elements to build the play on/he has a hard time finding them	E. create the play from his text/his experience E. vagueness/ uncertainty S. elements from his history/ from a painful event S. knowledge about theatre work	I. questions: how can he represent his experience? / I. question: how can he find the concrete elements to start the play?

ended when data saturation was reached and the interpretation of the results was validated by the participants and other researchers working in this field who were not involved in the study. Processing was carried out independently by the two researchers, with regular comparisons of the data coding and interpretations until consensus was reached; in cases of persistent disagreement, the item was removed from the corpus.

The results description focuses in particular on the experience of the participants, and presents a summary of its different components throughout the workshop.

An Accompanied Inquiry

The TLE workshop was a memorable experience for the participants (Salini & Durand, 2016b). We present excerpts from the verbatim of one of them, indicating the components identified during the semiological analysis and mapping them to the main steps of TLE (Table 10.3). We then summarise the elements that were typical for all the participants.

Table 10.3 Framework for the succession of TLE activities

Times and contents	Steps and experiences
A few weeks before the TLE: initial information	First contact with the person/institution proposing TLE
	Information sessions with the team of facilitators
First day: arrival at workshop and writing begins	Welcome, warm-up activities, trust-building, loosening of inhibitions
	Writing: in several phases, supported by diverse proposals to facilitate the work
	End of the day: each participant reads his/her text to the others
	Round table at the end of the readings
Second day—morning of third day: staging the play	Second reading (neutral) of the texts by the theatre professionals
	Round table
	Successive elaborations of the plays (almost two hours for each one)
	Round table after each elaboration of a play
Afternoon of the third day: the plays are performed and all leave the workshop	Viewing the finalised plays
	Final round table
The following days, weeks or months	DVDs of the recorded plays sent to participants
	The participants post-TLE reflection s
	The opinions of others (friends, families, caregivers)

Excerpts from J.'s Experience[2]

J. is a skilled worker in his 60s with chronic diabetes. He has somewhat unwillingly committed to this workshop and his expectations are measured: *I'm living with a burden that I have to lighten—try to share it—I need help to lighten it*[3] [E]. The burden is related to his wife's death six years ago and his inability to understand what has happened to him: *I'm always looking for an explanation* [E]. J. is nevertheless convinced that his suffering in inexpressible [K] and expects that this project to share it will end in failure [A]. The episode that he wrote about and then staged concerns this biographical juncture, which he describes as: *a very vague moment, the hardest of my life* [K], notably because it is associated with a haunting observation: *I didn't see her pass* [I] (his wife died during the night but not in their bed, while J. slept).

> Excerpts from J.'s text
> September 19th, 4 am
> Wake up with a start, groping next to me I don't feel my wife's body. Quick! Get up! Go see if she's outside. No! Her coat's here… I go back in and find her lying at the foot of her bed.
> I shout, I speak to her. No answer. She's dead.
> And from that moment when I opened the door on my sudden loneliness, a volley of questions started: What do I do? When? How? What? And above all, with whom?

As he wrote and staged his play, J. experienced the facilitators' actions [R] as comfortable and helpful [U—I]: *we compared ideas that weren't the same—they understood what I wanted—I felt surrounded and cared for*. What he wanted was precise [E]: *staging my experience* and subtle: *I don't want to stage this too strongly, too demonstratively* because he does not want [E] the re-enactment to be too realistic.

During this phase, J. wondered how to make his text concrete [U]—*it's a very vague moment* [R]—*how do I represent this experience?* [I] while

---

[2] Throughout the text, we use abbreviations of the components of experience presented in Table 10.1, as follows: Firstness: ([E], [A], [K]), Secondness ([R], [U]), Thirdness ([I]).
[3] Words and phrases in italics are typical excerpts from the verbatim in the corpus.

making sure it was coherent and clear [E]—*first of all I think about the story* [U] *how we're going to reproduce it* [U]. He approves of an initial suggestion to start with a simple and realistic scene [U]: *when they started talking about putting the material in order* [R] *I thought* [U] *"well, it's still going to look like something"* [A]. He feels a new impression [R]: that of *dealing with this lived moment as an object* [I]. He wants to express the duality of his experience [E]: the pain of discovery and his willingness to face it: *I held things in so I could start fighting right away* [K].

The metaphor of the final scene shook him [R] with its evocative power: the actress playing the role of his wife slowly leaves the scene, slowly walking to *Casta Diva*, the aria from Bellini's opera *Norma: the one my wife loved* [K]. This scene co-constructed in the interaction between J. and the director shows the inverted recovery from the past episode that was the theme of his text: *I didn't see her leave*. After the scene, he was able to say: *I saw her leave* [I]. Viewing the video of the play a few weeks later, as the light slowly faded away, he stated: *the light is going at the end… this shows the end of an era… really good* [I].

Typical Dimensions of the Participants' Experiences

The lived experience of every TLE participant was unique. However, we identified common or shared experiential components during our research, and J.'s experience serves as a kind of prototype: this case concentrated the most shared experiential components. We summarise these typical components below by generalising them, and we complete this description with some of the components not present in his experience.

At the start of the TLE workshop, most participants took the opportunity to reflect on a difficult past situation, one still present in their experience that they *come back to time and again*. Others wanted to relive something *beautiful, important, moving*. Healing was not the intention; rather they sought to use TLE to do something with what lived inside them—to find the words and gestures to express whatever haunted and unsettled them. Overall, they sought meaning. From the start, enticed by the light-hearted, respectful and generous atmosphere, the participants felt safe.

The texts covered many themes: (a) trigger events (illness, trauma, war, death of a loved one), (b) difficult family or professional relationships, or (c) inner states (loneliness, internal struggle, fear, anxiety, institutional responsibilities, spirituality).

As they scripted their plays, the facilitators' support lessened their fears and writing was often easier than expected. The readings at the end of the first day were moments of both emotional overload and emotional distance.

As their work continued, they focused on communicating the truth of their experiences and on finding the right tone to match what they had felt. The director's support was crucial: he made suggestions and offered reassurance while leaving them great freedom. The start of staging was facilitated by concrete elements that indirectly contributed to the veracity of the event: a sound recording of wind, canvas screens as an elevator, or miming gestures of work. The suggestions of the theatre professionals, whether accepted or not, were well received. A concern for aesthetics was ever-present: all the participants wanted their productions to be *beautiful*.

As they read their texts and then viewed their plays, everyone had the experience of being both the author and spectator of his/her work. As a spectator, the emotions returned, but as if grasped from the outside. The plays were a source of pain, pleasure and healing. Once finished, the authors dialogued with their plays, and new possibilities for understanding the past event emerged for each author and the others. Throughout TLE, an ephemeral but united community was built, strengthened by a sense of belonging and sharing and facilitated by the round table discussions.

In the weeks, months, and even years after TLE, all the participants expressed the feeling of having overcome an ordeal and described TLE's impact as positive. To varying degrees, all expressed gratitude and appreciation for their participation. Peacefulness and serenity were frequently felt, as well as a new-found frankness and emotional distance from their painful experience. They said they had a better grasp of their own life stories, thought they knew themselves better, and had clarified or confirmed their own values.

Thus, carefully, attentively and exactingly, the participants had exceeded their limits. Without prior initiation, they had staged plays, which they could never have done on their own. They had become authors, venturing into the unknown. In various ways, they described the opening of a future with potential worth.

Artistic Mediation and Developmental Training

The developmental effect of TLE can be interpreted on the basis of the six structuring elements that punctuate the course of the workshop: (a) an atmosphere with cycles of giving to and receiving from others, (b) the events-driven transformation of experience, (c) the creation of a space of playful and participative inquiry, (d) an amplification of imaginative activity, (e) the ambition of aesthetic and artistic creation, and (f) dynamics of transfer from "one's own" to the group and back (Durand & Salini, 2016; Salini & Durand, 2016a).

Giving Cycles

Activity in this educational space does not follow utilitarian, external prescriptions, but arises from an inner need. From the start, the participants have been given attention, competent help, time, support, confidence, new possibilities for action, and so on. All has been given without expectation or strategy. Although the facilitators/givers are demanding, everything is in the hands of the participants because receiving implies the acknowledgement of debt. Although the participants' artistic activity is modest for art specialists, it embodies an obligation to live up to what they have received according to an ethic of giving (Caillé, 2000).

Events-Driven Transformation of Experience

TLE encourages participants to grasp and re-signify a past experience lived as overwhelming by and in theatrical work. It encourages them to take a painful experience and turn it into an event (which is staged) by producing a fiction—the play—that becomes the event. This opens up the possibility of circularity between an *àlea* or unexpected event (object of the staging) and a *rendezvous* or intended event (staging) (Zarifian, 1995).

The *àlea* event is associated with uncertainty or crisis; unexpected and endured, it must be faced and absorbed into new meaning (Peirce, 1994). When this does not occur, questions without response may become compulsive, generating negative emotional states. The painful experience is not overcome and the person is plagued by suffering, feelings of incompleteness or incomprehension, or a sense of inexpressibility. The vital dynamics of meaning are at an impasse (Violi, 2014). The *rendezvous* event depends on the intention and desire for a future achievement. It is anticipated and taken as such in the course of existence. This planned for accomplishment is nevertheless uncertain and prediction is difficult. It has the power to transform meanings in a personal biography because it disturbs the established regularities and can be grasped by the individual (Zarifian, 1995).

When the participants choose what their theatrical work will be about, they point to something striking, a source of embedded suffering and an incomprehensible stalemate as the *àlea* event of reference. Yet with the support of the facilitators, its theatricalisation is a promise of a *rendezvous* event that can bring out new meanings.

The Enrichment of Expressive Possibilities

TLE amplifies imaginative activity by encouraging metaphor and fiction. The initial script is enriched by the possibilities of novel staging and mimetic phenomena. These are mainly expressed through the omnipresent metaphors and a telescoping of the fictional relationships between the work in progress and the personal experience, which we call *metalepsis* (Genette as cited in Pier, 2016).

Metaphors are not just artistic or rhetorical figures of speech: they involve human experience in its entirety, especially its bodily dimension (Lakoff & Johnson, 1980). They facilitate the viewer's comprehension and detach the staged play from the participants' original experience: they have a culturally loaded relationship to both direct and imaged meaning. Metaphors open up the possible outcomes for the staged play because, as miniature fictions, they prefigure and contain the directions for possible development (Fisette, 2009; Peirce, 1994; Pier, 2016). Through metaphor, the play can imaginatively account for the absence and emptiness of old meanings and provide a fictional epilogue to a situation of impasse.

The metalepses of authors (Genette as cited in Pier, 2016) are figures of speech that establish breaks in the modes of presence in a work. In TLE, participants are at once authors, readers, spectators and scriptwriters of the fictions that they stage and that stage them, as well as witnesses to and interpreters of the meaning of their own experience. Metalepses are sources for telescoping the registers of fiction that favour the changing relationship to the work in progress and personal experience. They disturb participants' relationships to their work and modify their place as authors and/or spectators, thus inflating the meaning of the ongoing story.

Painful experience is thus re-incorporated through fiction and represented on stage by the effects of mimetic. The theatrical play offers the possibility of an embodied simulation (Gallese, 2005) of the past and its experience, and this is conducive to another way of experiencing and signifying the staged event. It facilitates new and indirect access to an experience of suffering that is both re-incorporated with its emotional component and observed from the outside.

Aesthetic Ambition

TLE evokes an *aesthetic state of mind* with the assumption that each person is listening to his/her own sensitive perceptions (Fisette, 2009) in an amplified and more alive relationship to the world than in everyday situations. As Dewey (1934) noted about artistic experience in general, TLE participants undergo an experience of experience—that is, experience appreciated in itself. TLE preserves the generic features of ordinary experience but it amplifies and intensifies them through creative imagination. The participants' theatrical productions free a past experience that has remained unaesthetic and stunted because of impediments to its normal development. The participants are able to overcome these obstacles and bring the experience to term with closure or profound aesthetic pleasure. This experience of fulfilment can then be communicated and becomes an object for comment, reflection and analysis.

One's Own and What Is Shared

The accompaniment offered during the production and viewing of theatrical performances may explain the bi-directional dynamics: the phenomenal, physical and symbolic appropriation of the components of the experience of staging and the phenomenal, physical and symbolic expropriation of one's own experience of staging: this constitutes an other-ness that is likely to enrich the culture of each of these others, as well as the shared culture of the emerging TLE collective.

The appropriation dynamics are twofold. They consist of all the transformations by which the participants and their situations and cultures are mobilised and modified (Poizat, Durand, & Thereau, 2016) through mimetic processes as they view the other participants' plays. They also consist of the re-signifying and reconstruction of one's own experience by re-enacted suffering, which, by a boomerang effect, is re-appropriated by all the participants as they view their own staging.

Given the intensity of the mimetic and re-enactive processes, a phenomenon of externalisation and alienation occurs. This sense of becoming other is not freighted with negative values—in fact, it is quite the contrary. Expropriation signifies *de-individualed* sharing of the painful experience and spontaneously arouses debates as soon as the different but analogous experiences are viewed on stage. This empathetic interactivity lays the groundwork for co-constituting actors who act and a real collective through mutual appropriations. The process of expropriation-appropriation that is simultaneously individual and collective is such that the viewed experience potentially becomes external to the participant and can thus be shared by the theatre collective through mutual or collective appropriation.

Through theatre practices, the activity and experience that were unique to an individual are potentially projected, at a phenomenal level, into other individuals or into their shared cultural world. This simultaneous expropriation and sharing cause a community of practice to emerge (Lave, 2012). In the experience of suffering, its staging and viewing, there is *always already* a place for the experience of *other than oneself*. Each participant is affected by the experience of the others but is not in the place of the others; a relationship is established that is not a fusion, but a reciprocity that maintains difference. During the performances, the participants do not merely contemplate the staging of other experiences as similar to their own: what seems promising is the "slight and mysterious shift" that implies matching and opposition (and not identification) (Merleau-Ponty, 1992, p. 186). To paraphrase Merleau-Ponty, it can be said that, from an educational and therapeutic perspective, the staging of others' experiences operationalises the idea that the experience of others haunts one's own experience.

Conclusion

TLE is a theatrical practice in support of resilience-building. It is based on artistic mediation that is itself considered inseparable from dimensions of caregiving and education (Salini & Durand, 2016a). Resilience has been defined as a state or the process leading to it, and definitions also vary with the field of study (e.g., Fletcher & Sarkar, 2013). We understand it as the process by which a dynamic system that (a) has received a shock or been accidentally disturbed and (b) has thus been plunged into a more or less massive and permanent situation of breakdown, disorientation, or impasse, nevertheless (c) manages to recover its previous level of functioning and performance, (d) resuming a normal time trajectory and (e) recovering its capacities for development and projection into the future. In this conception, humans are one among many dynamic systems capable of resilience. A recent research stream in adult education focuses on the diversity of resilience dynamics and the design of educational systems for and through resilience (i.e., Durand & Salini, 2016; Flandin, Poizat, & Durand, 2018).

During the TLE workshop, artistic activity brings out *individual-artists* during the creation of the plays. The staging process imbues the events with value and meaning that go well beyond the here-and-now mini-plays, instead readdressing the participants' own—but also now shared—imaginary worlds. What emerges is both a *community of suffering* and an *artistic community* that bring together associated aesthetic experiences and a complex process of appropriation and expropriation. This occurs because, although the focus seems to be on the singularity of each participant's life story, what is shareable about these experiences is brought out, creating rich collective dynamics and promoting the emergence of a community (Durand & Salini, 2016).

The TLE workshop activity of creation, visualisation and artistic debate offers a powerful support for people in difficulty as they search for meaning and struggle to emerge from isolation and deadlock. This workshop seems to be an exemplary training dispositive that brings out artistic dynamics, which, as McNiff (2007) suggests, promotes a shift in the participants' inquiries from solipsistic to participative and dialogical. As a complement to other work, the research presented here contributes to the documentation on a broader program of training in and by resilience for developmental education for adults.

References

Assal, J.-P., Durand, M., & Horn, O. (2016). *Le Théâtre du Vécu—Art, Soin, Éducation*. Dijon, France: Raison et passions.

Assal, J.-P., Malavia, M., & Roland, M. (2009). *De la mise en scène à la mise en sens—Au croisement de la mise en scène de théâtre et de la médecine*. Paris, France: L'Harmattan.

Boal, A. (1985). *Theater of the oppressed*. New York, NY: TCG Edition.

Caillé, A. (2000). *Anthropologie du don*. Paris, France: Desclée de Brouwer.

Darmon, J.-C. (dir.). (2011). *Littérature et thérapeutique des passions. La catharsis en question*. Paris, France: Hermann.

Dewey, J. (1934). Art as experience. In J. A. Boydston (Ed.), *The later works of John Dewey* (Vol. 10). Carbondale, IL: Southern Illinois University Press.

Durand, M. (2013). Human activity, social practice and lifelong education. *International Journal of Lifelong Education, 32*, 1–13.

Durand, M. (2016). Des rapports triadiques entre soin, art et éducation. In J.-P. Assal, M. Durand, & O. Horn (Eds.), *Le Théâtre du Vécu* (pp. 250–256). Dijon, France: Raison et Passions.

Durand, M., & Poizat, G. (2015). An activity-centred approach to work analysis and the design of vocational training situations. In L. Filliettaz & S. Billett (Eds.), *Francophone perspectives of learning through work: Conceptions, traditions and practices* (pp. 221–240). Dordrecht, The Netherlands: Springer.

Durand, M., & Salini, D. (2016). Éducation à la résilience: une démarche événementielle. In J-P. Assal, M. Durand, O. Horn (Eds.), *Le Théâtre du Vécu* (pp. 303–315). Dijon, France: Raison et passions.

Fisette, J. (2009). L'icône, l'hypoicône et la métaphore. L'avancée dans l'hypoicône jusqu'à la frontière du non-conceptualisable. *Visual Culture, 14*, 7–46.

Flandin, S., Poizat, G., & Durand, M. (2018). Improving resilience in high-risk organizations. Principles for the design of innovative training environments. *Development and Learning in Organizations, 32*(2), 9–12.

Fletcher, D., & Sarkar, M. (2013). Psychological resilience. A review and critique of definitions, concepts, and theory. *European Psychologist, 18*(1), 12–23.

Fox, J. (1986). *Acts of service: Spontaneity, commitment, tradition in the non-scripted theatre*. New Paltz, NY: Tusitala.

Freire, P. (1970). *Pedagogy of the oppressed*. New York, NY: Continuum.

Gallese, V. (2005). Embodied simulation: From neurons to phenomenal experience. *Phenomenology and the Cognitive Sciences, 4*, 23–48.

Keats, J. (1899). *The complete poetical works and letters of John Keats*. Boston, MA: Houghton, Mifflin and Company.

Lakoff, G., & Johnson, M. (1980). *Metaphors we live by*. Chicago, IL: University of Chicago Press.

Lave, J. (2012). Changing practice. *Mind, Culture, and Activity, 19*(2), 156–171.

Mages, W. K. (2016). Educational drama and theatre. Paradigms for understanding and engagement. *Open Online Journal for Research and Education, (Special Issue 5)*. http://journal.ph-noe.ac.at

McNiff, S. (2007). Art-based research. In J. G. Knowles & A. L. Cole (Eds.), *Handbook of the arts in qualitative research: Perspectives, methodologies, examples, and issues* (pp. 29–40). Los Angeles, CA: Sage.

Merleau-Ponty, M. (1992). *La prose du monde*. Paris, France: Gallimard.

Moreno, J. L. (1959). *Psychodrama* (Vol. 2). Beacon, NY: Beacon House.

Peirce, C. S. (1994). *The collected paper of Charles Sanders Peirce (Volumes I–VIII)*. Charlottesville, VA: Intelex.

Peirce, C. S. (2014). *Illustrations of the logic of science*. Chicago, IL: Open Court.

Pier, J. (2016). Metalepsis. In P. Hühn, J. Pier, W. Schmid, & J. Jörg Schönert (Eds.), *The living handbook of narratology*. Hamburg, Germany: Hamburg University. http://www.lhn.uni-hamburg.de/article/metalepsis-revised-version-uploaded-13-july-2016

Poizat, G., Durand, M., & Theureau, J. (2016). The challenges of activity analysis for training objectives. *Le Travail Humain, 3*(79), 233–258.
Poizat, G., & Goudeaux, A. (2014). Appropriation et individuation: un nouveau modèle pour penser l'éducation et la formation? *Raisons Educatives, 14*, 13–38.
Salgado, M. (2008). Le théâtre, un outil de formation au management. *Revue Française de Gestion, 181*, 77–96.
Salini, D., & Durand, M. (2016a). Événement dramatique et éducation événementielle. In J.-P. Assal, M. Durand, & O. Horn (Eds.), *Le Théâtre du Vécu* (pp. 265–276). Dijon, France: Raison et Passions.
Salini, D., & Durand, M. (2016b). Participer au Théâtre du vécu: une expérience mémorable, une quête de sens. In J.-P. Assal, M. Durand, & O. Horn (Eds.), *Le Théâtre du Vécu* (pp. 119–134). Dijon, France: Raison et Passions.
Salini, D., Durand, M., & Goudeaux, A. (2016). Façonner une bulle d'art. La culture en action des « gens du théâtre ». In J.-P. Assal, M. Durand, & O. Horn (Eds.), *Le Théâtre du Vécu* (pp. 161–164). Dijon, France: Raison et Passions.
Sartre, J.-P. (1943/1983). *Being and nothingness*. New York, NY: Washington Square Press.
Simondon, G. (1992). The genesis of the individual. In J. Crary & S. Kwinter (Eds.), *Incorporations* (pp. 297–319). New York, NY: Zone Books.
Theureau, J. (2003). Course of action analysis and course of action centred design. In E. Hollnagel (Ed.), *Handbook of cognitive task design* (pp. 55–81). Mahwah, NJ: Lawrence Erlbaum Associates.
Theureau, J. (2006). *Le cours d'action: méthode développée*. Toulouse, France: Octarès.
Theureau, J. (2015). *L'enaction et l'expérience*. Toulouse, France: Octarès.
Varela, F. J., Thompson, E., & Rosch, E. (1991). *The embodied mind: Cognitive science and human experience*. Boston, MA: MIT Press.
Violi, P. (2014). *Paesaggi della memoria. Il trauma, lo spazio, la storia*. Milano, Italy: Bompiani.
Zarifian, P. (1995). *Le travail et l'événement*. Paris, France: L'Harmattan.

11

Clowning Training to Improve Working Conditions and Increase the Well-Being of Employees

Reinhard Tschiesner and Alessandra Farneti

Introduction

Some Preliminary Reflections on the Clown

To understand the reason why we started using clowning in education and training, we would like to outline first of all the profile of the clown as an artistic figure. It shows different nuances depending on the context in which the clown acts. The character is implicitly linked to the personality of an actor and a grotesque representation of his faults.

Each clown is therefore unique, as well as his performances, which are linked to special situations and characterised by improvisation. Despite numerous attempts to reconstruct the historical path that led to the birth of the clown, its origins remain unclear (De Marinis, 1980, 1993; Galante Garrone, 1980).

R. Tschiesner (✉) • A. Farneti
Free University of Bolzano/Bozen, Bolzano/Bozen, Italy
e-mail: reinhard.tschiesner@unibz.it; alessandra.farneti@unibz.it

There is no doubt that the clown represents — and has always represented — the culture of the paradox, and it is in the paradox that weaknesses and contradictions are revealed.

Many artists have considered the clown as a symbol of rupture, making it a spokesperson for important changes in artistic currents, in painting as well as in literature. From Seurat to Picasso, from Rouault to Ensor to Chagalle, from Flaubert to Musset to Sand to Marinetti, many artists were inspired by the circus and the clown as an expression of the avantgardes in the various artistic fields (Farneti & Tschiesner, 2012). The clown becomes a carrier of a message that many reject: *human beings are fragile and "stupid", they can easily fall and make mistakes* (Agosti, 2005).

The fact that some of the great masters of cinema, such as Charlie Chaplin or Federico Fellini, put the clown at the centre of their art shows that the clown is anything but a simple character as the media and the common culture often represent it. Also today, in a Faustian society where appearance, beauty and wealth are myths difficult to overcome, the clown becomes an uncomfortable character, an artist who entertains children, but who is boring or, worse, irritating for adults. Even though there are some great actors such as Slava Polunin or David Larible (to name but a few) who receive broad public consensus, it is still a selected audience, not always able to fully understand their importance. The clown artist has distant roots and reached us through jesters and buffoons, the masks of puppetry and the circus (Sallèe & Fabbri, 1984; Viganò, 1985).

The long training that allows an actor to become a clown today is well illustrated by Lecoq (2000) who underlines that not all actors can become clowns, as clowns are very particular actors who stage themselves, their own personality, their faults and their fears. And they do all this through a metaphorical body trained in mime and pantomime, a body that speaks without words, an emotional and emotive body that learns to act as a mirror for others (Sanguigno, 2001, 2004).

Psychodynamic, cognitive and social theories highlight the importance of the body as the basis of knowledge, self-image, self-esteem, communication and expression of emotions. We would like to mention just a few of the numerous authors of different backgrounds who wrote about the meaning and the development of the body image. The aspect on which all the authors agree is that the body represents not only the fundamental instrument of knowledge but also our "visiting card" in interpersonal communication (Boadella & Liss, 1986; Farneti & Carlini, 1981; Galimberti, 1983; Shilder, 1973).

The body of the clown is basically a body *without shame* in the strictest sense of the word, since the focus of the clown's artistic work is precisely the ability to play with his own physical, but also moral defects, slowly overcoming shame. Through exercise, one learns to know heaviness and clumsiness, in order to get rid of it through the comical processing of one's faults. Clowning, moreover, differs from other gymnastic activities, as it tends to become aware of the transience and fragility through a free and creative expression of the gesture (Farneti & Tschiesner, 2012, pp. 183–184).

Mime artists as Marcel Marceau, who expressed a rainbow of emotions through his clown called Bip, or clowns linked to the circus, like the great clown Grock, were able, in a variety of ways, to speak without words, to elicit in the audience reactions that seemed immediate, but were the result of longstanding training and exercise.

For this reason, some authors have analysed the most profound aspects of the clown's character, denoting it as a metaphor of the id, referring to Freud, or of the Shadow, in a Jungian perspective (Bala, 2010; Jung, 1934), by all means a provocative and desecrating emblem, sweet and bitter at the same time, weird and tragic, an aged child that disorientates without ever being banal or predictable (Farneti, 2004; Fellini, 1970; Fo, 1987; Starobinski, 1984).

Even though this is not the right place for a detailed analysis of the clown prototypes (the reader is referred to specialist texts about this topic), it is important to remember that there are two types of clowns: White or Louis, and Augustus or Tony or Red. The White (magister) stands always higher that Augustus and shows a stern and scornful face, while Augustus is the poor one, badly dressed, clumsy, incapable, persecuted and ridiculed by the White.

After having been considered only as a circus artist, the clown has stepped out of the circus a long time ago, in order to perform in movies, theatres, squares, streets, hospitals, prisons, nursing homes and care facilities in general. This has increased the clown's popularity, but it has not changed the simplified image that leads to see the clown first of all as a comedian capable of bringing joy where sadness dominates.

The great success of Patch Adams and the film inspired by him have increased the idea that one just has to put on a red nose and feel the impetus to help others in order to become a clown (Adams, 1998, 2002).

We use the concepts of *comic-therapy* or *gel-therapy* or *smile-therapy* in an all too superficial way, as if the art of the clown aimed only at entertaining, and the benefits deriving from his work were only due to the well-being elicited by laughter. Moreover, the concept of "therapy" is used referring to something that is, in our opinion, only a distraction with possible temporary positive effects. On this topic we have already expressed our doubts recently (Farneti & Tschiesner, 2014a, 2014b).

Training Through Clowning

Speaking of arts-based training practices aimed at changing participants means entering the complex world of education with all its multiple meanings, depending on its intended purpose and the methods used. Strictly speaking, the notion of *training* means "giving a form" or modifying the existing form.

We know, however, that there are training processes intended to transmit specific knowledge or particular skills necessary for a certain job, but not to change the personality structure or to reflect on the position of the subject in the world. Both from a philosophical and pedagogical point of view, education has been defined in very different ways, depending on the historical context and ideology, but this is certainly not the context in which to explore such a complex topic. For this reason, we refer to the extensive existing literature (Cappa, 2016).

When we talk about training through clowning, we refer to a process of personal and interpersonal change elicited through simple activities taken from the art of the clown and the related reflections with a psychologist. The training aims at creating the awareness of one's own communicative potentialities, of one's image and of a *metaphorical* body that connects the cognitive and affective sphere and is symbolically viewed as a means of expressing a particular paradigm. We would like to underline the fact that we don't aim at training professional clowns or volunteer clowns carrying out support activities, but at analysing and transmitting the "philosophy" of the character to the students, as illustrated before.

Talking about a "teaching" clown is a responsibility and at the same time a challenge, as no one has yet done it in a systematic way, even if there are many clowns who have been doing training activities for some time, especially at school. André Casaca, who has been working with children and young people in schools and on the streets for many years, is one of them (Farneti, 2010).

In our opinion, clowning has an extremely high potential and could offer, if well directed, a new strategy of interventions in many working environments.

We know that theatrical art has long been used both in the field of training as well as in therapy, starting from Moreno's psychodrama and the changes of his techniques into what is called theatre-therapy (Boria, 2011; Caterina, 2005; Fonseca, 2012; Lewis & Johnson, 2000; Orioli, 2007).

When we work with the techniques proposed by the clowns, we ask students to "put on stage" their own image of the Self, even if we do not use psychodrama in the narrower sense, nor theatre-therapy, since the courses we offer are short and have no therapeutic intent. We aim at getting students to express hidden parts of themselves through simple games that leave room for individual processing and allow participants to accept their faults. The main target of this work is therefore the development of self-irony. It is a question of rediscovering humility and stupidity as human conditions inherent to those who do not know, the Socratic *eironeia* [irony] as an awareness of not knowing, of finiteness as something inevitable.

Training is always done in groups and in a playful way, as playing is the privileged tool for the development of creativity, entering the so-called "realm of the possible" (Singer & Singer, 1995) and mirroring oneself in others that become children, expressing themselves freely.

Verbal language is rarely used; the main communication tools are facial and body expression, playing and creativity, awareness of one's own fragility, the exaltation of diversity, humility and self-irony.

A crucial part is nonverbal communication, a very complicated process that combines cognitive, emotional and relational aspects.

Communication always takes place in a certain time and space, defined by those who communicate. Communication can have different purposes (informative, training, declarative, solicitation, request, etc.). It can take place in real life, but also in the dimension of playing, pretending or imagination.

First of all, there is the fact that someone who creates a relationship and gets into communication with someone else takes up different positions: he or she can rank higher, at par or lower.

Sometimes, the terms used to define someone refer to his or her position in the communication process: if someone behaves as a teacher, etymology tells us that *magister* descends from *magis*, which means "more", and it is implied that the magister stands on a higher level than others (Farneti & Palloni, 2010).

The main character used for the courses is Augustus, even if the clown conducting the group sometimes plays the part of the White as a means of deliberate provocation, and the teacher might therefore rank lower than the others: he is not a magister, but a *minister*, a term descending from the Latin word *minus*, that is, "less".

The symbol used (and delivered at a certain moment of the training) is the red nose, defined by Lecoq "the smallest mask in the world", a small object that manages to drastically change the image of the Self (Farneti, 2004; Lecoq, 2000).

> The face is the manifesto that everyone proudly shows; it is a sign of recognition par excellence, the heavy seal of personal identity… The upright head and uncovered face symbolise autonomy and dignity: male dignity, denied to women by civilizations characterized by male dominance. This dignity seeks and finds consensus (or at least thinks so) in the gaze of another face… it is the meaning of communication based on mutual trust: a surface referring to intimacy and to the roots of being. It's this surface that counts more than words, and it's this surface where the truth of words is sought. The face becomes the guarantor of social order …. (Faenza, 2005, p. 55)

The clown, whose face does not express personal identity, triggers a completely different communication process. While looking at a clown, one does not seek his approval, as communication is somehow *unbalanced*, lacking the circularity of thought that starts with "I think you think" and continues with "I think you think I think", followed by "I think you think that I think you think", in an ever more complex interaction process (Battistelli, 1995).

The clown is nothing than a clown and gets not judged; his gaze does not confirm or disconfirm anything. The clown can thus break barriers that normal communication cannot scratch, getting straight to the heart of the other and to his emotions, without alarming him and without eliciting a defensive reaction. The clown uses the universal language of mimicry, empathy and sympathy. The clown looks like a slouch with his large shoes and impossible clothes, transmitting the idea of being stupid and clumsy. The message he transmits is "I'm worse than you, you can not be afraid of me".

This message has been used by many teaching clowns, as the clown Bano who helped deviant children, creating the Barabba's Clown (Giuggioli, 2001), or Miloud Oukili, who saved thousands of boys from the Budapest underground (Farneti, 2013; Mordiglia, 1999; Mussoni, 2003; Rivaroli, 2006).

In the first part of our article, we wanted to present in short the reasons why we believe that clowning can be used for many training processes. Despite a whole range of difficulties and even though we have not yet achieved homogeneous results supporting final conclusions, we consider this a topic deserving to be explored.

At this point, we would like to present some data from our research studies using the clowning-training as an instrument to improve the working conditions and the well-being of participants. This special kind of art is based mostly on bringing to awareness one's self-image and, furthermore, on the possibility of changing it by means of a series of steps that we would like to describe shortly.

Hypotheses and Research Methods Used to Date

Our hypothesis states that the simple games enacted by clowns and the metaphor of his mask can enhance intergroup relationships and help the participants to accept their small and fragile parts, thus reducing work-

and performance-related stress, improving communication, increasing emotional intelligence and reducing shame and fear of failure.

We know that shame is a complex and dangerous emotion that can inhibit or negatively modify behaviour in social relationships (Battacchi, 2002; Battacchi & Codispoti, 1992). We conducted our research with groups of medical doctors and nurses, physiotherapists, teachers, managers, and even patients from rehabilitation departments. The clowns leading the groups are always backed by a psychologist who provides tests and re-tests, organises focus groups and is available for individual interviews with the participants requesting them.

The course, which on average involves about fifteen meetings lasting two hours, has the following scheme (which, however, is adapted from time to time to the needs of the group of students):

Test Administration

1. **The ACL (Adjective Check List) of Ghough** can be used both as a clinical tool as well as for research. It provides varied information regarding personality traits of the subjects and their interpersonal relationships. The replication of the test allows detecting potential changes in the test results.
   It is composed of 300 adjectives that subjects must choose (without a numerical limit) to describe themselves or others. The combination of the adjectives leads to 37 scales that highlight different aspects of the perception of the self, from intra-psychic ones (male and female orientation, creative potential, self-control, originality, intelligence, etc.) to relational ones (need to understand, to take care, of dominion, to receive help, to command, etc.) (Gough, 1979; Lucchese, 1992).
2. **Bar-On's EQ-I (Emotional Quotient Inventory)** is a questionnaire composed of 133 short statements on a 5-point-Likert-scale. The test measures intra-personal dimensions (self-esteem, assertiveness, independence), dimensions related to adaptability (reality testing, flexi-

bility, problem solving), interpersonal dimensions (empathy, social responsibility) and the general dimension of stress (stress tolerance and impulse control) (Franco & Tappatà, 2009).
3. **Test of Shame of Battacchi** is composed of 46 statements with a 4-point response scale. It measures some dimensions of shame: shyness-embarrassment, anguish of shame in front of significant others, need of approval, self-blame for mental contents, self-blame for actions and omissions, need for dominance, "I try to exploit opportunities", normative-punitive fault, empathic-punitive blame, counter-deophilic attitude of unveiling (Battacchi, Codispoti, Marano, & Codispoti, 2001).
4. **Lesson about the purposes and methods of clowning:** the art of the clown, the character and how it evolved.
5. **Training with clowns:** The process involves the discovery of one's gait and postural defects, exercises of facial expression of different emotions (right up to the grotesque), group games and the discussion of sketches and gags with the group of participants.
6. **Training of simple conjuring tricks** and, if possible, the use of some simple musical instrument.
7. **Simple exercises to improve creativity**: Starting from everyday situations, we try to let the students rediscover *childishness* and the ability to see beyond reality. As in the symbolic play of children, where a cardboard box can become a bathtub, a boat, a bed and much more, also in the game of the clown objects are used to convey unusual meanings.
8. **The discovery of one's own clown:** This is probably the central and most important part of the course, in which the students focus on all the tools previously illustrated, giving life to their clownish character. First of all, we invite them to wear old clothes, shoes, hats, bags, ribbons, ties, and so on, then we invite them, one at a time, to choose the objects that seem best suited for expressing their hidden and comical parts. One by one the students disguise themselves and perform, asking for the approval of the tenant and the group. In this process of continuous changing of clothes and accessories, a clown-character that can be perfected and changed over time emerges.

9. **The universal language of the clown: the grammelot:** Speaking using a language that does not exist requires a very difficult technique. The grammelot maintains only the rhythm and the emotional intonation of spoken language. It is a very complex technique that requires a lot of exercise and that cannot be taught in a few lessons. However, approaching the grammelot allows us to understand better how many implicit components a message contains, among others the tone and the rhythm of the voice. A master of this art is Dario Fo: he is able to read an entire news program in German, French or English without ever using a single word that has a complete meaning (Fo, 1987).
10. **Weekly focus groups with the psychologist and documentation of the reflections on the work done.**
11. **Re-test: Submission of the questionnaires.**
12. **Final focus group with the students.**
13. **Students are also asked to keep a daily *comic diary*,** writing down all the funny situations they were faced with during the day and that could become sketches of a clown.

Results

As already stated, it is very difficult to obtain homogeneous results from groups of subjects that differ in terms of age, sex, work, personality, and so on.

It is not possible to keep all the variables under control, as these courses are in most cases offered by public institutions (schools, hospitals, etc.) and are sometimes imposed, sometimes freely chosen.

As a result, we obtain a lot of data from many different groups of subjects and included these in statistical analyses.

In addition to the individual variables of the students, there is also the personality of the clown conducting the lessons that has to be considered. As previously mentioned, clowns recite themselves and differ from each other, so even during the courses they express themselves in a very personal way, even though following a common path in the course.

The final evaluations of the students show that the *sympathy* and the *proximity* perceived differ depending on the clown that leads the group and depending on the students.

The work with the conducting clown is based on interaction, just us the work with a psychotherapist, and this interaction can't be planned and controlled. Another fundamental variable is the duration of the course: the shorter it is, the less obvious are the differences between test and re-test.

Despite all the difficulties that make our research "spurious", we dare to claim that a training in clowning changes the representation that the subjects have of themselves in a very fast way.

We would like to report only a few examples of the results obtained from the different tests and samples.

The first research was conducted with a sample of nine preschool teachers (aged 21–56 years, mean age 38 years) and a control group of nine teachers from another school that did not follow the course (the age of teachers ranged from 23 to 52 years, mean age 38).

Of particular interest are the results of the ACL test, which show that the self image of the subjects that participated in the course improves: the number of favourable adjectives chosen to describe oneself increases significantly comparing the results of the test submitted before the beginning of the course and at the end. After calculating various nonparametric tests, some significant differences were found in different scales, including those related to the ability to take care, the need to associate with others and the desire to improve psychologically. In the control group, no significant differences were found between the two measurements (Farneti & Palloni, 2010).

A second research was conducted with a sample of 11 subjects (10 females, 1 male) who work in hospitals as nurses or social-health-workers. The average age of the subjects is 41 years. The control group consists of 10 nurses from the same hospital who did not participate in the training (mean age: 45 years). In this sample (Farneti & Tschiesner, 2014a, 2014b), the results concerning emotional intelligence changed significantly on the scale of emotional self-awareness, using the Wilcoxon test. This implies that after the experience of clowning the participants are more able to describe, discriminate and understand the origin of their emotions and to express feelings in a verbal and nonverbal way.

Furthermore, many of the scales of the two tests show a strong tendency towards positive change even if the difference is not statistically significant due to the great variability of the samples.

The test of shame yielded contradictory results: in some subjects the sense of shame diminished significantly while it increased in others. This result is difficult to interpret; we hypothesised that in some cases shame increases due to a greater awareness of one's own defects and limits, while in others the possibility of "shaming oneself" helps to overcome the fear of exposure. Once again the individual differences and the many intervening variables make it difficult to draw final conclusions.

In all the samples, however, the comments and reflections of the students are homogeneous, regardless of the different conditions: there is almost total agreement in showing enthusiasm at the end of the path.

The impact on the work environment was so strong that—after a first research funded by the Free University of Bolzano and conducted at the hospital of Bolzano—the hospital asked us to propose it again to another group after a year, financing it entirely.

In the following section we would like to summarise the main observations of the students, drawn from the focus groups and written reports.

How Do the Students Describe the Effects of Clowning? Results of a Qualitative Analysis of Focus Groups

1. **The nonverbal communication of the clown** is a language that reaches everyone, due to the fact that it is universal and allows a more direct communication both with patients and with colleagues, especially in difficult situations occurring in hospital wards.
2. **Elementarity/essentiality of gestures** and body expression in general: in order to be effective, communication needs to cleanse the gestures and expressions of all the "rational" overlaps acquired over time. Returning to childhood expressiveness means rediscovering the "primeval" body that Galimberti (1983) speaks about.

3. **Mirror-neutrality function:** due to the absence of any "judgement", the clown acts as a neutral mirror in communication. Repeating exactly what the person in front is doing is an excellent exercise to acquire this ability.
4. **Unforeseen, open space that allows everything:** the space in which clown exercises are performed—a space far from the plane of reality—turns into a space of playing, where everything is possible. For adults, it is very difficult to act *as if* and to indulge in imagination, as we feel "displaced" and sometimes "in danger". Losing control of rationality and "being stupid" while performing as part of a group is very liberating, even though it is not easy. For this reason, the clown must be very careful not to force anyone to do what he or she does not feel like doing.
5. **Astonishment:** dropping the mask and unleashing infantile parts of the self conveys a sense of lightness that transforms our thinking about the world: it is the astonishment of the child who sees everything as new and interesting, and it is the astonishment that generates the creative process in adults, transforming everything "into something else" and everyone of us into someone new.
6. **A resource of different emotions:** experiencing the growing intensity of emotions in ad hoc games, mirroring oneself in others, transforming an emotion into a parody, allows us to understand the complex world of emotions and their expression.
7. **An insight that often accompanies the execution of a game or an exercise** (*when there are instants when you are yourself and then, all of a sudden, you are not anymore*): this is about the sudden awareness that comes with playing or doing exercises, something that might seem simple or even infantile, but that—precisely for this reason—creates awareness of our small and hidden parts, which suddenly and unexpectedly appear.
8. **The choice of the costumes** leads us to see our own clownish parts: wearing a costume chosen to express the comical aspects of the person, both physical and psychological, is an important moment because it is the concrete expression of the clownish part. Being a choice of the whole group and the result of the approval or disap-

proval of others, this moment almost turns into an "initiatory ritual" in which someone chooses his "uniform" to show and represent in a playful way the hidden and often denied parts of oneself. The costume ought to accentuate the defects and be perceived as a second skin by the wearer.

9. **Discovering parts that improve communication**: many students have emphasised the fact that the discovery of childish parts and the possibility of highlighting them allows a more direct communication with the others participating in the same game.
10. **Changes at work**: these new skills allow the participants, even while working in a hospital ward, to feel ease, to be less demanding towards themselves and others and to accept and forgive mistakes that are not seen as irreparable any more. Three nurses working at the same department also pointed out that it would be important for the entire team of a department to participate in the course, in order to change the emotional atmosphere of a work place. As long as only one of the team members participates, it is very difficult to make others understand this "new way of being". It is interesting to note that the change has effects both on the interaction between colleagues and between employees and patients.
11. **Course limits:** the main disadvantage pointed out by all the participants is the limited duration of the course. Thirty hours are not sufficient to pursue long-lasting goals, even if they cover several months. Many participants expressed the concern that the effects of the course might vanish quickly when returning to the frustrating reality of the work place.
12. **Considerations on the methods of different clowns:** the students noted significant differences between the methodologies used by the different clowns who led the courses. Some were seen as more "instinctive", others as more "technical". Some students said they felt better with one clown, some with the other. All the clowns, however, contributed to the change we described above. We were advised not to alternate two clowns but to make them work for a continuous period, one after the other, in order to avoid dissonance and to have enough time to elaborate both the relational aspects and the contents.

Conclusions

Unfortunately, there are no data on this topic to date, which is the reason why we can't place our findings into an empirical context.

In conclusion, we came to believe that training through clowning techniques is able to elicit positive effects in all the situations where it is necessary to modify the image of the self, often put to the test by difficult and/or competitive working environments. Many of the group representatives and doctors pointed out that all those working at a hospital should take these courses, underlining the extraordinary effects on the working atmosphere of the hospital departments.

The desire to play and laugh together, including colleagues and patients, made the work much more pleasant and improved the quality of service.

These changes in the workplace environment improve daily work and well-being. As a consequence, they have a positive impact not only on those who participated in the training, but also on people interacting with them on a daily basis.

What we do not know is how long the effects last. Follow-ups—which would be necessary—are difficult to obtain in environments such as schools or hospitals. Unfortunately, the long-term effects of training are a problem also in other fields. We hope that the experience of clowning might contribute to the capacity to look at oneself and others in a more benevolent way, despite or perhaps precisely because of our flaws and imperfections.

> The psychological risks associated with the values dominating our society have been highlighted by many authors: excessive competitiveness, ideals of megalomania, individualism, narcissism and consequent need for self-affirmation at the expense of others, exploitation of subjects, interpersonal conflicts, lack of listening and poor emotional intelligence are recurring topics in sociology, pedagogy, psychology and psychiatry... (Farneti, 2013, p. 11)

If our courses are a way of contributing—even on a small scale—to the desire to play and laugh like children, discovering a healthy self-deprecating stupidity and feeling united by frailty and transience (Freud, 1915), which makes us more similar than different, then we might contribute at least a bit to help bearing the "effort of living".

References

Adams, H. (1998). *Visite a domicilio* [House calls]. Milano, Italy: Apogeo.
Adams, H. (2002). Humour and love: The origination of clown therapy. *Postgraduate Medical Journal, 78*, 447–448.
Agosti, V. (2005). *La figura del clown. Metafora della condizione umana* [The figure of the clown. Metaphor of the human condition]. Firenze, Italy: Atheneum.
Bala, M. (2010). The clown: An archetypal self-journey. *Jung Journal: Culture & Psyche, 4*(1), 50–71.
Battacchi, M. W. (2002). *Vergogna e senso di colpa in psicologia e nella letteratura* [Shame and guilt in psychology and literature]. Bologna, Il Mulino: Cortina Raffaello.
Battacchi, M. W., & Codispoti, O. (1992). *La vergogna* [The shame]. Bologna, Il Mulino: Cortina Raffaello.
Battacchi, M. W., Codispoti, O., Marano, G., & Codispoti, M. (2001). Per la valutazione della suscettibilità alla vergogna e al senso di colpa: la scala SSCV [For the assessment of susceptibility to shame and guilt: The SSCV scale]. *Bollettino di Psicologia, Applicata, 233*, 19–31.
Battistelli, P. (Ed.). (1995). *Io penso che tu pensi. Le origini della comprensione della mente* [I think you think... The origins of the understanding of the mind]. Milano, Italy: Franco Angeli.
Boadella, D., & Liss, J. (1986). La psicoterapia del corpo: le nuove frontiere tra corpo e mente. Astrolabio.
Boria, C. (2011). *Psicoterapia psicodrammatica* [Psychodrama psychotherapy]. Milano, Italy: Franco Angeli.
Cappa, F. (2016). *Formazione come teatro* [Training as a theatre]. Milano, Italy: Raffaello Cortina.
Caterina, R. (2005). *Che cosa sono le arti-terapie* [What are the arts-therapies?]. Roma, Italy: Carocci.
De Marinis, M. (1980). *Mimo e mimi. Parole e immagini per un genere teatrale del Novecento* [Mime and mimes. Words and images for a twentieth century theatrical genius]. Firenze, Italy: La Casa Usher.

De Marinis, M. (1993). *Mimo e teatro nel Novecento* [Mime and theatre in the twentieth century]. Firenze, Italy: La Casa Usher.

Faenza, V. (2005). *L'arte di curare con l'arte*. Rimini, Italy: Guaraldi.

Farneti, A. (2004). *La maschera più piccola del mondo. Aspetti psicologici della clownerie* [The smallest mask in the world. Psychological aspects of clowning]. Bologna, Italy: Perdisa. ISBN 88-8372-217-5.

Farneti, A. (2010). Pagliacci a scuola. Principi educativi e metodi di intervento [Clowns at school. Educational principles and methods of intervention. *Psychology and School*]. *Psicologia e Scuola, 1–2*, 50–57.

Farneti, A. (Ed.). (2013). *Scarpe gialle per girare il mondo a testa in giù. Il clown al servizio della persona: una nuova figura professionale* [Yellow shoes to turn the world upside down. The clown at the service of the person: A new professional figure]. Padova, Italy: Libreria Universitaria.

Farneti, A., & Palloni, F. (2010). Clowning: The effects on self image and interpersonal relationships in nursery schools. *Procedia—Social and Behavioral Sciences Journal, 5*, 23–27.

Farneti, A., & Tschiesner, R. (2012). La metafora del clown, dall'arte alla psicologia. Il "saltimbanco delle emozioni". In A. Farneti & I. Riccioni (Eds.), *Arte, Psiche e Società* (Art, psyche and society) (pp. 171–190). Roma, Italy: Carocci.

Farneti, A., & Tschiesner, R. (2014a). *La clownerie come strumento di formazione per gli infermieri* [Clowning as a training tool for nurses]. Bressanone, Italy: Weger.

Farneti, A., & Tschiesner, R. (2014b). Il clown al servizio della persona: Una nuova figura professionale. In A. Dionigi & P. Gremingni (Eds.), *La clownterapia* (pp. 63–86). Roma, Italy: Carocci.

Farneti, P., & Carlini, M. G. (1981). *Il ruolo del corpo nello sviluppo psichico* [The role of the body in psychic development]. Torino, Italy: Loescher Editore.

Fellini, F. (1970). *I clowns*. Bologna, Italy: Cappelli.

Fo, D. (1987). *Manuale minimo dell'attore* [Actor's minimum manual]. Torino, Italy: Einuadi.

Fonseca, J. (2012). *Lo psicodramma contemporaneo* [Contemporary psychodrama]. Milano, Italy: Franco Angeli.

Franco, M., & Tappatà, L. (2009). *Emotional quotient inventory*. Firenze, Italy: Giunti O.S.

Freud, S. (1915). Caducità [Caducity]. In S. Freud (Ed.), *Freud Opere* (Vol. 8, pp. 173–176). Torino, Italy: Boringhieri.

Galante Garrone, A. (1980). *Alla ricerca del proprio clown* [In search of your own clown]. Firenze, Italy: La Casa Usher.

Galimberti, U. (1983). *Il corpo* [The body]. Milano, Italy: Feltrinelli.
Giuggioli, M. (2001). *Capriole fra le stelle. La favola dei Barabba's Clowns* [Capriolas among the stars. The fable of the Barabba's Clowns]. Varese, Italy: Editrice Monti.
Gough, H.-G. (1979). A creative personality scale for The Adjective Check List. *Journal of Personality and Social Psychology, 37,* 1398–1405.
Jung, C. G. (1934). Psicologia della figura del briccone [Psychology of the rascal figure]. In C. G. Jung (Ed.), *Opere* (Vol. IX, pp. 247–257). Torino, Italy: Bollati Boringhieri.
Lecoq, J. (2000). *Il corpo poetico* [The poetic body]. Milano, Italy: Ubulibri.
Lewis, P., & Johnson, R. (Eds.). (2000). *Current approaches in drama therapy.* Springfield, IL: Charles C Thomas Publisher.
Lucchese, D. (1992). *Guida allo scoring del Test* [ACL Adjective Check List]. Firenze, Italy: Organizzazioni Speciali, Giunti.
Mordiglia, P. (1999). *Randagi* [Strays]. Milano, Italy: Ed ADN Kronos.
Mussoni, L. (2003). *Miloud. Il volto non comune di un clown* [Miloud: The uncommon face of a clown]. Rimini, Italy: Fara Editore.
Orioli, W. (2007). *Teatroterapia* [Theatre]. Trento, Italy: Erickson.
Rivaroli, A. (2006). *Buongiorno, buonasera, ti voglio bene* [Good morning, good evening, I love you]. Milano, Italy: Fabbri.
Sallèe, A., & Fabbri, J. (1984). *Arte del clown* [Clown art]. Roma, Italy: Gremese.
Sanguigno, G. (2001). Un gioco molto antico [A very ancient game]. In A. Farneti (Ed.), *Psicologia in gioco: modelli ludici per la formazione degli educatori* (pp. 73–76). Bologna, Italy: Clueb.
Sanguigno, G. (2004). *Il corpo che ride* [The body that laughs]. Milano, Italy: Xenia.
Shilder, P. (1973). *Immagine di sé e schema corporeo* [Self-image and body schema]. Milano, Italy: Franco Angeli.
Singer, D. G., & Singer, J. L. (1995). *Nel regno del possibile* [In the realm of the possible]. Firenze, Italy: Giunti.
Starobinski, J. (1984). *Ritratto dell'artista da saltimbanco* [Portrait of the artist from Saltimbanco]. Torino, Italy: Bollati Boringhieri.
Viganò, A. (1985). *Nasi rossi, il clown tra circo e teatro* [Red noses, the clown between circus and theatre]. Lecce, Italy: Editore Del Grifo.

12

The Reflexive Practitioner; Using Arts-Based Methods and Research for Professional Development

Cecilie Meltzer

Introduction

Knowledge and new competencies need to be developed in education and training to ensure that the future social, cultural, economic and technological requirements of workplaces, organisations, homes and leisure can be met (NOU, 2015). The development of this knowledge and new competencies will require teachers and learners to be empowered. They, through this, will be able to contribute to local, national and global sustainable development, today and into the future. This requirement to develop skills for the future calls attention to the need to renew subjects and competencies at all levels in education. An essential element of this is the creation of learning environments in which we move from the inner places we normally operate within, towards a place where we can access the emerging future (Scharmer & Käufer, 2013 as cited in Darsø & Meltzer, 2020).

C. Meltzer (✉)
Oslo Metropolitan University, Oslo, Norway
e-mail: cecilie.meltzer@oslomet.no

Teachers that are sensitive to their own and to individual and group needs for learning and reflection are essential in teaching. Taylor defines reflective practice as "the skill of consciously learning how to get better at how you interact with other people" (Taylor, 2015, p. 10). An understanding of this interaction is reflected by teachers who, as reflectional-practitioners, support learners in their personal development. Educators are leaders and must, therefore, begin with themselves, look into their practices and ways of being and sense how they can create conditions for learning that will ensure sustainable social change (Scharmer in Schuyler, Baugher, & Jironet, 2016). These perspectives coincide with Childs' suggestions that "becoming reflective practitioners involves a process of on-going critical reflection and self-study, involving an in-depth look at our experiences and ourselves" (Childs, 2005, p. 143).

Arts-based methodological approaches are still relatively unknown in the educational system. So are the contributions these approaches can make to the development of the required new competencies and shifts in our ways of thinking. This chapter seeks to contribute to the closure of this gap by exemplifying how a teacher, in an ordinary classroom setting at a university, can include creative approaches into subject-specific topics. The ability of arts-based methodologies to enhance reflexivity and resilience and stimulate professional growth in facilitators and learners is no longer questioned (Antonacopoulou, 2018; Darsø, 2004). The question that remains is today solely how they should be applied. Two main issues are addressed by the question of how: (1) how the use of arts-based approaches can increase awareness of self and others, and (2) how dialogue and reflective writing combined with pictorial illustrations can enhance reflexivity.

The theoretical section of this chapter provides a brief outline of being a reflective practitioner and how this relates to arts-based action research. A description of how art-historians, arts-therapists and practitioners of arts-based approaches work to reach a deeper understanding of creative processes and artefacts is then laid out. This is followed by examples from teaching sessions at the Institute of Vocational Education (IVE) at Oslo Metropolitan University[1] (OsloMet). Four practical cases are presented

---

[1] Previously Oslo and Akershus University College (OAUC).

to show how this approach to learning can enhance teachers' and students' ability to reflect on themselves and their learning process, and so promote the development of four competencies needed in the twenty-first century (Erstad, Amdam, Arnseth, & Silseth, 2014). One competency is subject specific. The other three are transdisciplinary and are the ability (1) to learn, (2) to communicate, interact and participate and (3) to explore and create. The empirical material is derived from students' journals and reflective writing, classroom dialogue during the term and the feedback shared at the end of the year. Photos from classroom sessions were also used to verify parts of the groups' processes, their interactions and the created results. The discussion draws attention to the key role of reflexivity for teachers and the importance of the arts to support such reflexivity before the chapter's conclusion.

Theoretical Frameworks

The Reflective Practitioner and Arts-Based Action Research

Practitioners' knowledge is, according to Schön (1991), based on *knowing-in-action*, *reflection-in-action* and *reflection-on-action*. Knowing-in-action refers to their everyday routines of action. Reflection-in-action, however, signifies thinking about what they are doing while doing it. The later reflection-on-action, looking back and seeking to understand what was done, may lead to discoveries that in turn can lead to new actions that reframe previous problems. The situation, therefore "comes to be understood through the attempt to change it; and changed through the attempt to understand it" (Schön, 1991, p. 132).

Arts-based action research is described as being the merging of arts with the more traditional qualitative research methodologies. It is referred to as "the use of the arts, in various forms, as the basis for inquiry, interventions, knowledge production and/or information sharing" (Wilson & Flicker, 2014, p. 58). Arts-based action researchers, according to Leavy, speak from the heart of their relationship with their work and sculpt tools that open a more holistic, integrated perspective, "a space within research where passion and rigor boldly intersect out in the open" (Leavy, 2009, p. 1). These researchers are therefore not *discovering* new research tools, but are *carving* them. She suggests that arts-based research practices, and their attentiveness to *process* and emphasis on *meaning* and *doing*, are particularly useful in projects that seek to *describe*, *explore* or *discover*.

Arts-Based Methods, Visual Analysis and Understanding of Objects and Artefacts

Arts-based methods draw on a wide range of artistic mediums including the performing arts and representational forms. Bamford (2006) distinguishes between education *in* the arts and education *through* the arts. Austring and Sørensen (2010) go deeper into the matter and describe five ways in which art can be used in education. These range from the point at which creating art and aesthetics is a goal in itself, to using it as a learning tool, as an instrument for personal development, and as a source of life zest or as part of a socialisation. All these artistic methodologies intersect in arts-based approaches as they interconnect rather than exclude each other.

According to Riedel (1993), all symbolic expressions contain elements of longing, memories and utopia. Artworks are also representations of our living world, conveying multiple messages and providing broader perspectives to questions and ideas. This applies to both images that have occurred spontaneously and those created from an aesthetic consciousness.

The process of reaching a deeper understanding of an artwork or object involves several stages. These phases vary with the practitioner's professional background, focus, interest and goal. They vary not just with the theme in question or the symbols used, but also with the creator's choice of tools to express colour, shape and structure of space, and how these are used to create a specific composition.

The early stages of an art-historian's approach to works of art or architecture coincide with the methods used by practitioners of arts-based approaches and arts-therapy. The overall imprint of images or artefacts is studied objectively and without interpretation, to increase the observer's understanding and awareness of what is conveyed. The central parts of a painting and use of colours are considered before the nuances. The general features and construction of three-dimensional objects are also viewed before the details.

The arts-based or art-therapeutic approaches partly deviate from the visual analysis of art-historians. Practitioners of arts-therapy and arts-based learning, instead of delving into the historical background or an artist's psychological reasons for creating artwork, seek to reach an understanding of the symbolic value of the artefact to the creator. This may involve different forms of self-experience and artistic expression in performing arts (i.e., music, drama and performance) or in representational forms (i.e., drawing, painting, sculpting, creative writing) being used by the artist to discover new aspects of self.

The use of art-therapy and arts-based approaches, despite their methodological similarities, differ in focus, participants and the arenas in which these approaches are used. Art-therapeutic approaches are used in parts of healthcare for their therapeutic, restorative and empowering qualities. Arts-based approaches, which were inspired by the methods used in art-therapy, address a far wider group of participants such as pupils, students, managers, leaders and employees in schools, workplaces and organisations. The methods also involve personal development. They do not, however, intend to go deep into an individual's background and life history. They instead aim to cultivate personal and group development and creativity and emphasises the experience of creative processes, experimentation, developing skills and discovering new perspectives of self, a subject or theme (Darsø & Meltzer, 2020; Taylor & Ladkin, 2009).

Both approaches seek, however, to understand the reason behind the initiative to act and to examine experiences from the creative process. They also seek to understand how the subconscious material inherent in the artefact can give new insights to the themes in question and so cause a change in how individuals or groups solve perceived challenges in life and working life.

Betensky's phenomenological perspective (1995), which suggests how a deeper understanding of the tacit meaning in artworks can be reached, is central to this. She explains how the maker can identify with the artefact or object, sensing and fantasising what it is like to be part of it. The compositional elements mentioned earlier are studied but are now *seen with the intention* to clarify how the product may symbolically reflect the inner psychology of the creator and reveal new facets of self. These images, as symbols, come to represent the "tacit knowledge we hold in our bodies and at the edge of our unconscious, finding expression through feelings and non verbal forms of communication" (Grisoni, 2012, p. 14). Equally, deeper sensuous knowing can be reached through arts-based inquiry, where a chosen part or symbol may speak for itself, lending the voice of the spectator or creator (Meltzer, 2018). The following text will demonstrate how a reflective practice combined with arts-based approaches can be used to reach new places of knowing.

The Use of Arts-Based Approaches at the Institute of Vocational Education (IVE) at Oslo Metropolitan University (OsloMet)

Essential Frameworks to Enhance Reflexivity

The IVE students at OsloMet carry out developmental projects at their workplaces or in their work placements at schools, as part of their training and usually in groups. In 2014–2015, fifty-four students, divided into two different groups, took part in a one-day arts-based learning sessions. These students have different occupational backgrounds and work experiences and were now training to be teachers in vocational education. They often convey, at the start of this work on campus, ambivalent feelings, uncertainty around collaborating with fellow students and around agreeing on a joint project. The teacher should, at this point, assist them and help them to establish a sense of trust and security in one another before starting the group project.

Different arts-based approaches are used to reach this goal, students being challenged to explore, marvel, use their imagination and reflect on their experiences. This includes the selection of an animal figure as a representation of themselves, the creation of joint drawings and the sculpting of vessels from household waste. The students need to be prepared and motivated to engage, explore and reflect on perceived challenges through the arts. It is therefore worthwhile reminding them that the learning of something new requires a willingness to step out of their comfort zone. Emphasising and discussing this pedagogical perspective, however, usually generates the curiosity and courage needed for them to become involved in this way of learning. A further important factor in achieving this is including time for sharing and reflection in pairs, groups and plenum. These breaks also provide time and space for clarifying questions or uncertainties.

Sensing Oneself as an Animal

Using animal figures[2] to examine the relationship between individuals in a group is particularly compelling. The close connection between humans and other creatures and that all of us, in one way or other, relate to animals is one reason for this. We relate through this to encounters with animals in the real world, in our dreams and our fantasies and we recall fables, legends and folktales told in our childhood that describe the different character traits. Animals are also widely used as idioms in sayings to describe feelings or situations. Examples include "the elephant in the room", "letting the cat out of the bag" or "getting the lion's share". Animal qualities are also attributed to humans through idioms such as *copy-cat*, *pig-headed*, *loyal as a dog* or *silly as a goose*.

The students are therefore asked in the classroom setting to choose an animal that they identify with and that reflects how they feel at the start of the developmental project. Do they see and sense themselves as being a mouse or a rabbit, a horse, or maybe a kangaroo? They then pick out an animal figure and then study them in pairs, sharing with each other their knowledge of the animal from actual life. They use their imagination to project-specific qualities onto the animal figures and are attentive to how their descriptions might reflect themselves and their ways of being. They are also encouraged to be mindful of the qualities they project onto the

---

[2] I refer in this text to all the figures as animals, whether they are reptiles, wild, domestic, fantasy or prehistoric animals, birds or insects, fish or other water creatures.

animal figures, maybe through this discovering tacit resources and assets that might be beneficial in the work they are about to take part in.

Establishing Working Groups

The students are then invited to take part in a collaborative venture in which the figures are used to establish smaller groups. Four or five animals they feel can function well together are brought into a group. The students, in this process, share their opinions, make suggestions and jointly decide which animals might see each other as prey or equals in real life. They discuss which animals can fend for themselves and which have similar dominance and strength. Groups are formed based on the students' sense of parity between animal figures. The students are also to ensure that no one, as far as possible, feels vulnerable, trapped or afraid of being "eaten". Meat-eating animal figures are separated from the plant-eaters. Small rodent animal figures such as mice, rabbits and beavers come together in one group, lions, tigers and other predators in another. This process may take some time and require some discussion. The students, however, after reaching a collective agreement, group with their "animal" partners.

It can prove to be challenging to orchestrate the groups and safeguard all animals. Some animals can be the odd one out and have problems finding equals. They can be from a different continent than the animals in the groups already established or be from prehistory or the fantasy world. Authority that is perceived to be uneven can be an unintentional result of group composition. There is, therefore, a need to think creatively to ensure that animals have an escape route, for example, through envisioning that they can dive into the water or climb a tree if they feel threatened by meat-eating animals.

Creating a Joint Project

The students submit a joint paper at the end of term that presents the group developmental projects. The process of writing the paper often starts with establishing and defining a common topic, outlining the structure and delegating responsibility for the different text sections to group members. At the point where they need weave the text parts together and create a coherent report, they need to let go of ownership of their part of the text and become more deeply involved in the other group members' ideas and contributions.

Creating joint drawings is a good way of demonstrating the challenges involved in creating a collaborative text. I used this arts-based approach to give group participants' their first experience of working together. The group is asked to create a drawing without written text or recognisable figures and that they instead express themselves solely through lines, shapes and colours. This challenges them to draw as toddlers, creating spontaneous expressions of their emotions and sensations rather than describing them through familiar symbols and signs. This instruction challenges them to be aware of and examine their sensed experiences and the difference that altering the nuance, density or clarity of colour, varying the width, length or direction of a line or exploring the size and layout of a form can have.

They are encouraged to work in silence and be observant of their own as well as each other's actions. This methodological approach is used to enhance their inward focus and to give them the opportunity to sense to what extent they can create a space for themselves and equally be attentive to the needs of others. The sheets of paper should not be too large. Constraining the paper area may speed up the process at the point at which they need to unify their expression and co-create a single-piece result. Limited space can intensify the need to cross over into other sections and become involved in each other's work.

Examining Their Role in the Group

Each group then builds a vessel from different types of household waste, such as wrapping paper or empty cans. Using household waste reduces performance anxiety, the low value of the materials making it clear that the result does not need to be a work of art. The focus is, instead, on taking part in the creation of a three-dimensional sculpture and finding their animals' position on-board.

In the dialogue that takes place after they have created the vessel, they share their experiences of the process and clarify their expectations of each other. Expressing thoughts and feelings from the process may increase their awareness of habitual patterns of behaviour, what they experienced in the creation of the vessel, their involvement in the work and whether they instead stood back and left it to others.

Students create a visual illustration of their perceived roles in group work through positioning their animal figures on the vessel. Their reflection upon the initial positioning of their animal figures can also indicate the role they are prepared to play and the commitment they are prepared give to the developmental project. Questions asked at this point can include whether they see themselves as a *captain*, an *officer*, a *deckhand*, a *fellow passenger* or a *dodger* in the work they are about to begin. This provides a more indirect and playful way to study possible challenges in their group interaction. Their identification with an animal and their reflecting upon, through their placement on-board, the roles they are prepared to take, may open a new scope of opportunities. Drawing attention to the original positioning of animal figures may motivate them to move them, and thereby test whether this symbolic act clarifies their intentions or whether it challenges them to take on different roles in the group work.

Documenting the Process

Group collaboration and communication can be perceived as being complex in classroom settings of 20–40 participants. This can make it difficult for the teacher to gain an overview and to recognise and fully understand the subtle interactions that take place at the individual or group level. It can, therefore, be useful to use a camera to gain additional information on processes and group collaboration and to document moments of interaction and the creative results. These photos, however, cannot be considered to be visual "proof" as the person who reviews and analyses an image may impose their meanings onto the work, projecting or transferring their beliefs, impressions, ideas and feelings onto it. It is therefore important to remember that those who created the artefact are the ones that "own" the image and can determine what it means.

Still, snapshots of group work can provide valuable insights and provide thought-provoking material that can help verify the unfolding group processes even if they only capture a particular moment in time and do not document every move, incident or interaction that takes place. They can, when combined with students' log notes and reflective writing, enhance reflexivity. The snapshots can also be used at later gatherings to invite students to become involved in additional exchanges, to recall what happened and to reflect upon the process. Such feedback may again result in a readjustment of the content or focus of later teaching sessions.

Four practical cases will be shared in the following descriptions. The students' responses have been categorised and analysed based on what appeared to be the most obvious consequences of these specific approaches. Cases 1 and 3 retell two participants' encounters and their reflections from taking part in these activities. Cases 2 and 4 describe how photographs of group interaction and created results were used to support a teacher's reflections in- and on-action.

Results

The material presented in the following is taken from two classroom settings at IVE at OsloMet. Arts-based approaches were used in these classes at the beginning of a term to help initiate the students' developmental projects. At this start-up stage of the project work, there is a need to clarify individual resources and potential and to establish groups. Thoughts, ideas and wishes were therefore aired in each group, to find a joint problem formulation that all in the group could agree to.

Case 1: Using an Animal Figure for Self-reflection
Several of the students, in their reflective writings shared at the end of term, refer to seeing themselves through the lens of an animal as an important reference point. They, though this, review and assess their experiences, sharing what it was like to be, for example, the "dog" or "tiger" in the group. A participant describes, in this case, how her choice of animal moved her and made her more thoughtful. She shares how the exercise affected her self-perception and gave rise to thoughts about her

role in the group and about how she might be perceived in later education or work situations.

The participant chose an elephant as the symbol of her role in the group. She shares some of her thoughts about this choice in her text:

> At first, it surprised me that I picked this large and heavy animal. I was sure I would take a leopard, as I perceive myself as a fast and efficient person. Instead, I find myself holding an elephant in my hands. What did this tell me, and why did this animal appear?

She, furthermore, ponders her choice:

> An elephant is an animal that takes good care of its family. It doesn't hurry and has a firm grounded position. I can see these qualities in myself. They represent assets I would like to uphold after I graduate. I have learned a lot about myself in these years at university. To be considered as a good teacher, colleague and partner, I must come forth as a steadfast and solid person.

She contemplates how her attentiveness of her inner "elephant" increased her awareness of her role in the group project:

> As a human being, I normally like to work fast and purposefully without looking back. I, however, tried in this group project to stress down. I see myself as a minor control freak and feel that picking up an elephant made a point. If I am going to develop as a person on this course, I must take softer steps and take care of myself and the people around me. I might then become the teacher I want to be.

She speculates on how colleagues and pupils might perceive her as a teacher. As a stable, professional and consistent person, committed and caring? She also considers whether the elephant might suggest that she could be seen as being too slow and burdensome in a classroom setting, acknowledging the need to remain mindful of her way of being.

She furthermore gives thought to society's need for reliable teachers that see pupils as individuals and who are aware of the need to create safe and enjoyable classroom environments:

These pupils and the good relationships and experiences these environments foster, will in their future lives have a strong foundation on which to build positive relationships with fellow higher level students and workplace colleagues, so leaving a constructive trail of footprints through the arenas they move through.

She continues her line of thought, suggesting that future colleagues may find in her a reliable and collaborative sparring partner. Positive alliances may, furthermore, result in good working environments, which can, in turn, reduce staff sickness leave and thereby have an effect upon a school's reputation. She furthermore envisions the same effect in a company.

Case 2: Reflexivity Through the Lens of a Camera

Photos are presented in the following as sources of reflection. They can also demonstrate how snapshots from the classroom can provide additional information about classroom activity, and that this information may cause changes in future teaching. The images are first studied objectively and without interpretation, visually describing *what is seen*. The photographs are then used as sources for reflection and to reach an understanding of the nonverbal interaction that took place in the groups.

The groups were formed by bringing together well suited animals. Photos taken when the groups were creating joint drawings, revealed striking differences in participants' body language and their level of energy. The same differences in vigour and zest could be seen in their final drawings.

One group (Fig. 12.1) was of students who had chosen large and wild animals that were able to fend for themselves. Most of these animals were meat-eaters. The participants are all standing, bending over the sheet. Their attention is focused, at this point, on completing the drawing and making it "whole". Their final drawing (Fig. 12.2) is filled with bright and vibrant colours. There are no bare patches.

The snapshot (Fig. 12.1) gives the impression of five rivalling individuals, competing for their place on the paper. The outburst of energy and eagerness seems to be high, and they appear unaware of others' possible

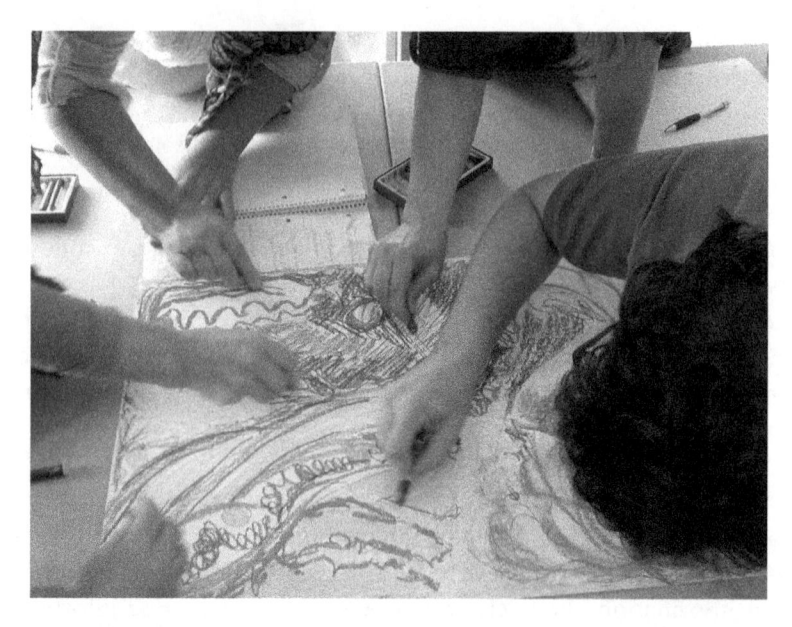

Fig. 12.1 'Predatory animals' competing for space

Fig. 12.2 A vibrant, coloured drawing expressing energy and zest

"ownership" of parts of the drawing. The lines in their drawing (Fig. 12.2) come forth as firm, and the forms are defined. Some parts have a second layer of colour, intensifying the impression of vitality, enthusiasm and liveliness.

A second photo (Fig. 12.3) contrasts the first. The participants of this group had chosen wild or tame hoofed animals. All in this group are seated. Some are leaning backwards, waiting and watching the others. Their final composition (Fig. 12.4) consists of several round forms of different sizes and of bands of circles. There are a lot of white areas and no double layers of colouring.

The snapshot of this group at work (Fig. 12.3) shows a more attentive setting, the participants conveying considerable sensitivity towards one another, seemingly taking turns to produce new marks on the paper. The photo indicates that they respect each other's parts of the drawing, joining forces and working together to strengthen each other's forms. Their drawing (Fig. 12.4) comes forth as far *lighter* and *airier* than the result in the first group. The colours are more delicate and subtle.

Fig. 12.3 'Hoofed animals', taking turns to draw on the paper

Fig. 12.4 A harmonious drawing filled with circles

Case 3: Examining Group Work Process

Animal figures are sometimes brought into groups that may be non-compatible in real life, and that may indicate an uneven feel of authority or strength. One student described, in her reflection paper, her experiences of taking part in such a group. The group consisted of three plant-eating and one flesh-eating animal. This alternative solution was chosen because the animals came from the same continent. She, in her log notes, describes feeling a lack of collaboration and common basis for understanding one another when they started creating the "vessel". She shares her initial reactions towards the group, her lack of a sense of security, equality and strength and discusses whether her feeling of unease came as a result of her set way of thinking about whom she knew and preferred to be in a group with.

The group members also represented different professions and cultures. She therefore also considers whether she was discriminatory. She, however, instead of guarding her feeling of intolerance, tries to see how the other participants' vocational or cultural backgrounds might widen her horizon and teach her something new. She reflects upon how her preconceived ideas affect her and cause her to misinterpret their gestures, facial expressions, tone of voice or use of language. She also acknowledges a need to learn more about nonverbal communication. She is aware that this kind of misread might result in wrong and unfair ideas and conceptions in a teacher/pupil relationship or between colleagues in workplaces.

Case 4: Studying One's Role in a Group Project

The photo documentation of two vessels was brought to mind after reading the students' journals and their reflective writing papers submitted at the end of term. They reflected, in their papers, on their experiences of group collaboration. A visual analysis of the vessels and the positions of the animals on board was used to cast light upon why the participants of the first group worked well together and the participants of the second group struggled to collaborate. The photos were studied thoroughly to understand whether the teacher could have intervened at an earlier stage to help the group that struggled. This analysis raises the question of whether their installation displayed their differences and a solution. The photographs are described and analysed in two steps, (1) what is seen, and (2) understanding how their results may portray their experiences.

The first vessel (Fig. 12.5) consisted of four parts, had an open construction and clearly defined sections that indicate the front and rear of the vessel. The four animals are all out in the open and placed so that their heads point in the direction of travel. The two predatory animals (the lion and white tiger) stand together at the rear of the craft. The elephant is positioned in the middle and the penguin higher up at the front, on top of a paper cup. The overall impression gained from this installation is that the participants in this group have a coherent strategy for their group work. The vessel's construction and form is simple but precise. The orientations of the animal figures mirror the direction of travel. Their elevated positions indicate a balance of power between them and that their roles are clarified. They all seem to hold a leadership role, such as "officers" of different ranks.

Figure 12.6 is a photo of the second vessel, which was made by the group that struggled. The vessel consists of many different parts, is fitted

Fig. 12.5 A group already 'on the move', ready to go

Fig. 12.6 A group with plenty of creativity but ambivalent to collaboration

with wheels and has a couple of "masts". A "cloth" is attached to one, indicating a sail. There are two small boxes at one end. The heads of the animals are all turned towards the same side of the vessel. The giraffe is on its feet, the zebra is lying down, the chimpanzee sits on top of the mast with something on its head, and the cheetah is at the rear, inside a box and partially concealed.

The general impression of this installation is more ambiguous and complex. The vessel comes forth as a patchwork of diverse ideas, indicating creativity, opportunities and resources. The overall feeling, however, is that there is no clear and consistent design and form. The positioning of the animals and their orientation does not coincide with the vessel's direction of travel. This may indicate that their roles "on-board" are unclear or undefined. Their postures signal that they do not relate to one another and that they are only coincidently together on the same vessel. The overall impression conveyed by their work at this point supports the feedback from the participants. It visually demonstrates that they had not, at this stage, found a common direction in their work or a way to collaborate.

Discussion

The student in *Case 1* reflected on her learning process. She described her choice of an elephant as "an incredibly useful animal for self-reflection"; this choice activating thoughts that made her more aware of herself and her resources (Meltzer, 2016). This demonstrates how identification with an animal figure may create a *potential space* (Winnicott, 1971); the distance that is needed to see oneself from a meta-perspective. The students were also surprised when her hand took command and picked up an animal that was different from that she initially expected. This act illustrates how entering into a world of pretence and play strengthens communication between the intellect and the body. This is the change of consciousness that is required to discover new perspectives and possibilities (Darsø & Meltzer, 2020).

The visual differences between the group of hoofed animals and the group of meat-eating animals were astounding, as shown in *Case 2*. The differences in bodily expression between the groups can, however, be interpreted in different ways. The students had "seen" through their and the other group members' choice of animal figures that the others possessed a strength that was equal to that they possessed themselves. This might have increased the sense of being well suited to the others, encouraging them to reveal more of themselves than they would without this visual confirmation. The drawing results can be seen as being a confirmation of the well functioning group collaboration.

The students had, by the time the figures were categorised into groups, turned their focus towards the imaginary world and how the different creatures might get on in real life. The student in *Case 3*, in her closing remarks, shared how participation in a non-compatible group took her out of her comfort zone and made her seek out what she could learn from this experience. She sees a parallel between her experience and that of future pupils who are required to collaborate with classmates they do not get on with. This experience encouraged her to be attentive to her feeling of discomfort and to be aware of possible solutions.

Case 4 led to an increased focus on this arts-based way of learning in later classroom gatherings. Groups that consisted of animals with uneven strengths or with positions that portray imbalances in their perception of responsibility were encouraged to reconsider their on-board positioning. They were given a chance to externalise a change by moving their animal figures, so creating a visual and artful solution of their forthcoming collaboration. This alteration coincides with Betensky's views (1995). She highlights how this approach, "offers a micro-world of experience, safe risks, and problems that can be solved, at first on the painting surface or with clay, then in the everyday life". Subsequent manipulation of art materials, to see them in new ways, can lead "to a renewed ability to look at and feel self-among-others in one's own world and in the larger world" (p. 13).

One question that arises from *Case 4* is whether the sense of frustration in groups that feel ill-matched can, at the very start of the group work, be altered by being mindful of and addressing what is seen in the installation. The group, through being attentive of and sharing and reflecting upon collaboration, upon their vessels and the positioning of the animals on board, might discern group resources and ways of working together that can change the initial frustration and feeling of mismatch. A willingness to move their figures can reflect a change in attitude, a belief that a solution is possible. According to Sparrer (2007, p. 323), "the actual change takes place in our attitude towards the world, not in the already existing world". Picturing a positive solution through a new position of their animal figures indicates a move away from the existing towards a new way of being.

Conclusion

This chapter has shown how learning via the arts stimulates and encourages deep learning, communication, exploration and creativity. These are the competencies that will be needed in future schools and workplaces. The photo documentation came to represent symbols. They, therefore, came to imply something more than the obvious and immediate meaning, conveying both the known as well as glimpses of possibilities for an emerging future. The end of term reflective writing combined with the photos acted as a source of reflection, a reflection-on-action through which aspects that might cast light on previous conceived challenges could be discovered.

The processes described in these four cases demonstrate how arts-based approaches that are integrated into an educational setting can stimulate learning processes in specific subjects. They also show that creative processes and aesthetic expression, where used as sources for reflection and self-study, can enhance the transdisciplinary competencies that will be required in the twenty-first century.

References

Antonacopoulou, E. (2018). Sensuous learning: What it is and why it matters in addressing the ineptitude in professional practise. In E. Antonacopoulou & S. Taylor (Eds.), *Sensuous learning for practical judgement in professional practice* (Volume 1: Arts-based methods) (pp. 13–44). Cham, Switzerland: Palgrave Macmillan.

Austring, B. D., & Sørensen, M. (2010). Æstetisk virksomhed i pædagogisk regi. *Dansk Pædagogisk Tidsskrift, 2*, 6–15.

Bamford, A. (2006). *The wow factor: Global research compendium on the impact of the arts in education.* Münster, Germany: Waxmann Verlag.

Betensky, M. G. (1995). *What do you see? Phenomenology of therapeutic art expression.* London, UK: Jessica Kingsley.

Childs, K. (Ed.). (2005). *Just where do I think I'm going?* London, UK/New York, UK: RoutledgeFalmer.

Darsø, L. (2004). *Artful creation: Learning-tales of arts-in-business.* Fredriksberg, Denmark: Samfundslitteratur.

Darsø, L., & Meltzer, C. (2020). Arts-based interventions as a series of methods to access presencing. In O. Gunnlaugson (Ed.), *Presencing Theory U: A book series. Book 2: Individual perspectives on presencing.* Vancouver, BC: Trifoss Business Press, in press.

Erstad, O., Amdam, S., Arnseth, H. C., & Silseth, K. (2014). *Om fremtidens kompetansebehov. En systematisk gjennomgang av internasjonale og nasjonale initiativ* [About the future's competence needs. A systematic review of international and national initiatives]. Oslo, Norway: Universitetet i Oslo

Grisoni, L. (2012). Poem houses: An arts based inquiry into making a transitional artefact to explore shifting understandings and new insights in presentational knowing. *Organizational Aesthetics, 1*(1), 11–25.

Leavy, P. (2009). *Method meets art: Arts-based research practice.* New York, NY: Guilford Press.

Meltzer, C. (2016). Life in Noah's Ark: Using animal figures as an arts-based projective technique in group work to enhance leadership competence. *Organizational Aesthetics, 5*(2), 77–95.

Meltzer, C. (2018). Using arts-based inquiry as a way to communicate creatively in uncovering the future. In E. Antonacopoulou & S. Taylor (Eds.), *Sensuous learning for practical judgement in professional practice* (Volume 1: Arts-based methods) (pp. 139–166). London, UK: Palgrave Macmillan.

NOU. (2015). *The school of the future. Renewal of subjects and competences.* Oslo, Norway: Ministry of Education and Research.

Riedel, I. (1993). *Bildspråket i terapi, konst och religion* [The imagery in therapy, art and religion]. Solna, Sweden: Centrum for Jungiansk Psykologi.

Scharmer, C. O., & Käufer, K. (2013). *Leading from the emerging future. From ego-system to eco-system economies.* San Francisco, CA: Berrett-Koehler Publishers, Inc.

Schön, D. A. (1991). *The reflective practitioner: How professionals think in action.* Aldershot, UK: Arena.

Schuyler, K. G., Baugher, J. E., & Jironet, K. (Eds.). (2016). *Creative social change. Leadership for a healthy world.* Bingly, UK: Emerald.

Sparrer, I. (2007). *Miracle, solution and system. Solution-focused systemic structural constellations for therapy and organisational change.* Cheltenham, UK: Solution Books.

Taylor, S. (2015). *You're a genius: Using reflective practise to master the craft of leadership.* New York, NY: Business Expert Press LLC.

Taylor, S., & Ladkin, D. (2009). Understanding arts-based methods in managerial development. *Academy of Management Learning and Education, 8*(1), 55–69.

Wilson, C., & Flicker, S. (2014). Arts-based action research. In D. Coghlan & M. Brydon-Miller (Eds.), *The SAGE encyclopaedia of action research* (pp. 58–61). London, UK: Sage.

Winnicott, D. W. (1971). *Playing and reality.* London, UK: Tavistock.

13

University Teachers' Professional Identity Work and Emotions in the Context of an Arts-Based Identity Coaching Program

Katja Vähäsantanen, Päivi Kristiina Hökkä, and Susanna Paloniemi

Introduction

Being a teacher is a complex process in the face of changing educational circumstances, as changing educational contexts often challenge teachers' professional role and cause tensions between their professional identity and work (Ruohotie-Lyhty, 2018). In the university context, external changes notably seem to threaten traditional academic values, missions and careers, and to challenge individuals to process their professional values and interests, for example, by moving from teaching towards research (Arvaja, 2018; Ylijoki & Ursin, 2013). In this sense, teachers are asked to undertake continuous identity work aimed at processing a distinct and integrated perception of who they are as professionals in relation to their changing work (Arvaja, 2018; Beijaard, Meijer, & Verloop, 2004).

K. Vähäsantanen (✉) • P. K. Hökkä • S. Paloniemi
University of Jyväskylä, Jyväskylä, Finland
e-mail: katja.vahasantanen@jyu.fi; paivi.hokka@jyu.fi; susanna.paloniemi@jyu.fi

According to Day (2018), teachers need to construct and sustain a meaningful, positive sense of identity to succeed over time as professionals. He also points to the significance of such professional identity for elaborating teachers' efficacy, well-being and resilience at work (see also Vähäsantanen, 2015). All of this implies that teachers' engagement in continuous identity work can produce a meaningful and coherent sense of professional identity that also promotes their resilience and well-being at work.

It is worth noting that identity work is an emotional and challenging process (Winkler, 2018), particularly without socioemotional support. Although some educational practices and arts-based methods exist to support teachers' identity work (e.g., Beltman, Glass, Dinham, Chalk, & Nguyen, 2015; Leitch, 2006), there is a need for empirical evidence of the underlying social and emotional identity processes related to the use of such methods in educational settings. This is essential if we are to understand resilience in adulthood and elaborate how arts-based methods support professional identity work.

Consequently, this study investigated professional identity work and emotions in the context of an arts-based identity coaching program. In line with the current discussion (Chemi & Du, 2017), we recognise the power of arts-based methods as stimulative means for learning, including professional identity work. The participants in this study were experienced university teachers in mature adulthood. The research questions were as follows: (i) *What kinds of emotional experiences emerged regarding arts-based methods during the program?* (ii) *In what ways were emotions part of the professional identity work while using a specific arts-based method called the professional body?* Here, arts-based methods are understood as including artistic forms, such as drawings, drama work and spoken storytelling (Wang, Coemans, Siegesmund, & Hannes, 2017). Since the professional body method was found to support professional identity work (Vähäsantanen, Hökkä, Paloniemi, Herranen, & Eteläpelto, 2017), this study was also aimed at elaborating this arts-based method in depth.

The chapter concludes with a discussion on the different perspectives of using arts-based methods in educational settings and the emotional nature of professional identity work. This chapter suggests that emotions can support and hinder professional identity work, but such identity work can also evoke both pleasant and unpleasant emotions.

Theoretical Viewpoints: Professional Identity Work and Emotions in Arts-Based Frameworks

Professional identity is seen as individuals' historically-based perceptions of themselves as professional actors (Arvaja, 2018; Beijaard et al., 2004). Particularly, it captures individuals' current professional interests, ambitions, values and commitments, their perceptions of meaningful responsibilities at work and their future orientations and dreams (e.g., Vähäsantanen, 2015). In this sense, professional identity is a temporal phenomenon that includes aspects related to an individual's past, present and future.

Owing to various changes that occur in different educational settings, teachers must constantly work on their professional identity in relation to their changing professional responsibilities and work practices, which might challenge their existing identity (Beijaard et al., 2004). This chapter addresses professional identity work among university teachers. Within the different conceptualisations in mind (e.g., Arvaja, 2018; Winkler, 2018), we understand professional identity work as a deep sense-making process. This process is aimed at enabling teachers to (re-) define, craft, maintain or strengthen a distinct perception of who they are as professionals and what is meaningful for them in their work, and negotiate a meaningful relationship between their identity and work. This implies that professional identity work is always an unpredicted and individual process that can result in different outcomes, varying from maintained identity to transformed identity, even in the same work context (Vähäsantanen, 2015). Overall, professional identity work can be seen as a process where an individual processes her/his understanding of oneself as a professional actor. Therefore, professional identity work differs from the more general learning goals and processes that are involved in the development of professional skills and knowledge.

Although individuals must often carry out professional identity work in changing work environments, identity work is not an easy, self-evident process. It is more difficult to redefine and craft the core aspects of one's professional identity (e.g., core professional beliefs, missions and values) than one's work-related activities (Korthagen, 2004). In particular, experienced teachers find it challenging to transform core aspects of their professional identity because they have defined this identity into something specific over a long period of time (Vähäsantanen, 2015). Therefore, individuals in mature adulthood particularly need special support for their professional identity work. In this study, we address professional identity work and emotions during such a life phase.

To explore emotions in identity work, we understand emotions as individuals' subjective experiences that emerge in relation to social events and context, other people and themselves (e.g., individuals' identities) in their professional lives (e.g., Uitto, Jokikokko, & Estola, 2015). This kind of conceptualisation emphasises the sociocultural viewpoint of emotions, including the interpersonal nature of emotions (Zembylas, 2007). Thus, we recognise emotions as emerging from and being constructed in social interaction and context instead of seeing them just as a product of an individual's internal state.

To date, Winkler (2018) has emphasised that emotions can play different roles in identity work: (i) emotions act as triggers for identity work, (ii) identity work is an emotional endeavour, and (iii) emotions emerge as outcomes of (un)successful identity work. This implies that emotions can, for example, boost or hinder identity work. Although we cannot ignore emotions in young teachers' identity work, we could assume that experienced teachers' professional identity work is even more emotional, since their identity work can be considered more challenging than the one of younger teachers, as noted above.

In particular, arts-based methods can offer a rich and fruitful recourse for identity work via enabling individuals to engage in constructing knowledge about themselves. One of their main premises is to enable individuals' conscious, unconscious and borderland experiences to be seen, recognised and elaborated (Leitch, 2006). Arts-based methods seem to offer a way to participate actively and express multiple truths, and the interaction of these truths enables new individual and collective meaning-making. In this meaning-making, the nature of embodied and tacit (non-articulated) knowledge, as opposed to merely discursive knowing, is important (Taylor & Ladkin, 2009). Embodied knowledge goes beyond logical and rational thinking, which traditionally has been defined as knowledge. Embodied knowledge offers a way to surpass the limits of language and become aware of unvoiced and unexpressed emotions and experiences (Leitch, 2006).

Such knowing and knowledge are closely interrelated with emotions. Art itself evokes emotions and thus offers a way to combine embodied knowledge with emotions, thinking and verbalisation. Artistic work also has the power to make identity work visible by offering possibilities for displaying emotions related to bodily stored experiences through externalisations and descriptions of experience. Thus, arts-based methods have the potential to open one up to express and process one's professional identity (Beltman et al., 2015; Chemi & Du, 2017) and perform new actions on the basis of emotions (Chemi & Borup Jensen, 2015).

Methodological Outlines

Arts-Based Identity Coaching Program

The specific aim of the arts-based identity coaching program under study (comprising six workshops offered over a six-month period, each lasting approximately 2.5–3 hours) was to prompt the participants to become aware of, re-explore and process their professional identity in relation to their (changing) work (Vähäsantanen et al., 2017). Consequently, the program aimed to support the participants' well-being and working in the challenging university context. The small group-based program was provided by an experienced coach. Its core was social interaction, as the focus of the coaching was on reflecting and processing one's experiences, perceptions and emotions with the support of other group members and coach in order to process one's professional identity. Although the program aimed to provide an arena for identity work, the participants were seen as active actors; that is, persons whose identity work was the result of their actions rather than the outcome of externally specified aims and forces. Furthermore, the participants were able to decide the nature and extent of their participation during the program.

In the program, several methods and techniques were used to support professional identity work, including drama work, sociometric practices, pair- and group discussions and visual methods, such as individual drawings and narrated, visual storylines. These were used for different purposes. For example, in the first workshop, to become aware and to process one's professional history as part of professional identity, each participant discussed their history with another participant. Furthermore, for these purposes, the participants illustrated the most significant experience for their professional identity development through means of drama work.

In the second and third workshop, one important method used was an archetype exercise that included an archetype test that the participants completed as homework (Pearson, 1991). Carl Jung introduced the concept of archetypes, pointing to universal themes of human existence that are evident in commonly shared storylines and characters in fairy tales, myths, poems and films. Pearson's archetype test assesses the characteristics of 12 different archetypes (e.g., Innocent, Orphan, Warrior, Creator) that are potentially active in a person's present life situation. These archetypes were explored through (i) sociometry to perceive and visualise one's childhood archetype to others, (ii) drama-based exercises to recognise and visualise what kind of an archetype each person is in their current work community and (iii) a group discussion to consider and share what kind of an archetype one would want to be in the future.

Furthermore, a method called professional body was used in the final workshop (see Fig. 13.1; Vähäsantanen et al., 2017). This method combines individual and collective processes of professional identity work. *As an individual process* (a home assignment before the workshop), participants were instructed to draw a professional body on a paper using various materials, such as clippings and drawings. They were able to select these materials by themselves (i.e., they were not provided for them). While personalising and visualising this body, the participants were instructed to address different themes, such as professional history, core commitments and values, and future dreams (see also Mahlakaarto, 2014). Therefore, they were asked to answer questions such as "Where I've come from?", "What are my current values and mission at work?" and "What are my future goals and dreams?". During this individual phase, the participants were not asked to interact, but some participants helped each other to draw their body lines on the paper.

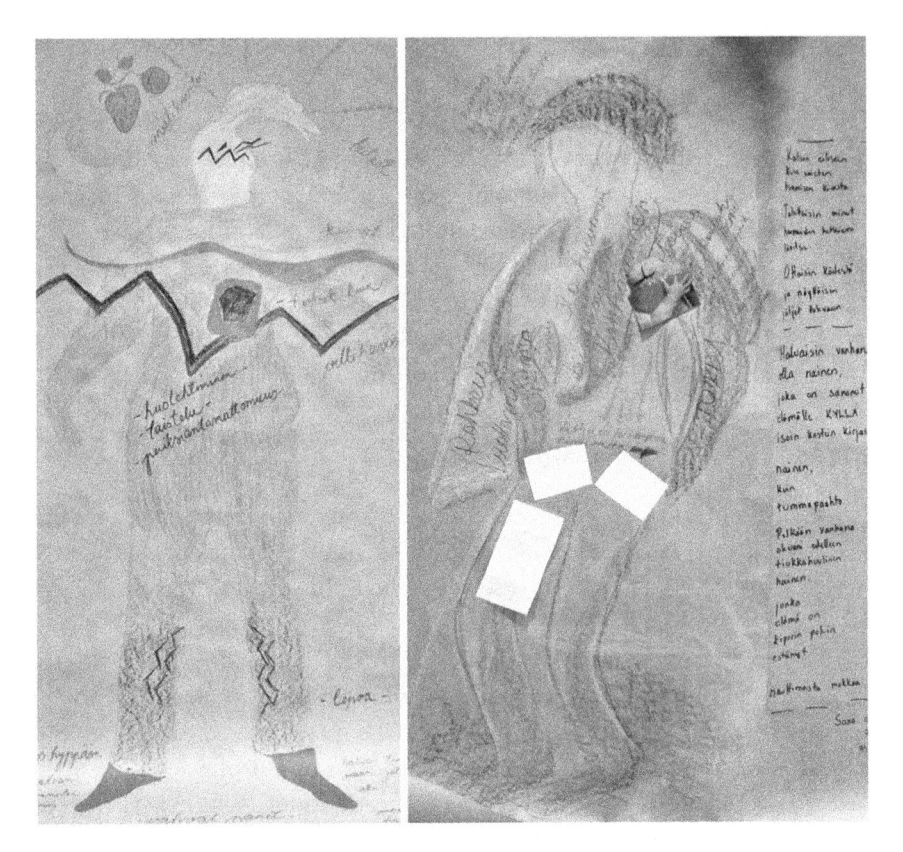

Fig. 13.1 Examples of professional bodies

Afterwards, the completed bodies served as material for a *collective process* in the workshop. First, the participants described the process of creating their professional bodies and shared their experiences. After hanging the drawings of the professional bodies on the walls, the participants were able to comment and ask questions concerning the drawings, followed by the creator's answers. Furthermore, each participant narrated the storyline of their body in more detail, to which the others responded through embodied, drama-based activities (such as the mirror technique) either by using words or silently. The whole process (lasting about an hour in the case of six teachers) was guided by a coach who gave comments, asked questions, and provided the participants with empowering viewpoints.

Participants and Datasets

The participants were six experienced Finnish university teachers who had participated in the program. The average age of these female participants was 51 years (46–57 years). All of them had at least a master's degree in their field, and they had worked in the field for an average of 18 years (16–28 years). While the program was organised for ten university teachers in total, we utilised the research material from six participants, because they were the ones who were able to engage in all data collection phases. In this multimethod study, we utilised the following datasets:

i. Six *professional bodies* that illustrate professional identity from a temporal viewpoint.
ii. *Video recordings* (57 minutes in total) from the workshop where the professional bodies were narrated and processed in the group. In these recordings, each teacher also described the process for producing one's professional body.
iii. Six *post-interviews* (396 minutes in total) were conducted shortly after the program and six *follow-up interviews* (in total 292 minutes) were carried out some years after the program. Both interviews focused in particular on teachers' emotions and professional identity work during the program. They also captured teachers' experiences of the program, including its methods.
iv. Six *stimulated recall interviews* (310 minutes in total) were conducted shortly after the follow-up interviews. In these interviews, each teacher viewed video-recorded episodes of her professional body work in the group and was encouraged to reflect on these episodes after watching them.

Data Analysis

To answer the *first research question*, we applied the principles of narrative analysis (e.g., Lieblich, Tuval-Mashiach, & Zilber, 1998). First, we read the post-interviews and follow-up interviews in their entirety with each teacher. This narrative holistic content reading was aimed at identifying the most meaningful contents of each interview regarding the emotional experiences of arts-based methods. By comparing the similarities and differences between teachers' narrations, it became clear that their emotional experiences of the arts-based methods varied. Overall, we were able to categorise these experiences into three groups. The experiences of each teacher could be placed fairly unambiguously in one of these groups. Second, a single core narrative was created and named for each group so that each narrative formed a coherent and chronological unity. One narrative was constructed by using research material from one teacher, and the two other narratives were based on the interviews of two or three teachers.

To answer the *second research question*, we applied qualitative content analysis (Saldaña, 2013) to analyse all of the datasets. First, we identified all relevant accounts of professional identity work using the professional body, moving from one participant to the next. These accounts were re-read to group them into different categories illustrating professional identity work. Altogether, we identified and named two main categories to illustrate the individual and shared parts of professional identity work. Second, we re-read the accounts of professional identity work to uncover the most common emotions regarding identity work processes.

To follow ethical guidelines, to increase trustworthiness and to decrease the bias of this qualitative study, the participation in the program and in the study was voluntary, the interviews were open-ended so that the participants were able to express their experiences and emotions openly without strict frameworks, the datasets were coded through a collective process, the findings were verified with different datasets, and the participants were able to read the chapter before its publication.

Emotional Experiences of Arts-Based Methods

The findings indicate that the participants' emotional experiences of the program's arts-based methods varied considerably, most notably in the case of drama-based methods. Here, we present three different narratives to demonstrate the different emotions, participation and identity work associated with these methods. It is also worth noting that the participants' accounts of their participation in arts-based working included similar descriptions. All participants felt *safe* and *confident* in the group and were *satisfied* with the considerable opportunities for being heard and seen and for expressing their experiences and thoughts with other people. The group meetings were also full of *joy*, *empathy*, *kindness* and *togetherness*, and such meetings refreshed participants.

Courageous Adventurer

Before the coaching program, the courageous adventurer was interested especially in its thematic contents. The arts-based methods also fascinated her because of her previous experiences and because she perceived herself as a kinaesthetic and embodied person rather than as a rational one.

Through the program, the adventurer was *satisfied* with the methods used. In particular, she *enjoyed* and felt *inspired* by the drama-based methods, as they were useful for working deeply with her identity and other meaningful matters in (working) life at the unconscious, un-cognitive and emotional levels:

> Well, I really liked the drama-based methods; I think they were really good. Somehow, the fact that we don't act on such a conscious level… So, I felt that the unconscious layers of myself began to move and become visible with the help of those methods, that when in the university world we often work so much with reason and consciousness. So, it feels really healthy and good that there's also another layer that moves, other than just the conscious side. I felt that those drama-based methods were really nice. And it was refreshing and fun, but also touching. You get in touch with emotions—your own emotions.

In this sense, the adventurer recognised the arts-based methods as attractive, and she threw herself open-mindedly and sincerely into different exercises with an "adventurous feeling about what's going to happen and what it is that we're going to do". Although she felt positively about the methods, it was not self-evident that she was throwing herself into the coaching processes. Instead, conscious decision framed her participation—additionally, *courage* was strongly present in this decision. Courage was necessary for revealing her weaknesses to others and for jumping into change processes despite being unsure of their course and outcomes:

> When we went through different kinds of situations through the means of drama. Situations that I participated in, you had to think about whether you have the courage or not. So, there was this question of courage, if you have the courage to throw yourself into the situation and what the consequences are. So that you have the courage to clearly decide that, "Oh well, now I'll just go and see what's going to come of it".

In addition to courage, the *confident* and *safe* atmosphere of the group encouraged creativity and throwing oneself into involvement.

The adventurer was extremely *satisfied* with the contents and methods of the program. The methods were empowering and helped her to process her professional identity (through working on and redefining more profoundly what being a researcher means to her), deal with the meaningful matters in her private life and modify her acting in the work community. For example, demonstrating Pearson's archetypes through drama expressions was meaningful to her. In particular, the presence of a strong emotional trace and un-cognitive processes enabled deep and comprehensive learning—including professional identity work—better than ordinary lectures and group discussions did. Several powerful emotions also emerged while seeing others' drama-based exercises. Unpleasant emotions, such as *sorrow* and *irritation*, emerged especially when the adventurer learnt about, for example, the mistreatment of others at work. Such emotional experiences enhanced one's clarity about one's own professional values and facilitated to change one's behaviour at work.

Surprised Experiencer

Before the coaching program, the surprised experiencer had no extensive experience of arts-based methods, including drama methods. She perceived herself strongly as a verbal learner, and she had notably worked in dialogical environments that supported acting at conscious levels. Although she was *suspicious* of unfamiliar arts-based methods, she decided to participate in the program due to its interesting thematic contents.

During the program, the experiencer was not suspicious, reserved and cautious anymore while participating in drama-based methods. Instead, she recognised that she participated actively and threw herself spontaneously into different exercises. She was extremely *surprised* about such participation because she did not see herself as a drama person. Due to this surprise, she was *confused* and reflected on the methods and her unexpected activities. It seems that the experiencer was riveted by unfamiliar drama methods that activated her to participate spontaneously:

> I noticed being amazed that wow, how you act in a way that you can't know in advance, and don't understand afterwards how it went... But it's good to acknowledge that people probably behaved spontaneously in these situations and probably wouldn't have done so if they had thought about it more carefully. At least I felt like that at some point... I was really surprised that I found myself, for example, in that situation, where the coach said that please come here, and I just went and talked about a co-worker openly in a negative way. So, I think I screwed up there a little bit. I was ashamed afterwards, and I was thinking how in this kind of dramatisation you can exceed yourself, go beyond your own limits.

Afterwards, she felt at least some *shame* and *regret* when thinking about situations where she felt that she had revealed too much about work-related matters and persons. Consequently, she thought that she should have been more cautious without throwing herself headlong into coaching: "Yeah, I was annoyed afterwards that I should have been more careful, but I just somehow fell into such situations. I didn't like much myself afterwards". Although the experiencer felt that the drama-based methods, in a sense enticed her to participate without making a clear and conscious decision to do so, she emphasised that she, not the coach, was in charge of her own activities.

Overall, the drama-based methods did not convince the experiencer. After the program, she still felt that such methods did not suit her, although she noted that arts-based methods can lead towards novel expressions that can reveal unconscious matters:

> Those exercises were very captivating. In a way, I did more than I had thought to do. The action swept you away. And then some things came out

which you sometimes should take up. Probably, you could express yourself very differently through the means of drama compared to mere words, like in which position you are or how. Those moves are very meaningful, such as facial expressions and expressions in general.

Although arts-based methods caused some unpleasant emotions, the experiencer was overall quite *satisfied* with the coaching program. The program helped her reflect her core professional interests; consequently, her professional identity as a teacher was strengthened and socially accepted. In particular, she was pleased with the discussion with other participants, as they supported her identity work and brought, for example, *joy* and *empowerment* to her private life.

Cautious Observer

The cautious observer had previous experience of arts-based methods, and she was not convinced of their suitability for her as a learner and a person, since she was not such an artistic and visual person. Instead, she was quite critical and cautious of such methods because she felt that they were not the most suitable method for learning and handling matters.

After the program, the observer felt that discussions with other participants were the best part of the program, whereas arts-based methods, such as drama methods, did not motivate her. The main reason for this was that she did not understand their actual and profound idea and intention:

> Those drama exercises didn't really touch me. I somehow couldn't get into them at all. I couldn't really tune myself into them. Those drama-based things, because I just don't see the point… Like with some movement, you describe something you want to communicate to another person. I just don't understand it at all…

In these kinds of situations, *irritation* and *frustration* also emerged.

Since drama-based methods did not motivate and inspire the observer, they did not provoke her to participate actively and throw herself spontaneously into different exercise processes. Rather, she was mainly reserved and consciously controlled her participation. In particular, she avoided situations where she might get too involved in situations or offend other participants. She also refused to participate in some exercises because they were against her values and ways of acting. For example, she did not want to say something nasty to another person in the drama exercise as she was supposed to. That is, it seemed that the observer made conscious decisions not to participate actively in arts-based exercises. She also mentioned that the safe atmosphere of the group gave her *courage* to refuse to do exercises.

Overall, the arts-based methods did not please the observer because they were outside of her comfort zone. Such methods might have helped her describe previous events in life and work, but did not make it truly possible to gain new inspiration about her (professional) identity:

> I think the drama exercises, they didn't really give me anything. I guess it was interesting to get to know about them, but I didn't find them very useful… It was nice to be able to deal with an earlier event in this drama-based moment. But that it would've advanced something or created some new understanding, that didn't happen.

In this sense, the utilisation of drama-based methods did not provide a very successful learning experience for the observer. However, the other methods—mainly discussions with other participants—provided an arena for reflecting and strengthening her professional identity (including a perception of her strengths and weaknesses, as well as her core mission as a teacher) while gaining others' acceptance of core aspects of her professional identity.

Emotional Professional Identity Work via Creating and Sharing One's Professional Body

Despite the contradictory experiences of the arts-based program reported above, all participants experienced the professional body method mostly as positive. In relation to the second research question, we concentrated on the ways in which emotions were part of the professional identity work while using this method. Here, two categories are presented: (i) Individual professional identity work that demonstrates different emotions and forms of identity work via processing one's professional body; and (ii) Collective emotional experiences in a group while sharing one's professional body.

Emotional Identity Work as an Individual Process

All of the participants described the core elements, grounds and future aspirations of their professional identity through their professional body. Using this method in a safe and creative environment evoked particularly pleasant emotions and supported participants' commitment and well-being at work, as we shall demonstrate next.

The method allowed for identifying and explicating the core elements of one's professional identity. In creating and processing their professional bodies, the teachers used and highlighted the meanings of colours and symbols (e.g., scout scarf, rock, thunderbolt). Creative and illustrative ways were especially helpful in expressing the emotional and embodied aspects of identity work better than via writing.

> When I was making this, there were a lot of colours. I also added some words, but different feelings and everything on top of my drawing. Then I was wondering how I ended up in this profession and so on, but there's a lot of this emotional side. In place of the heart, there's a big black stone, but there's also red. The head has light, but there are also black, painful thunderbolts coming out of it, so in this kind of moment, you learn to walk by taking small steps.

Ultimately, the professional body method was a powerful way of shaping and strengthening one's professional identity, where visualising was a central way to process and express one's inner thoughts and emotions. The process of creating one's professional body evoked various pleasant emotions, such as *satisfaction, joy* and *inspiration*. Inspiration boosted the process of creating one's professional identity through elaborations on one's professional strengths, commitments and future dreams. Satisfaction and joy supported the strengthening and shaping of professional identity through becoming aware of the core elements in one's own professional identity. Thus, these pleasant emotions offered a foundation for their professional identity work.

However, some participants felt *uncomfortable* with the professional body method because they did not see themselves as artistic or visual persons. For them, the identity work was hindered because of the *frustration* towards the arts-based ways of working that they did not find helpful for themselves. For some participants, the unpleasant emotions emerged especially as outcomes of the identity work. Despite regarding the creation of the professional body as a pleasant task, some participants assessed the outcome as "quite modest, since this is not a natural way of working for me". In this case, the university teachers expressed *shame* as an outcome of quite unsuccessful arts-based identity work.

In their professional bodies, the teachers also recognised their values and described the (im)balance between their current professional duties (e.g., research and teaching) or between different life areas—most typically work and family life:

> The professional body image, while creating it or afterwards… I was thinking what my mottos for coping or working really are, which values are important to me, the values that carry me in my work and life, and also what my options considering work are, if there are any options. So, I acknowledged these, and I sometimes go back to these things. It was somehow nice that they were in the body. Through the body image, I think about doing research and teaching; those are my two hands. And then I can ponder if they're in balance or not and what the ideal situation would be. Like, it's very easy to perceive identity-related issues as a part of your body.

For some participants, finding a work– private life balance was one of the main issues reflected in their professional bodies and also in relation to their current life situation. Here, they experienced more *courage* in making wise decisions according to their personal values to strike a balance between their professional and personal lives. They also expressed more *compassion* towards themselves. Thus, these comfortable—one could also say relieving—emotions were evoked as a consequence of identity work, especially when elaborating the current goals and future aspirations.

Since the participants were in mature adulthood, the issue of ageing was evident, and professional identity was reflected in terms of this shared life phase. In the group discussion, participants created and used the narrative of *a mean old hag* and gave it a very positive connotation of a strong woman who knows and respects herself and is an agentic actor in defining herself.

> It's like about defining yourself and what's important to you. Before everything went according to different kinds of needs, when the children were small… other people's needs and the needs at work. Now, I'm beginning to be like a mean old hag, who takes her own space.

Professional identity work was an emotional endeavour that, besides evoking pleasant emotions, included tensions and unpleasant emotions. Processing one's professional body was accompanied by emotions of *frustration*, *confusion* and *compassion* in relation to one's identity work. This was typically the case when participants reflected and realised that they were still working with the very same issues that they had experienced previously. Consequently, this evoked frustration regarding the slowness of the change process, and the lack of learning was accompanied by "irritation, because it is still the same. No learning at all". In this sense, emotions emerged from slow and even unsuccessful identity work. However, at the same time, they also felt compassion towards themselves when accepting their identity redefining to be a slow and time-consuming process.

Collective Emotional Experiences in a Group Through Sharing Identity Work

The professional body method also offered ways and space for collective sharing and experiencing among the participants. Verbalising its contents and meanings offered a new way to elaborate on one's professional values, core commitments, main strengths and expectations and dreams. Although the professional body task was an individual one, it was not possible to complete without help. Some participants drew their body lines on a paper with other participants. They found the drawing of their figure with colleagues to be a *joyful* situation with togetherness. The physical and embodied nature of being drawn by a colleague and seeing one's actual-size body figure was also a powerful experience. This offered tools to see oneself from a new angle and also to work on and redefine one's own identity.

> I didn't want to take the position that I had been drawn into because it looked horribly speedy. So then I drew myself in a slightly calmer position. I'm somehow really happy about this discovery, and I'm probably gonna work on this in my life now.

An essential part of the process was sharing one's professional body in a workshop through visual and spoken storytelling. This enabled collective identity work in two different ways during the workshop meeting. This happened, first, through sharing one's professional identity work process and the professional body, and getting feedback from the others. As one of the participants describes below, collective working offered new reflections of oneself through the eyes of others:

> It was also very good when we got comments on these bodies through the mirroring technique. Somehow, the fact that the mirror is given to you, how you've been heard and how others understand you. So, I think, as a situation, it was extremely efficient—a really good and functional situation… The fact that I've been seen and heard.

Second, collective experiences were enabled through hearing and relating to other participants' identity stories. The process of sharing revealed similarities in the core elements of the teachers' professional identities. At the same time, since there were no strict rules regarding the format of the professional body, the various ways of undertaking professional identity work were made known. Commenting on each other's professional body was meaningful not only to the presenter but also to the feedback giver. Thus, the sharing of one's professional body was a journey, during which *excitement, joy, courage* and *compassion* were present and caused by the collective identity work.

However, the process of describing and sharing one's professional body within a group of colleagues was not only a pleasant journey; it was a rollercoaster of emotions where *fear* and *shame* concerning the quality and goodness of one's professional body were followed by *courage* and *joy* when sharing one's story with the group. This was the case for all participants, but especially for those who felt uncomfortable with the method and who described feeling unpleasant emotions. Although the participants were satisfied with being *encouraged* to throw themselves into the process of creating the professional body, they had doubts about accomplishing and presenting their task to the group. On one hand, presenting oneself through the professional body caused doubts about the quality and contents of the outcome, accompanied by *shame* and *guilt* owing to poor performance. On the other hand, the task fostered the agency to act according to one's choices.

> When I quite heavily threw myself into creating the professional body, I was wondering what people in the group were thinking of me, that I made it in this way. But, on the other hand, it's good that you also have the courage to let go. Because there were no rules and I don't have to tell the whole truth, I've just chosen this path and this particular way of creating it. It was a nice exercise; it also gave me an opportunity to show my own creativity.

Eventually, sharing one's professional body with the group made the teachers feel *encouraged, inspired* and *happy*. The feedback that they received from the others enabled them to see themselves through the others' eyes. Eventually, the emotional mode turned back into a pleasant one via shared and collective meaning-making within the group.

Discussion and Conclusions

The findings of the study reported in this chapter contribute to the understanding of arts-based practices and enrich the theoretical understanding of the role and range of emotions in professional identity processes. The strength of this study was its utilisation of different datasets collected over time. The weakness of this study was the utilisation of self-reports as data. Nonetheless, self-reports are potentially the most suitable method for revealing participants' actual experiences and nuanced emotions (Pekrun, 2016).

First, this chapter provided a discussion of arts-based methods from the viewpoint of emotional experiences. Although all participants felt safe and confident in the group, the findings depict their different emotional journeys via using arts-based methods, notably drama-based methods. The nature of their participation varied: conscious decisions involved both throwing oneself into action (*adventurer*) and cautious (*observer*) participation, whereas unconsciously active participation was a result of the methods (*experiencer*). Different emotions emerged via engagement in arts-based working. Emotions such as courage and cautiousness framed the teachers' participation, but such working also evoked emotions such as satisfaction and shame. In the case of the adventurer, drama-based methods with pleasant and unpleasant emotions helped in processing and redefining one's core aspects of professional identity. In the case of the experiencer and observer, professional identities were strengthened and accepted mainly via shared group discussions. The drama-based methods evoking unpleasant emotions were not so supportive for identity work.

Second, this chapter approached professional identity work through the use of the professional body method from an emotional perspective. The findings reveal that the method supported participants' creative professional identity work, particularly in terms of balancing teaching and researching duties, becoming aware of what is most important in their work and learning how to navigate towards a meaningful future. Professional identity work was found out be a rich emotional endeavour, during which emotions both supported and hindered identity work and emerged as outcomes of the process (see also Winkler, 2018). Pleasant emotions (e.g., inspiration) supported the identity work of the teachers, whereas unpleasant emotions (e.g., fear) hindered the process. Here emotions played a role in affecting the ways the teachers approached, assessed and completed their professional body. In addition, emotions emerged as an outcome of the identity work process. Similarly, both pleasant (e.g., compassion) and unpleasant (e.g., shame) emotions were present.

The findings further underline the meaning of this kind of navigation particularly in mature adulthood. Through individual and shared identity work, the participants created the narrative of a mean old hag representing the power, acceptance and appreciation of oneself as an individual and professional actor. In addition, the collective part of the professional body work provided information about how one is seen in the eyes of others. This fostered a powerful arena for professional identity work in terms of receiving supportive feedback from the other participants and the coach. Through this feedback, the teachers were able to become aware, accept and appreciate themselves as professional actors and human beings. In this collective process, both pleasant and unpleasant emotions were salient in the professional identity work.

All in all, the findings emphasise the meanings of both pleasant and unpleasant emotions in arts-based professional identity work especially in adulthood. These emotions were intertwined with the substance of the identity work, but also the arts-based methods per se. Taking part in participatory arts-based practices arose joy and enthusiasm, but also a wide range of anxiety, fear and pressure to accomplish the tasks and to "perform" in the right way (Chemi & Borup Jensen, 2015). To conclude, arts-based methods were not the most suitable working methods for all participants, but at best, they promoted fruitful professional identity work by enabling participants to go beyond language and cognitive ways of knowing and being. Arts-based methods offered new frontiers for participants to become aware of their core professional beliefs, missions and values and to refine or strengthen their professional identities. At best, such professional identity work can enhance individuals' well-being at work, particularly in terms of energising and increasing their empowerment at work and in their private lives.

Despite being fruitful and effective, there are pitfalls of using arts-based methods in identity work (Brady & Brown, 2013). These methods have the power to reveal unconscious and unexpressed issues of which the individual is not aware. When these issues are worked through in collective processes, there is a possibility of revealing something that one will regret afterwards, as was the case of the *experiencer*. In addition, there must be a safe and confident atmosphere in the group without, for example, any severe conflicts between participants. This highlights the importance of the expertise and ethical responsibility of the coach and her/his understanding of the power of these methods. Overall, the coach must be an expert to guide participants of different backgrounds and orientations on their journeys in individual and ethical ways.

To conclude, we need to remember that our research findings cannot be generalised for other arts-based learning contexts, since this study was conducted within a specific program with specific aims and methods. However, our study is able to contribute to the discussion on professional identity work and arts-based methods. This chapter encourages to explore these topics more comprehensively, including perspectives on unpleasant emotions. It would also be important to explore emotions (as an embodied responses and reactions) in respect with professional identity work through using physiological data collected with real-time measurements.

Acknowledgements This work was supported by the Academy of Finland under Grant number 288925 [The Role of Emotions in Agentic Learning at Work]. We wish to thank the university teachers for sharing their individual experiences.

References

Arvaja, M. (2018). Tensions and striving for coherence in an academic's professional identity work. *Teaching in Higher Education, 23*(3), 229–306.
Beijaard, D., Meijer, P. C., & Verloop, N. (2004). Reconsidering research on teachers' professional identity. *Teaching and Teacher Education, 20*(2), 107–128.
Beltman, S., Glass, C., Dinham, J., Chalk, B., & Nguyen, B. (2015). Drawing identity: Beginning pre-service teachers' professional identities. *Issues in Educational Research, 25*(3), 225–245.
Brady, G., & Brown, G. (2013). Rewarding but let's talk about the challenges: Using arts based methods in research with young mothers. *Methodological Innovations Online, 8*(1), 99–112.
Chemi, T., & Borup Jensen, J. (2015). Emotions and learning in arts-based practices of educational innovation. In B. Lund & T. Chemi (Eds.), *Dealing with emotions: A pedagogical challenge to innovative learning* (pp. 21–36). Rotterdam, The Netherlands: Sense.

Chemi, T., & Du, X. (Eds.). (2017). *Arts-based methods in education around the world*. Gistrup, Denmark: River Publishers.
Day, C. (2018). Professional identity matters: Agency, emotions, and resilience: Mapping challenges and innovations. In P. A. Schutz, J. Hong, & D. Cross Francis (Eds.), *Research on teacher identity: Mapping challenges and innovations* (pp. 61–70). Cham: Springer.
Korthagen, F. A. J. (2004). In search of the essence of a good teacher: Towards a more holistic approach in teacher education. *Teaching and Teacher Education, 20*(1), 77–97.
Leitch, R. (2006). Limitations of language: Developing arts-based creative narrative in stories of teachers' identities. *Teachers and Teaching: Theory and Practice, 12*(5), 549–569.
Lieblich, A., Tuval-Mashiach, R., & Zilber, T. (1998). *Narrative research: Reading, analysis and interpretation*. London, UK: Sage.
Mahlakaarto, S. (2014). Työidentiteetit pelissä ja peilissä—Menetelmällisiä ratkaisuja toimijuuden vahvistamiseen [Work identities at stake and in the mirror—Practical tools for supporting agency]. In P. Hökkä et al. (Eds.), *Ammatillisen toimijuuden ja työssä oppimisen vahvistaminen—Luovia voimavaroja työhön! [Strengthening professional agency and learning at work—Creative resources to work!]* (pp. 47–65). Jyväskylä, Finland: University of Jyväskylä.
Pearson, C. S. (1991). *Awakening the heroes within: Twelve archetypes to help us find ourselves and transform our world*. San Francisco, CA: Harper.
Pekrun, R. (2016). Using self-report to assess emotions in education. In M. Zembylas & P. A. Schultz (Eds.), *Methodological advances in research on emotion and education* (pp. 43–54). Cham, Switzerland: Springer.
Ruohotie-Lyhty, M. (2018). Identity-agency in progress: Teachers authoring their identities. In P. A. Schutz, J. Hong, & D. Cross Francis (Eds.), *Research on teacher identity: Mapping challenges and innovations* (pp. 25–36). Cham, Switzerland: Springer.
Saldaña, J. (2013). *The coding manual for qualitative researchers*. London, UK: Sage.
Taylor, S. S., & Ladkin, D. (2009). Understanding arts-based methods in managerial development. *Academy of Management Learning and Education, 8*(1), 55–69.
Uitto, M., Jokikokko, K., & Estola, E. (2015). Virtual special issue on teachers and emotions in teaching and teacher education (TATE) in 1985–2014. *Teaching and Teacher Education, 50*, 124–135.
Vähäsantanen, K. (2015). Professional agency in the stream of change: Understanding educational change and teachers' professional identities. *Teaching and Teacher Education, 47*, 1–12.

Vähäsantanen, K., Hökkä, P., Paloniemi, S., Herranen, S., & Eteläpelto, A. (2017). Professional learning and agency in an identity coaching programme. *Professional Development in Education, 43*(4), 514–536.

Wang, Q., Coemans, S., Siegesmund, R., & Hannes, K. (2017). Arts-based methods in socially engaged research practice: A classification framework. *Art/Research International, 2*(2), 5–39.

Winkler, I. (2018). Identity work and emotions: A review. *International Journal of Management Reviews, 20*, 120–133.

Ylijoki, O.-H., & Ursin, J. (2013). The construction of academic identity in the changes of Finnish higher education. *Studies in Higher Education, 38*, 1135–1149.

Zembylas, M. (2007). Theory and methodology in researching emotions in education. *International Journal of Research and Method in Education, 30*(1), 57–72.

14

"Colouring Outside the Lines": Employment and Resilience for Art-Makers with Disabilities

Tanya Riches, Vivienne Riches, and Bruce O'Brien

Introduction

This chapter explores the possibilities and complexities for unemployed and underemployed Australian artists with disability undertaking arts-based work. Internationally, artistic endeavours have been used as acts of self-definition but the literature also notes they also play a role in meaning-making for wider society. By promoting the visibility of marginalised groups they can be tools for successful advocacy. However, there are challenges to turning art-making into paid employment. Here, ten artists with disabilities are interviewed to explore the potential of the Arts in building resilience amongst adults.

Disability is contested and complex in definition but incorporates bodily impairment and is associated with economic and social disad-

---

T. Riches (✉) • V. Riches • B. O'Brien
Centre for Disability Studies, Northern Medical School, University of Sydney, Sydney, NSW, Australia
e-mail: tanya.riches@sydney.edu.au; vivienne.riches@cds.org.au; cds@cds.org.au

© The Author(s) 2020
L. McKay et al. (eds.), *Arts-Based Research, Resilience and Well-being Across the Lifespan*, https://doi.org/10.1007/978-3-030-26053-8_14

vantage. Thus, the preamble of the United Nations' Convention on the Rights of Persons with Disability (CRPD) (UN, 2006) defines disability as "the outcome of the interaction between a person with an impairment and the environmental and attitudinal barriers he/ she may face." This broadens an individual's biological and psychological impairments to include their social (and therefore cultural) context, called the *bio-psycho-social model* by the World Health Organization (WHO, 2011).

Using a constructionist approach as presented by Runswick-Cole and Goodley (2013), it is possible to define resilience for people with disability as "negotiation between individuals and their environments for the resources to [view] themselves as healthy amidst conditions collectively viewed as adverse" (Ungar, 2004, p. 342). Furthermore, Ungar (2007, p. 19) maps out a network of resources including access to employment alongside the availability of financial, educational, medical and other opportunities or assistance.

This chapter explores this negotiation; in particular: how arts-based activities (defined here broadly as all visual and performing arts) may allow people with disabilities to lead more resilient and meaningful lives. It adopts an arts-based approach, here defined as "research that uses the creative arts as a design method in various stages of investigation, as well as a methodology that is defined by a creative worldview that forms the philosophical foundation for an inquiry" (Viega & Baker, 2017, p. 239). This paradigm includes all "poetic insights, echoes, layerings, assemblages" (Currans, Heit, & Kuppers, 2015, p. 372).

The disability arts movement amplified disability rights internationally (Barnes, 2003; Eisenhauer, 2007; Kuppers, 2014). Correspondingly, Wexler and Derby (2015, p. 127) propose that all "artworks of disabled people are bonded in a common socio-political experience." Here, ten Australian *disabled people doing art* within the mainstream are interviewed. These individuals work in similar ways to other able-bodied artists, rather than as *disability artists*, a distinction made clear in disability studies (Eisenhauer, 2007, p. 9; Kuppers, 2014).

Artworks selected by the participants were discussed during semi structured interviews with the researchers and the data analysed using grounded theory, resulting in four themes that highlight a range of issues meaningful to the lives of people with disability. Finally, the conclusions of this study in regards to resilience are presented.

Theoretical Underpinnings: Cultural Representation and Resilience

Social narratives often create ableist stereotypes that exclude and limit the performance of people with disability (Snyder & Mitchell, 2001; Wilde, 2014). Thus, sociologist and disabled self-advocate Tom Shakespeare in his watershed publication, *Cultural Representation for Disabled People: Dustbins for Disavowal* (1994, p. 295) distinguished "the difference between having an impairment (a common experience) and being disabled (a specific social identity of a minority)." For him, although people with impairment experience discrimination in interpersonal relationships, it is their depiction as "other" in culture that results in the social category of "the disabled." This phenomenon deems them to be subjects rather than actors in the cultural domain. To epitomise the cultural significance of disabled (as opposed to abled) bodies Shakespeare uses Western literary examples including King Lear and Richard III. He cites Kreigel:

> the cripple is the creature who has been deprived of his ability to create a self. [...] He is the other, if for no other reason than that only by being the other will he be allowed to presume upon the society of the "normals." He must accept definition from outside the boundaries of his own existence. (Kreigel as cited in Shakespeare, 1994, p. 286)

Similarly, the popular media also often omits disabled people from broadcasting or disables them in varied ways.

> Disabling stereotypes which medicalise, patronise, criminalise and dehumanise disabled people abound in books, films, on television, and in the press. They form the bedrock on which the attitudes towards, assumptions about and expectations of disabled people are based. They are fundamental to the discrimination and exploitation which disabled people encounter

daily and contribute significantly to their systematic exclusion from mainstream community life. (Barnes as cited in Shakespeare, 1994, p. 286)

People with disability are objectified by cultural representations and rendered passive by this process.

Shakespeare (1994, p. 295) noted, "Disabled people are seen to be ambiguous because they hover between humanity and animality, life and death, subjectivity and objectivity." By stereotyping the performance of disability, he claims, society acts to "[reduce] ambiguity; by physically controlling it; by avoiding it; by labelling it dangerous; by adopting it in ritual." However, he asserts, such liminality can be an advantage for work in the Arts. Here, he uses Victor Turner's depiction of the court jester to suggest that liminal peoples have particular resonances for cultural representation, and a licence to criticise or to strip off the pretensions of the power-holders. Ambiguity forms a rich resource that interrogates questions of culture, representation, and meaning. Taking back the means of production through alternative and more inclusive images, disabled people can incorporate but also invert and resist the dominant cultural norms. Creative production is therefore a way in which a self can be created (or, perhaps, recreated).

The conscious (and unconscious) disruption of cultural scripts subverts audience expectations (Kuppers, 2014). Interaction between the artist and the viewer (via the created work) can be a means of changing society. This resonates with the work of Brazilian educator Paulo Freire (1990, p. 60), who speaks of *conscientização* or self-consciousness, as the process of becoming "a being for itself." For Freire (1990, p. 28), the oppressed must liberate themselves, and therefore also their oppressors. In this way, arts-based activities may increase visibility of disabled peoples, and reverse dominant cultural ideology.

By Ungar's definition cited earlier (2004, p. 242) such work may, therefore, stage a negotiation (or renegotiation) between the individual and society to build resilience. Resilience is also defined by Gordon as:

> … the ability to thrive, mature and increase competence in the face of adverse circumstances. These circumstances may include biological abnormalities or environmental obstacles. The adverse circumstances may be chronic and consistent or severe and infrequent. (1998, p. 7)

Benard (in Arrington & Wilson, 2000) claims that resilience generates traits—such as self-esteem, self-efficacy, autonomy and optimism—which enable people to develop social competencies or skills in problem solving. If true, then arts-based activities may build resilience amongst disabled artists by fostering self-esteem, self-efficacy, autonomy and optimism.

Art-Making: Employment or Leisure?

However, any increased resilience gained through the Arts must be considered in light of the marginalisation experienced by people with disability. Often, forms of "speaking back" to society are channelled or controlled. One of the particular challenges of art-making is that it has been used as therapy for people with disability (Snyder & Mitchell, 2001). Rather than a paid activity supported by its audiences, disabled people are often encouraged to make art for leisure's sake. Funding in the Arts is precarious, and it can be challenging to turn a passion into a paid role. Therefore, there is need to evaluate the role the Arts play for people with disability.

Association between being "disabled" and unemployment or underemployment arose during industrialisation with the professionalisation of the workforce (Barnes, 1991; Humpage, 2007). Although unemployment rates in the Western world have reduced dramatically, this is less true for people with disabilities who still today have: drastically low workforce participation; high likelihood of being unemployed/underemployed; or long-term unemployed; and often experience relative poverty (Carter, Austin, & Trainor, 2011; Dempsey & Ford, 2009; International Disability Rights Monitor, 2004; Nord, Stancliffe, Nye-Lengerman, & Hewitt, 2016; Simonsen & Neubert, 2013). Australian data from 2015 reveal only 48% of working-age people with disability (and 22% with severe or profound disability) were employed compared with around 79% of the general population (ABS, 2016; AIHW, 2017). People with cognitive or intellectual disabilities were three to four times less likely to be employed than those without (ABS, 2014). In addition, about 18% of school leavers with disability transitioned to unemployment, compared with about 5% of those without disabilities (in Dempsey & Ford, 2009, p. 234).

An indicator of a healthy society is the ability for all people to exercise their right to work. The UNCRPD enshrines this right for people with disabilities in Article 27. Employment not only brings economic benefits but is recognised as a social determinant of health and wellbeing (Kirsh et al., 2009). Work activities often structure the relationships adults have with their peers and with the wider community. They are an important part of adult life and identity, and a resource from which we draw self-understanding. Work leads to a variety of resources often used to build resilience. For example, playing a meaningful role in the community can increase social equity. This in turn can interact with cultural and environmental factors to enhance our ability to thrive, rather than only survive.

Like other Western nations, Australia now encourages the participation of people with disabilities in community life. However, in the Neoliberal paradigm, individual responsibility is emphasised. The Australian welfare system still reinforces a medical model of disability as the "problem" is located with the individual rather than society. Humpage (2007, p. 216) describes its "systems of surveillance, compliance and coercion" that often characterise the lives of the unemployed. The state places responsibility upon an individual to build their skills and pursue employment, with any failure to do so ultimately seen as a personal weakness rather than a structural issue.

Further, the idea that humans can draw meaning from any type of labour is short-sighted. Often employment opportunities for people with disabilities are entry level jobs that reduce their power and control. There is a general loss of unskilled work in the changing global economy and the rise of fixed-term, casual, and part-time roles, which increase the chance of precarious employment, or underemployment. Therefore, for adults with disabilities, finding *meaningful* work is often an area of concern (Honey, Kariuki, Emerson, & Llewellyn, 2014; Strong, 1998).

In the past, the state encouraged sheltered employment where people with disabilities worked for "little pay" (Kuppers, 2014, p. 39). Alternatively, they attended day activity centres where art therapy was used (Derby, 2013). Consequently, the Arts have often been viewed as paternalistic activities for people with disability, as Barnes outlines:

Those disabled people viewed as inadequate and incapable have been given art as therapy in the context of special schools, day centres, and segregated institutions. Such initiatives have not just individualised and depoliticised creativity, advocates have also sometimes used them for commercial purposes, such as charity Christmas cards. Whilst there is arguably a place for art therapy, disabled people do not deserve this presumption of perpetual infantilization. (2003, p. 8)

Art-making can be used in multiple ways. It can be enjoyable. However, the notion of art as *only* therapy promotes individual over social (intrinsic over extrinsic) benefits. Although it allows for the expression of the self, this is unconnected to any viewing audience. Any potential for resilience is through transforming others, as well as transformation of the self, and its "internal states of being" (Wexler & Derby, 2015, p. 131; Wilde, 2014).

Today, Art Centres have opened some opportunities for people with high and complex disabilities to communicate with the world. Wexler and Derby (2015) note:

The communicative behaviour of disabled people—which can include bodily tics, atypical gestures, compulsive rituals, and verbal perseveration—may seem foreign and incomprehensible in social settings while the artworks of such people articulate thoughtful, intentional, and valuable lived experiences and ideas about the importance of our social connection to others. (p. 138)

They argue that art *can* assist people with disabilities to function more independently and contribute their unique perspective to society. However, this relies on them being able to explore their own artistic vocabulary rather than learning the formalism of traditional art educators. In this context, art-making can become a sociopolitical activity to reverse dominant or stereotypical cultural notions of disability in public space.

An individualised market approach such as Australia's National Disability Insurance Scheme (NDIS) is often promoted as contributing to more meaningful social and economic inclusion. This occurs via individualised, person-centred, and flexible paid and unpaid support opportunities that are "built around the skills, strengths and interests" of people with disabilities (Thoresen, Thomson, Jackson, & Cocks, 2018, p. 164). Many individuals with high/complex needs require creative and innovative entrepreneurial approaches in order to meet the requirements of working life. Recently, Curtin University researchers examined small business enterprises (SBEs) to demonstrate how a person-centred approach may bring meaning to not only a person with a disability but also their community. Through social entrepreneurship individuals were found to have gained pride, and positive self-image (Thoresen et al., 2018). These attributes qualify as the kinds of resources presented by Ungar (2007). Although not all SBEs are profitable, they may provide valued social roles for persons with disabilities to build resilience. This chapter sought to explore whether similar outcomes are possible for art-makers.

Method

The design of the study was a qualitative research project with a convenience sample of ten artists with a range of disabilities who were interviewed using an arts-based approach through a semi-structured questionnaire. Here, arts-based refers to "using any form of art (visual, music, poetry, dance, etc.) in the data collection, analysis and/or reporting of research" (Lawrence, 2015, p. 142).

This investigation was initiated as an inclusive research project in which three co-researchers—two without disability (a psychologist and an anthropologist) and one with a learning disability—sought to design an inclusive study to address this topic. *Inclusive research* includes people with disability and promotes outcomes that matter to them (Johnson & Walmsley, 2003; Nind, 2016, p. 24). Realistically, many researchers do not identify (or want to identify) as "disabled." Therefore, the term is often applied to people with intellectual disabilities (or learning difficulties), who tend to experience increased barriers to participation and require support in the scholarly community. Our co-researcher Bruce O'Brien stated his interest was in employment. Having worked at CDS since 1998, he explained that employment was an important feature of his life, which he recognised as having built resilience for him as he transitioned from youth into adulthood. This provided the research team a thematic focus to explore representation and work for disabled persons in greater depth, seeking how employment may contribute to resilience amongst art-makers, particularly across adult life stages.

Following ethics approval from the University of Sydney, potential participants were identified as Australians with disabilities working in the Arts. Individuals were approached via publicly listed emails or websites, however none responded. So, colleagues publicised this study further afield, inviting contacts with disability to volunteer as study participants. This led to the identification of a convenience sample of ten consenting adults with disability who engaged the Arts in various ways. Six were female and four male.[1] Six were visual artists; one worked exclusively in sculpture, and another in photography. Two were performing artists. Two worked in sound using technology and music. In addition, the range and severity of their disabilities were similarly diverse: one participant had dyslexia and learning difficulties; two had Down Syndrome and learning disabilities; one was Deaf; another visually impaired; one had acquired a physical disability; one had spastic/dystonic cerebral palsy; one had dissociative identity disorder, and another an autoimmune disorder chimera. One participant listed Depression and Anxiety but also ADHD, Graves' Disease, Fibromyalgia pain, and Chronic Fatigue.[2]

Viega and Baker's (2017) proposal is that art is useful for explicating meaning and enhancing thematic material drawn from data generation. Artists were asked to provide two examples of their *art-making* (in mediums including music tracks, videos, or photographs of their sculpture, acting, music or circus performance). They were invited to discuss these in relation to themselves and their work. This allowed the lived experience of participants to be explored in a focused discussion using an *arts-based* approach. Eight artists complied. The researchers conducted open listening/viewing of the art sample. Then, artists were given a choice to begin with semi-structured interview questions or discuss these pieces—including composition and subjective meaning.

---

[1] Some artists consented to use of their names for this study.
[2] Descriptive data have been summarised to preserve the identity of some participants.

Using grounded theory, the discussion was analysed to determine what the art-maker wanted to convey about their craft. This produced initial then focused coding for comparison with data and content analysis of the semi-structured interview responses. Four broad complex, themes emerged from the art works provided as discussed by participants. These represented tensions negotiated by the art-makers as they created in their various mediums. Following are exemplar artworks that represent these themes.

Theme 1: Art-Making as Defining Disabilities and Abilities

The first theme highlighted by participants related to how they saw themselves as people with disabilities and as art-makers. For example, Lisa Lanzi described herself as *a performing arts worker*. Since completing her Bachelor degree at the Australian Theatre for Young People (NIDA), her career has spanned a number of decades (and artistic mediums). Despite the challenges of her visual impairment and working in the often struggling Australian arts industry, Lanzi created many opportunities for both herself and others to engage in artistic endeavours via movement, theatre, and voice initiatives. The image Lanzi presented for the study was a photograph of herself acting in a Bakehouse Theatre play entitled *Fefu and her Friends* (Fig. 14.1). This character is captured hallucinating in bed. She says of the image,

> It was a role that was quite mercurial and deep. …that particular image … was when I was doing a ten minute monologue …with the audience all around me on a platform looking down at me in very close proximity. So, it was incredibly raw and very challenging. But … I was able to deliver that performance given all those challenges. So it was a really precious memory for me.

Lisa's description highlighted the character's disability and complexities. Paradoxically, this difficult role enabled her to reflect upon her own abilities, and to therefore define herself through her successes rather than any diagnosis or label.

Fig. 14.1 Lisa Lanzi in *Fefu and her Friends*. (Photograph by Michael Errey, 2018)

Theme 2: Art-Making as Therapy

The second theme emphasised by participants was that their art had intrinsic rewards, particularly therapeutic ones. For example, Justin Lampson, a Nungawal man with dystonic cerebral palsy, lives in Sydney, Australia. He says "I talk a lot about mental health, I talk a lot about my faith… I talk a lot about pain… [it's] a way of getting crap off my chest." He declared "pain produces power."

Within the song *Arsonist* (provided by Lampson, personal communication, 2019) he rapped,

> … *Don't rap for attention, it's suicide prevention*
> *Not to fucking mention intellect ascension*
> *No respectful mentions, when I'm with my henchmen*

> *Don't ever fucking lie lad, don't even fucking try that*
> *More like a triad, decisions with precision, my vision is clear*
> *Was driven by fear coz collision was near*
> *I diverted the path never perverted my craft or deserted my past*
> *I'm an arsonist*

He is passionate about "classic" hip hop which he considers a lost art. The main stated benefit of refining his craft was to his own well-being. However, he had also found his audience gained from his music. His listeners had told him they received "strength, a lot of resilience, and a lot of stoicism from [his music]… a sense of maybe being a hard bastard, and not wanting to give up."

Theme 3: Art-Making as Liminality in a Finite Body

The third theme identified in the art-makers' discussions was liminality or the ability to change. For many of them, making art had been a transition—exploring the more creative side of their persona or experimenting with new parts of themselves. This enabled them to move through social space and find new identities even as their bodies remained impaired. For example, when Keith Chidzey experienced an injury to his hand and wrist 18 years ago, he realised he could not continue working as a dentist. So, he approached his insurer with a proposal—that of a career change into the Arts. His insurer backed him and funded his training in the skills he needed to become a full-time sculptor, working primarily in timber and bronze. His sculpture explores themes that range from highlighting beauty in our world to the finiteness of human existence, suffering, and death. Although sculpting was perhaps financially a less secure pursuit than he would have hoped, his sculpting work also proved a catalyst for further study including an application for a PhD, which may lead to further exploration of the topics which interest him, and a future lecturing position.

The image *Franciscan Beauty* (Fig. 14.2) is a holding bowl made of old timber and glass. Its dual qualities evoke nature but also spirit, with a recurring symbol of hands common in Chidzey's work.

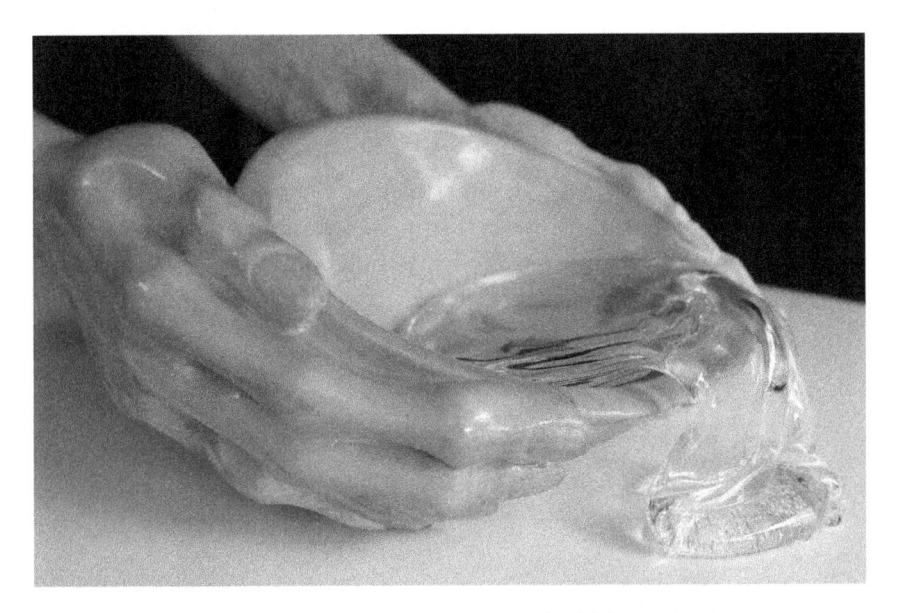

Fig. 14.2 *Franciscan Beauty.* (Photograph by Keith Chidzey, 2017)

The researchers noticed a juxtaposition of medium and movement, which echoes the prominent transitions in Chidzey's interview. Liminality or the ability to change was perceived as important by many art-makers who spoke about the difficulty of labels that society often placed upon them due to their disabilities.

Theme 4: Art-Making as Opportunity and Focused Work

Finally, many art-makers discussed the opportunities their art had provided, contrasted with the narrow or focused detail of their work. For example, for Kym Thomson, navigating her learning disability was an unavoidable reality throughout the creation of her commercial photography business, which has now run successfully for 14 years. In reflecting upon her time as Director and Senior Photographer, she noted that the income from her art had facilitated the formalising of the supports she needed, allowing her to gain accountancy skills and understand the legal documentation that is an ordinary part of managing a small enterprise. Thomson's first image had gained acclaim as it was chosen as a finalist for the Art Gallery of NSW City Bank Portrait Prize—part of the Archibald Exhibition in 2005.

Her second chosen image, depicted here, is her portrait of paralympian runner Amy Winters, described as "strong," a reversal of the cultural stereotypes of disability and femininity as inherently fragile. She says, "I wanted to show her disability without it being the first thing you see" (Fig. 14.3).

Fig. 14.3 Amy Winters. (Photography by Kym Thompson, 2017)

Thomson noted that ironically most of her work in corporate and product imaging requires meticulous attention to detail. She explained that while some people may consider this unenjoyable or menial work, it facilitated exciting opportunities—to meet Olympians, to win awards and engage in more creative aspects of her role.

Study Findings

This section expands the themes uncovered via the art-works, using the interview data. Our participants openly declared their art as a way of redefining themselves but also often their disabilities. They described their lived experiences of disability in varied terms, from "it affects everything" through to "nobody would ever know because I manage it." Their physical impairments affected their work ("I'm constantly unwell") but also social lives ("socialising in the way that hearing people socialise can be very difficult, so I do struggle a bit at work"). Participants emphasised the structural difficulties; they "[faced] a lot of barriers" or "hiccups", in daily life, for example, "the biggest one is that I can't drive." Hip Hop musician Justin Lampson explained that "having my music and my voice not be taken seriously" was one of the greatest limitations that he felt, but he also empathised with his audience "I wouldn't want to listen to me for an hour either." His disability had affected his own perception of his contributions.

But visual artist James Cross also described how the label of disability was significant as,

> … people … assume you've got everything wrong with you… they assume that you are hard of hearing, you've got an intellectual disability, everything …they bend down, they speak slowly, they speak loudly.

In contrast, art-making offered alternative ways of interacting with the world that were not prescribed by an impairment. Cross noted that membership in an art factory not only gave him access to tools and resources but also allowed for recognition not centred around his disability: "you get a moment where people aren't looking at you as a person with a disability. They're just looking at you as a peer… You're just another artist."

The participants described the intrinsic benefits of Art-making activities as being "relaxing," making them "feel creative," and helping them process their experiences. Justin Lampson explained his music as "mental immersive release." This was also true for James Cross who said, "in Darwin, when in palliative care [I created art] just basically as a sort of distraction from the pain. I couldn't really read or watch TV or anything, it was just something that I could do." However, as an Aboriginal man, art-making was meditation and offered a cultural reconnection. His mother had been a part of the Stolen Generations and placed with a Sydney family at the age of eight, effectively severing her ties to the Tiwi community. Cross stated. "I started spending time at the university … with some of the Elders from mum's community… a group of women living on campus and studying." He identified that his line doodling had cultural significance. Art created on the islands was often done in sand and was therefore temporary rather than for external audiences. Consequently, he often provided meditations alongside his art in order to emphasise this aspect of his work.

Although Lisa Lanzi had suffered deep bouts of depression, she found that work with a colleague in community choirs provided her great joy, with the therapeutic benefits extending out to others. She says,

> the work I was able to build up… was fantastic for me because it kind of gave me more of a purpose, as well as being able to earn …part of a living. [It] gave me a sense of myself again—that I actually was worthwhile as an artist… I was working as a professional [and] having amazing community outcomes. The people that were taking part in all of these projects … normally could not access the arts easily—so people with dementia, people with Parkinson's, people in prison, women experiencing homelessness or at a certain stage of that journey, people with mental health issues.

She noted that the outcomes included increased confidence ("the way that people walked into a room, or the way they could converse with others," and "ease in public situations") as markers of resilience. However, Lanzi had to make the difficult decision to quit this initiative she loved so much, despite a significant loss of income. She explained, "it was better for my mental health to … not to be dealing with the powers that be."

Many artists emphasised the opportunities and future possibilities of art-making for people with disabilities, rather than their impairment. Visual artist Sue Stergo noted that many of her collaborations were via mental health organisations, whose art groups intentionally exhibited together. Elizabeth Seares identified as Deaf and sought to translate sound into a visual or tactical medium. She described her work as

> a different way of expressing myself … enabling people who are 'd/Deaf' to experience sound, and also enabling people without a Deaf Gain to experience deafness and sound differently.

Her art intended to communicate that

> d/Deaf and Hard of Hearing people can do anything, especially when the world is made more accessible to everyone through universal design rather than forcing people with a disability to change.

Similarly, visual artist Kylie Scott cited her paintings of refugees as an inspiration because they were "invisible" in the same way she had felt in the past. She noted, "they're not 'boat people', they're talking and have fun." She continued, "people with disabilities like me… are afraid to speak out… I suppose. It's for them if I sell stuff, the cards… make them realise, 'oh I can do that too'; that sort of attitude."

The complexities of working in the arts were clear. One participant highlighted the additional costs of a person with disability participating in any activity; "basically… it's the challenge of medications, food, paint." Whether formalised or not, most participants ran their own small business enterprise (SBE). Two had successfully commercialised their art-making to support them and their families. Another two used their skills to generate a range of income streams and had won significant arts grants, although their work did not provide a full-time salary. One artist wryly noted that this meant settling for less than ideal arrangements with companies, stating, "I had to change my ideology, my point of view … sometimes it's more important to make a living than to be starving and on

Centrelink!" Another noted that her husband's regular income assisted in ensuring that her bills were met on a weekly basis. Neither were looking for additional work. Two participants who had spent significant time working on their art were now exploring education to get additional income. Of these, one had decided to transition into a full-time teaching position that now restricted her art-making. For another three, their impairment affected any work activities, so while their performance/art offered them *some* possibilities of making money, it was also a way of engaging with the community despite these limitations.

All participants required support to engage in their artistic endeavours. Some contracted the skills that were needed, just as any other person would. This could be done via SBEs or their NDIS funding packages. The level of support required was often linked to their ambitions for their art. Some admitted they weren't marketing themselves effectively, mainly because they lacked the skills to do so. James Cross noted that while he could doodle with pencils and paper on his own (and often did so), he needed his support workers to assist by squirting paints and with other more physical activities. At people's request, he had finally entered a local exhibition and sold a number of pieces. This event left him "shocked" but had boosted his confidence in his ability to sell his artwork. He noted, "if art is actually going to be displayed or visible to other people, that takes a lot of production."

Sue Stergo had been greatly aided in art-making via her recent NDIS package. She had incorporated her relationship with support workers into her latest exhibition. Describing her style as "a cross between Vincent Van Gogh and Disney" she noted that she had chosen a Superhero theme. She explained,

> I've got four workers, from able organisations, and, and [I have portrayed] them like superheroes in helping me… [but] at the same time as honouring my workers in this exhibition I've brought out old paintings …of different superheroes of myself as well.

Other participants described being heavily reliant on informal supports for their art-making; such as the effort and time of family members. For example, Scott explained that she enjoyed creating multimedia canvases of an evening while watching television. Together she and her mother turned original work into digital prints to place in frames or create cards. In order to sell enough pieces the family had tried market stalls, which her mother noted as less successful than Scott's public speaking events. Another visual artist noted that for a small irregular job he would rather be paid in art supplies which did not reduce his income benefits for other things.

Many artists in the study had decided to give back to other people with disabilities in unpaid ways. But the expectation to do so was often a burden. They were often expected to teach others with disabilities without payment. For some, volunteering provided positive social interactions. However, it was often seen by the artists as diminishing the value of their time and efforts.

Conclusion

Although our artists represented a wide range of disabilities and used various art mediums, the convenience sample was small so ability to generalise these findings is limited. For many, art was not a means to financial security. However, responses showed that art-making provided participants various capabilities that improved their lives and ordered their external life worlds by providing them relational networks of resources. They were slowly working to change the perceptions of their limitations in the Australian environment, exposing and removing barriers through acts of resistance to abled norms. They could be said to be achieving good outcomes despite their challenges, defined as resilience by Runswick-Cole and Goodley (2013, p. 2).

More specifically, when assessed against the eight domains adapted by Runswick-Cole and Goodley (2013) and Ungar (2004, 2007), various observations can be made. First, although individualised funding assisted some people with disabilities in their art-making, the material resources that could be expected from art-making were not automatic and required a measure of risk. If their SBEs succeeded, this allowed artists to lead better lives. Their second domain was clearly improved, with evident potential for relationships to be formed based on shared interest in art, rather than merely upon a participants' physical/psychological limitation. Third, it was clear that art provided the artists a sense of self and purpose. Although affected by their impairments, the fourth domain of their body and mind was enriched through art-making activities. Fifth, such activities also clearly increased their power and control in the domain of community participation. In addition, many of the participants were able to also contribute towards society by creating initiatives for others, thus increasing the sixth domain of community cohesion. Finally, these activities contributed to social justice, as all ten participants played a meaningful role in assisting Australian society in better understanding disability, and in removing barriers to others with impairment. Therefore, this study found that the Arts do hold potential for building resilience amongst unemployed and underemployed adults with disabilities.

References

ABS (Australian Bureau of Statistics). (2014). *Intellectual Disability, Australia*. Cat. no. *4433.0.55.003*. Canberra, ACT.

ABS (Australian Bureau of Statistics). (2016). *Disability, ageing and carers. Summary of Findings, 2015. Cat. no. 4430.0*. Canberra, ACT.

AIHW (Australian Institute of Health and Welfare). (2017). *Disability in Australia: Changes over time in inclusion and participation in employment. Cat. no. DIS 68*. Canberra, ACT.

Arrington, E. G., & Wilson, M. N. (2000). A re-examination of risk and resilience during adolescence: Incorporating culture and diversity. *Journal of Child and Family Studies, 9*(2), 221–230.

Barnes, C. (1991). *Disabled people in Britain and discrimination: A case for anti-discrimination legislation*. London, UK: C. Hurst & Co. Publishers.

Barnes, C. (2003). Effecting change: Disability, culture and art? *In Finding the Spotlight Conference*. Conference Paper delivered at Liverpool Institute for the Performing Arts. Available at: https://pdfs.semanticscholar.org/3083/66015761b54b390ea7fc7b714318373ef596.pdf

Carter, E. W., Austin, D., & Trainor, A. A. (2011). Factors associated with the early work experiences of adolescents with severe disabilities. *Intellectual and Developmental Disabilities, 49*, 233–247.

Currans, E., Heit, S., & Kuppers, P. (2015). Arts-based research sharing and disability culture methods: Different ways of knowing. *Research in Drama Education: The Journal of Applied Theatre and Performance, 20*(3), 372–379.

Dempsey, I., & Ford, J. (2009). Employment for people with intellectual disability in Australia and the United Kingdom. *Journal of Disability Policy Studies, 19*(4), 233–243.

Derby, J. (2013). Nothing about us without us: Art Education's disservice to disabled people. *Studies in Art Education, 54*(4), 376–380.

Eisenhauer, J. (2007). Just looking and staring back: Challenging ableism through disability performance art. *Studies in Art Education, 49*(1), 7–22.

Freire, P. (1990). *Pedagogy of the oppressed.* New York, NY: The Continuum Publishing Company.

Gordon, K. (1998). Resilience from poverty and stress. *Human Development and Family Bulletin, 4*(1), 7–26.

Honey, A., Kariuki, M., Emerson, E., & Llewellyn, G. (2014). Employment status transitions among young adults, with and without disability. *Australian Journal of Social Issues, 49*(2), 151–170.

Humpage, L. (2007). Models of disability, work and welfare in Australia. *Social Policy & Administration, 41*(3), 215–231.

International Disability Rights Monitor. (2004). *Regional report of the Americas.* Chicago, IL: International Disability Network.

Johnson, K., & Walmsley, J. (2003). *Inclusive research with people with learning disabilities: Past, present and futures.* London, UK: Jessica Kingsley Publishers.

Kirsh, B., Stergiou-Kita, M., Gewurtz, R., Dawson, D., Krupa, T., Lysaght, R., & Shaw, L. (2009). From margins to mainstream: What do we know about work integration for persons with brain injury, mental illness and intellectual disability? *Work, 32*(4), 391–405.

Kuppers, P. (2014). Outsider histories, insider artists, cross-cultural ensembles: Visiting with disability presences in contemporary art environments. *TDR: The Drama Review, 58*(2), 33–50.

Lawrence, R. L. (2015). Dancing with the data: Arts-based qualitative research. In V. C. Wang (Ed.), *Handbook of research on scholarly publishing and research methods* (pp. 141–154). Hershey, PA: IGI Global.

Nind, M. (2016). Inclusive research as a site for lifelong learning: Participation in learning communities. *Studies in the Education of Adults, 48*(1), 23–37.

Nord, D. K., Stancliffe, R. J., Nye-Lengerman, K., & Hewitt, A. S. (2016). Employment in the community for people with and without autism: A comparative analysis. *Research in Autism Spectrum Disorders, 24,* 11–16.

Runswick-Cole, K., & Goodley, D. (2013). Resilience: A disability studies and community psychology approach. *Social and Personality Psychology Compass, 7*(2), 67–78.

Shakespeare, T. (1994). Cultural representation of disabled people: Dustbins for disavowal? *Disability & Society, 9*(3), 283–299. https://doi.org/10.1080/09687599466780341

Simonsen, M. L., & Neubert, D. A. (2013). Transitioning youth with intellectual and other developmental disabilities. *Career Development for Exceptional Individuals, 36*(3), 188–198.

Snyder, S. L., & Mitchell, D. T. (2001). Re-engaging the body: Disability studies and the resistance to embodiment. *Public Culture, 13*(3), 367–389.

Strong, S. (1998). Meaningful work in supportive environments: Experiences with the recovery process. *American Journal of Occupational Therapy, 52*, 31–38.

Thoresen, S. H., Thomson, A., Jackson, R., & Cocks, E. (2018). Meaningful social and economic inclusion through small business enterprise models of employment for adults with intellectual disability. *Journal of Vocational Rehabilitation, 49*(2), 161–172.

Ungar, M. (2007). Contextual and cultural aspects of resilience in child welfare settings. In I. Brown, F. Chaze, D. Fuchs, J. lafrance, S. McKay, & S. Thomas Prokop (Eds.), *Putting a human face on child welfare* (pp. 1–24). Toronto, ON: Centre of Excellence for Child Welfare.

Ungar, M. A. (2004). Constructionist discourse on resilience: Multiple contexts, multiple realities among at-risk children and youth. *Youth & Society, 35*(3), 341–365.

United Nations (UN). (2006). *Convention on the rights of persons with disabilities*. Geneva, Switzerland: United Nations. Retrieved from May 16, 2009 http://www2.ohchr.org/english/law/disabilities-convention.htm

Viega, M., & Baker, F. A. (2017). What's in a song? Combining analytical and arts-based analysis for songs created by songwriters with neurodisabilities. *Nordic Journal of Music Therapy, 26*(3), 235–255.

Wexler, A., & Derby, J. (2015). Art in institutions: The emergence of (disabled) outsiders. *Studies in Art Education, 56*(2), 127–141.

Wilde, A. (2014). Spectacle, performance, and the re-presentation of disability and impairment. *Review of Disability Studies: An International Journal, 6*(3), 34–43.

World Health Organization. (2011). *World report on disability*. New York, NY: United Nations.

15

Beating Stress, the Swedish Way: Time for a 'Fika'

Liisa Uusimäki

In the depth of winter, I finally learned that within me there lay an invincible summer.
—Albert Camus

Introduction

This chapter relate to my experiences as senior executive of the Occupational, Health and Safety (OHS) team at the University of Gothenburg in Sweden 2014–2016. My work involved development and analysis of psychosocial environmental surveys, the implementation and follow-up of well-being programs and participating in safety inspections and investigating incidents relating to occupational injuries. The work also involved confidential meetings with academics experiencing stress. To support me in this role required participation in numerous interesting and mandatory workshops. I learnt about the role of Swedish Trade

L. Uusimäki (✉)
Gothenburg University, Gothenburg, Sweden
e-mail: liisa.uusimaki@gu.se

Unions, Swedish laws on health and safety and well-being, stress, alcohol and drug abuse, policies relating to gender equity, discrimination, bullying, violence and threat of violence in the workplace. I also participated in several leadership courses and a yearlong course on conflict resolution that was to prove especially effective when mediating in staff conflict. I am using a narrative inquiry approach (Connelly & Clandinin, 2006) reflecting and understanding my experiences while knowing that "engaging in narrative inquiry requires attentiveness to the stories of other professionals as well as to the larger social, institutional and professional narratives in which individuals are embedded" (Clandinin, Cave, & Berendonk, 2017, p. 94).

According to Poalses and Bezuidenhout (2018), stress-related disorder among academics is a growing phenomenon worldwide. Research has identified that university academics (both research and teaching staff) are among the occupational groups with the highest risk of stress-related disorders along with classroom teachers, health care workers and emergency service personnel (Guthrie et al., 2017; Madsen, Hanson, & Rugulies, 2014; Pignata, Winefield, Boyd, & Provis, 2018). This unfortunately, suggests that universities no longer provide the low-stress working environment they once did.

The role of today's academics is highly complex that require skills in several areas such as, leadership, teaching, research, grant applications, supervision, administration, communication, collaboration, consultancy, community service, establishment of international networks, time management, budgeting, and to some extent marketing (Coates & Goedegebuure, 2010; Melin, Astvik, & Bernhard-Oettel, 2014). Of concern is that there seem to be assumptions and expectations that academics are resilient by nature. For example, abilities to adapt "quickly" to changes, such as, organisational or leadership changes, keeping up with government reforms, adapting to new technology, conducting research, teaching and supervising a growing number of students, manage conflict among both students and colleagues and meeting endless deadlines (Blix, Cruise, Mitchell, & Blix, 1994; Guthrie et al., 2017; Watts & Robertson, 2011).

Resilience is often associated with developmental psychology and with behavioural sciences and within stress research. The American

Psychological Association (2014) defines resilience as "the process of adapting well in the face of adversity, trauma, tragedy, threats or even significant sources of stress (para. 4)." Southwick, Bonanna, Masten, Panter-Brick, and Yehuda (2014a, 2014b) states that the "determinants of resilience include a host of biological, psychological, social and cultural factors that interact with one another to determine how one responds to stressful experience" (p. 2). Burnout on the other hand is defined "as a state of physical, emotional and mental exhaustion caused by long-term involvement in situations that are emotionally demanding" (Harrison, 1999, p. 25). Hence, resilience is not a trait that individuals are born with or that stress and burnout only affect some individuals and not others. What one person, experience as stressful another person may not. Similarly, recovering or bouncing back from highly stressful and challenging situations and the ability to adapt to new circumstances differ among individuals. The recovery time from burnout varies among individual academics and is dependent on the support from the academic workplace, that is, time off from work to recover and reintroduction or reassignment to other duties, counselling and professional advice on physical training activities as well as the support from family and friends.

Dealing with Stress in the Nordic Countries

A major reason why people living in the Nordic countries score high on *Happiness* measures relate to a deep respect for democracy and the rule of law, together with principles of universality and egalitarianism. These underlie the so-called Nordic model. The Nordic countries are Sweden, Finland, Norway, Denmark, Iceland, the Faroe Islands, Greenland and Åland. *The Three Basic Pillars of the Nordic Model* developed by Dølvik (2013) (Fig. 15.1) is a visual representation of a shared social-democratic welfare model.

Each of the Nordic countries' governments share a commitment to universal social rights and to the well-being of their citizens. There are differences among the countries in implementation of laws and policies but in general, all citizens are entitled to free comprehensive education, free childcare, free age-care and healthcare. The Nordic countries are

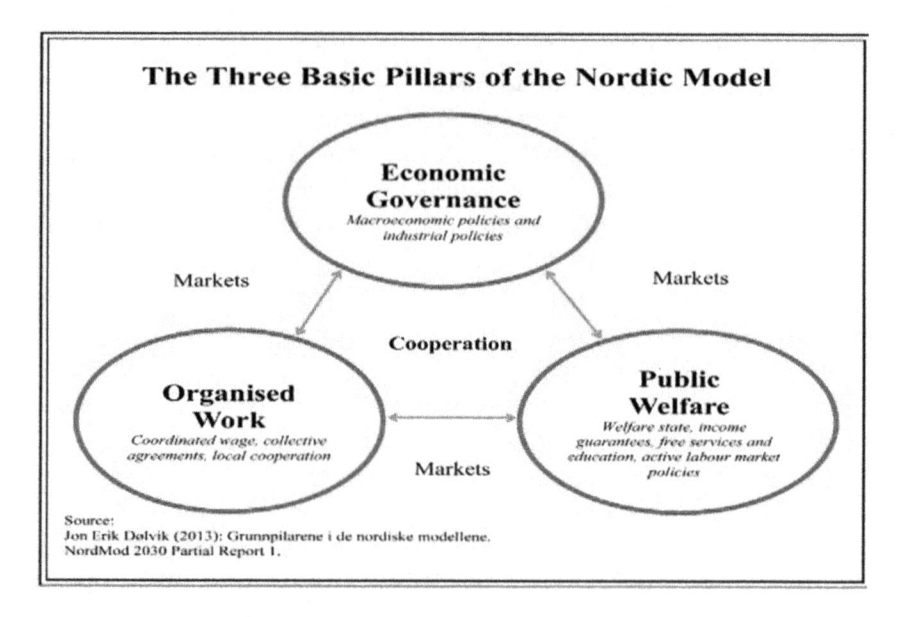

```
┌─────────────────────────────────────────────────────────────┐
│          The Three Basic Pillars of the Nordic Model        │
│                                                             │
│                      ╭─────────────╮                        │
│                     │   Economic    │                       │
│                     │  Governance   │                       │
│                     │ Macroeconomic policies and│           │
│                     │  industrial policies │                │
│                      ╰─────────────╯                        │
│         Markets         ↗      ↖        Markets             │
│                                                             │
│                       Cooperation                           │
│       ╭─────────────╮              ╭─────────────╮          │
│       │  Organised   │              │   Public     │         │
│       │    Work      │ ←─────────→ │   Welfare    │         │
│       │ Coordinated wage, collective│ Welfare state, income │
│       │ agreements, local cooperation│ guarantees, free services and│
│       │              │   Markets    │ education, active labour market│
│       │              │              │   policies   │         │
│       ╰─────────────╯              ╰─────────────╯          │
│                                                             │
│  Source:                                                    │
│  Jon Erik Dølvik (2013): Grunnpilarene i de nordiske modellene.│
│  NordMod 2030 Partial Report 1.                             │
└─────────────────────────────────────────────────────────────┘
```

Fig. 15.1 The Nordic Model, Dølvik (2013)

unique in the world because of the close partnership between employers, trade unions and the governments to ensure that a well developed social safety net is in place for anybody who finds themselves excluded from the world of work for whatever reason (West Pedersen & Kuhnle, 2017). Each of the Nordic countries has their own take on self-care and antidotes to stress based on both culture, tradition and history. Below are examples of typical antidotes to stress in Sweden Denmark and Finland.

The Swedish idea about catching up for a fika to enjoy coffee and a piece of cake is common practice as already established has another dimension relating to the word *lagom*. *Lagom* translated to English means "everything in moderation". For example, enjoying a fika means to enjoy only *one* piece of cake and not *two*. Overindulgence is frowned upon, as the expected behaviour is to show restraint. For Swedes, lagom is central to ensuring a happy work-life balance, it means to participate in fika breaks, social gatherings, and to take advantage of the work place policy encouraging all staff a free hour per week for exercise during office hours.

The Danish word *Hygge* relates to cultivating feelings of contentment that leads to a sense of happiness (Internations, 2018). For the Danes it is about quality time with family and friends. Hygge is celebrated particularly during the dark months to combat feelings of sadness common to all Nordic citizens, with lots of candles and lights enjoying hot chocolate and Danish pastries, it is about comfort and relaxation. Hygge during summer means bike rides, street festivals, and picnics ensuring a happy, healthy and well balanced life style.

The Finns secret to self-care is cultivating *sisu*. Sisu translated into English refers to persistence, stoicism, resilience and determination (Lahti, 2019). Development of sisu is about nurturing a healthy body and mind that starts at birth. Sisu is central to the Finnish identity: it refers to not giving up when things are tough and includes honesty, humility and integrity. The antidote to immediate stress relief practised by *all* Finns is about enjoying a sauna night with family and friends and that often depending on access to one of the thousand lakes includes a dip or swim in freezing water regardless of the season.

Understanding Swedish Higher Education, Universal Labour Laws, and Rights

The Swedish Government has the overall responsibility for the 14 Swedish Universities and 17 University Colleges found in Sweden. The funding for all universities and colleges come from government sources. The government's role is to provide the goals, guidelines and the allocation of resources to the university sector while universities are independent public authorities where each university decide and organise courses and programs they offer and research priorities.

The Swedish Ministry of Employment are responsible for labour law and work environments. There are several legislated acts protecting all employees in Sweden. Table 15.1 below provides some examples of rights of *all* Swedish employees.

Table 15.1 Swedish universal rights and benefits

Rights	Details
Holidays	Five weeks paid vacation after one-year full-time employment. (For academics 40 years and over, 7 weeks)
Maternity and paternity leave	Parents in Sweden have the right to 480 days of leave from work to care for their children, equally shared between the mother and father and is non-transferrable
Childcare allowance	Monthly childcare allowance is paid till children turn 16. Or for sick or disabled children till they turn 19
Caring for sick children	To *vab* is staying home caring for your children when they are sick. In Sweden, it is not only the mother but also the father who stays home to care for their children. Grandparents and friends are also eligible for time off (fully paid) from work to step in to support families with care needs
Public Holidays	Swedes call public holidays for *röda dagar* [red days], public holidays are always written in red font in calendars. These are of course days in addition to the holidays
Subsidies for gym membership or other training	To support Swedish full-time and part-time employees to maintain a good physical and mental health all full-time employees are offered 2000.00 Swedish crowns each year towards some form of memberships e.g., strength training, swimming, bowling, table tennis, tennis, squash, dance, tai chi, qigong, office massage and so on. Even activities such as singing, dancing, acupuncture, are included
One paid hour a week to keep fit (Some employers)	All employees are entitled to one hour per week to train or to attend some form of physical activity during working hours, as long as it does not interfere with work commitment. For academics this relates to, for example, teaching or meetings
Fika breaks	A cherished and a common tradition in Sweden is to catch up with friends for a coffee for *fika*. While all Swedish employees are entitled to 30 minutes morning and afternoon fika breaks, fika can take place any day or time

Source: Swedish for Professionals (2018)

Swedish Work Environment Authority

In Sweden, the Work Environment Act (Arbetsmiljölagen, 1978) provides direction and sets the goals for achieving a good work environment. The Work Environment Act applies to all areas of occupational life in Sweden, including students, self-employed persons, military conscripts and inmates in institutions. The Swedish Work Environment Authority support the Swedish government overseeing that all universities, businesses and organisations follow the Organisational and Social Work Environment (AFS, 2015) Act. Their research have found that there are two main causes of work related stress, an increase in workloads and the workplace culture (psychosocial environment) and aligns with international research (Melin et al., 2014; Pignata et al., 2018). Other causes that are known to cause stress include, shift work, isolation, bullying, victimisation, threats and threats of violence. The role of the Swedish Work Environment Authority is to inspect workplaces, ensure employers commit to regular work environment inspections, to promote cooperation between employers and employees, supporting overseeing policies are in place to encourage disabled employees in the work place.

Each place of work in Sweden has Health and Safety and Well-being officers who are also union representatives and elected by the personnel of each work place or university faculty's department. These Health and Safety and Well-being officers are required to undergo regular training in all matters relating to Health and Safety and Well-being policies. They collaborate with the Head of School to oversee that government policies are in place, develop reports, document incidents and resolve issues or conflicts threatening the health and well-being of employees. Each of the Health and Safety delegates has the power to report any incident relating to health and safety and well-being to the Swedish Work Environment Authority.

All university staff have opportunities to meet individually with one or two of the Health and Safety officers during the yearly inspection of the workplace environment. For example, ensuring that the academic's workspace is safe, checking to make sure the office lighting, the condition of the air, office desk and chair as well as computer are all in working order. Additionally, and relating to the psychosocial environment all staff are encouraged to express any concern they may have, relating to workload, or social communication and support. Where a staff member want to discuss issues of sensitive nature a date is set for a separate and a longer meeting. The official visit usually ends with a reminder of the upcoming yearly psychosocial environment survey that all staff are encouraged to fill in.

Workplace Health and Well-Being at the University of Gothenburg, Sweden

Responses to a workplace health and well-being survey from 2415 academic teaching and research staff working at the University of Gothenburg (Leffler & Schaller, 2015), found that 1956 (80%) of the academics stated that they enjoy their work. Causes relating to academic stress, included; increase in workload (75%), not being able to let go of thinking about work at the end of the working day (71%), not being able to say no to extra work (68%) and not doing a good job (72%). These finding are in line with international research identifying sources of stress (Guthrie et al., 2017; Madsen et al., 2014).The findings also noted that (72%) of academics experienced frustrations for not having the time to complete work during normal business hours. Working outside business hours seem to have become the norm for many academics and has shown to impact negatively on family and private life (Melin et al., 2014; Pignata et al., 2018). Regardless of policies on discrimination, research has found that female academics relatively new or in the middle of their academic careers with children and particularly children or other family members needing care are particularly vulnerable to stress and may contribute not only to lower quality job performance but can result in denial of tenure or promotion (O'Laughlin & Bischoff, 2005).

Reflecting on the above findings confirm the sources to the growing number of academics experiencing work place stress at the Faculty of Education. In meeting with academics in my role as the senior executive of OHS team it was not surprising to find that most of the academics stated that they highly enjoyed their work but found the continuing increase in their workload stressful. They mentioned that the extra workload prevented them from doing a good job and that taking home extra work had a detrimental impact on their family and private life. What became apparent was that while most academics wanted to open up and voice their concerns about the heavy workloads and long working hours to their supervisor or head of school they chose not to, fearing repercussions. They did not want to be seen as "trouble makers", fearing that to discuss concerns with their supervisor may influence negatively on their future promotional prospects. Academics who "complained" about the workload and or long working hours were met with comments from colleagues (and supervisors) such as *we all work long hours* or *it is part of the job description*. There was and continue to be a perception among some academics about the academic who "complains" that they are not *resilient* enough; they are "unprofessional", and even lazy. This fear of not being able to discuss, question, or challenge work related issues openly in a workplace is a reflection of a *culture of silence* (Freire, 1972) and sadly, the "strongest predictor of the culture of silence is the attitude of the direct supervisor" (Vakola & Bouradas, 2005, p. 451).

Most of the conflicts among academics were work-related, for example, some related to disagreements about changing responsibilities in projects. Being isolated or "cut" out from participation in a successful research grant application, (this related to a senior academic who had a significant part in writing of a major grant application), or where new academics were denied co-authorship. However, the bullying and harassment reported to me was particularly challenging to bring to the attention of the faculty leadership. The confidentiality clause in relation to my role meant that I could not disclose the name of the person (s) who was experiencing bullying or harassment. The unfortunate response from the leadership was that "it was impossible to provide support for the person if [they] did not know who the person was". Interestingly, there is a zero tolerance policy against bullying at the university and it is against the law in Sweden, yet it continues to persist, as does a *culture of silence*. Academics being afraid to discuss their concerns to their immediate supervisor or head of school related to a distrust in a fair, transparent and honest process. Unfortunately, the lack of support from the leadership resulted with several competent academics transferring to other institutions, resign or take sick leave.

Kaya Cicerali and Cicerali (2016) state that poor leadership is often responsible for why individual staff members are afraid to stand up to bullying, victimisation, or discrimination whether directed at himself, herself, or a colleague. The effects of not sharing frustrations or about feeling overwhelmed whether with a trusted colleague or an empathetic supervisor or head of school has led some academics resorting to unhealthy coping strategies to deal with their stress. For example, self-medication with alcohol, prescription drugs or illegal drugs, smoking, an overindulgence in unhealthy foods and so on. Feeling under severe and prolonged stress can also result in changed behaviour, irritability, inappropriate and unintended verbal abuse towards colleagues, friends and family. It is the interference of work competing with family and private life that are associated with stress, depression and burnout and a reason why committed academics choose to leave the profession or in extreme cases have known to commit suicide (Flaherty, 2017; Hughes, 2018).

Leadership in Sweden

There are particular leadership styles that have shown to be contributing to academic stress and burnout. Madsen et al. (2014), in their study from Denmark and Sweden found that an autocratic leadership style is particularly detrimental to academic psychological well-being. This leadership style increase employees' symptoms of burnout, stress, sleep related disorders, reduced job satisfaction, absenteeism, job performance, and intentions to leave. Autocratic leadership is often associated with managerialism and accountability (Heystek, 2007). Leffler and Schaller (2015) noted that Swedish academics are highly critical of the managerial style of leadership who they describe as being "driven by results, control and self-interest by the departments' leadership rather than contributing to the common good of the society" this autocratic leadership style is in direct contrast to the traditional Swedish Democratic leadership style.

Democratic Leadership

Primus inter paras or "first among equals" [translated from Latin] has been associated with a "typical" Swedish leadership style. For example, in successful Swedish organisations while titles are recognised, it is the leader, who sees him or herself as *equal* to that of others who is accorded unofficial respect traditionally owing to the seniority in office.

Democratic leaders emphasise consensus and collaboration, they encourage innovation, open discussions and especially consensus in decision making at team meetings. This is in direct contrast to autocratic leaders whose leadership style encourage a *culture of silence*.

A popular model of leadership in Sweden and other Nordic countries that build on the democratic leader model is the Transformational leader.

Transformational Leadership

Transformational leadership style is associated with positive employee mental health outcomes and sense of well-being (Madsen et al., 2014). The characteristics of transformational leadership is the ability to inspire, motivate and support individual employees to find novel and better ways to reach goals. Transformational leaders provide feedback and are committed to quality and fairness. This leadership style is associated with reduced stress and job satisfaction among academics that encourage, academic autonomy, control, involvement in decision making as well as providing time for research and professional development. Interestingly, transformational leaders have abilities to intervene in conflict-ridden interpersonal situations as these become apparent and that has shown to lead to improved employee psychological well-being.

Work-Life Imbalance vs. Sustainable Work-Life Balance

It should not come as a surprise that universities with *work-life imbalance* (Sheppard, 2016), experience high staff turnover, high absenteeism, poor staff morale and motivation, an increase in staff grievances and disputes, poor quality in student learning, and learning outcomes and low productivity in relation to publications. On the other hand, universities promoting *sustainable work-life balance that include family-friendly policies* where care and fairness permeate the culture show that academics not only are motivated and committed to their work. There is greater job satisfaction, with less job burnout, and less work-to-family conflict (Sheppard, 2016). There are many good examples of successful university-supported programs, programs that include, organised on-campus activities during lunch such as, walking, jogging, or joining a gym and mindfulness training to release stress. The university to offer special programs targeted to support the faculty or institutional leadership, for example, improving workplace culture, recognising the symptoms of workplace stress and burnout, implementing and evaluating *effective* and *non-threatening* interventions.

Swedish Fika Breaks in Academia

The equivalent to catching up for morning or afternoon tea in Sweden is *fika*. Fika breaks are a serious part of Swedishness, part of workers' rights, and health and safety that has been negotiated by the Swedish trade unions with employees (Morley, Angervall, Berggren, & Dodillet, 2018). The rationale for fika breaks is that it provides a space where university staff have opportunities to develop inclusive and supportive communities, a non-threatening environment to socialise, share and discuss things other than work over a cup of coffee. In addition, some Swedish universities provide fruit twice a week as well as a social afternoon fika break, once a week, normally on a Monday afternoon, where all departmental staff are invited to enjoy some time away from their offices as such, a recognition by the faculty of the importance of staff well-being.

Unfortunately, while every day fika breaks is highly welcomed and valued by all university staff, not all academics have the time to attend. For academics with heavy workloads fika breaks is not about relaxing over a cup of coffee while chatting with colleagues about mundane things to relieve work stress. Fika break is about catching up on urgent matters relating to work. Similarly, lunches once leisurely enjoyed by most academics, have turned into so-called *working lunches* where the conversation between the bites of one's salad or sandwich is work related. Regular attendance at the 30-minute morning and afternoon fika breaks are mainly the university administrative staff. Morley et al. (2018, p. 12) argue that fika breaks today at the university has become "a management tool for surveillance and regulation, and the relay of social, organizational and occupational norms" rather than what it should be intended for, an enjoyable, and social short break to support happiness and positivity among colleagues.

There is no doubt about the importance of health and safety and well-being in the Swedish work environments. The growing stress and burnout among in Swedish employees has fortunately seen a growth in research into mental health disorders including stress and burnout (Hjärnfonden, 2017; Swedish Work Environment Authority, 2018). For example, the establishment of Stress Research Institute at the Stockholm's university, Hjärnfonden, (2018), Institute of Health and Care Sciences at the University of Gothenburg. Even so, the regulated working hours, conditions and holidays by the country's trade unions and overseen by the Swedish Work Environment Authority (2018) seem not to be enough to stop the growing trend of academic burnout as seen in some universities.

Recognising When Enough Is Enough

Most academics seem to believe that the attainment of a sustainable work-life balance is their personal responsibility alone. While this is true to some extent it is not entirely so. In Sweden and in all Nordic the responsibility for a work-life balance and well-being for all employees (including university staff) is the responsibility of the employer. It is legislated in laws (AFS, 2015, p. 4; Arbetsmiljölagen, 1978).

University leadership that support sustainable work life balance, inclusion and well-being recognise the harm caused by heavy workloads and long working hours to the mental health and well-being of academic staff members. The good news is that there are universities that go beyond formal policies and have in place and available support measures for all academics authentic with or without family responsibilities, whether sole-parent, or married, caring or not caring for sick children or other family members' work-life balance and well-being.

Nonetheless and importantly, recognising the signs of stress and burnout may not be that easy, especially for some individuals "used" to high workloads, who have high expectations and enjoy the challenges of multitasking. There are also academics with family responsibilities such as caring for family members who are not well and who do not recognise when they may need to take time out. These high achieving academics and especially female academics may simply consider their academic workload and family responsibilities as a norm. They believe they are resilient and tough enough to handle both work and family commitments regardless of the actual cost to their own sense of well-being if they do not allow some time out for relaxation.

Recognising the signs of burnout early is crucial, especially since studies (Melin et al., 2014) suggest that the recovery time from burnout after the second or third time is that much longer for some individuals. Some signs to look out for include: feeling exhausted, experiencing anxiety, forgetfulness, feeling detached, emotional, sense of isolation, insomnia and depression. Again, these signs may differ in both strength and duration and does not apply to every individual experiencing stress or are on the verge of burnout. It is though important to take a step back to consider whenever one or more of these symptoms arise. Take a day or two off from work and deliberately do not engage with anything remotely relating to your work.

There are numerous if not an overwhelming amount of self-help material available on the internet for self-diagnosis for many mental health disorders and in particular relating to stress, burnout, and anxiety. Problem is that self-diagnosis in the midst of a crises can be misleading and can be detrimental to ones state of mind if not outright depressing (Pillay, 2010).

Stress

Sweden's Karolinska University in Stockholm provides comprehensive information relating to stress. Stress manifests itself in a number of ways and Table 15.2 provides a description of stress and their consequences:

It is of course important to know that what one person may experience as stressful another person may not. Stress like burnout is highly individual as is their recovery time.

Table 15.2 Causes of stress and symptoms

Causes of stress	Manifest in
Emotional reactions—teary, anger, irritability	Worry, anxiety, low mood, tiredness, feelings of inadequacy, isolation, and sleep disturbances
Intellectual functions	Impaired concentration, difficulties with problem solving, making decisions, visualising goals and organising work. Lowered involvement and stamina
Lowered immune function	Increased susceptibility to infection
Gastro-intestinal problems	Increased formation of gas, intestinal noises, constipation, diarrhoea, nausea, vomiting and various levels of aches and pain. These symptoms can occur even if dietary habits are good
Cardiovascular disease	Palpitations, high blood pressure, heart attack. Increased risk for stroke. A negative effect on blood lipids
Headache, in specific areas or more general	Migraine and tension headaches can be caused by stress and tension
Skin rashes	Eczema and herpes infections usually appears at times of fatigue and stress
Pains and discomfort in joints	Neck and shoulder blade problems (stress can often lead to round shoulders, hunching, poor working posture and fewer breaks during work). Lumbar back pain and repetitive strain injuries

Hjärnfonden

Translated from Swedish to English and based on suggestions by Hjärnfonden (2017), a well known and highly regarded Swedish organisation specialising in mental health disorders. The following very simple and effective steps can help identifying initial stress symptoms while supporting awareness and a sense of personal calm, (1) Relax and breathe, (2) The art of saying no, (3) Let's get physical, (4) Fika for mental well-being, and (5) Sleep.

Relax and Breathe

We can handle periods of stress better if we remind ourselves to relax. To check how relaxed you are take a moment to check your breathing (not, the smartphone). Place your hand on your stomach and breathe normally, did you find your stomach rise? If so you are breathing from your diaphragm or stomach (called deep breathing). This is how we breathe when we are calm and how we calm ourselves. On the other hand, if you are breathing from the upper part of your body especially around your throat area (referred to as shallow breathing) this is often how we breathe when we are anxious and stressed.

Now take another breath and note how your stomach is rising, hold your breath and count to three, exhale and let go of all air (it does not matter whether let go of air through your nose or your mouth) and as you do, allow yourself to relax. Continue breathing from your diaphragm for a few minutes and you will note a sense of calm. Just allow yourself to relax and simply do nothing for a short while.

If you concentrate on remembering to breathe deeply whenever you get tense or feeling stressed, you will *immediately* begin to notice the area or areas where you hold onto any tension. Breathing correctly allows your muscles to relax. This simple technique allows for a simultaneous recovery of your mind and body.

The Art of Saying No

Multitasking is common among academics and it is both ridiculous and harmful and really does nothing to a job well done. When asked to take on extra duties on an already full workload can be stressful and for many academics, difficult to say no. Yet, learning to say no (in a nice way) is crucial to not let symptoms of stress or burnout get hold. A good idea when asked to take on extra tasks is to ask for a day to think about it. This extra time allows you to think about the influence this might have on your mental and overall well-being. Not getting that promotion. This extra thinking time might also help you think of ideas how to share the work with a colleague, or delegate the work. Importantly, it is all about communication, so do not be afraid to share your concerns, ideas and there is nothing wrong asking for help. You might be surprised at the response.

Let's Get Physical

The dangers of sitting in front of the computer for hours on end is well documented, as are the benefits of regular short 7–15 minute walks each couple of hours. The benefits of short walks outside in the fresh air allow clarity in thinking and a sense of overall well-being. Why not get together with colleagues and friends for a regular 15-minute walk before lunch. The message here is to trust the benefits of moving your body even if only for a short time, (regardless of your age). Of course there is no reason why you cannot join a gym, yoga classes, dance classes, a gospel choir, swimming, gardening, and so on.

Fika for Mental Well-Being

Inviting colleagues or getting to know new colleagues from other faculties for fika is a good way of relaxing and developing and enjoying new friendships. Find a nice café or buy take away coffee and go for a walk. Why not begin a conversation explaining the meaning of fika. Keeping conversation light hearted and happy, enjoy having a good laugh and you will ensure a happy and positive outlook towards work and an appreciation of learning about others.

Sleep

There is nothing more crucial to physical and mental health than a good night's sleep and nope, no drugs needed. Undisturbed sleep (or a good night's sleep) is necessary in the recovery process of body and mind disorders. Unfortunately, bad habits such as checking and keeping the mobile phone next to our beds, the staring at computer or TV screens are habits that keep us from settling down. Simple things such as, ensuring a regular bedtime, keeping the bedroom dark and the room temperature cool (not cold), having a warm bath after a particularly stressful day followed by perhaps a warm cup of milk or tea are just some ways to unwind. Suffering from insomnia and trying to force sleep only adds to stress. Rather than worrying about sleep why not read a book, or listen to easy listening or calming music. Relax and trust that sleep will follow naturally.

Swedish research suggest that our addiction to checking our smartphones constantly, staring at our mobile phones screens or laptop screens is detrimental to our eyesight and mental health disorders such as anxiety and depression, and especially is known to interfere with a good night's sleep.

Conclusion

Stress-related disorders among academics is a growing global phenomenon and does not differentiate between the socioeconomic statuses of countries (Poalses & Bezuidenhout, 2018). Reasons such as, continuous governmental reforms, managerial accountability, cuts in university funding, technological changes, and organisational changes are cited as causes in the increase in work related stress disorders and burnout not only among Swedish academics but among academics worldwide (Melin et al., 2014; Pignata et al., 2018). The intensification of academic work is concerning to all universities regardless of the high work satisfaction among academics. A way forward to ensure quality education and research is to allow autonomy, freedom, control, challenge, and genuine support for all academics with family commitments before experiences of stress and burnout. This means (1) overseeing and decreasing academic workloads where necessary, (2) implement programs to develop understanding resilience as culturally, socially and temporally bound, and (3) understanding that to support develop resilience and well-being, can be facilitated through individual support in the development of protective factors, for example, hope, efficacy, social networks and family.

Here's hoping your resilient university provides you with the necessary support to ensure a happy, sustainable healthy and safe work-life balance.

If All Else Fails

Finally, regardless where you live or work is to remember and accept that you and you alone are responsible for your own happiness and well-being.

It may be about proudly accepting support from mental health care professionals recommended and offered by the workplace. It may be about trying out new activities to de-stress. Meditation/Mindfulness twice a day can help with stress and anxiety as can deep breathing, similarly, hitting the gym or at least making sure you are walking 20–30 minutes or 10,000 steps each day whether the weather is crap or not, is good. Make sure to sleep and eat well (and choose healthy foods). And, heaven forbid if you decide to ditch the gym and head for the pub to have that forever dreamt-of and, to you, well earned sirloin with a glass or four after work all by yourself and to top it off with cake with two dollops of cream. A true anti-dote to stress is a good laugh, allowing yourself a treat is part of happiness, health and well-being. Be kind to yourself and those around you.

References

American Psychological Association. (2014). *The road to resilience*. Washington, DC: American Psychological Association. Retrieved November 25, 2018, from http://www.apa.org/helpcenter/road-resilience.aspx

Blix, A. G., Cruise, R. J., Mitchell, B. M., & Blix, G. G. (1994). Occupational stress among university teachers. *Educational Research, 36*(2), 157–169.

Clandinin, D. J., Cave, M. T., & Berendonk, C. (2017). Narrative inquiry: A relational research methodology for medical education. *Medical Education, 51*(1), 89–96.

Coates, H., & Goedegebuure, L. (2010). *The Real Academic Revolution. Why we need to reconceptualise Australia's future academic workforce, and eight possible strategies for hot to go about this*. Melbourne, VIC: Research Briefing, LH Martin Institute.

Connelly, F. M., & Clandinin, D. J. (2006). Narrative inquiry. In J. Green, G. Camili, & P. Elmore (Eds.), *Handbook of complementary methods in education research* (pp. 375–385). Mahwah, NJ: Lawrence Erlbaum.

Dølvik, J. E. (2013). *Nordic models facing European crisis: Still flexible adapters?* Oslo, Norway: FAFO.

Flaherty, C. (2017). Aftermath of a Professor's suicide. *Inside Higher Ed*. Retrieved October 21, 2018, from https://www.insidehighered.com/news/2017/04/21/recent-suicide-professor-sparks-renewed-discussions-about-access-mental-health

Freire, P. (1972). *Cultural action for freedom*. Harmondsworth, UK: Penguin Books.
Guthrie, S., Lichten, C., van Belle, J., Ball, S., Knack, A., & Hofman, J. (2017). *Understanding mental health in the research environment: A rapid evidence assessment*. Santa Monica, CA: Prepared for the Royal Society and the Wellcome Trust; RAND Europe.
Harrison, B. J. (1999). Are you destined to burn out? *Fund Raising Management*, *30*(3), 25–27.
Heystek, J. (2007). Reflecting on principals as managers or moulded leaders in a managerialistic school system. *South African Journal of Education*, *27*(3), 491–505.
Hjärnfonden. (2017). *Stress och stressrelaterad psykisk ohälsa. Ett bakgrundsmaterial* [Stress and stress-related mental illness. A background material]. Retrieved October 17, 2018 from https://www.hjarnfonden.se/wpcontent/uploads/2017/12/171214_M_Stress_bakgrundsmaterial.pdf
Hjärnfonden. (2018). *Stress: Vad händer i kroppen när vi stressar* [Stress: What happens in the body when we stress]. Retrieved October 17, 2018 from https://www.hjarnfonden.se/vad-ar-stress/
Hughes, M. (2018). University says lecturer who died was 'loved and respected by students and staff'. *Wales Online*. Retrieved December 17, 2018, from https://www.walesonline.co.uk/news/wales-news/university-says-lecturer-who-died-14329099
InterNations. (2018). *Denmark: Balancing job, family & hygge*. Retrieved December 20, 2018, from https://www.internations.org/denmark-expats/guide/denmark-balancing-job-family-hygge-17495
Kaya Cicerali, L., & Cicerali, E. E. (2016). A qualitative study on how Swedish organizations deal with workplace bullying. *Nordic Psychology*, *68*(2), 87–99.
Lahti, E. (2019). *Sisu begins where perseverance ends*. Retrieved January 15, 2019 from https://finland.fi/life-society/sisu-begins-perseverence-ends/
Leffler, M., & Schaller, J. (2015). Arbetsmiljöbarometer 2015. [Work barometer] Resultat från en undersökning av anställdas arbetsmiljö. Göteborgs Universitet. Retrieved July 3, 2018 from https://medarbetarportalen.gu.se/digitalAssets/1557/1557500_arbetsmiljobarometer-2015.pdf
Madsen, I. E. H., Hanson, L. L. M., & Rugulies, R. (2014). Does good leadership buffer effects of high emotional demands at work on risk of antidepressant treatment? A prospective study from two Nordic countries. *Social Psychiatry and Psychiatric Epidemiology*, *49*(8), 1209–1218.
Melin, M., Astvik, W., & Bernhard-Oettel, C. (2014). New work demands in higher education. A study of the relationship between excessive workload,

coping strategies and subsequent health among academic staff. *Quality in Higher Education, 20*(3), 290–308.

Morley, L., Angervall, P., Berggren, C., & Dodillet, S. (2018). Re-purposing fika: Rest, recreation or regulation in the neoliberalized Swedish University? *European Journal of Higher Education, 8*(4), 400–414.

O'Laughlin, E. M., & Bischoff, L. G. (2005). Balancing parenthood and academia: Work/family stress as influenced by gender and tenure status. *Journal of Family Issues, 26*(1), 79–106.

Pignata, S., Winefield, A. H., Boyd, C. M., & Provis, C. (2018). Qualitative study of HR/OHS stress interventions in Australian universities. *International Journal on Environmental Research and Public Health, 15*(103), 1–16.

Pillay, S. (2010). *The dangers of self diagnosis. How self-diagnosis can lead you down the wrong path*. Retrieved October 17, 2018 from https://www.psychologytoday.com/us/blog/debunking-myths-the-mind/201005/the-dangers-self-diagnosis

Poalses, J., & Bezuidenhout, A. (2018). Mental health in higher education: A comparative stress risk assessment at an Open Distance Learning university in South Africa. *International Review of Research in Open and Distance Learning, 19*(2), 169–190.

Sheppard, G. (2016). *Work-life balance programs to improve employee performance* (Walden dissertation and doctoral studies). London, UK: Walden University Scholar Work.

Southwick, S. M., Bonanno, G. A., Masten, A. S., Panter-Brick, C., & Yehuda, R. (2014a). Resilience definitions, theory, and challenges: Interdisciplinary perspectives. *European Journal of Psychotraumatology, 5*(1), 25338.

Southwick, S. M., Bonanno, G. A., Masten, A. S., Panter-Brick, C., & Yehuda, R. (2014b). *Resilience definitions, theories, and challenges: Interdisciplinary perspectives*. European Traumatology. Proceedings paper. Retrieved November 17, 2018 from https://www.ncbi.nlm.nih.gov/pmc/articles/PMC4185134/pdf/EJPT-5-25338.pdf

Swedish for Professionals. (2018). *Benefits of working in Sweden*. Retrieved November 11, 2018 from http://swedishforprofessionals.com/benefits/

Swedish Work Environment Authority. (2018). *Health and safety*. Retrieved December 2, 2017 from https://www.av.se/en/

Vakola, M., & Bouradas, D. (2005). Antecedents and consequences of organisational silence: An empirical investigation. *Employee Relations, 27*(4/5), 441–458.

Watts, J., & Robertson, N. (2011). Burnout in university teaching staff: A systematic literature review. *Educational Research, 53*(1), 33–50.

West Pedersen, A., & Kuhnle, S. (2017). The Nordic welfare state model 1 Introduction: The concept of a "Nordic model". In O. P. Knutsen (Ed.), *The Nordic models in political science: Challenged, but still viable?* (pp. 249–272). Bergen, Norway: Fagbokforlaget.

16

Using Clay in Spiritually Ecological-Existential Art Therapy: To "See", to "Listen" and to "Understand" by Hands

Jaroslava Šicková-Fabrici

Introduction

This chapter draws on the work of neurologists Cozolino, who believes that traumatic events rejected as unbearable by consciousness are stored in the implicit memory system in the unconscious. The tactile stimulation provokes forgotten memories and builds a bridge between consciousness and unconsciousness and offers the change and transformation of negative feelings and attitudes through artistic creation (Landgarten, 1981). The process is guided by art therapists providing a safe place for reflection, a place of fiction and imagination (Horovitz, 2009).

Background to the Study

In the following text, I introduce the reader to some of my experiences from my art therapy praxis. Growing up in the family where my mother was a sculptor I fell in love with clay as a child. Then when studying

J. Šicková-Fabrici (✉)
University J. A. Komenský, Bratislava, Slovakia

sculpture at the Academy of Art my favourite material became clay, again. Several years after finishing at the academy I started to work as an art therapist with teenagers with mental disorders. Again clay became the most expressive material for art therapy with all kinds of populations. There is no doubt that clay, from the Earth, is fascinating art material not only in art, but also in art therapy.

Clay is a very appropriate material for use in art therapy, especially in its existential therapeutic context (Petzold & Orth, 1991). The mystery of creation of the world and of man is similar in the sense of the mystery of creating, whether the creator is a professional sculptor or child with a disability, clay can provide the perfect avenue for therapeutic outcomes (Šicková-Fabrici, 2002).

I have been witnessing that as in the summer thunderstorm, where it is possible to conduct an immense energy of lightning into the ground, into earth; it is the same earth, clay, which is able, in an art therapeutic context, to eliminate, or to *earth* the explosions of aggression, anger, rage, as well as grief and sorrow. Healing earth (*Heilende Erde* in German) is a fine powder. It is ground earth, which in Germany is sold at the chemist's for external use against insect stings, or as a medicine for minor injuries. Fine earth is an absorbent of toxic matter and a constituent part of pharmaceutical preparations treating digestive disorders. I believe in the same therapeutic effect of earth on injured souls. Beside the smoothness of this material, it is also haptic pleasure in the process of touching (Elbrecht, 2013) as a way of communicating.

Work at the Clay Field, a sensory-based therapy, was founded in 1972 by Professor Heinz Deuser. It is a proven and effective method to support children, adolescents and adults in their personal development. Deuser (2009) reports on the beneficial effects of clay therapy for children and adolescent with disabilities or challenging behaviour. Cornelia Elbrecht (2013) who was the assistant of Deuser describes how clay therapy helped her clients to work through their experiences of trauma. Peter Levine (2010) calls this approach *somatic experiencing* because trauma is stored in our body memory. He also has confirmed that "a kinestetic, sensory aware psychodynamic art therapy was beneficial in the context of trauma healing" (p. 21). It is evident that people react to trauma with survival instincts not with the intellect (Levine, 2010).

Looking back over more than 35 years of working in clay in art therapy, my experiences are the same: The bodily oriented experience of haptics and kinaesthetic "doing" in clay reportedly supported many of my clients to reduce aggressive behaviour, and to gain insight and various perspectives into their problem solving.

In art therapy with clay it is crucial to rely more on the hands than on the head (Elbrecht, 2013). During this process, the motor impulses are more important than cognitive ones. Through the moulding of figures, especially one's own figure, can help the art therapists to evaluate the different attitudes of clients towards themselves, other people, their problems and their environment. Dutch art therapist and the priest Hilarion Petzold (Petzold & Orth, 1991) describes work with clay with young drug addicts. He stressed its therapeutic potential, which lies in the reformation of the self-aggressive impulses of drug addicts, whereby instead of injecting drugs, they transmit these aggressive impulses into clay.

Clay is suitable also for family art therapy. The art therapist can gain lots of valuable information from family sculptures and their spatial constellation during the working in clay by family members. One can get better acquainted with the family dynamics and the hierarchy of family authorities (Kwiatkowska, 1978).

Another of Petzold's case studies (1991) describes work with dying patients. They are fascinating. One speaks about a young woman, dying of breast cancer. When moulding with an art therapist's help, she managed to convey in clay, during the last passage of her life, all her negative emotions, anger, remorse, reproaches, unresolved conflicts, and through the expression of these emotions, and find reconciliation and peace. Her last sculpture portrayed a nest with an egg in it. This motif expressed, besides her health problem, (she has suffered under the breast cancer) the desire that the earth may accept her in the same way. Clay, as art therapy material, with its activities like throwing, squeezing, shaping, hand modeling, re-modeling correction, and casting is suitable for: breaking barriers of fear; as a substitution for verbal communication; the elimination of aggressive behavior; the development of imagination, and three-dimensional perception; creating space for overview, as the background for changing attitudes towards oneself and others. Work with clay strengthens self-confidence; is a medium of compensation for absent or damaged senses (sightless, impaired sight); offers relaxation and rehabilitation for people with distorted fine motor skills; gives opportunity for mentally disabled children to physically perceive and understand various contexts, which are complex abstractions for them, in both graphic and verbal forms.

Research Design and Case Studies

In the following section, I describe the art therapy process using clay in an example from my experience.

> A nine old Romany boy was adopted, when he was three, by a couple, who were parents of another child. In spite of their loving care the boy was often very aggressive. He did not respond to expressions of affection, and could not bear a tender touch. His adoptive mother explained that she often felt he treated her rudely and insensitively. He was not submissive to discipline at school, and had no friends. His behaviour and learning problems, might be, in the first place, connected with attachment disorder (AD) and the ability to develop the prime relationship with his biological mother. He was not able to adapt and attach to a new family. The boy had endured a double trauma. Shortly after birth, he had been placed in a nursery institute and later, into children's home. He was adopted by his previous stepparents for a trial period. As the boy had to undergo an appendectomy, he was taken to hospital. The family, however, did not take him back home. He was returned to the orphanage.

> At one of our sessions I asked the mother to model together with her son—each one, his or her own self-portrait. Then they were asked to present it to each other and then correct it according to their own conceptions. The boy was apparently more skilful than the mother. He kept intervening in her work, improving her self-portrait. Having finished his portrait complete with a neck, he made a neck for his mother's head, after he had taken real measurements. Standing by his mother, he huddled by her, touched her, measuring his height with his palms, and so created a real, proportionally correct image of both his and his mother's breasts. I suggested that they should attach their portraits together. The boy refused.

But he suggested that the portraits after being baked in the ceramics kiln "can stand close side by side". Only after several weeks of art therapy work he spontaneously modelled Madonna. It was actually one body with two heads—a woman's head and the baby's one. He was suddenly able to picture an attachment to mother—be it only in clay, but in reality the correction of an impaired attitude to his adoptive mother, had begun. The transfer of what he has learned by my intervention and re-moulding of clay, into the area of behaviour, communication and attitudes to other people was remarkable.

Praise Be to Touch and Tactile Feeling

When seeking a bridge between the art expressions of non-disabled people and of people with disabilities in art therapy, it will certainly be in the tactile and not in the visual area. After Czech social psychologist Bohuslav Blažek, the optical attitude towards the space conceals in itself the danger of slipping along the surface, whereas the perspective of tactile space is a perspective of value (Blažek & Olmrová, 1986). A couple of years ago, during an exhibition I had in Sweden, I saw a scene which expressed very clearly how important *touch sensing* is for children, in order to become familiar with the world. The children learn about the world through hands.

Like a bright beam of light that penetrates the darkness, a little girl, about five years old, appeared in, actually danced into the hall of the art gallery. She stopped, looked around, and suddenly came running to one of the exhibited sculpture, a stylised head of a young girl. The surface of the wood sculpture had been coloured using a medieval technique; discovered by the Slovakian Gothic master, Pavol from Levoča, using natural materials chalk, fine pigments, gold leaf and beeswax. The eyes of the girl said that she was satisfied with her spontaneous choice, which, I suppose, was not accidental.

She was feeling the natural smooth surface of the sculpture and expressed her feeling with a joyful laugh. I was filled with amazement at her intrinsic, even physiological sense for beauty of shape, surface, and her need to feel, to touch the world, where she is learning how to exist and how to live. I strongly wished that this child of twenty-first century civilization would always remain faithful to genuine, pure natural shapes and materials, as well as relationships. I wished that her senses should not be deceived by substitutes, or by artificial, plaster imitations of all kinds of pure, genuine materials, ideals, and attitudes. After a while, the little girl ran out of the gallery hall, but in no time she returned, bringing her mother to the wood sculpture. She took her mother's hands and put them on the smooth shapes of the sculpture.

Touch

Scientists are convinced that there exists a direct relation between touch and the *degree of physical proximity* and that children perceiving is evidently connected with their mental health (Servan-Schreiber, 2012). To touch, to be physically close, is something, that our culture, and particularly American culture, "has reserved for sexual contact only, or for tragic events in our life – in a hospital bed or at a funeral" (Buscaglia, 1984, p. 133). We are afraid to show our interest by touching.

The child, whom nobody touches, who no one pets, will make close contact with whatever is at hand, with stuffed toys, with an artificial compensation for his mother. If a child is deprived of all touch, he will die. The dysfunction in touch, perception and tactile systems cause problems with writing, with own body care, with social interaction. The touch influences how we perceive ourselves, how we react to our surroundings and our social interaction. Increased sensitivity to tactile impulses is linked with ADHD and Autism. But of course through inappropriate touching our own boundaries can be invaded.

Work in clay in art therapy involves an intensive tactile experience. It can link to the preverbal stage in the life client. Its regressive qualities allow art therapists to address the attachment issues or traumatic events in nonverbal way. The verbal way could be either problematic or unnecessary bypassing the problem. The need for physical contact, for touch, remains throughout life. Psychologists, psychiatrists and sociologists write about the emotional and intellectual benefits of touch. It has been proven that chemical functions in the human body change if someone touches an individual, if he/she is physically close with someone

(Buscaglia, 1984). A lack of touch leads to depression, to a loss of appetite, and to apathy, and suppresses life processes, and well-being (Servan-Schreiber, 2012). A physical shortage of touch, and of contact, is connected with emotional alienation. Specialists have acknowledged the need for touch, for emotional stimulation, especially among children and old people (Servan-Schreiber, 2012). Working with clay with different populations has highlighted to me its value in how to stimulate touch sensitivity, or to compensate for a deficit in touch perception. Victor Löwenfeld (1982) the German art therapist and art teacher worked with children who had a visual impairment, stressed that the physical experience with concrete forms among children is more important than visual perception. Art activities are not only the reproduction of what was seen, but first of all, they are creative processes. This is confirmed by the fact that drawings made in early childhood and drawing schemes made by healthy children are composed of identical formations of children who are sightless or who have impaired eyesight. He assumes that the tactile world is their only world of expression and subjectivity.

Art therapeutic activities of moulding out of pliable materials, in particular, with clay, are one of a number of very important techniques and procedures, particularly for children, but for adults, as well. They bring back the third dimension lost in our present computer era, to create a relationship with and respect for manual work, build tactile authentic experiences of subjective, individual perceptions.

The Significant Attributes of Working in Clay

The following are the attributes of clay moulding, which are significant for art therapy:

- **Self-reflection:** Melding with clay offers a unique possibility for self-reflection
- **Correction:** In contrast to correction in graphic expression, the advantage here is the possibility of permanent correction and change without any trace of the previous shape. Consequently, moulding makes it possible for even less capable "artists" to experience success; thus, it strengthens their self-assessment and self-confidence. Psychoanalytically

oriented therapists consider clay moulding as an appropriate medium for expressing inner feelings, unconscious issues that facilitates the reconstruction and rebuilding of the new function of "I" (Petzold & Orth, 1991). Projection of unconscious material through creating in clay is an expressive process. Art therapists aim to differentiate between the unconscious and consciousness (Skov, 2017). It is easier to interact with the unconscious through the dialogue with the three-dimensional object as it connects the two hemispheres of the brain. The benefit is in integrative process, symbolic communication and transformation and the potential for positive changes.

- **Regression:** Clay is a medium of regression, in the following sense. Through this mouldable material, emotions from the past can be processed again, worked out and destroyed. Humanistic oriented therapists assume that this is the most significant process, which, due to its dynamic features, may facilitate changes in the development of the client's personality. The person who is moulding and reshaping the clay, can, to some extent, reconsider his/her life and his/her problems and create new possibilities and solutions.
- **Learning:** The blind and children with impaired sight can learn to distinguish space and situational and relational terms, that are easily comprehensible for sighted children, for example, *before*, *behind*, *inside*, *outside*.
- **The structure of the human figure:** To create a human figure by moulding, which is done through bodily concrete, is easier for children than drawing and painting. Children, who during drawing were permanently in the stage of under-developed drawing where the human figure comprised only head and feet without neck of shoulder, even though their chronological age would suggest a more detailed drawing should be possible, benefit from moulding. Through moulding children can represent the body in closer proportion and with accurate parts than how they represent it through drawing.
- **Self image:** Clay is an important tool in creating one's own self-image. In this way, a child learns how to perceive his body. Clay moulding is a part of therapy called *eutony* (Steiner, 2010), where by means of physical therapy the art therapist corrects the way of holding the body during clay moulding. It is often the case, that both children and adults transfer their handicaps to their moulding—their wrong bodily posture.

- **Physical stimulation:** Bodily stimulation through tactile expression and through strengthening expressive perceptions is a way of self-realisation using mouldable material.
- **Projective value:** As children progress developmentally and when the given materials are also expanded, the projective value of work with clay increased as well. This means that the shapes that are made are less and less accidental. The artwork created is more and more a message from the child, about the child, for the child and for others.

Methods of Aesthetic—Tactile Stimulation

In order to build and promote the awareness of one's own body and to develop tactile sensations, it is advisable to include the following in art therapy work:

- finger plays with clay, and play with string
- playing with hands (tickling, clapping, squeezing)
- touching hard and soft objects
- filling plastic bags with various materials (sand, small stones, rise, cotton)
- painting with finger colours, and painting with thin clay
- painting on the wall with both hands simultaneously
- drawing with fingers on misty windows
- painting and drawing on a smooth base or on a stretched canvas with feet dipped in thin clay
- promoting perceptions of body parts (wrapping in paper rolls, curtains)
- playing with water and sand
- making clay balls and shaping clay rolls
- printing on parts of the body
- making a pot from clay rolls and clay balls

Such a variety of aesthetic-tactile stimulations bring into play various psychodynamics, which stimulates the impaired functions of perception of oneself and one's surroundings.

I refer to art therapeutic "play" with clay which emphasis on tactile experiences as *Terra therapy*. Terra means in Latin *clay* but also *earth*.

As inspiration I will introduce some concrete activities with clay that are not bound by age or ability. All these activities support visual-motor coordination.

Clay Throwing

The therapist takes out of a box, pieces of clay approximately the size of an orange, warms them in her hands and gradually throws them to the participant. In this way, eye-hand coordination is trained. Participants face the situation, where they have to catch in their hands something unknown to them, something they may fear. They often worry that they may get dirty. The process of getting dirty and then washing has a diagnostic and therapeutic value.

Moulding with Fingers

I recommend finger moulding for younger school children, as well as for preschool children, or for children with anxiety or children on the Autism spectrum. About a two-centimetre thick layer of ceramic clay is rolled out on a table with a smooth surface. The children press their fingers into the clay, making a relief mosaic. They make, for example, flowers, leaves, the sun, snail shells, roads, small houses, and trees.

The following are suggestions drawn from my own work using *Spiritually Ecological Existential Art-Therapy* (Šicková-Fabrici, 2002).

Seeking for One's Own Shape

At the onset of my work with a group of adults, I often apply the therapeutic game, *Seeking for my own shape*. Each participant is to take a piece of clay from a shapeless pile on the table, but no more than his hand can hold. In case there are some individuals who are afraid to touch the clay, I apply the principle of *mediated touch-clay throwing*. I warm the clay in my hands and then throw it in an arch-like manner so that the client should catch it. Even anxious individuals accept the clay and the atmosphere is relaxed and pleasant.

When all the participants have clay in their hands, I ask them to meld a ball. I clarify each next step in the procedure, which builds a feeling of openness between the client and me, and eventually any distrust towards the therapist or her method is overcome. After moulding the ball, we talk about what ideas this shape evokes. Their associations are usually pleasant. The ball reminds them of the sun, space, a head, a globe, an egg, an apple, or the beginning. We consider the words of Steiner (2010) who once said that everything that is important is round. Likewise Cézanne (Micko, 1975) states that the ball is the prime shape of everything. After making shapeless scribbling, a young child begins his first drawing—he makes a round shape. A circle is a symbol of wholeness, a symbol of psyche, infinity, and the family.

Later the clients re-model the ball into a cube. Re-moulding a round shape into an angular one evokes different associations and different tactile experiences. Cubes are associated with a house, a room, and a table; with stability. After circles, a further shape in a child's drawing is a square. It is a symbol of self-awareness in a certain closed space.

Next, the clients model from the cube, a many-sided object, by moulding off each of the cube's eight angles. Eight triangles are formed. This, again, brings further associations and new touch feelings. A triangle is a symbol of the superiority of the spirit over matter, the symbol of man and woman, and of a triad.

The participants hold this crystal shape in their hands, made by the same procedure, and yet, each somewhat different from the others.

We get to the point that each of the clients is to create something individual, distinctive, something of one's own. It should be the shape that suits his touch, his imagination, and his need to take life in his own hands, and to shape it by his image.

I demonstrate to the clients the possibility of utilising negative space, as well (in the same way as the "holes" of English sculptor, H. Moore), in order to form and make one's own unique form. Negative space, too, has its shape and sense. Negative things form our lives, as well.

Following these steps, each one gives a name to his artwork and by doing this; he or she gives it life. The shape, the sculpture, placed in the light, has its own real shadow. A shadow is a phenomenon carrying duality in itself and its interpretation through the introspection of each individual is unique.

Searching for and finding one's own shape is a method well suited especially for clients with depression, as this activity entails a great number of changes, and dynamic alterations, which every man, the creator of his own existence and shape, can partly influence. We are not dealing with static, unchangeable life. To *find out how to be in good shape—to find one's own shape* is a significant act. This therapeutic method can be extended and modified, so that participants create a common sculpture, or a group of sculptures by joining single pieces of artwork. The names of the artworks written on pieces of paper, may serve to give ideas for a plot of a story.

Every client is asked to write a short story, which should include the titles of all the participants' sculptures. Then the stories are read aloud. In the beginning, there had been only a bit of shapeless earth, but in the end, there are stories, on which every client has bestowed his imagination, skills and creativity. Thus, the more participants, the richer the story.

Moulding a Common Country

Both children and adults can benefit from this technique. On the table we prepare an area of clay about three cm thick and about sixty centimetres in diameter. It should form a large pancake shape, which need not necessarily have straight edges.

1. Tell the participants that this is *no man's land*.
2. Ask them to identify themselves with immigrants or asylum seekers or first settlers, and they can each work in a homestead and take possession of a portion of it.
3. Each one cuts out a portion of the clay territory. The shape does not matter. It is more important that everyone will have his own part, and should remember who his neighbour is. From a diagnostic point of view it is interesting to watch how the children manage to share the earth, the country.
4. Following this, the instruction is given: *On this piece of earth build your new existence. Everything that you think is important should be there.*

The clients often build dwellings, caves, houses, towers, lighthouses, wells, and fireplaces.

5. After their "country-islands" have been filled with all that is important to them, they are instructed to form again one unit, one land, or one country, out of all their little lands put together. This is not always as simple as it seems to be. The border areas of the single parts must remain unchanged in order to fit back together again. The larger the number of participants present, the more complicated the putting together is, but the whole artwork is more interesting. Together we are trying to create a functional country. We set communication in place between single parts. It sometimes happens that a citizen offers his neighbour to remove the fence dividing their fields, and that they should rather build a road which would connect them. This is therapeutically a very precious moment, because it builds cooperation, cohesion, and democracy.

Conclusion

To summarise the importance of using the clay I would like to stress how spontaneous shaping is important for healthy development of the child. It plays an important role in reducing aggression, depression and to gain the positive changes in the life (Šicková-Fabrici, 2002). It contributes towards the integration, harmonising, healing and enriching of the personality. The main goals are to stimulate spirituality, creativity, authenticity, responsibility in approach to oneself, other people, nature, country: Art is understood as the medium for personal and social changes and growth. The methods of SEEA are focused on supporting integrity and complexity of bio-psycho-social-ecological context of people. The working in clay facilitates the stimulation of the touch sense, rehabilitates the fine motor, brings about the opportunity of corrections and change, allows the creation of three dimensional shapes, signs, objects and symbol which have projective value through implicating sensory memory (e.g., in the cases of trauma). In a haptic process, it also carriers the emotional and memory experience. Three dimensional art expressions represent the bridge from the world of the healthy population to a population with special needs, in the paradigm of inclusion. The clay moulding in SEEA is holistic. It enables the approximation of three sensual modalities: touch, sight, hearing (verbal—words). It means the three sensual centres are approached simultaneously: temporal lobe—hearing, occipital lobe—the sight, centre of touch and proprioception in the brain has been located in the parietal lobe. For all these reasons, using clay while working with people of different age and problems is a very powerful art material.

References

Blažek, B., & Olmrová, J. (1986). *Krása a bolest*. Praha, Czech Republic: Panorama.
Buscaglia, L. (1984). *Loving each other: The challenge of human relationships*. Robbinsdale, MN: Fawcett Columbine Books.
Deuser, H. (2009). *Der haptische sinn* [The haptic sense]. Keutschach, Germany: Verlag Tonfeld-Anna Sutter.
Elbrecht, C. (2013). *Trauma healing at the clay field*. London, UK: Jessica Kingsley Publishers.
Horovitz, E. (2009). *The art therapists' primer: A clinical guide to writing assessments, diagnosis, and treatment*. Springfield, IL: Charles C Thomas Publishers.
Kwiatkowska, H. Y. (1978). *Family therapy and evaluation through art*. Springfield, IL: Charles C Thomas Publishers.
Landgarten, H. B. (1981). *Clinical art therapy: A comprehensive guide*. New York, NY: Bruner.
Levine, P. A. (2010). *In an unspoken voice: How the body releases trauma and restores goodness*. Berkley, CA: North Atlantic Books.
Löwenfeld, V. (1982). *Creative and mental growth*. New York, NY/London, UK: Macmillan Publishing.
Micko, M. (1975). *Paul Cezanne*. Prague: Odeon publisher.
Petzold, H. G., & Orth, I. (1991). *Die neue Kreativitätstherapien*. Padernborn, Germany: Junfermann Verlag.
Servan-Schreiber, D. (2012). *Healing without freud or prozac: Natural approaches to curing stress, anxiety and depression*. Prague: Pan Macmillan.

Šicková-Fabrici, J. (2002). *Základy arteterapie* [Spiritually ecological existential art-therapy]. Prague Czech Republic: Portál.
Skov, V. (2017). *Shame and creativity: From affect towards individuation.* New York, NY: Routledge.
Steiner, R. (2010). *Duchovní hierarchie* [Spiritual hierarchy]. Prague: Michael Publishing.

17

Picturing Childhood Connections: How Arts-Based Reflection and Representation Strengthen Preservice Early Childhood Teachers' Understandings About Well-Being, Belonging, and Place

Alison L. Black

Introduction and Focus

This chapter considers early childhood educators, the significance of their own formative and lived experiences, and the significance of the early environments they subsequently provide for the young children they teach. Early childhood educators have daily opportunities to support and enhance young children's well-being though responsive relationships and environments. Developing and communicating their personal and professional commitments about working with young children toward sustainable, well, and resilient futures is therefore important.

The context of this chapter is a sustainability-focused course in an Australian undergraduate early childhood education teaching degree.

A. L. Black (✉)
The University of the Sunshine Coast, Sippy Downs, QLD, Australia
e-mail: ablack1@usc.edu.au

Over the last four years, as part of coursework and assessment tasks, preservice teachers have used narrative and arts-based methods to explore personal childhood experiences and memories linked to being in relation with people, place, and the more-than-human world. Remembering and representing significant relational experiences has assisted preservice teachers' articulation of ideas about early relationships, including their own sense of belonging, well-being and connectedness. Supported by their stories and creative and historical artefacts, preservice teachers have engaged in reflection about their personal/professional commitments and hopes for children.

This chapter is interested in the telling and sharing of preservice teachers' stories, stories made possible through reflective inquiry and arts-based methods. The stance taken on theory building is that experience generates knowledge. The researcher role here is not to produce propositions and analysis of preservice teachers' personal conceptions. Rather, this chapter privileges the shared stories, the life histories, and the personal perspectives of the storytellers. Throughout the chapter, I employ, and ask to the reader to employ, a listening approach to preservice teachers' ways of knowing and being, to their descriptions of childhood and relational experiences, the influence of these experiences, and their visions for their work with children. This chapter is focused on remembering and attending to experience; remembering and attending to relationship and connection; remembering and attending to early experiences in the natural world.

Examples and fragments of preservice teacher stories are scattered across the chapter and between chapter sections. They are invitations to attend; they are invitations to pause and respond to relationships and experiences (Figs. 17.1, 17.2, 17.3, 17.4, 17.5 and 17.6).

Rena: Memories of childhood

I remember spending most of my days as a child outside. I have fond memories of days in the garden planting with my father and mother. I remember the sensation of the dirt on my fingers as I dug small holes and planted flowers with my mother, and herbs and vegetables with my father. I checked on the plants' growth most days. Going outside to find a new flower or vegetable had bloomed in the garden inspired wonder. I used the flowers as decorations for my creations in the sand pit and loved taking the herbs and vegetables inside for dinner.

17 Picturing Childhood Connections: How Arts-Based Reflection...   319

Fig. 17.1 Rena: Fond memories

Fig. 17.2 Rena and her mother

Fig. 17.3 Rena's Nan and father

Fig. 17.4 Rena: Connecting with clay

Fig. 17.5 Rena's handmade bowls

Fig. 17.6 Rena's finished art making

I have fond memories of exploring clay with my mother. We owned a pottery wheel and always had clay on hand. I remember the feel of the clay and the water between my fingers. I often watched mum make sculptures and pieces of art that she entered in the local pottery show. I remember walking around the gallery and admiring the various ceramics on display.

I had a very strong sense of connection with my family and was lucky to grow up surrounded by creative, caring adults. My nan lived across the road. I would cross the road daily with my brother and often find nan in the garden, caring for her flowers.

These relationships provided a safe base for exploration and learning and shaped my understanding of myself and the world around me. As an educator I know I play a vital role creating a sense of belonging and place for children.

These early experiences have supported my connections with nature. After reflecting on my early years, I have been eager to start using clay again. I purchased some clay to reconnect with some of the feelings I had in my childhood. When I played with the clay I remembered some of the techniques I learnt when I was younger. I rolled out coils to form the structure of a bowl and made a second bowl by kneading and shaping the clay with my hands.

I walked into my mother's garden and picked leaves, flowers and gumnuts. As I sat in the grass and pressed these natural materials against the surface of the clay I also sat with precious memories of my father and recalled the influence he was in my life. I thought back to days of gardening, smiles, sharing stories and laughter. I pressed the leaves against my newly made bowl and admired the unique details.

When my bowls had dried, I filled them with soil. I picked rosemary, basil and thyme from the garden and planted them in one bowl in memory of my father and his garden. I picked pink and white periwinkles and planted them in the other bowl, for since I was little my mother's garden has always bloomed with these flowers.

Sometimes I miss those moments in my early years, the times in nature where nothing was expected or demanded of me and I could just be free. I remember the times I believed fairies lived in the garden, the hours of playing in the backyard with my siblings, climbing trees, chasing my cat, and the smell of the soil as it became darker as I dug. As children we see the world in a different way, as children we have the ability to see, feel and hear more intensely than adults. I feel a sadness because I think as adults, somewhere along the way, we lose this magical capacity to see the world as we did as children.

Reflecting on these moments has become a reminder to myself, a reminder that my own experiences outdoors as a child inform and illuminate the significance of children's time in nature.

I plan to offer experiences for children that allow them opportunities to just be in nature, where they can anticipate the changes in the seasons, observe and care for living things, explore natural elements, play and create games. After reflecting on my early years and establishing the meaningfulness of my own connections, I am motivated to create rich environments for children – environments where children can have endless opportunities to have an emotional and physical release through their connections with nature and people.

Well-Being and the Natural World

Whilst many educators know it is so, there is growing empirical evidence that children's well-being and learning is supported through nature connections and outdoor play (Bratman, Hamilton, & Daily, 2012; Dillon & Dickie, 2012; Maller, Townsend, Pryor, Brown, & St Leger, 2006; Malone & Waite, 2016; Russell et al., 2013).

Research encompassing the lifespan documents that time spent in the natural world, be it viewing, interacting with, or living in natural environments, has a positive effect on human mental health and well-being including recovery from mental fatigue, enhancing levels of generosity and caring, and advancing the ability to cope with distress (Maller et al., 2006; Russell et al., 2013; Weinstein, Przybylski, & Ryan, 2009; Wells & Evans, 2003). Deep interconnections have been found between mental well-being and living in close relationship with animals (Melson, 2019; O'Haire, 2010; Sable, 1995). Time in the natural world supports children's inspiration, creativity and imagination (Fjørtoft & Sageie, 2000; Louv, 2008; Russell et al., 2013), with connection to physical places an important component of well-being (Russell et al., 2013).

Memories of places often reflect place attachment and connections with people and ecosystems (Kudryavtsev, Stedman, & Krasny, 2012; Louv, 2008). The literature shows our early identities and sense of belonging can be intertwined with ecosystems and landscapes and the activities we experience within nature (Grimley, 2006; Howell, Passmore, & Buro, 2013; Mayer & Frantz, 2004; Post, 2007; Stairs, 1992). In short, connections between people and their environment are necessary for human well-being (Russell et al., 2013).

Positive human connections in the natural world also benefit the earth. A child's direct experience in nature and spending time in nature with someone close (such as a parent, grandparent or trusted teacher) are two factors that most contribute to a child choosing to take action to benefit the environment as an adult (Charles & Louv, 2019; Chawla, 2015) (Fig. 17.7).

Amber: Finding my way back

This creative artefact explores the relationship I have with the natural environment and how it has contributed to my wellbeing. It illustrates my personal struggle with anxiety as a child and how my experiences with the natural environment led to my recovery.

Fig. 17.7 Amber: Finding my way back

When I was young I was happy, adventurous and full of positivity. I enjoyed dancing, playing with my siblings, swimming, surfing, skateboarding and netball. I was just like every other kid my age. Then, I experienced severe anxiety. I remember waking up each morning with crippling nausea. I couldn't eat or attend school some days.

To help me, my dad would take me for a run through the bushland near our house. As I ran through the trees following my dad the nausea would leave me. I started to feel like myself again, happy again. I started to see the beauty around me. I noticed the breeze cooling my skin and the smell of the callistemon trees, and my thoughts calmed. This experience helped me feel grounded, safe, secure, reassured. Being in nature was such a relief. I gained an immense appreciation for the environment. The trees, long grass, cool breeze gave me motivation to keep pushing through, it was almost like seeing the light at the end of a tunnel again. It somehow recalibrated my mind, so I could put strategies into place before spiralling back into anxiety.

Relationships with nature support wellbeing. I want to support children's connections and make their wellbeing a priority. I want to provide natural spaces where children can relax and calm their thoughts and play outdoors where they are surrounded by the natural world.

Early Childhood Education and the Third Teacher

Early childhood education is recognised as critical for formative experiences. There is growing recognition of the value of quality early learning experiences and interactions in environments where the natural world has a central place, and where a love of and relationship with nature is fostered (Davis, 2009).

Children act as one part of a complex mesh of relations, relating and relationships (Rautio, 2013a).

Early childhood educators know this. Many work under a socioculturally framed curriculum, which is influenced by a complex range of factors including: children themselves; relationships and environments; values and principles about what matters for children and their futures;

a personal teaching philosophy; sensitivity to the diverse range of family and community contexts that children live and learn in; commitments to connectedness and collective well-being; and consideration of the current and future life-worlds that children are citizens within (Shulman & Shulman, 2008).

Unfortunately, educator capacities to support children's development, well-being and resilience in early childhood is currently under challenge as governments pressure educators to hurry and test children's learning to demonstrate academic attainment (McCree, Cutting, & Sherwin, 2018). Yet, early childhood educators know the importance of following children's interests and development, of engaging in slower, unhurried, creative, connected, affective and restorative learning processes and invitations for learning, many of which are presented through the learning environment (Roe & Aspinall, 2011; Rose, Gilbert, & Smith, 2012). The role of environments as a *third teacher* (the first two teachers being *parent* and *teacher*), in early childhood education has been illuminated beautifully by the scholars of Reggio Emilia. Their emphases on place, culture, relationships and responsive and aesthetic learning environments (Gandini, 1998; Rinaldi, 2012) have become foci for early years settings globally. Attention to the role of natural materials and outdoor spaces that incorporate natural elements such as plants, animals, rocks, water and insects can also be seen.

Outdoor play, experiential play, and learning in nature are significant contributors to children's potentials for learning and development (Rinaldi, 2012).

Natural areas provide opportunities for children to engage in creative play alone and with friends, set self-paced challenges, find quiet retreats, learn about the environment from direct experience, and form emotional bonds with places and the natural world (Chawla, 2015). Recent research also shows when adults take a more hands-off approach—instead of organising and planning specific activities—more spontaneous, child-initiated, unstructured and self-directed play occurs—generating in children a more emotional, sensuous and embodied engagement with nature (Skar, Wold, Gunderson, & O'Brien, 2016; Stordal, Follo, & Pareliussen, 2015) (Fig. 17.8).

Fig. 17.8 Cherished connections

Deborah K: Cherished connections

Growing up, my parents grew strawberries. I have many memories of conversations with my mother about how the plants grew and how to care for them. This was our way of life and the success of the season was imperative to our livelihood. If we had a particularly wet season, or a frost ruined the berries, it directly affected how we were to live day-to-day.

We also had goats on our farm. Not only were they beloved pets, they were a food source providing milk. The chickens were hand raised by us and provided both eggs and meat. This was our way of life and how my family survived.

I did not realise until now the values I have come to cherish. I have a love and appreciation for the land and a strong sense of connectedness and belonging to the world around me. Something I value is not taking for granted the resources we have available to us. I believe in living seasonally and sustainably. Even now, I still have my own chickens, ducks, and a goat. The conversations I have with my children focus on the importance of every living thing, and an appreciation for the food and resources we have—developing a sense of place and connectedness to the land and the importance of supporting and maintaining this for future generations.

Teacher Education as a Site for Remembering and Representing Significant Experience

My current workplace, The University of the Sunshine Coast, is one of many universities including courses about early childhood education for sustainability in their teacher education programs. As a result, our preservice teachers are recognising that they, with children, have an important contribution to make to the world.

For the last four years, preservice teachers in their second year of their early childhood degree have engaged in a course I have developed about early childhood education for sustainability. Julie Davis' (2015) book *Young Children and The Environment* is a core text. As part of assessment and coursework, preservice teachers engage in reflection, writing and art-making about their relationships with people, place, and the more-than-human world. The rationale is, our own childhoods and relationships can be an important starting point for education for sustainability, especially as we come to realise our knowing and our *being* are inseparable (Rautio, 2013b). Recent research highlights quality environmental education occurs when it is grounded in children's experiences and lives and connected to specific localised contexts and nearby nature (Gundersen, Skår, O'Brien, Wolda, & Follo, 2016). And so similarly, the course assessment is grounded in preservice teachers' own experiences and lives, *their* localised contexts and nearby nature, and in *their* sensory impressions and emotional responses. They connect to their values, perceptions and understandings of the opportunities afforded by natural environments (Torquati & Ernst, 2013) as they return to their own foundational experiences and recall the potentials and opportunities of teaching and learning in natural environments that they encountered (Fig. 17.9).

Fig. 17.9 Grounded in the earth

Deb T: Grounded in the earth

As a child my life was lived outside. From sun up till sun down I roamed our property, engaging in the myriad of adventures the Australian bush and my vast imagination invited. I would lie on my horse's back as he would graze. I would get lost in the sky. I was invincible. I loved the feel of the earth beneath my bare feet. It calmed me.

This carefree life came to an end when I started school. The classrooms were loud and crowded and I couldn't concentrate. I longed for the weekends.

But then I experienced a different kind of teacher. Her name was Mrs. Thompson, and she took us outside where we would learn about the world around us, how each one of us had a responsibility to look after the environment. She helped me to understand the connection I felt with nature and how it could ground me during those times when I felt like my mind was running too fast. She encouraged us to take off our shoes and concentrate on what we were feeling beneath our feet. She taught me that focusing could calm and bring me back to where I needed to be. I started to understand my connection to the earth.

Now, as an adult, when my mind races and I feel a need to escape, I take off my shoes and let the earth ground me. I have taught my own children how to use the earth to ground them in times of stress, passing on the knowledge I was born with but didn't understand until a teacher cared enough to understand me. I too will be that teacher, supporting every child's connection with the earth, helping them experience how the earth can ground them, showing we have this strong foundation we all share and rely on, and that we must protect.

Using Arts-Based Methods

As a narrative and arts-based researcher, I value arts-based forms and methods for collecting data, analysing data and reporting research, so possibilities for accessing knowledge and raising awareness are expanded (Lawrence, 2015; Leavy, 2009). The experiences of our lives are essential to our meaning-making and to our understanding of relationships, their interconnectedness and interrelatedness (Eisner & Powell, 2002), with the processes and products of creative approaches offering catalysts for deep thinking and reflection (Black & O'Dea, 2015; Bullough, 2006).

The goal of my course is for preservice teachers to consider their own experiences with nature, how these have influenced them, and will influence their educator roles. Arts-based methods are essential to this reflection. The course outline offers the following advice:

> Create a narrative or creative work to capture the connections, interconnections, and disconnections of your personal experiences with nature and the natural world, as well as your holistic thinking in relation to values, commitments, learning, living and wellbeing. You might consider how your experiences and relationships with nature and the natural world have supported your experiences of belonging, wellbeing and connectedness. You could consider the effects, positive or negative, your experiences of the natural environment have had on your sense of self, your connectedness to other people and the world around you; or on your physical, mental and spiritual health. In your reflection, consider how these experiences might influence and enhance your role as a professional working with young children.

Fig. 17.10 The Big Fig Tree

Preservice teachers are able to use any form of art they feel would support their meaning-making processes. Over the years they have chosen a range of formats and methods to share their stories and histories, including visual art, photography, metaphor, poetry, film, digital storytelling, written narratives, installations and artistic displays, storybooks, and hybrid works incorporating a mix of the above with music and effects (Fig. 17.10).

Renee: The big fig tree
The tree in this painting was inspired by the fig tree in my Poppy's yard. I spent numerous weekends and holidays at my grandparent's house playing

in and around this tree with my brother and cousins. I recall having so much fun and being so carefree. Upon reflection, being at my Poppy's and in nature provided me with a place where I could socialise and build relationships through play with my cousins, and just be – without worry or fear – something I didn't always have at home.

The tree represents how I see myself now as a parent to my own children, as well as in my role as a future educator. The tree's roots, seen growing throughout the red, yellow and black of the aboriginal flag in the soil, represent my identity as a proud aboriginal woman and my always-deepening connection to country. As an educator, I am going to embrace my aboriginality and provide children with knowledge of and respect for country, by embedding cultural values and experiences into my practice. I was not brought up learning the ways of my people—the Ngaringman people from the Fitzmaurice region of the Northern Territory. I am, however, on a journey of self-discovery, with the goal of making the trip up to the Northern Territory to meet my family and connect with my country before I finish my degree. This, I believe, will enable me to appropriately and respectfully embed indigenous perspectives into my practice and the early childhood settings I work in.

The tree visible above the soil has withstood many years out in the elements, and with a sturdy, well-developed trunk, branches, and large leafy canopy, it provides shade, shelter and structure for people and creatures alike.

This symbolises my growth and development as a person and future educator. I have faced much throughout my life, but am able to stand strong and provide children with a safe, supportive environment. I will give children time to engage in play both with, in, and for nature, in meaningful ways. I will achieve this through the designs of the learning environments – outdoor and indoor, and bring aspects of the outdoors inside. I will provide children with opportunities to connect with the natural world to facilitate their healthy development both physically and mentally.

The Value?

These methods have been significant tools scaffolding preservice teachers own connections with nature, supporting recall and awareness, and supporting their intentions to engage children with/in natural environments in their future teaching.

Arts-based approaches have enabled opportunities for preservice teachers to create work that holds their unique signatures of experience, embodies their unique style and expresses meanings that matter to them in new and deeper ways than an essay would have done (Barone & Eisner, 1997; Lawrence, 2015; Merriam & Tisdell, 2016). The inquiry has offered time and ways to attend to their lived and relational lives and the significance of those experiences.

Their storying and representation of human and more-than-human relationships makes visible the significant early experiences that contribute to physical, mental and spiritual health. Their creations document intimate interactions and individual/affective components of favourite person-place relationships.

This space of learning is about *being* and knowing. It provides aesthetic-affective ways for preservice teachers to perceive again their people-place relationships, and to connect again with their felt and embodied experiences, to recognise the relevance of these, then and now. The recalling of connections strengthens both their own sense of connectedness and their desire to promote opportunities for children's connections (Howell et al., 2013). Preservice teachers are remembering they belong to a universe that articulates through them and extends beyond them (Bennett, 1994).

Their stories highlight that children's or our own connections to nature are built through experiences, and these in turn predict well-being, positive emotions and feelings of connectedness (Howell et al., 2013). This knowledge has supported new insights and directions for the experiences they offer children and deepened understanding of human interconnectedness and interdependence with the more-than-human world (Green & Somerville, 2015; Lenz-Taguchi, 2011; Torquati & Ernst, 2013).

Emma: Thinking deeply

It wasn't until I started this course that I began to understand how blessed and lucky I was. I have a new-found connection to my dad, my grandparents and great grandparents that I didn't realise was there before—we share memories and connections with the same land. The same tree I used to climb and pretend was my little house, my grandfather broke his arm falling out of 50 years before me, and his father before him would sit under and roll his cigarettes. The same land, the same tree, but different meanings for us all.

I can recognise these childhood experiences contributed greatly to a wonderful upbringing. I can link all these things to my development of independence and agency, how I understood and contributed to my world, my curiosity and wonder for the environment around me, and my connectedness to place.

This task has made me think more deeply about my experiences with nature and how this links to my professional development as a pre-service teacher. The outdoors is a place of spiritual and emotional connection and physical release and play in nature just seems so 'absurdly logical' now.

Conclusion

Engaging preservice teachers in reflection about people-place relationships seems critical given teachers play a lead role in shaping young children's experiences and understandings.

For these preservice teachers, engaging in reflection about their own experiences has supported articulation of commitments and desires to contribute to social change. Reflection has supported deeper understanding and appreciation of self-environment-people-place relationships which have then become integrated into identified educator commitments.

This chapter has brought into focus the value of arts-based methods, including narratives of lived experience. It has offered a reflective exploration and collective sharing of childhood encounters through an assemblage of preservice teachers' memories of childhoods and relationships within nature; a collection of senses and feelings and perceptions and dwelling (again) in significant experiences and relationships. And, it has invoked recognition about the importance of attending to such experiences and relationships *with children*.

These future teachers now have a deeper understanding of what they are a part of. They are connected to their hopes for children and the planet and realise the importance of their role in bringing these hopes to life (Fig. 17.11).

Fig. 17.11 Remembering and reconnecting

Liam: Remembering and reconnecting

The memories portrayed in this collage represent moments of connection and building my sense of well-being and resilience in the face of challenges. It highlights my interactions with nature itself.

When my sister and I were kids, we regularly went to Tickle Park in Coolum Beach. In this park was a massive tree we always gravitated towards. We were enchanted by this huge marvel that offered so many possibilities for play. My sister, being the confident person she is would always climb the tree without feelings of fear or hesitation. I always approached the tree with caution.

One day I tried climbing as high as I could. As I took hold of the branch, I remember the feeling of dirt and bark on my skin. I remember holding on so tight that marks and imprints of the dirt and bark were left on my hand. I made it to half way when I slipped from the tree and fell to the ground. At this moment in time, I felt defeated and incapable. However, I discovered it is important to take risks and learn from them. I learned that when you fall it is important to get back up again. I did get back up again and kept trying. Although I never reached the top I learned to be persistent and optimistic about my abilities.

On the days my parents had to work, we spent them with our grandmother. We would go to the beach to walk her dog, Muffin. I can remember walking along the beach and feeling the individual grains of sand which were soft, smooth and solid. I remember my sister and I would stand on the edge of the water and wait for waves to come rushing in and wash over our feet. I recall this therapeutic feeling. We discovered so many shells, ones that were small, big, curved, sharp and that made unique sounds.

These moments were some of the best moments in my childhood. They opened my eyes to the natural wonders of the beach and created a connecting bond that I would always share with my grandmother. This bond is significant as it represents the relationship I hope to create with the children in my care.

As an educator, I want children to be in nature and learn from it. I want to create spaces where children can explore, create and form a strong identity. I want to design environments that utilise natural resources and materials, where natural elements intertwine with other aspects of the space. I want children to develop their capacities to cope with day-to-day stresses and challenges, and I believe the natural environment offers a great platform for children to build these capabilities. Like my grandmother was for me, I want to be a co-learner and respond with curiosity and wonder as children explore their environments.

My connection with the environment is an aspect of my life I lost over the years. However, through these processes of reflecting on my childhood experiences within nature, I have been able to reconnect with my natural environment. I want to keep reforming this relationship with nature to benefit myself as a person and as an educator who enriches children's experiences and connections.

References

Barone, T., & Eisner, E. (1997). *Handbook on complementary methods for educational research*. Washington, DC: American Educational Research Association.

Bennett, J. (1994). *Thoreau's nature: Ethics, politics, and the wild*. London, UK: Sage.

Black, A. L., & O'Dea, S. (2015). Building a tapestry of knowledge in the spaces in between: Weaving personal and collective meaning through arts-based research. In K. Trimmer, A. L. Black, & S. Riddle (Eds.), *Mainstreams, margins and the spaces in-between: New possibilities for education research*. Abingdon, UK: Routledge.

Bratman, G. N., Hamilton, J. P., & Daily, G. C. (2012). The impacts of nature experience on human cognitive function and mental health. *Annals of the New York Academy of Sciences, 1249*(1), 118–136.

Bullough, R. V., Jr. (2006). Developing interdisciplinary researchers: What ever happened to the humanities in education? *Educational Researcher, 35*(8), 3–10.

Charles, C., & Louv, R. (2019). Wild hope: The transformative power of children engaging with nature. In A. Cutter-Mackenzie, K. Malone, & E. Barratt Hacking (Eds.), *Research handbook on childhood nature: Assemblages of childhood and nature research*. Dordrecht, The Netherlands: Springer International Handbooks of Education.

Chawla, L. (2015). Benefits of nature contact for children. *Journal of Planning Literature, 30*(4), 433–452.

Davis, J. M. (2009). Revealing the research 'hole' of early childhood education for sustainability: A preliminary survey of the literature. *Environmental Education Research, 15*(2), 227–241.

Davis, J. M. (Ed.). (2015). *Young children and the environment: Early education for sustainability* (2nd ed.). Port Melbourne, VIC: Cambridge University Press.

Dillon, J., & Dickie, I. (2012). *Learning in the natural environment: Review of social and economic benefits and barriers* (Natural England commissioned reports, 092). London, UK: Natural England.

Eisner, E., & Powell, K. (2002). Special series on arts-based educational research. *Curriculum Inquiry, 32*(2), 131.

Fjørtoft, I., & Sageie, J. (2000). The natural environment as a playground for children: Landscape description and analyses of a natural playscape. *Landscape and Urban Planning, 48*(1–2), 83–97.

Gandini, L. (1998). Educational and caring spaces. In C. Edwards, L. Gandini, & G. Foreman (Eds.), *The hundred languages of children: The Reggio Emilia approach—advanced reflections* (2nd ed., pp. 161–178). Greenwich, CT: Ablex Publishing Corporation.

Green, M., & Somerville, M. (2015). Sustainability education: Researching practice in primary schools. *Environmental Education Research, 21*(6), 832–845.

Grimley, D. M. (2006). *Grieg: Music, landscape and Norwegian identity*. Woodbridge, UK: Boydell.

Gundersen, V., Skår, M., O'Brien, L., Wolda, L. C., & Follo, G. (2016). Children and nearby nature: A nationwide parental survey from Norway. *Urban Forestry and Urban Greening, 17*, 116–125.

Howell, A. J., Passmore, H. A., & Buro, K. (2013). Meaning in nature: Meaning in life as a mediator of the relationship between nature connectedness and well-being. *Journal of Happiness Studies, 14*(6), 1681–1696.

Kudryavtsev, A., Stedman, R. C., & Krasny, M. E. (2012). Sense of place in environmental education. *Environmental Education Research, 18*(2), 229–250.

Lawrence, R. L. (2015). Dancing with the data: Arts-based qualitative research. In V. C. X. Wang (Ed.), *Handbook of research on scholarly publishing and research methods* (pp. 141–154). Hershey, PA: IGI Global.

Leavy, P. (2009). *Method meets art: Arts-based research practice.* New York, NY: The Guilford Press.

Lenz-Taguchi, H. (2011). Investigating learning, participation and becoming in early childhood practices with a relational materialist approach. *Global Studies of Childhood, 1*(1), 36–50.

Louv, R. (2008). *Last child in the woods: Saving our children from nature-deficit disorder.* Chapel Hill, NC: Algonquin.

Maller, C., Townsend, M., Pryor, A., Brown, P., & St Leger, L. (2006). Healthy nature healthy people: 'Contact with nature' as an upstream health promotion intervention for populations. *Health Promotion International, 21*(1), 45–54.

Malone, K., & Waite, S. (2016). *Student outcomes and natural schooling.* Plymouth, UK: Plymouth University. Retrieved from http://www.plymouth.ac.uk/research/oelres-net

Mayer, F. S., & Frantz, C. M. (2004). The connectedness to nature scale: A measure of individuals' feeling in community with nature. *Journal of Environmental Psychology, 24*(4), 503–515.

McCree, M., Cutting, R., & Sherwin, D. (2018). The Hare and the Tortoise go to Forest School: Taking the scenic route to academic attainment via emotional wellbeing outdoors. *Early Child Development and Care, 188*(7), 980–996.

Melson, G. (2019). Rethinking children's connections with other animals: A childhood nature perspective. In A. Cutter-Mackenzie, K. Malone, & E. Barratt Hacking (Eds.), *Research handbook on childhood nature: Assemblages of childhood and nature research.* Dordrecht, The Netherlands: Springer International Handbooks of Education.

Merriam, S. B., & Tisdell, E. J. (2016). *Qualitative research: A guide to design and implementation.* San Francisco, CA: Jossey-Bass/Wiley.

O'Haire, M. (2010). Companion animals and human health: Benefits, challenges, and the road ahead. *Journal of Veterinary Behavior, 5*(5), 226–234.

Post, J. C. (2007). 'I take my dombra and sing to remember my homeland': Identity, landscape and music in Kazakh communities of western Mongolia. *Ethnomusicology Forum, 16*(1), 45–69.

Rautio, P. (2013a). Being nature: Interspecies articulation as a species-specific practice of relating to environment. *Environmental Education Research, 19*(4), 445–457. https://doi.org/10.1080/13504622.2012.700698

Rautio, P. (2013b). Children who carry stones in their pockets: On autotelic material practices in everyday life. *Children's Geographies, 11*(4), 394–408. https://doi.org/10.1080/14733285.2013.812278

Rinaldi, C. (2012). *In dialogue with Reggio Emilia: Listening, researching and learning*. London, UK: Routledge.

Roe, J., & Aspinall, P. (2011). The restorative outcomes of Forest School and conventional school in young people with good and poor behavior. *Urban Forestry and Urban Greening, 10*(3), 153–256.

Rose, J., Gilbert, L., & Smith, H. (2012). Affective teaching and the affective dimensions of learning. In S. Ward (Ed.), *A student's guide to education studies* (3rd ed., pp. 178–188). Abingdon, UK: Routledge.

Russell, R., Guerry, A. D., Balvanera, P., Gould, R. K., Basurto, X., Chan, K. M. A., … Tam, J. (2013). Humans and nature: How knowing and experiencing nature affect well-being. *Annual Review of Environment and Resources, 38*(1), 473–502.

Sable, P. (1995). Pets, attachment, and well-being across the life cycle. *Social Work, 40*(3), 334–341.

Shulman, L. S., & Shulman, J. H. (2008). How and what teachers learn: A shifting perspective. *Journal of Education, 189*(1/2), 1–8.

Skar, M., Wold, L. C., Gundersen, V., & O'Brien, L. (2016). Why do children not play in nearby nature? Results from a Norwegian survey. *Journal of Adventure Education and Outdoor Learning, 16*(3), 239–255.

Stairs, A. (1992). Self-image, world-image: Speculations on identity from experiences with Inuit. *Ethos, 20*(1), 116–126.

Stordal, G., Follo, G., & Pareliussen, I. (2015). Betwixt the wild, unknown and the safe: Play and the affordance of nature within an early childhood education and care institution in Norway. *International Journal of Early Childhood Environment Education, 3*, 28–37.

Torquati, J., & Ernst, J. A. (2013). Beyond the walls: Conceptualizing natural environments as "third educators". *Journal of Early Childhood Teacher Education, 34*(2), 191–208.

Weinstein, N., Przybylski, A. K., & Ryan, R. M. (2009). Can nature make us more caring? Effects of immersion in nature on intrinsic aspirations and generosity. *Personality and Social Psychology Bulletin, 35*(10), 1315–1329.

Wells, N. M., & Evans, G. W. (2003). Nearby nature: A buffer of life stress among rural children. *Environment Behavior, 35*(3), 311–330.

18

Arts-Based Research Across the Lifespan and Its Contribution to Resilience and Well-Being

Loraine McKay, Georgina Barton, Viviana Sappa, and Susanne Garvis

---

L. McKay (✉)
Education and Professional Studies, Griffith University, Brisbane, QLD, Australia
e-mail: loraine.mckay@griffith.edu.au

G. Barton
School of Education, University of Southern Queensland, Springfield, Brisbane, QLD, Australia
e-mail: georgina.barton@usq.edu.au

V. Sappa
Swiss Federal Institute for Vocational Education and Training, Lugano, Switzerland
e-mail: viviana.sappa@iuffp.swiss

S. Garvis
University of Gothenburg, Göteborg, Sweden
e-mail: susanne.garvis@gu.se

Bringing the Research Together

As editors, we have been given the privilege of bringing together a diverse range of researchers across the world who are interested in arts-based research methods, well-being and resilience. We all feel very excited about the final contributions to this book and hope that our readers gain a greater insight into how the arts can be a powerful tool in supporting resilience and well-being across the lifespan. A number of major themes have revealed themselves across the chapters and we present this final chapter as a summary of these themes.

Our purpose in bringing together *Arts-based research, resilience and well-being* was to illustrate the positive contribution and potentialities of arts-based research methods to participants' lives. Illustrated throughout this text are examples of the positive contributions of arts-based research to resilience and well-being. In summary, arts-based research supported well-being and resilience of individuals, groups and organisations by:

1. **Providing agency through the foregrounding of participants' voices.** Riches et al. (Chap. 14) shared examples of agency and advocacy for people with disabilities. Garvis (Chap. 2) highlighted the role arts can play in early childhood in supporting children to express their emotional needs, especially for those children who might not yet have developed the language skills to express complex emotional needs. Coad's (Chap. 4) research highlighted how arts can provide valuable information to health care professionals working with children of all ages. The arts allows young patients to feel more included in the decision making related to their own health care needs and the effectiveness of services provided. Similarly Macdonald et al. (Chap. 3) and Yohani (Chap. 6) noted how, through the arts, young people can take agency following events of trauma or circumstances that may lead to disengagement.
2. **Affording transformational learning opportunities.** Transformational learning opportunities related to professional identity development were notable in the teacher education research of McKay and Gibbs (Chap. 7), Vähäsantanen et al., (Chap. 13) and Black (Chap. 17). Furthermore, Salini and Durand's chapter (Chap. 10) emphasised the potential of arts to bring together groups as a collective to transform personal views about one's self and one's circumstances.

3. **Creating opportunities for relationship building in a world where the more connected we become the less connected we feel.** Ho and Wong's chapter (Chap. 8) illustrated how more positive relationships between mother and son were developed through arts. On a broader scale, Tschiesner and Farneti's (Chap. 11) work related to clowning helped to develop stronger collegiality between staff but also supported stronger relationship with those who were being served in a range of contexts and work environments.
4. **Supporting creativity and new ways of thinking.** Garvis (Chap. 2) suggests the arts allow a new way of considering resilience and development of resilience for children. Previously considered from an adult's view, she suggests using arts-based research allows new ways of understanding resilience in an early childhood setting. Meltzer (Chap. 12) demonstrated the potential for developing creative thinking skills required for success in twenty-first century workplaces as well as future thinking that generates new perspectives and possibilities that can support hope.
5. **Generating aspirations and hope.** The preceding chapters illustrated how arts-based research supported hope for a brighter future. People at risk of marginalisation from their community due to adversity or displacement (Garvis, Chap. 2; Yohani, Chap. 6); related to disability (Riches et al., Chap. 14); or work related stress (Uusimaki, Chap. 15) have been seen to benefit from the hope generated through arts-based research.
6. **Encouraging forms of communication that exposes ideas, emotions and feelings that previously might not have been known or known how to be expressed.** The arts has been illustrated in this text as a means of channelling thought processes linked more with the senses and emotions rather than logic. Šicková-Fabrici (Chap. 16) illustrated the power of natural materials such as clay to evoke strong emotional responses. Drama in various forms, such as clowning (Tschiesner & Farneti, Chap. 11), forum theatre (Sappa & Barabasch, Chap. 9), theatre of lived experience (Salini & Durand, Chap. 10) were also seen to generate dialogical spaces that stimulated emotional and reflective processes and resources, essential for resilience.
7. **Enhancing reflection and reflexivity.** Arts-based reflection includes reflection of self (Black, Chap. 17; McKay & Gibbs, Chap. 7), reflection of experience (Coholic, Chap. 5; Salini & Durand, Chap. 10);

reflection on practice (Meltzer, Chap. 12); and reflection on context (Sappa & Barabasch, Chap. 9). The value of the arts in supporting resilience and well-being is in the opportunity to develop and strengthen the ability to reflect and be reflexive. As the editors we complete this text with our own reflections drawing from the experience of preparing this book.

Reflections from Loraine

I chose to represent the key themes of this book through collage, first as a tribute to my current research participants who I have watched struggle with a range of emotions as they trust me with their stories that they tell through collage. Second, because it felt right in a cathartic sense (Fig. 18.1).

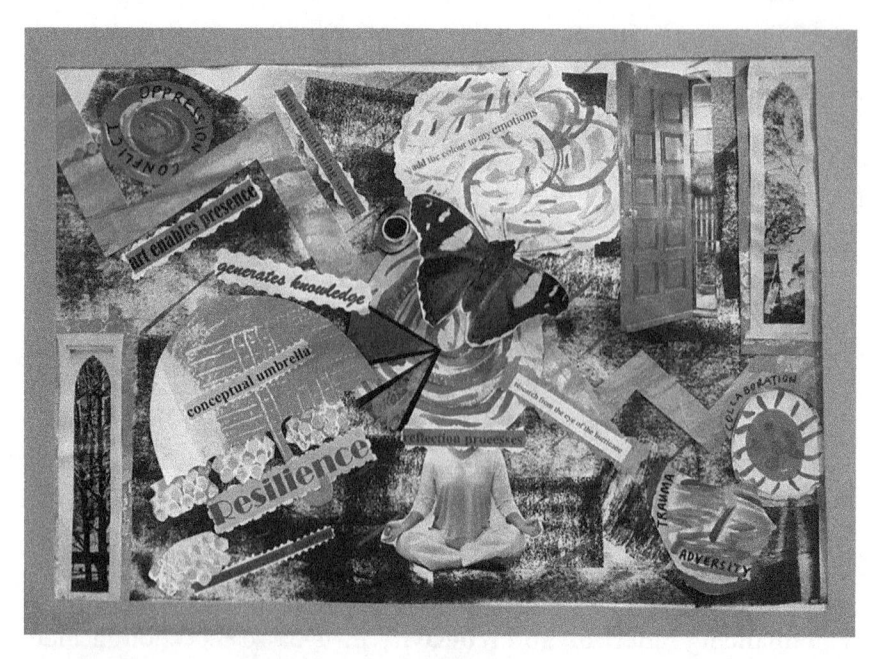

Fig. 18.1 Using collage for self care and reflection

Life has a way of sending a curve ball every once in a while, maybe as a means to ward off complacency. At the time of constructing this collage I was struggling to balance the responsibility and requirements of my work, with the love and desire to support my family. Both were overloaded by circumstances of the moment and each was deserving of my attention. It can be argued that the resources drawn upon to navigate the peaks and troughs of life can be strengthened through this navigation. Also important is some form of reflection, that highlights the strategies and resources successfully utilised in given situations. Being part of a team to bring together this book and making time to create art, in collaboration with my colleague, friend and co-editor was a means of supporting my own well-being and the created image is a reminder to me of self-care and well-being.

Shades of dark and light form the background of this collage reminding us that from dark we can find light but we should never take the light for granted. Glimpses of hope radiate through in shades and shapes of orange. Orange is the colour of career highlights from a previous time working with children and families from diverse backgrounds. Over twenty years ago they taught me so much about overcoming adversity, trauma, oppression and conflict. Whether it was making a life after escaping war, exploring ways to work with disability, or overcoming sociocultural barriers within schools and communities, those children and families are my orange. I wish I had known then about the potential value of arts.

I love how the collage process (and other art making) brings one's thinking to the here and now: centring and slowing the mind. The images in this collage highlight alternatives, new ways of thinking when we open out mind, hearts and eyes. We are awoken to new possibilities if we remain open minded. Like the butterfly we have the potential to shed the burdens or reinvent ourselves when we understand what we are capable of doing and being. Being able to undertake this metamorphosis may be required to flourish in a changing world.

If we are to get into the heads of others, to research in the eye of the hurricane (Vist, personal communication, 2018), it is clear within these chapters it requires the establishment of a non-threatening environment where we feel safe to expose, examine and explore confrontation. Building trust between and within the researchers and participants is part of the process of opening doorways to new potentialities and to explore and add the colour to emotions (Coholic, Chap. 5).

This collage represents the themes from this book that resonated with me at the time and some phrases are taken from conversations with authors at the early stages of planning this book. As you engaged with the stories within these pages perhaps you too reflected on how arts-based methods could be useful to support resilience and well-being in your own life and the lives of those around you.

Reflections from Georgina

The arts have always been a large part of my life. My mother was always dabbling in visual art, my grandmother was a dress maker and I was drawn to the beauty of the violin at the age of six. As a parent I have also encouraged my own children to participate in the arts and now my daughter is a fashion designer and visual artist and my son a fine musician. I have always known about the power of the arts and how they can transform people's lives for the better. I have felt so proud to be part of this project, knowing that the pressures in our everyday lives seem to becoming more and more complex and particularly for young people with whom we work. Reading each chapter as we were receiving them kept reinforcing for me, how important this work is in academia. I will continue to do arts practice for my own creative self and often for relaxation and rejuvenation. Please enjoy.

Reflections from Susanne

I cannot remember my life without the arts. They have been a constant in my life and still form part of my daily habits. From an early age, music, dance and visual arts were encouraged by parents to ensure a *well rounded person*. Today I also ensure my daughter is surrounded with arts experiences to help support her in her daily endeavours and to learn more about her own social and emotional well-being. The arts have an amazing power for the *entire body* as a cathartic experience that is responsive to human need and emotion. The book has been able to highlight the importance of arts for resilience across the lifespan and show the importance across cultures and contexts. I hope that as readers engage with the book, they also become stronger advocates for the arts across education systems and society to allow all children and adults to have access. Equal access to arts participation can then be provided to everyone in society to benefit.

Reflections from Viviana

This book gave me the opportunity to rouse my creative soul that has been too often obscured by rationality. The academic mainstream pressed me to be rational and close to the quantitative-oriented scientific standards. This book offered me the opportunity to combine artistic and scientific thinking by showing me the extraordinary potential of arts for both research and interventions in the field of well-being and resilience. Consistently with the theme of the book, I would like to represent such a potential by means of an artistic medium, that is sculpture I created with modelling clay (Fig. 18.2). I chose a tree as a symbol of empowerment. Arts are the nourishment of such empowerment. The multiple satellite dishes in the sculpture aims at representing the opportunity of arts to approach the life and experiences in a multi sensorial way. Rational thinking and emotions are intertwined in arts like colours in the bark of my tree. As reported in some chapters of this book, arts can support individuals to look inside themselves, to reflect on their own identity, to see himself or herself through a sort of mirror. By making art individuals can express themselves in an unusual way and discover new facets of their identity.

Arts help people think outside the box. Arts help people break the box they are "trapped" in. Arts can help people cross social and cultural boundaries or constrains. I hope readers of this book realise the importance of cultivating arts in academic, education and care settings as an essential component of the human being.

Fig. 18.2 Thinking outside the box

Index[1]

A

Adolescence, 8, 35, 149
Adults, 9, 16, 17, 23, 49, 51, 52, 55–57, 59, 65, 69, 71, 82, 84, 89, 153, 156, 169–187, 192, 203, 257, 262, 265, 276, 302, 307, 308, 310, 312, 321, 323, 325, 329, 341, 345
Agency, 18, 19, 64, 68, 98, 123, 150, 153, 251, 333, 340
Art, 4, 14, 30–32, 39–41, 49, 69, 83, 111, 127–144, 148, 182, 192, 211, 257, 293, 301–314, 340
Arts-based, 2–10, 13–24, 29–41, 47–60, 63–76, 82–99, 105–124, 128, 134, 142, 143, 148, 158, 163–165, 194, 209–229, 233–254, 257, 258, 260, 261, 264, 265, 317–335, 340–345

Aspirations, 33–35, 37–38, 116, 247, 248, 341
Attitude, 107, 143, 153, 162–164, 199, 229, 259, 273, 287, 301, 303, 305, 306

B

Balance, 2, 18, 106, 118, 171, 225, 248, 282, 289–291, 296, 343
Beliefs, 6, 16, 52, 107, 115, 173, 174, 218, 229, 235, 253
Belonging, 9, 13–15, 17, 18, 21, 51, 69, 71, 106, 107, 123, 150, 181, 317–335

C

Childhood, 35, 64, 66, 90, 134, 143, 202, 215, 238, 317–335

---

[1] Note: Page numbers followed by 'n' refer to notes.

© The Author(s) 2020
L. McKay et al. (eds.), *Arts-Based Research, Resilience and Well-being Across the Lifespan*,
https://doi.org/10.1007/978-3-030-26053-8

Clowning, 9, 191–206, 341
Collaboration, 38, 63, 154, 218, 224–226, 228, 273, 280, 288, 343
Collage, 48, 55, 57, 84, 85, 91, 97, 110–113, 115, 334, 342–344
Colleagues, 39, 63, 115, 129, 131, 149, 150, 155, 160, 162–165, 202, 204, 205, 220, 221, 225, 250, 251, 265, 272, 280, 287, 288, 290, 291, 294, 295, 343
Community, 3, 4, 7, 13, 14, 22, 24, 30, 34–41, 55, 56, 58, 97, 148, 150, 153, 181, 186, 187, 238, 243, 260, 262, 264, 272, 274, 276, 280, 290, 325, 341, 343
Context, 2, 3, 6, 7, 9, 19, 21, 24, 30, 32–35, 38–40, 69, 76, 82–85, 88, 90, 107, 112, 153, 161, 170, 171, 191, 194, 205, 233–254, 258, 263, 302, 304, 313, 317, 325, 327, 341, 342, 345
Creative, 5–7, 20, 34, 35, 38, 68, 69, 71, 75, 76, 84, 89, 90, 96, 144, 173, 184, 193, 198, 203, 210, 213, 218, 229, 247, 252, 258, 260, 264, 268, 271, 272, 307, 318, 321, 323, 325, 329, 341, 344, 345
Culture, 15, 17–19, 38, 39, 98, 151, 175, 176, 185, 192, 224, 259, 260, 282, 285, 287, 289, 290, 306, 325, 345

D
Disability, 9, 257–276, 302, 305, 340, 341, 343
Dissonance, 21, 152, 159, 161, 204
Diversity, 18, 33, 69, 76, 186, 195
Drama, 4, 9, 18, 130, 144, 148, 151, 161–165, 169–187, 213, 234, 237, 238, 243–246, 341
Drawing, 5, 7, 19, 21, 48, 51, 52, 56, 68, 70, 72–74, 81, 84, 130, 135, 140, 141, 213, 214, 217, 218, 221–224, 228, 234, 238, 239, 247, 250, 307–309, 311, 342

E
Early childhood, 2, 8, 9, 13–24, 307, 317–335, 340, 341
Education, 2–4, 7–9, 13–24, 30, 32–35, 37, 38, 67, 98, 105–124, 129, 149, 169–187, 191, 194, 209, 212, 214, 220, 274, 281, 283–284, 296, 317, 324–329, 340, 345
Emotions, 5, 7–9, 36, 37, 64, 66, 94, 107, 109–111, 122, 128–133, 135–137, 139–143, 150, 152, 153, 157, 158, 164, 173, 181, 192, 193, 197–199, 201, 203, 217, 233–254, 303, 308, 332, 341, 342, 344, 345
Empathy, 6, 40, 63, 64, 67, 69, 152, 158, 160, 197, 199, 242
Experience, 5, 13, 30, 51, 64, 82, 105, 128, 148, 169–187, 201, 210, 234, 258, 281, 301, 317, 341

Index

F

Factors, 3, 6, 13, 14, 19, 30, 33, 96, 107, 108, 113, 116, 123, 133, 137, 160, 215, 262, 281, 296, 323, 324

Families, 8, 13–24, 30, 33, 53, 54, 66, 67, 75, 96, 106, 107, 109, 111, 113, 115, 117, 118, 122, 132, 155, 176, 181, 220, 248, 272–275, 281, 283, 286, 288, 291, 292, 296, 301, 303, 304, 311, 321, 325, 326, 331, 343

H

Health, 3–5, 7, 8, 14, 15, 17, 34–36, 38, 39, 47–60, 66, 70, 71, 98, 129, 149, 170, 262, 267, 272, 273, 280, 285–293, 295–297, 303, 306, 322, 329, 332, 340

Hope, 7, 10, 64, 82–99, 205, 296, 318, 333, 335, 340, 341, 343, 345

Humour, 107, 119, 123, 150, 152, 161, 163, 164

I

Identity, 5, 9, 18, 19, 39, 106, 123, 164, 196, 233–254, 259, 262, 265, 265n2, 268, 283, 322, 331, 335, 340, 345

Inclusion, 15, 22, 24, 170, 263, 291, 314

K

Knowledge, 5–7, 15, 19, 20, 23, 41, 56, 68, 71, 72, 83, 85, 86, 89, 97, 106, 108, 116, 120, 121, 163, 164, 172, 192–194, 209, 211, 214, 215, 235–237, 318, 329, 331, 332

M

Mature-age, 105–124

Meaning-making, 8, 9, 36, 236, 251, 257, 329, 330

Multimodal, 22, 23, 40, 130

N

Narrative, 14, 15, 17–23, 53, 70, 88, 95, 97–99, 151, 240, 241, 249, 253, 259, 280, 318, 329, 330, 333

Nature, 93, 153, 161, 234, 236, 237, 250, 252, 268, 280, 285, 313, 321–325, 327–329, 331–335

O

Opportunity, 5, 6, 15, 16, 18, 21–23, 34, 36, 37, 40, 48, 82, 106, 111, 115, 135, 137, 140, 153, 160–165, 180, 217, 218, 227, 242, 251, 258, 262, 263, 266, 269–271, 273, 285, 290, 304, 313, 317, 322, 325, 327, 331, 332, 340–342, 345

Oppression, 82, 343

Index

P

Performance, 4, 107, 131, 151–155, 158–164, 171, 185, 186, 191, 213, 217, 251, 259, 260, 265, 266, 274, 286, 288
Personal resource, 3, 4, 107, 108
Photo, 90, 91, 93, 110–112, 211, 218, 221, 223, 225, 229
Presence, 90, 135, 138, 184, 243
Profession, 113, 123, 149, 151, 247, 288

R

Reflection, 6, 8–10, 34, 41, 57–59, 65, 92, 93, 98–99, 105–124, 137, 139–141, 150, 153, 158, 162, 164, 173, 185, 191–194, 200, 202, 210, 215, 218, 219, 221, 224, 229, 250, 287, 301, 317–335, 341–345
Reflexivity, 171, 210, 211, 214–219, 221–223, 341
Refugee, 8, 14–24, 81–85, 273
Relationships, 8, 9, 13, 16–18, 33, 35, 49, 52, 66, 67, 71, 75, 82, 106–108, 112, 113, 116, 122, 123, 127–129, 131, 134, 135, 137, 139–144, 149–151, 155, 160, 163, 164, 171, 173, 174, 181, 183, 184, 186, 196–198, 211, 215, 221, 225, 235, 259, 262, 274, 275, 304, 306, 307, 317, 318, 321, 322, 324, 325, 327, 329, 331–333, 335, 341
Resilience, 2–10, 13–24, 29–41, 47–60, 63–76, 83, 105–124, 127, 129, 147–165, 169–187, 210, 257–276, 280, 281, 283, 296, 325, 334, 340–345
Role play, 143

S

Sculpting, 213, 214, 268
Sculpture, 89, 217, 265, 268, 302, 303, 305, 306, 311, 312, 321, 345
Self-efficacy, 13, 261
Self-esteem, 8, 13, 37, 40, 66, 67, 87, 192, 198, 261
Stress, 3, 15, 21, 34, 37, 66, 107, 108, 122, 148, 155, 159, 198, 199, 220, 279–297, 313, 329, 335, 341

T

Teacher, 8, 9, 16–20, 38, 55, 72, 94, 105–124, 132, 133, 147–165, 196, 198, 201, 209–211, 214, 218–220, 225, 233–254, 280, 307, 317–335, 340
Theatre, 8, 131, 147–165, 170, 171, 181, 185, 193, 266, 341
Therapy, 2, 55, 130, 131, 142–144, 194, 195, 261, 263, 267–271, 302–310
Transformation, 6, 8, 21, 37, 39, 107, 123, 143, 144, 162, 170, 172, 174, 182–183, 185, 263, 301, 308
Trauma, 35, 66, 68, 81, 82, 84, 85, 98–99, 176, 181, 281, 302, 304, 313, 340, 343

V

Voice, 23, 40, 41, 49, 52, 59, 71, 99, 115, 144, 200, 214, 225, 266, 271, 286, 340

W

Well-being, 2–10, 15, 20, 24, 29–41, 47–49, 51, 52, 54, 55, 59, 60, 66, 69, 71, 83, 105–124, 147–149, 154, 158, 160, 191–206, 234, 237, 247, 253, 262, 268, 279–281, 285–297, 307, 317–335, 340

Workplace, 2, 9, 10, 108, 155, 205, 209, 213, 214, 221, 225, 229, 280, 281, 285–288, 290, 297, 327, 341

Y

Youth, 8, 30, 33, 34, 41, 63–76, 82–99, 265

CPSIA information can be obtained
at www.ICGtesting.com
Printed in the USA
LVHW081503170320
650314LV00011B/212

9 783030 260521